Children of the Holocaust

Children of the Holocaust

PAUL R. BARTROP AND EVE E. GRIMM

BLOOMSBURY ACADEMIC
NEW YORK • LONDON • OXFORD • NEW DELHI • SYDNEY

BLOOMSBURY ACADEMIC
Bloomsbury Publishing Inc
1385 Broadway, New York, NY 10018, USA
50 Bedford Square, London, WC1B 3DP, UK
29 Earlsfort Terrace, Dublin 2, Ireland

BLOOMSBURY, BLOOMSBURY ACADEMIC and the Diana logo
are trademarks of Bloomsbury Publishing Plc

First published in the United States of America by ABC-CLIO 2020
Paperback edition published by Bloomsbury Academic 2024

Copyright © Bloomsbury Publishing Inc, 2024

Cover Photo: A boy in the street with his hands up during the Holocaust. April 30, 1943, Warsaw, Poland. (Keystone Press/Alamy Stock Photo)

All rights reserved. No part of this publication may be reproduced or transmitted in any form or by any means, electronic or mechanical, including photocopying, recording, or any information storage or retrieval system, without prior permission in writing from the publishers.

Bloomsbury Publishing Inc does not have any control over, or responsibility for, any third-party websites referred to or in this book. All internet addresses given in this book were correct at the time of going to press. The author and publisher regret any inconvenience caused if addresses have changed or sites have ceased to exist, but can accept no responsibility for any such changes.

Library of Congress Cataloging-in-Publication Data
Names: Bartrop, Paul R. (Paul Robert), 1955- author. | Grimm, Eve E., author.
Title: Children of the Holocaust / Paul R. Bartrop and Eve E. Grimm.
Description: Santa Barbara, California : ABC-CLIO, [2020] |
Includes bibliographical references and index.
Identifiers: LCCN 2020005161 (print) | LCCN 2020005162 (ebook) |
ISBN 9781440868528 (hardcover) | ISBN 9781440868535 (ebook)
Subjects: LCSH: Jewish children in the Holocaust. | Jewish children in the Holocaust—Biography. | Holocaust, Jewish (1939-1945)—Sources.
Classification: LCC D804.48 .B37 2020 (print) |
LCC D804.48 (ebook) | DDC 940.53/18083—dc23
LC record available at https://lccn.loc.gov/2020005161
LC ebook record available at https://lccn.loc.gov/2020005162

ISBN: HB: 978-1-4408-6852-8
PB: 979-8-7651-2965-4
ePDF: 978-1-4408-6853-5
eBook: 979-8-2160-5985-1

To find out more about our authors and books visit www.bloomsbury.com and sign up for our newsletters.

To
Michael and Danielle
Heather and Ken
Don and Trish

Success is not final, failure is not fatal: it is the courage to continue that counts.
—Winston S. Churchill

Contents

List of Entries	xi
List of Primary Source Documents	xiii
Preface	xv
Introduction	xix
Entries	1
Primary Source Documents	263
Chronology	303
Glossary	311
Bibliography	317
Index	325

List of Entries

Abadi, Moussa
Adelsberger, Lucie
André, Joseph
Anne Frank House
Association of Children of the Holocaust

Barkman, Frances
Bauman, Janina
Berg, Mary
Białystok Children
Birenbaum, Halina
Blatt, Thomas "Toivi"
Border Crossings
The Boy: A Holocaust Story
Brundibár
Budisavljević, Diana
Bullenhuser Damm

Château de la Hille
Chevrier, Félix
Child Euthanasia
Child Survivors
Children and Film
Children's Concentration Camps, Croatia
Children's Literature of the Holocaust
The Cigarette Sellers of Three Crosses Square
Circumcision
Cohn, Marianne
Comité de Défense des Juifs

Daman, Jeanne
David, Janina
Deceptions
Deffaugt, Jean
Diaries and Journals
Dunera Boys

Éclaireurs Israélites de France
Edelweiss Pirates

Education in the Third Reich
Elli: Coming of Age in the Holocaust
Errázuriz, María

Flinker, Moshe
Frank, Anne
Freier, Recha

Garel Network
Garnethill Hostel
Gerlier, Pierre-Marie
Getter, Matylda
Geulen-Herscovici, Andrée
Geve, Thomas
Gies, Miep
Glas-Wiener, Sheva
Glasberg, Alexandre
Gunden, Lois

Haining, Jane
Hana's Suitcase
Hart, Kitty
Helga's Diary
Heyman, Éva
Hidden Children
Hirsch, Alfred (Fredy)
Hitler Youth
Hübener, Helmuth
Hulst, Johan van

Infanticide

Jewish Youth Movements
Joffo, Joseph
Jonas, Regina
Jospa, Yvonne

Kerkhofs, Louis-Joseph
Kertész, Imre

LIST OF ENTRIES

Kidnapping
Kindertransport
Kor, Eva Mozes
Korczak, Janusz
Kraus, Dita
Kraus, Gilbert and Eleanor
Küchler-Silberman, Lena
Kulski, Julian Eugeniusz

La Colline aux Mille Enfants
Lapid-Andriesse, Mirjam
Le Chambon-sur-Lignon
Le Voyage de Fanny
League of German Girls
Lebensborn
Leszczyńska, Stanisława
Liberation
Loinger, Georges
Lore

Maison d'Izieu
Marceau, Marcel
Medical Experimentation
Meed, Vladka
Mengele, Josef
Mischling

Ninas Resa

Œuvre de Secours aux Enfants
Oslo Jewish Children's Home

Passing
Père Jacques
Perl, Gisella
Piepel
Pritchard, Marion

Racine, Mila
Ranjitsinhji, Digvijaysinhji
Reynders, Henri
"Rhineland Bastards"
Rubinowicz, Dawid
Rudashevski, Yitskhok

Salomon, Andrée
Sauvage, Pierre
Schink, Barthel
Schonfeld, Solomon
Screaming Silence
Second Generation
Sendler, Irena
Sierakowiak, Dawid
Sletten-Fosstvedt, Ingebjørg
Smuggling
Süskind, Walter
Swing Kids
Sztehló, Gabor

Theresienstadt
Tiefenbrunner Orphanage
Trocmé, André
Twins

Weiner, Pavel
Westerweel, Johan
Wiesel, Elie
Winton, Nicholas
World Federation of Jewish Child Survivors of the Holocaust and Descendants

Yad Vashem Children's Memorial

Żegota

List of Primary Source Documents

1. *The Jewish Question in Education* (1937)
2. *The Poisonous Mushroom* (1938)
3. Heinrich Himmler on the Responsibility to Beget Children (October 28, 1939 and January 30, 1940)
4. Testimony of John Freund
5. Testimony of Ann Szedlecki
6. Mordecai Chaim Rumkowski, Łódź Ghetto (September 4, 1942)
7. Heinrich Himmler: "The Difficult Decision" (October 4 and 6, 1943)
8. Affidavit of Szloma Gol on the Killings at Ponary (1944)
9. Sir Herbert Emerson: Memorandum on Refugee Children in France, Belgium, and Switzerland (December 11, 1944)
10. Testimony of Fanny Lesser

Preface

The Holocaust was the most horrific crime any group of people ever perpetrated against another. It spoke of a human dream: of how, in the Nazi view, humanity could be perfected. In attempting to reach this perfection, the Nazis concluded that it was necessary to eliminate those they considered to be an impediment to achieving this goal—the Jews. Amid the many political and philosophical discussions that took place considering how this should take place, Jewish children featured significantly: if the Jewish future could be cut off in the current generation, Nazism would be much closer to realizing its racial ambitions.

Nazi ideologues and politicians thus concluded that they were acting with the best of intentions to guarantee the future of the Aryan people. Their Jewish victims, they reasoned, possessed neither a present nor a future, other than as a people who, until now, had avoided their intended (and inevitable) fate. As the Holocaust's perpetrators, the Nazis planned, perpetrated, and presided over that fate. They were committed, for reasons clear to them, to realizing the dream of achieving racial and national homogeneity for the German people, a pure society comprising only others like themselves, a place representing the closest possible approximation to human perfection. The deeds carried out by those perpetrating the Holocaust were vicious, violent, inhumane, and, from the perspective of Western morality at least, utterly wrong.

The current volume, examining a broad range of issues relating to children during the Holocaust, is not meant as the last word on each of the topics it covers but rather as an introduction to a variety of people, ideas, movements, and events. It is, therefore, a reference work designed to assist others in their own research.

When we began our search for topics relating to children and the Holocaust, we thought the process would be relatively easy; after all, there were so many cases we could have identified for inclusion that were automatically self-selective. It took us no time at all to find an initial list, but this only fed our desire to dig deeper. We began looking for others—and additional themes—to add. Sometimes it was sheer accident or luck by which we found names that had been little studied up until now. On other occasions, dealing with one topic inevitably led to uncovering another—and, just as with the layers of an onion, we kept peeling back without ever reaching a central core. And the process of discovery continued right up to the very last days.

In the long run, our selections were conditioned by our preference to choose examples representative of the wide range of children's experiences during the

Holocaust. For every person included here, however, there were dozens more we could have added.

This presented an added problem—that of space. We simply could not include the experience of every child, as the publishing process could not allow for this in a single volume. This has meant that practical considerations have led to many topics being omitted—though this can count as a positive for students and researchers seeking to undertake their own projects. The field, in many respects, remains wide open.

That said, it is our hope that the entries we have included here provide a profile broad enough to enable readers to derive some measure of understanding. In this context, we anticipate that the entries will be sufficiently illustrative of an experience that is thousands of times greater in expanse than the current volume suggests.

The entries have been organized in such a way as to provide maximum accessibility for readers. It is a straightforward alphabetical listing, by last name or theme, of a variety of people and issues relating to children during the Holocaust. To assist readers where cross-references occur, we have placed terms in **bold** when they appear in the entries of others featured in the volume. Most entries in the book have at least one reference listed for further reading. In some cases, these works are intended to serve as further reading on a specific topic or a broader context in which it can be placed.

In writing this work, we have employed a wide range of sources, ranging from books and documentaries to a massive range of internet sites that could not be listed even if we were to try. Often, while researching a person's life, we might consult up to 30 or more sites, only to find three or four key facts. Sometimes, despite all efforts, some data simply could not be found. On other occasions we might be lucky and hit the information "mother lode" after consulting only five or six sites. In every case, however, we would only consider a piece of data legitimate after corroboration from two or more sources independent of each other. Internet sites are notorious for the extent to which they lift the work of one or two generic sites and then just keep replicating the same information, uncritically, again and again. It is our hope that the standards of corroboration we have applied have dealt with the issue satisfactorily and eliminated the worst excesses of inexactitude.

Europe in the 1930s and 1940s was a continent in flux, in which countries and regions changed borders, and towns and cities often changed names. To preserve the contemporaneity of the situations under examination, we have preserved the names of the localities by which they were best known within the context of the Holocaust (for example, Vilna), with their modern renditions in parenthesis alongside (Vilnius). Our hope is that this will enhance clarity for modern readers and cut through what might otherwise be a confusion of names.

A few other points of explanation are needed. Unlike most other nonfiction or reference works, we have chosen to refer to children (and some adults) by their first names rather than their surnames when recounting their stories. The essential reason for this has been to emphasize the youth of the subjects under discussion, or the nature of the efforts on their behalf by others who were older. It should not be forgotten that in studying children, we are looking at a very special type of subject, requiring a different approach from that usually associated with more traditional academic themes.

Use of the term *antisemitism*, an umbrella term for a variety of negative beliefs or actions held or taken against Jews for the sole reason that they are Jewish, has been preferred in this volume. In line with much contemporary scholarly practice, this is not to be spelled as "anti-Semitism," as there is no such thing as "Semitism" against which hostility can be directed. In like manner, because the Nazis used the term *Aryan* to describe people of Northern European "racial" background, application of the term here has been employed without placing it in quotation marks. It is, simply, a term that is as much a part of the Nazi worldview as many others for which quotation marks are also not used.

It will also be seen in the text that from time to time, a name is mentioned with another name in quotation marks and parenthesis alongside. This is used in cases where a member of a resistance movement had a code name or alias—for example, Georges Garel ("Gasquet") or Fela Perelman ("Denise Dumont").

When reading about the children in this volume, it is worth noting that with the passage of years, they aged. A child born in 1927 or 1928, who would not yet be a teenager when war broke out in 1939, would be close to young adulthood by the time it ended in 1945. As a result, the nature of their perspectives and experiences underwent changes as the years of the Holocaust unfolded, and this should be considered when contemplating the nature of the trials though which they lived.

Finally, the bibliography here has been designed as more than just a list of relevant works. While it is intended as a starting point for researchers and students of the Holocaust, with a specific focus on children, it does not pretend to be a complete listing of all works relating to children the Holocaust but, rather, an aid for deeper investigation.

As this project has developed, we have been fortunate in receiving encouragement and support from several people, who now deserve our public thanks. Florida Gulf Coast University (FGCU) is a vibrant center of educational excellence, and the opportunities presented for us to develop and extend our thoughts regarding those listed in this work have been many. Associate Vice-President of Research and Dean of Graduate Studies Dr. T.C. Yih and former Dean of the College of Arts and Sciences Dr. Robert Gregerson were steadfast in the confidence they showed in us as we worked through this often-difficult project.

The library staff at FGCU, in particular our subject librarian, Rachel Tait, have assisted in numerous ways throughout the project and deserve our deep respect and gratitude.

We have been fortunate throughout the writing of this book to have a remarkable editor at ABC-CLIO who has shown faith in the project from its inception. To Padraic (Pat) Carlin, we are pleased to express our appreciation for his help, ideas, and forbearance. The book would not have been completed without his assistance.

Introduction

On November 10, 1945, Hermann Graebe, a German manager and engineer in charge of a building firm in Ukraine, swore an affidavit before Major Homer B. Crawford of the United States Army's War Crimes Branch. In this, Graebe described the process by which the Rowno (Rivne) ghetto in Poland was liquidated in July 1943. He related that many of the people living there were driven onto the street just as they were, regardless of whether they were dressed or in bed. "Since the Jews in most cases refused to leave their houses and resisted, the Schutzstaffel (SS) and militia applied force. They finally succeeded, with strokes of the whip, kicks and blows with rifle butts in clearing the houses. The people were driven out of their houses in such haste that small children in bed had been left behind in several instances. In the street women cried out for their children and children for their parents."[1]

Jewish children during the Holocaust were denied choices over their fate. As infants, juveniles, and adolescents, they had to rely on their parents, families, or other caregivers for sustenance and shelter; as Jews, they were caught in a net cast deliberately in their direction by Germany's Nazi regime and its collaborators in other parts of Europe.

The experiences of Jewish children were just as varied, within this awful uncertainty, as they were for adults—varied, and also different. As the examples in this volume show, those who were younger than 18 underwent a range of trials often quite different from those who were older. Their ordeals were many, their fates mostly dependent on others. What they experienced cannot be explained according to the standard classifications of victims, perpetrators, and bystanders; rather, because of their specific circumstances, it can be argued that it is more appropriate to describe the events to which children were subjected according to a different taxonomy, that of vulnerability, morality, and rescue.

The Vulnerability of Children

The French historian Marc Bloch, reflecting on the vulnerability of children in World War II, wrote that it is "intolerable that war should involve the very young," because "in their weakness and irresponsibility they make so confident an appeal to our protection."[2] This weakness and irresponsibility rendered them completely at the mercy of those who would destroy them. In a social environment where it was expected that children would be seen but not heard, they were already at a disadvantage; with the onset of the war, and persecution in which they were deliberately targeted *because* they were children—albeit of a special, Jewish, kind—they stood little chance of being able to withstand their tormentors.

Despite this, the resilience of children (and the quick thinking of their parents, themselves conflicted and tormented) often provided opportunities to overcome their state of helplessness. A few examples will suffice to show how their vulnerability could be overcome.

In the city of Simferopol, in the Crimea, a young girl, Ekaterina Danova, hid in a cupboard for two and a half years in order to avoid being picked up by the Nazis. Her ordeal lasted until the tide of war began to shift and she was able to resurface. Managing to reach the forest, she joined up with a partisan unit, survived the war, and was able to return to the house where she had obtained her original refuge.[3]

An eight-year-old boy in 1938, Fred Antman came from a Berlin Jewish family. He was subjected to various antisemitic measures at school, and then, in October 1938, he witnessed the arrest and deportation of his Polish-born father—part of the much larger events leading, eventually, to the *Kristallnacht* pogrom of November 9–10, 1938. Fred's young age precluded his appreciating fully the significance of what was happening.[4]

Donald Berkman was only an infant when the Nazis attacked the Soviet-occupied part of eastern Poland in the summer of 1941. Moved from his hometown of Druysk to ghettos at Vidzy and then to Swieciany, Donald and those with him eventually arrived at the much larger ghetto of Vilna (Vilnius), where almost all the inhabitants were murdered in the enormous bloodletting that took place in the Ponary Forest. While Donald was too young to be fully cognizant of the broader details of his and his family's experience, he later remembered certain things—such as his survival with his mother, being hidden as a result of the efforts of a friendly priest, and roaming the woods around Vilna until the end of the war.[5]

Marika Goldfayl's father was initially from Hungary and arrived in France in 1924 while in transit to the United States but decided to remain. The onset of war, and the collaborationist Vichy government, combined to render the family vulnerable. By 1942, when Marika was eight years old, her parents decided that she would be safer if hidden as an orphan in a convent school, where she remained for the duration of the war.[6]

In the aftermath of *Kristallnacht*, Jews all over Germany scrambled to try to find a way out of the Nazi trap, if not for their whole family, then for their children. A little girl aged only five, Ruth Fisch Kessler was given up by her parents to one of the **Kindertransport** transfers, which took her to safety in Britain where she lived out the war.[7]

A native of Gdov, Poland, Arnold Weitzenhof was only 12 years old when the Nazis invaded in September 1939. By 1940, the SS had rendered the town *Judenfrei*, or "free of Jews." Arnold and his brothers were taken to a hastily improvised concentration camp at Stalowa Wola and from there to a succession of other camps as the war unfolded. Eventually, he was the only member of his family to survive the Holocaust.[8]

For the most part, however, examples such as those shown here, where Jewish children of occupied lands survived, were exceptional. Most did not experience anything remotely approximating an end leading to survival. Their exposed situation —the "weakness and irresponsibility" to which Marc Bloch referred—rendered most Jewish children prime targets for the Nazis and their allies, resulting in catastrophic outcomes for these children throughout Europe.

Morality: Nazism and Mass Murder

In a remarkable documentary made in 2005, Danish film maker Ove Nyholm sought to learn what the motivations were of mass murderers in a time of war. Interviewing Serbian killers from the Yugoslav wars of the 1990s, he showed how such men, through their actions, acquired ancestors—the SS murderers of the Holocaust. He was, he said, attempting to plumb the depths of heartlessness. Quoting one of the *Einsatzgruppen* killers who was confronted by a victim just before he gunned the victim down in a pit killing, Nyholm reached what he considered to be the quintessential justification of genocide: "You must die," the SS officer said, "so that we can live."[9]

During the Holocaust the Nazis murdered over 1,500,000 children under 18 years old. In addition, vast numbers of Roma children, German children with physical and emotional disabilities, Polish children, and many thousands of others were also murdered. Children from all over occupied Europe were deported to their deaths in the German extermination camps situated in Poland. Tens of thousands of Polish children with Aryan features were stolen from their families and given to German couples.

In Germany from 1933 onward, Jewish children were subjected to a bewildering array of new rules and regulations that must have been incomprehensible—and, to their young sensibilities, deeply hurtful. At school they were separated from their non-Jewish friends and classmates, prior to being expelled altogether if the schools they attended were state institutions. They would then be denied membership in the sports clubs to which they had belonged before the Nazis took office. Inevitably, name-calling and bullying of Jewish children by others became acceptable forms of behavior. At home, Jewish children saw their parents descend into a welter of despair, as adult worries penetrated the fabric of family life.

Once the war broke out and Germany began to expand its territory, Jewish children became especially vulnerable to murder and death. Not only were they considered nonproductive, but they also symbolized the very Jewish future the Nazis were determined to destroy. On the principle that "nits make lice," children were frequently among the first victims sent to their deaths—or killed outright—when a Nazi unit entered a Jewish area, or when deportations to death camps took place. Babies, infants, and small children were, for obvious reasons, exceptionally vulnerable; not only were they themselves incapable of self-defense, but their parents, in trying to shield them from harm, often inadvertently took them into harm's way. Their parents often had their businesses stolen from them and "Ayranized," so the families faced difficulties in meeting their basic needs. Older children and adolescents had more of a chance of survival if they could convince the Nazis of their ability to work as slave labor.

After the Nazis established ghettos throughout Poland, Jewish children were especially susceptible to starvation, disease, and the ravages of climate—particularly when winter came, and there was a lack of heating and housing. When the ghettos were liquidated from 1942 onward, children were among the first (along with the elderly and the sick) to be "selected" for deportation to the death camps. With their mothers, they were also in the forefront of those murdered when the *Einsatzgruppen* came rampaging through the Soviet Union. On other occasions, children were selected to fill the deportation trains as a result of deliberate decisions made by the Jewish Council (*Judenrat*) leaders, working from the awful premise that by holding back stronger and more robust sections of the population, the ghetto might be spared on account of its labor productivity.

Jewish children were killed when they arrived at the death camps, and babies were murdered at birth. Those capable of labor were worked to death; they were abused and tormented by local Nazis or collaborators; they were murdered during reprisal raids and antipartisan operations. The Nazis murdered Jewish children on the grounds of racial ideology or because they possessed (or were perceived to possess) physical or psychological disabilities.

Although children were among the first to be murdered, at Auschwitz some were deliberately spared, to be exposed to pseudoscientific **medical experimentation**. Here, SS doctor **Josef Mengele** ran a laboratory for such purposes. Mengele's research subjects were better fed and housed than other prisoners, and they were temporarily safe from the gas chambers. But he was personally responsible for the deaths of an unknown number of victims, whom he killed via lethal injection, shootings, beatings, and through selections and deadly experiments. Mengele was especially notorious for his experiments on **twins**, and in his pseudo-scientific endeavors, he amputated limbs or infected one twin with typhus or other diseases to see how it would impact upon the other. He experimented with trying to artificially change a child's eye color by injecting chemicals into his or her eyes and engaged in blood transfusions from one twin to the other to see what would happen. Most of the victims died while undergoing these procedures or were killed once an experiment was over. Mengele would then routinely dissect their bodies.

This was a world in which usually accepted standards of morality were overturned, where the torture and killing of children became a state virtue. Such was the nature of Nazism that actions of this kind were the clearest expression of its antihuman views on society.

Rescue: Struggles and Risks

The oppressive environment in which Jewish children found themselves gave rise to a desperate need for rescue, and in this regard, some non-Jews risked their lives to help them survive. Throughout Europe they constituted only a fraction of the population that might have helped, but their importance transcends their numbers.

Rescuers came from all walks of life: rich and poor, religious and nonreligious; Catholics, Protestants, and Muslims; women and men; young and old; educated and uneducated. Most remain unknown to the larger public, though several thousand have been honored by Israel's Yad Vashem in Jerusalem as Righteous among the Nations for their efforts in saving Jewish lives. They were ordinary people who nonetheless performed extraordinary deeds, and, consistent with their quiet heroism, many in retrospect refused to see that what they did was anything more than "the right thing to do." Their actions were undertaken in secret, and not known generally, as there were people in the community willing to denounce them to the authorities (often for a bounty).

What did rescuers do? As Jews were progressively stripped of their rights, segregated, and isolated from the rest of the community, rescuers sustained them materially and emotionally. They conspired to hide Jews and smuggle them out of harm's way, and as it became clear that Jews were marked for extermination, rescuers helped them maintain an underground existence, often sheltering them within their own homes for at least part of the time.

Any of these activities could, depending on the circumstances, result in death for the rescuers if caught. In addition to this very real threat, rescuers carried other burdens. Forced to keep their activities covert, deception dominated their lives. Some helped manufacture new identities for the victims, obtaining or forging false papers and then coaching those they were helping so they could play their new Aryan roles appropriately. Finding hiding places, as well as obtaining food, frequently taxed their ingenuity and resources. Many deprived themselves of the routine intimacies of family and friends to avoid revealing secrets accidentally. They often enlisted their older children in their illicit activities and sometimes deceived the younger ones who might talk about the strangers living with them. In the atmosphere of the day, no one could be fully trusted, and they had to constantly be on guard.

Rescuers sometimes (though by no means always) undertook their activities for little reward and (again, by no means always) performed their activities voluntarily. Regardless, the potential risks involved in all such undertakings were very high, not only to those engaging in the rescues but also to their families. In addition, they often acted in an environment that was at best ambivalent about Jews and at worst virulently antisemitic; the perils of betrayal by neighbors and acquaintances were ubiquitous.

Jewish activists also created networks that rescued thousands of other Jews, often working alongside non-Jews for the common good. Sometimes Jewish rescuers of children could be found among underground fighting groups; in all, across Europe, there were more than 200 active Jewish rescue organizations. Some were deep in the heart of occupied territory, whereas others operated outside of the Nazi grip. Hundreds of Jews participated in these rescues, risking their lives on both an organizational and an individual level, assisting in smuggling and hiding activities, obtaining or creating false documentation, providing food and medical supplies, warning their fellow Jews about impending actions and deportations, establishing welfare societies, and harboring children in orphanages.

It is important to realize, in this context, that rescue was itself a form of resistance: an active, ongoing process of opposition to all aspects of life as intended by the Nazis. It could take many forms and arise over any issue. It was as much an attitude as a physical process, and it sought to negate the commands, rules, intentions, actions, statements, and deprivations imposed by the occupiers. Its numerous forms enabled men and women to take some measure of control over their fate in an environment in which survival and success were in no sense guaranteed. Every act of helping, encouragement, and cooperation that took place disproved the claim that an attitude of self-reliance could not be maintained, and individuals, groups, and movements all sought to establish and maintain this attitude. This was particularly the case in saving the lives of Jewish children. As resistance activities, these actions fused into a joint endeavor that sought to outlive the Nazis and ensure Jewish survival despite the odds.

Children of the Holocaust

In a work of this kind, thought must be given to those who are its focus. It was decided from an early date that the subject would best be served by reference to children *of* the Holocaust, rather than children *in* the Holocaust, as the best way to describe the general topic. Whether Jewish or German, it was agreed that in one way or another, all children had a relationship to the murderous dark that dominated Europe between 1933 and 1945 and that, as a result, "of the Holocaust" was a more appropriate way to describe those caught up in the terrible events of that time. Children from both sides of the Holocaust were inextricably intertwined, innocents in a world dictated by forces over which they had no influence (even less, control) and in which their fate was, all too often, predestined.

Notes

1. *Nazi Conspiracy and Aggression*, Office of the United States Chief of Counsel for the Prosecution of Axis Criminality. Washington, D.C.: U.S. Government Printing Office, 1946, Red Series, vol. V, pp. 700–703, Doc. 2992-PS.71222.
2. Marc Bloch. *Strange Defeat: A Statement of Evidence Written in 1940*. New York: Norton, 1968, pp. 129–130.
3. Ekaterina Danova. "A Ghetto in the Cupboard." In Julie Meadows and Elaine Davidoff (Eds.), *Memory Guide My Hand: An Anthology of Life Stories by Members of the Melbourne Jewish Community from the Former Soviet Union*. Caulfield South, Victoria: Makor Jewish Community Library, 2008.
4. Fred Antman. *A Tale of Three Cities: Berlin, Shanghai, Melbourne*. Caulfield South, Victoria: Makor Jewish Library, 2011.
5. Donald (Chipkin) Berkman and Maryann McLoughlin. *Two Voices: A Mother and Son, Holocaust Survivors*. Margate, NJ: ComteQ Publishing, 2010.
6. Marika Goldfayl. "The Orphanage." In *Memory Guide My Hand: An Anthology of Autobiographical Writing by Members of the Melbourne Jewish Community*, vol. 3. Caulfield South, Victoria: Makor Jewish Community Library, 2004, pp. 113–125.
7. Ruth Fisch Kessler and Maryann McLoughlin. *The Blue Vase: A Memoir of a Vienna Kindertransport Child*. Margate, NJ: ComteQ Publishing, 2013.
8. Arnold Weitzenhof. *This I Remember: A Polish Youth Survives the Shoah*. Margate, NJ: ComteQ Publishing, 2006.
9. *Anatomy of Evil (Ondskabens anatomi)*, Angel Films, dir. Ove Nyholm; prod. Janne Giese, 2005.

A

ABADI, MOUSSA (1910–1997)

Moussa Abadi was a French Jew from Syria who created a Jewish rescue network operating in Nice, France. Between 1943 and 1944, the Marcel Network, as it was called, saved 527 Jewish children ranging in age from babies to teenagers.

Moussa was born in Damascus on September 17, 1910, to Nassim Abadi and Farida Katran. When Moussa was 12, his mother died, and he was raised by his maternal grandparents in a strict Jewish religious environment. Attending school at the *Alliance Israélite Universelle*, he obtained a scholarship to enter the Sorbonne, and after arriving in Paris in December 1929, he proved to be an excellent student. In June 1933 he obtained a bachelor of arts degree and a certificate of child psychology, after which he became a graduate student in theater.

In December 1939 he met Odette Rosenstock, a young Jewish woman who had qualified as a medical doctor during the Spanish Civil War—during which time she supported the Republicans and assisted refugees. The two fell in love and became engaged. Because of the Nazi occupation of Paris in the summer of 1940, they fled south to the Italian-occupied zone of France, settling in Nice. Here, Moussa taught in a Catholic theological seminary, while Odette practiced medicine until anti-Jewish laws forced her to stop, after which she worked as a midwife.

Around the same time, Moussa published an antifascist article under the pseudonym Marcel Samade. He would use the name "Marcel" again in the future.

During his time in Paris, Moussa had begun a doctoral thesis, studying under a French medievalist, Gustave Cohen. After each had moved to Nice, they were reunited; Moussa then began attending some of Cohen's lectures. At one of these, Cohen introduced Abadi to a French cleric, Bishop Paul Rémond.

In 1942, after speaking with an Italian army chaplain fresh from the Eastern Front, Moussa learned that the Nazis were murdering Jews in Poland, Russia, and elsewhere. This gave him pause; if the Nazis had a systematic agenda in place, it was only a matter of time before they began killing Jews in France, too. Thus, when German troops and Vichy French police began to round up Jewish children in 1942, he decided the time had come to do something about it.

Accordingly, in November 1942 Moussa and Odette organized a rescue operation to prevent the deportation of this most vulnerable segment of society. There was one important logistical question that needed to be answered, however: How was it to be done?

Early in 1943 Moussa approached Bishop Rémond and asked for his help. Without hesitation Rémond swung into action, giving the young couple official roles within the church. Odette, under the alias "Sylvie Delattre," became a diocesan social welfare representative; Moussa became superintendent of Catholic education under the alias Monsieur Marcel, and with this, the Marcel Network was born.

To help facilitate their work, Rémond provided them with the assistance of several priests and office space at his official residence where forged papers and baptismal certificates could be produced. He signed a letter of appointment, giving them freedom to circulate freely and access to Christian institutions where children could be hidden.

Appropriately prepared, the Marcel Network began operations. After the Italian surrender in September 1943, the Nazis moved into Nice, and the full force of the Holocaust descended on the Jews of southern France. Moussa and Odette began rescuing Jewish children whose parents had already been deported or were in hiding and found them safe hiding places among the church institutions offered by Bishop Rémond.

Moussa also obtained support from Protestant ministers in the area, such as Pastors Pierre Gagnier and Edmond Evrard, who worked hard to find Protestant families prepared to shelter Jewish children. Throughout this entire time, the lives of the children, as well as of Moussa and Odette, were in constant danger.

While allocating children to welcoming families, a problem was presented in the form of how best to camouflage them so they would not give themselves away. Moussa saw that each child would have to undergo fundamental changes, with their names and personal histories altered. They consequently must lose their Jewish identity and learn a new, Christian one. Moussa called this "depersonalization" and found it one of the more difficult aspects of his rescue initiative—the more so because, when the war came to an end and surviving parents came to collect their children, often a new (and painful) reintegration process would have to begin.

In April 1944 Odette, who continually stayed in touch with "her" children, was denounced and arrested by the Gestapo. Tortured during her interrogation, she refused to reveal anything about the Marcel Network. Deported initially to Auschwitz, she was then sent to Bergen-Belsen, where she managed to survive until liberation in 1945. After a period of recuperation, she joined Moussa, who had managed to avoid capture in Nice during the final year of the war. Later, they were married.

In early 1948 they returned to Paris, where they remained for the rest of their lives. Odette resumed her work as a doctor, becoming director of social hygiene, while Moussa spent several postwar years facilitating the reintegration of Jewish children with their families.

In sum, the Marcel Network saved the lives of 527 children, hidden in sanctuaries throughout southeastern France. After the war neither Moussa nor Odette spoke about their work, and when it was revealed, many people were taken by complete surprise.

On September 15, 1997, Moussa Abadi died two days short of his 87th birthday and was buried in Montparnasse Cemetery. His wife committed suicide on July 29, 1999, at the age of 85, unwilling to live without her beloved husband.

Further Reading

Coleman, Fred. *The Marcel Network: How One French Couple Saved 527 Children from the Holocaust.* Washington, D.C.: Potomac Books, 2013.

ADELSBERGER, LUCIE (1895–1971)

Lucie Adelsberger was a German Jewish physician imprisoned at Auschwitz during World War II. There she provided medical care to Roma families (especially children) and to pregnant Jewish women, giving them midterm abortions and killing newborns in order to save their mothers' lives.

She was born on April 12, 1895, in Nuremberg, studied medicine at Erlangen, and began practice as a certified physician in 1920. She then moved to Berlin's Wedding district, where she worked at the Friedrichshain municipal hospital, receiving a postgraduate diploma in internal medicine (1925) and pediatrics (1926).

Lucie went into private practice as a pediatrician, specializing in immunology and allergies. In 1927 she joined a serological research group at the Robert Koch Institute, where she published some 15 scientific papers between 1924 and 1933. In 1933 she was dismissed due to the introduction of Nazi antisemitic laws that year. Harvard University in the United States then offered her a prominent faculty post in bacteriology, but she rejected it because she was unable to obtain a visa for her mother, who would be forced to remain in Germany if she accepted the position.

Lucie was able to maintain her private medical practice in Berlin but was stripped of her medical license in 1938 and could no longer call herself a doctor. Instead she was known as a *Judenbehändler*, an attendant of Jews. In 1938, after a 10-day visit to Harvard University undertaking research, she returned to Berlin. In 1939 she tried unsuccessfully to move with her mother to the United States.

Her mother died in early 1943, and on May 6, 1943, during a Nazi crackdown on Jews living in Berlin, Lucie was arrested. As one of the last Jews to be deported from Berlin, she was sent to Auschwitz on May 17, 1943. On May 19, the Nazis declared Berlin to be *Judenfrei*, that is, completely emptied of all Jews.

Upon arrival she had her head shaved and was deloused, disinfected, registered, and tattooed with the inmate number 45171. All her clothes and property were taken, and she was given a camp uniform. She and two other German Jewish physicians were selected to work as prisoner-doctors in the so-called Gypsy camp in Birkenau and in the woman's camp. Lucie's job was to issue rations, write detailed reports on her patients (which had to be updated every three days), and ensure the head count conformed to the number of prisoners registered. Losing count meant instant death.

The faces of the Roma children had lost all signs of childhood, and like the adults, they quickly became enfeebled. They were covered in scabies, and their stomachs were bloated by starvation. Many were no longer hungry due to having not eaten. They did, however, crave water, but this was forbidden because it was contaminated. Hunger, thirst, cold, and pain gave these children no peace, day or night.

On May 30, 1943, on just her second Sunday in the camp, there was a carnival-type atmosphere in the "Gypsy camp." Five Roma violinists played, another had an accordion, and there was dancing. After a period of festivities, the crowd was driven back into their barracks and put under lockdown. Later that night trucks drove up, and the SS called out names and numbers; that night, possibly as many as 2,000 Czech Roma were sent to their deaths.

Lucie continued to minister to the ills of surviving Roma, along with those in the women's camp. The "Gypsy camp" ended when the remaining Roma were gassed in the last week of July 1944, ending with the emptying of the camp on August 1, 1944. The camp was soon filled with Russian and Hungarian Jews. Lucie provided medical care in the camp's infirmary, particularly for prisoners suffering from a typhus epidemic then ravaging the camp.

At Auschwitz the general assumption was that all Jewish children automatically condemned their mothers to death. Prisoners who had been in the camp for any length of time would often try to move a child from its mother to its grandmother when the family was facing a selection. Grandmothers were already doomed, as were the children, but by removing a child from its mother, she might be able to survive.

Pregnant women were often admitted to Lucie Adelsberger's infirmary. They included women from mixed marriages (non-Jewish women who were married to Jewish men and who were generally spared the gas chamber) and childless full Jews whose pregnancies were not detected when they arrived. Often, where a Jewish child was delivered full term, both the mother and child were sent to the gas chamber within a week. A number of these had abortions as late as the fourth and fifth months. Lucie performed many of these secret abortions, often without anesthesia.

Moreover, the dangers to pregnant women came from another source: the medical experiments of Dr. **Josef Mengele**. His interest lay in how pregnant women suffering from typhus might pass the disease onto their children. Accordingly, he infected women with typhus in the final stages of their pregnancy to see if the placenta might serve as a barrier to infection. On other occasions he sent both the mothers and their newborn babies straight to the gas chamber. Knowing that newborns would not on any account be allowed to live, prisoner-doctors, including Lucie, chose to kill the babies so the mothers might live. They preferred to poison the babies, but when poison was unavailable, they—or the mothers themselves—would strangle or drown the newborns.

On January 18, 1945, as Soviet troops approached, Lucie was put on a death march out of Auschwitz. She walked in a column of emaciated prisoners through the deep snow, one step ahead of death. On January 21, 1945, after marching three days in freezing weather, the prisoners who were still alive traveled in open coal cars on a train for the next six days and nights as it progressed to Ravensbrück. On May 2, 1945, Lucie was liberated.

In 1946 she migrated to the United States and resumed practicing medicine as an immunologist at Montefiore Medical Center in the Bronx, New York. She published a memoir about her time in Auschwitz in 1956; it was translated into English in 1995. Lucie Adelsberger died in New York on November 2, 1971.

Further Reading

Adelsberger, Lucie. *Auschwitz: A Doctor's Story*. Boston: Northeastern University Press, 1995.

Waxman, Zoë. *Women in the Holocaust: A Feminist History*. Oxford: Oxford University Press, 2017.

ANDRÉ, JOSEPH (1908–1973)

Father Joseph André was a Belgian Roman Catholic priest from the diocese of Namur who helped save hundreds of Jewish children from deportation, and likely death, during the Holocaust.

He was born in in Jambes, in the Namur district, on March 14, 1908. In 1926 he joined the Jesuit order as a postulant, but after two years, plagued by poor health, he left. He still felt a religious calling, however, so after a period of contemplation and reflection, he entered the seminary of Namur and was ordained in 1936. He then taught at a Catholic high school in Floreffe for several years before being named curate of St. Jean-Baptiste Church in Namur.

Father André was committed to helping the poor and marginalized and was especially drawn to aiding Jews in need, which by extension came to include Jewish refugees from Nazism. Indeed, he had an abiding respect for Jewish religious and cultural traditions and was a strong advocate of religious freedom; given this, he did not attempt to convert Jews to Christianity. In 1933 he met Arthur Burak, a Jewish lawyer who had fled with his family from Nazi Germany, and the two became good friends. Later, in the summer of 1942, when deportations from Belgium started, Father André arranged a hiding place for Burak and took his two sons to his father's home in Jambes, close to Namur.

In the months leading up to the outbreak of World War II, Father André operated a parish youth center. When war came to Belgium, this would provide him with an ideal cover behind which to build a network designed to shelter and hide Jewish children. Known as the Home de l'Ange community center, it was located across the street from the local Gestapo headquarters. By early 1941 it had become the hub of a secret organization that aimed to hide Jewish children and save them from deportation. The Home de l'Ange served as a transit house where up to 20 children at a time were sheltered for a few days before being entrusted to monasteries or private homes where they could remain in hiding. Father André did this at great personal risk, as aiding Jews could have resulted in his own arrest and deportation. To feed the children in his care, he and those with whom he worked traveled throughout the region, seeking the assistance of local farmers and village folk. Although the Gestapo periodically suspected him and interrogated him on several occasions, he managed to elude serious scrutiny. On the many occasions when a search took place, the children escaped to the building behind the center. In most instances, the searches passed without incident, but sometimes Jews were arrested in the building or in nearby homes.

In December 1943 there were 35 Jewish children hidden at the Home de l'Ange, aged from 8 to 12 years old. Older children, aged 15 to 17, generally found work and lodging with local families. Father André was supported in his work largely through donations, while André-Marie Charue, the Bishop of Namur, not only favored his activities but also provided him with financial assistance. Through this connection Father André could remain in touch with other parishes as well as convents and monasteries to where he could transport Jewish children; through their silence and cooperation, the children's rescue network was never uncovered and remained active until Belgium's **liberation** after September 1944.

In 1943 Father André began working with Belgium's clandestine Jewish resistance organization, the *Comité de Défense des Juifs* (Committee for the Protection of Jews, or CDJ). Though never formally a member, he was thoroughly sympathetic to their goals, and he personally arranged for 66 CDJ members to be hidden. He kept sufficient distance, however, to not compromise the secrecy of his work.

With an intensification of Allied bombing in May 1944 and the occupying Germans becoming anxious at the prospect of an Anglo-American invasion of Europe, the situation for both Jews and resisters became imperiled. It was decided to disperse the children still in Father André's care, while he was himself forced to go underground. He found a hiding place in Moorsel, in east Flanders, where he stayed until Belgium's liberation in September 1944. After this, the Home de l'Ange again became a transit center, this time to reunite children with their returning families.

It is not possible to say for certain how many Jewish children Father André helped from mid-1942 onward, but certainly several hundred passed through the Home de l'Ange on their way to more permanent places of refuge. Father André's informal organization, *L'Aide Chrétienne aux Israélites* (Christian Assistance to Jews), was organized loosely, with no fixed hierarchy. It is estimated that this group alone helped up to 250 children find hiding places, and several other priests, including Father **Bruno Reynders**, were also involved in the network.

In 1948 Father André followed closely the birth of the new state of Israel, and for the rest of his life, he maintained an active involvement with the Belgian Jewish community. Then, in 1957, he became chaplain of the Namur jail, where he was able to further exercise his devotion to those in need of pastoral care.

On November 26, 1968, Yad Vashem in Jerusalem recognized Father Joseph André as one of the Righteous among the Nations, and he was present to receive the honor in person. He also traveled to New York at the invitation of the United Jewish Appeal, where he was lavishly praised for his efforts during the Holocaust.

Father Joseph André was found dead in his office in the Namur jail on June 1, 1973, aged 65.

Further Reading

Paldiel, Mordecai. *The Path of the Righteous: Gentile Rescuers of Jews during the Holocaust.* Hoboken, NJ: KTAV, 1993.

Vromen, Suzanne. *Hidden Children of the Holocaust: Belgian Nuns and Their Daring Rescue of Young Jews from the Nazis.* Oxford: Oxford University Press, 2008.

ANNE FRANK HOUSE

The Anne Frank House is a museum dedicated to **Anne Frank**, the Jewish girl who kept a diary while in hiding during the Holocaust. The building is in Amsterdam at Prinsengracht 263.

The house was built in 1635 and underwent several renovations. During one of these, a small extension was built on the back, shielded from view by buildings in a quadrangle. Originally a private residence before becoming a warehouse, in the early 20th century, it became the site of a small factory catering to various businesses. On December 1, 1940, Anne's father, Otto Frank, relocated the offices of the Opekta spice company to this location, which was still used for apartments. By this stage the German invasion had taken place, and the persecution of Jews in the Netherlands had begun.

This area of the building was known as the Secret Annex. The first floor served as the operational area of the business, while the second floor housed Frank's office and those of his employees. The Secret Annex was the rear extension of the building, concealed from view by houses on all four sides of a quadrangle. As arrests of Jews intensified under the Nazi occupation, the sheltered location of the Annex made it an ideal place for Otto Frank; his wife, Edith; their daughters, Margot and Anne; and four other Jews seeking refuge from persecution. Frank's employees helped with the deception. During their time in hiding, Anne kept a diary chronicling her hopes, fears, and daily life. The little group remained hidden here for two years and one month until, on August 4, 1944, the Annex was raided by Nazis acting on a tip. Everyone was arrested and deported to concentration camps where all, save Otto Frank, died.

Shortly after the raid, the hiding place was cleared by the Nazis, and all traces of the Frank

The Anne Frank House is a museum located in Amsterdam dedicated to Anne Frank, the Jewish girl who kept a diary while hiding in this building during the Holocaust. The third most-visited museum in the Netherlands, it preserves Anne's hiding place and has a permanent exhibition on her life and times. An exhibition space also addresses all forms of persecution and discrimination. (Courtesy of Massimo Catarinella)

family's belongings were removed. **Miep Gies**, one of Otto Frank's employees who had aided the family in the deception, returned to the location and retrieved the scattered pages of Anne's diary. Fearful that the Gestapo would find it and hunt down those mentioned in it, Gies kept it in her home in an open drawer, which she guessed would cause the least suspicion.

After the war, Gies returned the papers to Otto Frank. The diary was then published in edited form in 1947 and became an immediate international bestseller, eventually appearing in 50 languages. Soon after this an informal traffic began in which Otto Frank's employees showed visitors the secret rooms in the Annex. By 1955, however, the building was in danger of demolition, and it was only saved as a result of a public campaign seeking to have it listed as a protected monument, as well as a protest on the site on the scheduled day of demolition.

On May 3, 1957, Otto Frank and Johannes Kleiman established the Anne Frank Foundation with the aim of collecting funds to purchase and restore the building, protecting it from developers. In October of that year, the building was donated to the Foundation, and the funds that had been collected to that point were used to purchase the house next door.

On May 3, 1960, the Anne Frank House was established as a museum to the public. In its first year, about 9,000 visitors came to bear witness to Anne's experience. Within a decade, there were twice as many, and since the mid-2000s the Anne Frank House has seen over a million visitors per year. The apartment has been left as it was at the end of the war, stripped of furniture but with many reminders of the family throughout. Anne's movie-star posters are still pasted on the wall, along with a few mementos. The museum preserves the hiding place and has a permanent exhibition on Anne's life and times, with an exhibition space addressing all forms of persecution and discrimination. Visitors usually fall silent as they move through the Annex. The Anne Frank Foundation, which owns the building, also engages in antiracist education programs and organizes traveling exhibits.

After a refurbishment, Queen Beatrix of the Netherlands rededicated the museum on September 9, 2001. To this day, it is the third most-visited museum in the Netherlands, after the National Museum (*Rijksmuseum*) and the Van Gogh Museum. It now incorporates not only the entire building, but also exhibition spaces, a bookstore, a cafe, and the reconstructed front offices as they were in the 1940s.

Further Reading

Frank, Anne. *The Diary of a Young Girl*. New York: Doubleday, 2003.
Gies, Miep. *Anne Frank Remembered*. New York: Simon and Schuster, 1987.
Lee, Carol Ann. *The Hidden Life of Otto Frank*. New York: HarperCollins, 2003.

ASSOCIATION OF CHILDREN OF THE HOLOCAUST

The Association of Children of the Holocaust (*Stowarzyszenie Dzieci Holocaustu*) is a Polish organization whose primary aims are to create a community of persons who survived the Holocaust and give them support, to never forget the experiences of the Holocaust, and to preserve the memory of Jewish life in prewar Poland.

Membership of the Association is defined through reference to survivors who, at the outbreak of World War II, were 13 years of age or younger, or were born during the war, and who, because of their Jewish origins, "were targeted for extermination by the Nazi occupiers, were incarcerated in ghettos, concentration camps or death camps, or had to conceal their identity."

The origins of the Association date to 1991, when, at the First International Gathering of Children Hidden during World War II, held at the Marriott Marquis Hotel in New York on May 26–27, there were 19 Polish survivors and three Polish rescuers recognized by Yad Vashem as Righteous among the Nations. At that time the decision was made to create a Polish organization of children who had survived the Holocaust.

When the founding meeting took place at the headquarters of the Jewish Historical Institute in Warsaw on June 27, 1991, 45 people attended. On September 25, 1991 the Warsaw Provincial Court registered the Association formally, and by the time of the first General Assembly on October 11, 1991, membership had doubled, from the initial 45 to 90 members. The first chairperson (remaining in this position until 2000) was Professor Jakub Gutenbaum, who, as a 13-year-old, survived by hiding in a basement during the Warsaw Ghetto Uprising of 1943. Since its establishment, branches of the Association have been established in Kraków, Wrocław, Łódź, and Gdańsk. The Association has honorary members and several supporters who live abroad but have Polish and Jewish roots.

The most important commitments of the Association include the following: increasing and disseminating knowledge of Nazi crimes perpetrated during World War II, especially against Jewish children; preserving and consolidating the memory of Holocaust victims and of persons who risked their lives in rescuing the persecuted; condemning expressions of intolerance, particularly those relating to antisemitism in public life; organizing various forms of assistance for Association members; and initiating and stimulating attempts by Association members to obtain benefits stemming from relevant legislation in Poland as well as compensation for moral and material harm suffered during World War II.

To achieve these aims, the Association undertakes several activities. One of the most important, in view of the survivors' advancing age, is to pursue efforts to improve the material well-being of the membership. Part of this requires the provision of programs designed to help members overcome a sense of loneliness and isolation. Given the nature of its membership, furthermore, the Association is aware that some members are still traumatized by their wartime and postwar experiences and, increasingly, can be living alone. Association activities and meetings are thus, frequently, the only place where members can talk freely about their concerns.

An area of great importance to the Association relates to the ongoing task of honoring the Righteous among the Nations, those who risked their lives to save Jews during the Nazi years. This became one of the Association's major tasks after its formative years, and a breakthrough in the Association's quest for recognition came when the Polish government acknowledged that those classed as Righteous should be accorded the status of war veterans.

The early years of the Association were devoted to increasing the number of members and giving them financial support. Since then, its activities have branched out in a variety of directions, always with an eye to achieving its fundamental objectives. As a result, the Association organizes psychotherapy sessions for those needing them, as well as medical and social care, and opportunities for stays in sanatoria and rest houses. Visits to health centers and holiday excursions (in Poland and Germany) are also organized, made possible by the support of the Maximilian Kolbe Foundation in Freiburg and the social welfare program of the Union of Jewish Religious Communities. Trips have been organized to Israel under Association patronage.

Beyond this, monthly meetings for members are held in all branches, in which special guests are featured such as artists, politicians, writers, and journalists. Every year a General Assembly takes place attended by Association members from all over Poland and abroad, which brings together up to 150 people (though numbers have been declining in recent times). Honored guests at the Assembly, when they attend, are those designated as Righteous among the Nations. Another important area of the organization's activity is an educational program called "Memory for the Future" (*Pamięć dla przyszłości*), which familiarizes young people with the history of the Holocaust. This meets another of the key objectives of the Association, which is to preserve the memory of the Holocaust and pass on its legacy to future generations.

Another way to place this last goal into practice has been for members of the Association to publish their memoirs, produce films, deliver lectures and talks, and organize exhibitions. The Association operates a speakers' bureau and educational programs aimed at teachers and school children.

Most Association members are women. Jewish boys during the Holocaust were much more vulnerable to detection by the Nazis, and therefore to murder, due to the fact of their **circumcision** and the historical reality that this was not generally practiced among non-Jews in Poland.

With the advance of years, the number of Association members diminishes, keeping in mind that most were born between about 1927 and 1939, with relatively few born during the war years. Members of the Association are acutely aware that they represent the last generation of those who survived and are the only remaining Jewish eyewitnesses, in Poland, of the Holocaust. They understand fully that the mission of the Jewish children who were saved is to communicate what they experienced and to tell people of the enormous crime of genocide suffered by the Jewish people.

Further Reading

Sliwowska, Wiktoria (Ed.). *The Last Eyewitnesses: Children of the Holocaust Speak*. Evanston, IL: Northwestern University Press, 1998.

B

BARKMAN, FRANCES (1885–1946)

Frances Barkman was a teacher and Jewish welfare worker. A child refugee, she was born in March 1885 in Kiev, Russia. Most of her family had been massacred in pogroms, and she escaped with her parents, Joseph and Anna Barkman, prior to migrating to Melbourne, Australia, in 1891 at the age of six. She was educated at the Rathdowne Street State School and the Melbourne Training College, and while teaching in the Victorian Education Department, she graduated from the University of Melbourne with a diploma in education and a bachelor of arts degree.

From an early age, Frances developed cultural interests, which she later demonstrated by convening the dramatic circle of the Lyceum Club. As a young teacher in suburban state schools and then at Melbourne's Continuation School, between 1911 and 1936, she was energetic in organizing dramatic performances. Her major academic area was French, in which subject she was appointed an examiner for the university's public examinations. For her "outstanding interest and promulgation of French literature, art and teaching," she received two awards in the 1930s from the government of France. Throughout her career she was a leading member of the *Alliance Française* in Victoria.

To help alleviate the distress of Jews who had fled from the Nazis, the Australian Jewish Welfare Society was established in Sydney in 1936, with a separate Victorian organization founded in Melbourne soon after. Frances served as the Victorian honorary secretary.

In this capacity, on December 13, 1938, she proposed furthering the immigration of Jewish refugee children to Australia, and she was largely responsible for initiating schemes to bring them into the country. She also arranged local assistance for the new arrivals once they were admitted, seeing to it that representatives from the Welfare Society met incoming ships with refugees on board. Older children were then looked after by guardians identified through the Welfare Society, while those who were younger were accommodated at a special home created in 1939 for 32 refugee children at Frances Barkman's initiative. Larino, an old mansion in the then–outer Melbourne suburb of Balwyn, was acquired by the Australian Jewish Welfare Society and became the permanent location of the relief services offered to juveniles. An initial group of 17 Jewish refugee children managed to arrive and were housed at Larino before war broke out in September 1939.

Frances was known as a tough disciplinarian and a stickler for rules, but at the same time, she sought to make Larino as much like a home as possible for the children, given that most of them had left parents behind in Germany. Always concerned to ensure that the children in her care would obtain the best advantage for entering Australian society, she habitually forced new arrivals to anglicize their names, and she imposed these changes unilaterally. Larino was organized on strict Jewish lines, with mandatory Shabbat observance, visits to the St. Kilda synagogue, and the availability of kosher food. Frances was also an astute user of the media to win support for her causes, fighting to create sympathy for Jewish refugee children whenever possible.

What Frances Barkman began at Larino turned into a Welfare Society norm, and when Larino was sold in 1965, two new homes, designated "Frances Barkman Houses," were established to commemorate their founder.

During World War II, Frances became an inaugural member of the Free French Movement in Australia and was a leading advocate of its cause throughout the German occupation of France. From 1942 she taught at MacRobertson Girls' High School, where she took charge of war relief organization, "bullying" (it was said) her students into raising money for the patriotic fund and producing vast quantities of khaki wool so the girls could knit their quota of balaclavas. Following the liberation of France in 1944, she initiated a scheme to obtain French educational materials for Australian schools and was keenly supported by the French government.

After years of selfless work at the expense of her health, Frances Barkman died of cancer on September 1946 at St. Vincent's Hospital, Fitzroy, and was buried in Fawkner cemetery. As she had never married, her will named the University of Melbourne and the Australian Jewish Welfare Society as her chief beneficiaries and provided educational bursaries for students in the Jewish refugee homes.

Further Reading

Bartrop, Paul R. "Barkman, Frances (1885–1946)." *Australian Dictionary of Biography*, vol. 13. Melbourne: Melbourne University Press, 1993, p. 114.

Palmer, Glen. *Reluctant Refuge: Unaccompanied Refugee and Evacuee Children in Australia, 1933–1945*. Sydney: Kangaroo Press, 1997.

BAUMAN, JANINA (1926–2009)

Janina Bauman was a girl of 13 when Germany invaded Poland on September 1, 1939. Soon after this, together with her mother and sister, Zosia, she was imprisoned in the Warsaw Ghetto until escaping to the country where they were given shelter by a peasant family.

Born as Janina Lewinson in Warsaw to a surgeon, Szymon Lewinson, and his wife, Alina *née* Fryszman, on August 18, 1926, she came from an assimilated, educated, well-off Jewish family and enjoyed an idyllic childhood, embracing a certain measure of privilege. The family lived outside the Jewish area of the city.

When war came to Warsaw, Janina and her family sheltered in their cellar from the constant bombing and shelling. Her father, a reserve officer in the Polish Army, was deployed to a military hospital but was captured by the Red Army after the Soviet invasion of September 17, 1939. Taken to the Kozielsk officers' camp, he was later murdered by Soviet troops in the Katyn Forest massacre of April and May of 1940.

By the end of September 1939, Polish resistance to the twin invasions had been crushed, and Warsaw was occupied by the Germans. Janina was forced to wear a white armband with a blue star; Zosia, her sister, aged nine, was not. Janina recalled later that the Jews of Warsaw were anything but confident that they would not be targeted by the Nazis, as they were aware of what the fate had already been for Germany's Jews. With the likelihood that a ghetto could be established, some Jews tried to run away to the Soviet side, at a time when the border between the two occupations was still somewhat porous. Janina's family did not move, however, as they were awaiting news of her father; her grandmother was also seriously ill and unable to travel.

After the ghetto was established in 1940, Janina, Zosia and their mother were forced to relocate there, and for the next 26 months, they did the best they could to make do. They lived in a tiny, overcrowded apartment without a bathroom. Food was in short supply and would become scarcer as time went by. Despite this, the girls were able, for a time, to continue their education with other children in private homes. Going to these classes through the streets of Warsaw, Janina saw corpses lying on the pavements and people dying of starvation. Homelessness was near-universal, and begging characterized much of what she witnessed daily.

To try to help alleviate the distress she saw, Janina joined *Towarzystwo Popierania Rolnictwa*, or *Toporol*, a prewar organization sponsored by the American Joint Distribution Committee. In its attempts to support and encourage agriculture, *Toporol* had created an agricultural school for young people in which small patches of ground were transformed into vegetable plots. The produce grown there was handed across to the Jewish Council (*Judenrat*) for the soup kitchens created to help those who were starving.

As the war against the Jews intensified, deportations from the ghetto started to take place, increasing in intensity throughout 1942. Calls for resistance organized by **Jewish youth movements** started circulating, culminating in a first strike against the Nazis in January 1943. Janina, now aged 16, wanted to join this movement, but, coming from a largely assimilated background with few prior contacts in the Jewish community, she had no idea how to connect. So, after this first expression of organized resistance, Janina, her mother, and Zosia escaped the ghetto on January 25, 1943. For the next two years, they were constantly on the run, moving from one safe house to another and depending on the kindness of sympathetic Poles.

At the time of the Warsaw Uprising between August and October 1944, Janina contracted tuberculosis—a legacy of living in the ghetto. The little party of three were hidden with other families in a cellar, while their neighbors brought in food for them. After Janina's recovery, they moved to southern Poland, hiding in the house of a peasant woman in the country. It was here that Janina, while peeling potatoes over a newspaper spread on the kitchen floor, learned of the death of her father in the Katyn Forest. The shelter they found with the old woman—and her son, a priest—enabled them to survive until Soviet troops arrived.

After the **liberation**, Janina, her mother, and sister returned to Warsaw. Janina studied journalism at the Warsaw Academy of Political and Social Science, where she met her future husband, sociologist Zygmunt Bauman. Zosia and her family left for Israel in 1957 with her mother, but Janina remained in Warsaw and worked in the film industry as a translator, researcher, and script editor. She left Poland for Israel with her husband and three daughters in 1968, but after three years there, they decided to settle permanently in the United Kingdom, where Zygmunt took the chair of sociology at the University of Leeds. Janina worked as an assistant school librarian and upon her retirement she wrote her autobiography, *Winter in the Morning*, based in part on diaries she had kept as a young girl. A second volume of memoirs focusing on her life in postwar Warsaw, *A Dream of Belonging*, was published in 1988.

Janina Bauman died in Leeds on December 29, 2009, aged 83.

Further Reading

Bauman, Janina. *Winter in the Morning: A Young Girl's Life in the Warsaw Ghetto and Beyond, 1939–1945*. New York: Free Press, 1986.

BERG, MARY (1924–2013)

Mary Berg was a child who survived the Warsaw Ghetto and wrote, in 12 notebooks, a diary of her experiences in the Holocaust. Her entries were written between October 10, 1939, and March 5, 1944, during which Poland was occupied by Germany.

Mary Berg was born Miriam Wattenberg on April 20, 1924, to Shaya (Sruel) Wattenberg, a local gallery owner in prewar Łódź, and his wife, Lena, who was a U.S. citizen living in Poland. Her birthday was changed to October 10, 1924, after the Nazis made it illegal for a Jew to share the same birth date as Adolf Hitler. Mary and her younger sister Anna were qualified for U.S. citizenship because of their mother's American nationality.

On September 1, 1939, Germany invaded Poland. Beginning October 10, 1939—her 15th birthday—Mary commenced writing a diary, setting down the everyday events affecting her family and the community. The diary detailed the sufferings experienced during the Warsaw Ghetto, the siege of Warsaw, the Warsaw Ghetto Uprising and its defeat, forced labor, deportations, and the final destruction of the ghetto.

When the Germans entered Łódź, the family fled, walking and bicycling the 70 miles to Warsaw. A year later they were living in the Warsaw Ghetto. Mary wrote that she was aware that the funds her family had brought with them from Łódź saved them from the hunger and sickness of other ghetto residents. Just prior to the German moves on July 22, 1942, to liquidate the ghetto in what was codenamed *Grossaktion Warschau*, Mary, her parents, and Anna were moved to a prison in Pawiak, before being transferred to an internment camp for British and American citizens.

In January 1943 the family was sent to an internment camp in France, where they awaited a German prisoner exchange that would allow them to be relocated to the United States. Mary had smuggled out of Warsaw the diary she had begun four years earlier.

She could not have known that by the time she filled her 12 small notebooks, she would have experienced four years of Nazi terror and that she would have chronicled the details of certain key events of World War II. She was a caring, sympathetic child haunted by memories of the many thousands of innocent people who died in Warsaw. In a very moving entry in her diary, she described Dr. **Janusz Korczak** walking and leading the orphans in his care to the train that took them to Treblinka, where they were all killed.

Mary Berg's journey to freedom began on March 1, 1944, when the family took a train to Lisbon, Portugal. There, they boarded the ocean liner S.S. *Gripsholm* for the voyage to the United States. When they arrived later that month, Mary was 19 years old. There she met Samuel L. Shneiderman, a Polish journalist who worked as a reporter in Warsaw, Paris, and in Spain during the Civil War, until he left Europe in 1940. She allowed him to edit her notebooks. Two months later, her memoir was serialized in 10 monthly installments in a leading New York Yiddish newspaper, *Der Morgen Zshurnal*.

Translations of Mary's account were published by several other papers—an English-language afternoon paper, a German-language paper with a Jewish readership, and *Contemporary Jewish Record*, the forerunner to *Commentary* magazine. In February 1945, L. B. Fischer, a former German publishing firm that established temporary wartime headquarters in New York in 1942, produced the diary in book form. One of the first accounts of the Holocaust to appear in English, Mary Berg's account of life in the Warsaw Ghetto was highly successful. On the strength of its exposure, she appeared at New York City Hall to urge action to save the Jews of Poland. She was a sought-after speaker and gave interviews to live audiences and on the radio.

The diary went out of print in the 1950s, however, and Mary disappeared from public view thereafter. She refused to take part in any Holocaust-related events and took many steps to preserve her privacy, even dissociating herself from her own diary. It is understood that she lived in York, Pennsylvania, for many years, where she married William Pentin and called herself Mary Pentin. She died in April 2013, aged 88.

The diary was adapted into a play by Polish actor Jan Krzyżanowski, entitled *A Bouquet of Alpine Violets*, and was republished in its original form in 2006 (and reprinted in 2009) as *The Diary of Mary Berg: Growing Up in the Warsaw Ghetto*.

Further Reading

Berg, Mary. *The Diary of Mary Berg: Growing Up in the Warsaw Ghetto*. London: Oneworld Publications, 2006.

BIAŁYSTOK CHILDREN

Located in northeastern Poland, the city of Białystok, with a Jewish population prior to 1939 numbering approximately 50,000, was the site of a ghetto established in mid-1941. It is estimated that fewer than 1,000 Jews survived the war. It was also here, in August 1943, that the second-largest ghetto uprising took place, only behind that of Warsaw.

On August 15, 1943, the ghetto was surrounded by SS troops supplemented by Ukrainian, Estonian, and other auxiliary forces, and all Jews were ordered to report on the next day for evacuation. It was then that the revolt began. For the next five days, the poorly armed and undermanned Jews fought the Nazis, but on August 20, the inevitable happened; and with the death of the last of the Jewish resisters, the Białystok ghetto uprising came to an end. Over the next three days, deportations robbed the ghetto of virtually its entire population, with most of the Jews deported to death camps, including Treblinka and Auschwitz.

On August 21, 1943, during the ghetto liquidation, some 1,196 children from Białystok were deported to **Theresienstadt** (Terezín) in Bohemia. The oldest of these children was 14; the youngest was just four years old. The reason for this is in dispute and has been the subject of speculation ever since.

In the summer of 1941, an underground Jewish organization of public figures was formed in Bratislava, Slovakia, to be known as the "Bratislava Working Group." In the spring of 1942, the Working Group attempted to stop deportations of Jews from Slovakia to Poland. The group members were of different ideological and religious persuasions, and included Zionists, Orthodox Jews, and assimilated members. They were supported by a larger group of public figures and activists in the various youth movements.

In their attempt to halt the deportations, members of the group bribed key figures in the Slovakian regime and the German embassy. The summer of 1942 saw members of the group negotiating with Dieter Wislieceny, Eichmann's representative in Slovakia, whom they provided with large bribes. This temporary halt convinced the members of the Working Group of the effectiveness of bribery when dealing with the Nazi authorities. Following this, one of the leaders of the Working Group, Rabbi Chaim Michael Dov Weissmandel, initiated the Europa Plan, an ill-fated attempt to save all the Jews in Europe by ransoming them. The group trusted Wisliceny and believed that if world Jewry could come up with the money, the deportations would cease. Protracted negotiations between members of the group and figures in the SS were undertaken, beginning in November 1942 and lasting until August 1943.

It is still unclear how the Białystok children fitted into the larger scheme of Nazi-Jewish negotiations ongoing at the time. The Working Group was still negotiating for the ransom of European Jews, and in early 1943, a Swiss diplomat, Anton Feldscher, forwarded a British proposal to the German Foreign Office seeking permission for 5,000 Jewish children to be transferred to Palestine via Sweden.

In the spring of 1943, Mohammed Amin al-Husseini, the Grand Mufti of Jerusalem and an ally of Adolf Hitler, learned of the negotiations then taking place and hastened to prevent the rescue operation that would see Jews going to Palestine, with protests directed at the Germans and Italians as well as at the governments of Hungary, Romania, and Bulgaria. Demanding that the operations be scuttled, he suggested that the children be sent to Poland, where they would be subject to "stricter control" (that is, exterminated).

Dieter Wisliceny was later to attest that al-Husseini's intervention was a key to the scheme falling through. On the other hand, there were some in the Nazi hierarchy—reaching all the way to *Reichsführer-SS* Heinrich Himmler—who held that some Jewish children could be held in reserve for possible later negotiations. It was therefore decided that a consignment of children would be sent from Białystok to Theresienstadt, there to await a fate yet to be determined. Probably on August 21, the children were gathered near the train station, waiting to be deported. Rumors circulated that they would be exchanged for German prisoners of war and sent to safety in Switzerland, and some parents, hoping to save their children's lives, gave them up voluntarily. The Białystok children, together with a few medical helpers, arrived in Theresienstadt on August 24, 1943. These chaperones continued to Auschwitz, where some 20 were selected for forced labor and the rest gassed.

The children were not registered into the camp records. They were held in relatively good conditions and given extra food, while 53 Czech volunteers, mostly doctors and nurses, could cross the barrier to attend to them. They remained there in a special barracks called Kreta until October 5, 1943. During this time complex negotiations took place to save these children through some sort of "exchange" or "transfer," perhaps to Switzerland and then Palestine. When negotiations failed, the children, together with the volunteer doctors and nurses who accompanied them, were deported to Auschwitz, where they were gassed and burned on the eve of Yom Kippur (the Day of Atonement), October 7, 1943.

The order to do so came directly from Adolf Eichmann, Nazi Germany's head of the Gestapo's Department IV B4, who planned and carried out the Final Solution. It can be surmised that he did this after consultation with Heinrich Himmler and that the decision was, in fact, strongly influenced by the protests coming from Haj Amin al-Husseini. The children were kept alive as bait for possible Allied agreement to the idea, however, until it became obvious that the ransom initiative would not materialize. Only after that was the operation canceled by the Nazis, and the children, no longer considered useful, were murdered.

Further Reading

Bauer, Yehuda. *Jews for Sale? Nazi-Jewish Negotiations, 1933–1945*. New Haven, CT: Yale University Press, 1994.

Bender, Sara. *The Jews of Białystok during World War II and the Holocaust*. Boston, MA: Brandeis University Press, 2008.

BIRENBAUM, HALINA (b.1929)

Halina Birenbaum is a survivor of the Holocaust, born in Warsaw on September 15, 1929, to Jakub Grynsztajn and Pola, formerly Perl, née Kijewska. She was the youngest of three children in the family. On September 1, 1939, just days before her 10th birthday, Germany invaded Poland, and Halina's otherwise carefree childhood was shattered.

With Poland's defeat and the German occupation, the family found itself confined in the Nazi-imposed Warsaw Ghetto. Halina was to write later that her survival there was due exclusively to her mother's efforts when working at slave labor in a workshop where she sewed uniforms for the German army. Halina accompanied her mother to the workshop every day, where she hid under a sewing machine or a chair and benefited from the little soup her mother was granted by way of wages.

During the Warsaw Ghetto Uprising of spring 1943, Halina and her mother hid wherever they could find shelter, in bunkers, basements, and attics. In one bunker they managed to survive for three weeks, until they were discovered and taken to the *Umschlagplatz*, the assembly point for those going on trains to the death camps. When the train on which they were traveling arrived, they found that they had been sent to Majdanek. Halina's immediate thought was that they would survive imprisonment there due to the popular wisdom that it was only at Treblinka that Jews were killed. Still, caution was needed, and Halina again credited her mother for her survival. Perceiving—correctly—that children had little chance of surviving the process known as selection, she took a pair of high heels from a woman who had not survived the train trip and gave them to Halina to make her look taller and older. Halina retained the shoes for the duration of the war. When the selection at Majdanek took place, Halina, then aged 13, was passed as fit for labor, but her mother was sent to the gas chamber to be murdered.

Halina and her sister-in-law, Hela, remained in Majdanek for two months until, one day in July 1943, it was their turn to be killed. After surviving a night in the gas chamber, however, they were released, as that very night, the supplies of gas at Majdanek had run out. The next day, those whose lives had been spared were placed on a transport to Auschwitz.

Later, Halina would say that she was lucky in being transferred to Auschwitz, for she had been destined to die at Majdanek. Yet at Auschwitz her opportunities of survival, though slim, held out. On one occasion, a selection took place presided over by Dr. **Josef Mengele**. Hela, who was already very weak, was marked for the gas chamber. On hearing this, Halina began to shout that she would not allow Hela to be taken. Her insistence so impressed the SS overseeing the operation that both Hela and Halina were spared, though Hela, debilitated by the experiences she had undergone, succumbed soon after this.

In January 1945 Auschwitz was evacuated, and Halina was sent to Ravensbrück, where she stayed until being evacuated to her final camp, Neustadt-Glewe, in February 1945. It was here that she was liberated by the Red Army in May 1945. Now aged 15, she had no idea what she should do with her newly gained freedom. She was, however, fortunate in having found her eldest brother, Marek, who was the only other surviving member of her family.

By 1947 she decided that, owing to the rising tide of antisemitism in Poland, she would have to leave for Israel with the aid of a Zionist organization. Here, she married Chaim Birenbaum, started a family, and began a new life on a kibbutz.

She also turned to writing. As a poet and prose writer, much of her work has since focused on life and death under the Nazis, always with the underlying intention of promoting understanding and reconciliation between Jews, Poles, Germans, and others. She became best known in the English-speaking world for her autobiographical memoir *Hope Is the Last to Die: A Personal Documentation of Nazi Terror* (1971), first published in Polish as *Czytelnik* in 1967. It was a powerful work, informed not only by a desire to come to terms with what she and others experienced but also to proclaim the existence of good as well as a powerful affirmation of hope and faith. After the publication of *Hope Is the Last to Die*, Halina continued writing and speaking to young audiences in various parts of the world about her experiences during the Holocaust.

In recognition of her work, in 1999 the Polish president, Aleksander Kwaśniewski, awarded her the Order of Officer of Polonia Restituta, and in March 2001, she received the "Reconciliation Person of the Year" Award by the Polish Council for Polish Jewish Dialogue, for her "patient service to the sacred and difficult cause of reconciliation." Other awards she has received include the Freedom of the City of Warsaw, bestowed in 2018.

Further Reading

Birenbaum, Halina. *Hope Is the Last to Die: A Personal Documentation of Nazi Terror*. New York: Twayne, 1971.

BLATT, THOMAS "TOIVI" (1927–2015)

Thomas (Tomasz) "Toivi" Blatt was born to a Jewish family in the small Polish town of Izbica on April 15, 1927. As a 16-year-old at Sobibór in 1943, he participated in, and survived, the prisoner uprising that eventually led to the camp's closure.

In 1941 the Germans created a ghetto in Izbica with the intention of having it serve as a transit point for the deportation of Jews from Central Europe to the death camps at Sobibór and Bełżec. On April 28, 1943, Toivi and his family were taken to Sobibór. Within an hour of their arrival, his father, mother, and younger brother were gassed and burned. Toivi, with a few dozen others, was chosen to work in the camp—a place not intended to have a large permanent prisoner population. On one occasion, a group of Jews from Lublin who had been working at Bełżec were transferred to Sobibór. Some, realizing that they were about to be murdered, wrote notes that they left in their clothing, knowing that Jews would be sorting through their belongings after their death. One of them wrote, "We know we are being killed and the same thing will happen to you. We will not be defeated. Avenge our deaths." Toivi Blatt, who was to be imprisoned at Sobibór for half a year, had the job of sorting through the clothes of the dead. He found one of the notes left by the men from Bełżec and passed it to members of a resistance group that had been forming.

BLATT, THOMAS "TOIVI" (1927–2015)

It is estimated that more than 250,000 persons were murdered at Sobibór, located near the town of Włodawa in eastern Poland, after gassing operations began there in May 1942. Its victims were primarily Polish Jews, but Czech, Slovak, German, Austrian, French, Lithuanian, and Dutch Jews were also murdered there. The bodies of the victims were "processed" (that is, removed from the gas chambers, examined for valuables, and then burned in huge crematoria) by Jewish *Sonderkommandos*, or "special work squads." Toivi Blatt was in one of these.

Sobibór is best remembered for the successful revolt that took place there by Jewish prisoners led by Alexander Pechersky and Leon Feldhendler on October 14, 1943, in which 11 SS and several Ukrainian guards were killed. Some 300 prisoners escaped, though only about 50 survived World War II. Toivi was to write later that they did not anticipate their liberation, only that their actions would destroy the camp and that they would die from bullets rather than gassing. During the revolt, Toivi managed to evade the mines surrounding the camp, and he made a mad dash for the forest that lay beyond. He and a few others were successful, though many of those who had escaped were hunted down and killed within the coming days. Immediately after the revolt, every Jew who had remained there during the revolt was executed. *Reichsführer-SS* Heinrich Himmler ordered the camp dismantled; it was demolished and converted into a farm so that no trace remained.

Toivi and two fellow escapees then bribed a Polish farmer to hide them in his barn. This sanctuary did not last, however, for after a few months, the farmer, fearful of being caught, shot them and left them for dead. Toivi's companions died, but he survived with a gunshot wound to the jaw. He gathered his strength and moved on, surviving nearly a year of deprivation in the forest while waiting out the war in hiding. He then resumed his life in postwar Poland.

In 1957 Toivi emigrated from Poland to Israel, and then, in 1958, he moved to the United States. Making his living through the establishment of three electronics shops, he started a family of his own and settled in Santa Barbara, California.

Toivi Blatt saw it as his life's mission to document what took place at Sobibór. In the late 1970s and early 1980s, he was commissioned by American journalist and author Richard Rashke to help locate and interview Sobibór survivors for the story he was writing about the revolt. This led to the subsequent publication of a bestselling book, *Escape from Sobibor* (1982). By 1987 this had been adapted into a movie of the same title, directed by Jack Gold and featuring British actor Jason Norman as Toivi Blatt. The film also highlighted another child survivor of the camp and the revolt, Stanisław "Szlomo" Szmajzner (played by Simon Gregor), who, with Toivi Blatt (and another survivor, Ester Terner), contributed to the screenplay.

Around the same time as Rashke's book was released, Toivi returned to Europe to interview one of the SS guards at Sobibór, Karl Frenzel. He had been convicted and sentenced to life imprisonment after the Holocaust for war crimes (on evidence provided by Toivi and others) and served 16 years in prison but was ultimately released early on the grounds of ill health. Toivi later claimed that this interview was the first time an extermination camp survivor had spoken directly with one of the mass murderers from a death camp.

Toivi traveled regularly to the site where the camp once stood and used his recollections and observations in order to write two books about Sobibór. The first, *From the Ashes of Sobibor* (1997), dealt with his life before the war, the German occupation of Izbica, and the deportation of his family to Sobibór. The second was entitled *Sobibor, the Forgotten Revolt: A Survivor's Report* (1998).

On October 31, 2015, Thomas "Toivi" Blatt, then aged 88, died at his home in Santa Barbara of complications resulting from dementia. He was survived by three children and several grandchildren.

Further Reading

Blatt, Thomas (Toivi). *From the Ashes of Sobibor*. Evanston, IL: Northwestern University Press, 1997.
Rashke, Richard. *Escape from Sobibor*. Boston: Houghton Mifflin, 1982.

BORDER CROSSINGS

Fleeing the Nazi terror, with the intention of moving to a neutral or Allied country, was fraught with difficulty. To say that Jews faced obstacles when seeking sanctuary elsewhere is a massive understatement. In fact, given the difficulties of crossing the border it is less surprising that there were so few successes than that there were so many. Often the decision to attempt the crossing would be long-contemplated, but rarely did the opportunity arise to choose when it should be made. In a vast majority of cases, the urge to flee was sudden, forced upon Jews due to changed circumstances over which they had no control. Plans might be made carefully in advance, but rarely could they be acted upon; all too often the run for the border had to be an improvised, sudden affair.

Only a few European countries were able to maintain their neutrality throughout the war; being able to find ways to reach any of them successfully became the goal for many Jews on the run. For those in the occupied countries of Western Europe, Sweden, Switzerland, and Spain were within relatively easy reach and consequently offered the best chances of safe havens. Jews in Eastern Europe, on the other hand, had far fewer lands to which they could flee.

The decision having been made to flee—whenever the opportunity presented itself—the next realization that had to be faced was that crossing the border was invariably not something that could be done without help. Most of those seeking sanctuary were alien to the region; indeed, many might not originally be local at all, but had fled earlier from other parts of the Nazi empire. Success demanded the assistance of a third party (at least), to which the refugee was obliged to entrust his or her life (and often the lives of their family members if they were accompanying them). Usually, neither the refugee nor the rescuer knew each other, which could intensify the risk for the person in flight.

This extreme level of trust was often to prove ill-founded. People movers (in French the term was *passeurs*) rarely undertook the high-risk practice of taking people through the lines out of the goodness of their hearts, and frequently they would exact recompense for their efforts. Such payment occasionally ran to very high sums; how much, they reasoned, was a Jewish refugee prepared to pay for their life and that of their family? The money handed across, moreover, did not always result in the sought-after salvation. In too many cases, unscrupulous *passeurs* blackmailed the refugees for more money as payment against denunciation; sometimes, once the money had been handed over, the *passeur* would abscond with the cash, abandoning the refugee and leaving him or her either to make their own way or, more likely, to be picked up by a passing patrol.

Presuming successful transportation to the border, a further problem arose once the refugee arrived. *Passeurs* rarely crossed the border with "their" refugee, as their own major issue—that of getting back undetected—was the foremost of their concerns; after all, their home was in the area through which the refugee was simply traveling. It should also be kept in mind that border crossings were often dangerous for reasons beyond the prospect of capture (or worse) by the Nazis, with formidable geographical barriers such as the Alps or the Pyrenees or exposed seas such as the Kattegat or the Skaggerak.

Moreover, upon reaching the border (which was problematical enough), the question was invariably one of what to do next. In most neutral areas, the authorities had established a wide border zone in which refugees who were caught had to reckon with being turned away. On either side of that zone were barbed wire fences. And then what? Turn left, turn right? Go to the nearest village or town and declare oneself? Go to the first house seen and hope for the best? The issues were complex and accumulating for Jewish refugees who managed to cross the border. Getting there was only part of the problem. Traversing it and then negotiating next steps led to additional dilemmas that did not always have a successful outcome.

Saving Jewish lives was always perilous. What is often not considered is that evading the authorities formed only one part of the equation. Reaching the border undetected was obviously crucial, but getting across it brought its own problems. Immediate sanctuary was far from a given; in fact, the likelihood of being turned around and thrown back into the country of origin was an ever-present possibility. And thought must also be given to how the refugees were to hold body and soul together should they be allowed to stay. The problems, in short, did not end once a person reached the border or even once they managed to step over it.

It must never be forgotten, further, that rescuing Jews was an illegal act in both Nazi-occupied Europe and in the neutral countries. Violating the law requires a certain frame of mind willing to rebel against what is deemed to be legitimate authority, and not everyone is brave enough, or committed enough, to act when their moral conscience is challenged to the extent of standing out from the crowd and facing the consequences of doing so. If being a resister had its drawbacks, so also did being a rescuer.

Crossing the border with children presented greater problems still, as the cases of **Mila Racine** and **Marianne Cohn** show. Although collectively they saved hundreds of Jewish children by passing them across the French border into Switzerland, their clients made them highly vulnerable to being apprehended—which, in the long run, was what sealed their fate. On the other hand, cousins **Georges Loinger** and **Marcel Marceau** carried out innumerable crossings with children in ingenious ways, always with a view to their ultimate salvation.

All in all, the risks taken by people movers to rescue children were immense. Border crossing was an endeavor fraught with dangers, and without local community support networks, those taking care of the children could not expect any quarter if captured. Having to ensure their own freedom, and always on the run from gendarmes or soldiers, they assigned themselves the task of saving the lives of as many children as they could.

Further Reading

Bartrop, Paul R., and Samantha J. Lakin. *Heroines of Vichy France: Rescuing French Jews during the Holocaust*. Santa Barbara, CA: Praeger, 2019.

Paldiel, Mordecai. *Sheltering the Jews: Stories of Holocaust Rescuers*. Minneapolis: Fortress Press, 1996.

THE BOY: A HOLOCAUST STORY

The Boy is the title of a book by Israeli historian and author Dan Porat, published in 2010. Taking as its motif what is arguably the most iconic photograph to come out of the Holocaust—an unnamed little boy of about eight years old, with his hands upraised during the Warsaw Ghetto Uprising of 1943—Porat wove together a narrative in which he examined the horror of the Warsaw Ghetto from the perspectives of five different people whose lives intersected in the photograph of the boy.

Porat was not able to identify the little boy, though there have been numerous claims made about him: that he was killed soon after the photo was taken, that he was deported to Treblinka and murdered, that he survived, that he lives in the United States or Israel. Yet the book is not really an attempt to trace the fate of the boy himself but, rather, to show what he has come to symbolize regarding the overall Holocaust experience. In looking at the fear and bewilderment on his face, he embodies the horror facing all those who lived and died as innocent victims of the Nazis. As such, *The Boy* combines literary imagination with observations and evidence from letters, journals, and official reports.

The image of the little boy does not focus only on the boy himself or the other victims in the picture; standing behind him are two SS guards (presumably there are others nearby), their submachine guns at the ready. The SS man staring at the camera has been identified, and he features in Porat's masterful reconstruction of events. His name is Josef Blösche, and in the book, his story is told in detail. Obsessed with obeying orders no matter what they might be, Blösche has become just as much a symbol of the dreadfulness of the Holocaust, in his way, as the little boy has in his.

Porat's identification of Josef Blösche is balanced by a detailed study of two Nazis whose stories intersect with that of the little boy: Franz Konrad, who took photographs in the ghetto, possibly including that of the boy; and SS General Jürgen Stroop, who was most responsible with unleashing the terrible forces employed to liquidate the ghetto. To round out the picture, Porat also examines two Jews: another young boy, Zvi Nussbaum; and Rivkah Trapkovits-Farber, a teenage girl who was seemingly everywhere during the killing times and managed to survive to bear witness. Linking these five stories, Porat provides a focus by which we can appreciate something of the little boy beyond just looking at his terrified face.

The Boy is illustrated with 60 photographs chosen carefully for what Porat clearly intended to be a didactic purpose. Those reading the book and looking at the photographs cannot help but stop and consider many of the issues about reading such images that Porat raises. And although the boy is the central figure in the photograph, it is those on whom Porat rests his study who expose us to the true essence of what happened during the Warsaw Ghetto Uprising and what it represents for the overall history of trying to come to grips with the Holocaust narrative more broadly.

Many of the photographs in the book were taken directly from Jürgen Stroop's official report that recorded the end of the Warsaw Ghetto. He created a detailed 75-page report, covering the period April 24, 1943, to May 24, 1943, with 69 photographs and documents. Carefully bound in black leather and entitled *The Jewish Quarter of Warsaw Is No More!*, the Report was intended as a souvenir album for Heinrich Himmler. Franz Konrad, Stroop's personal photographer, snapped the photograph with the little boy; as Porat shows, it was Stroop himself who provided the caption: "Pulled from the bunker by force."

As this is a study as much of photographs as it is of text, Porat gives attention to how those beholding such images are to consider them. Adopting a critical eye when evaluating the photograph of the little boy—indeed, of all the images in this volume—he has actually composed a scholarly detective story. He wants to know not only about the little boy and the circumstances in which he found himself at this terrible time in April 1943 but also the identity of the man behind the camera and who authorized (or ordered) that he take this photograph. Therefore, *The Boy* is not only about the little boy. We will probably never know conclusively the identity of this young, terrified child, hands upraised and with sheer terror on his face. Dan Porat undertook an immense amount of research to try to piece together the narrative dominating this story, and his descriptions—of Jewish victims, of Nazis, and (so far as he could) of the little boy himself—deliver a remarkable piece of historical reconstruction that takes the Holocaust into new realms of understanding for future generations.

Further Reading

Porat, Dan. *The Boy: A Holocaust Story*. New York: Hill and Wang, 2010.

BRUNDIBÁR

Brundibár—the colloquial name in Czech for a bumblebee—is a children's opera by the Czech composer Hans Krása, usually considered to be an allegory of the triumph of good over evil. It tells the story of a brother and sister, Pepiček (Joey) and Aninka (Annette), who manage—with the help of three animals and many other children—to defeat *Brundibár* (a metaphor for Adolf Hitler), an evil organ grinder, who will not let them sing in the marketplace to raise money to buy milk for their sick mother. With *Brundibár* defeated the children can finally sing, and as a result of their singing, they earn enough money to buy the milk needed. As an allegory of good defeating evil, it relates a lesson that this can happen, not through violence but rather through solidarity and perseverance. The opera is divided into two short acts and can be staged in less than 40 minutes.

Poster designed by Walter Heimann, who died in 1945. *Brundibár* is a children's opera by the Czech composer Hans Krása. Composed in 1938, the opera was most successful at the Theresienstadt (Terezín) concentration camp during the Holocaust. It became the camp's greatest musical success, completing 55 performances before the last transports left Terezín in the fall of 1944. (Poster by Walter Heimann)

The opera was composed in 1938 and first staged in Prague, but where it was most successful was at the **Theresienstadt** (Terezín) concentration camp, which became operational as a combination ghetto and camp on November 24, 1941. That same month, *Brundibár* was staged in secret at a Jewish orphanage in Prague. In 1942, the Nazis sent some of that orphanage's directors and children to Terezín. The opera's composer, Hans Krása, was also deported at the same time.

In 1943 *Brundibár* arrived at Terezín when a well-known Czech pianist, Rudolf Freudenfeld-Franěk, was deported and managed to smuggle a piano arrangement in with him. Hans Krása then orchestrated the opera for the instruments available in the camp, and rehearsals began in secret in the attic of the Dresden Barracks. Theater director Frantisek Zelenka built the scenery with stolen timber; Kamila Rosenbaum, a famous dancer from Vienna, choreographed it; and on September 23, 1943, *Brundibár* opened in the Magdeburg shack at Terezín. It went on to become the camp's greatest musical success, completing 55 performances before the last transports left Terezín in the fall of 1944. It bore witness to the day-to-day life of the prisoners, and, amid suffering, violence, and death, provided some hope and encouragement, particularly for the children who were watching and those performing in it.

Brundibár, indeed, was Terezín's foremost attraction. Although admission was free, people could only see it through possession of a ticket—and demand for these remained high right through to the last performance. Not only was the music easily accessible and enjoyable for those listening, but the story line was one that advanced a positive attitude even in the midst of a subtext that was clearly political in tone. While the villainous character of *Brundibár* was the personification of evil, the children's victory chorus that ends the opera told the audience:

> *We won a victory*
> *Over the tyrant mean.*
> *Sound trumpets, beat your drums,*
> *And show us your esteem!*
> *We won a victory,*
> *Since we were not fearful,*
> *Since we were not tearful,*
> *Because we marched along*
> *Singing our happy song,*
> *Bright, joyful, and cheerful.*

This left no room for doubt: the children were singing loudly and clearly about the eventual defeat of Hitler and the Third Reich.

Jews had earlier been forbidden to attend concerts, but at Theresienstadt the Nazis relaxed this sufficiently to be able to show off the camp to the outside world as a place in which Jews were looked after. Accordingly, musicians, actors, artists, poets, and writers—among them Hans Krása—staged a variety of performances. This, of course, played into the hands of the Nazis in their exploitation of the camp as a model location of humanity and goodwill. Red Cross commissions passed through the area, and the reports they made were based on Terezín. It was also at the camp that the Nazi propaganda film *Der Führer Schenkt den Juden eine Stadt* (*The Führer Gives the Jews a City*) was filmed, using *Brundibár* as an illustration of its children's activities.

Between January and October 1942, the number of prisoners at Theresienstadt increased almost tenfold. As well as the Jews coming in from the Czech lands, increasing numbers were arriving from Austria, Germany, Hungary, and elsewhere. The camp's population grew to 140,000, including no fewer than 11,000 children. They made the best of their situation, with an extraordinary flourishing of artistic and creative activity taking place. All this artistry—musical productions, paintings by the children (of which over 4,000 were recovered after the war), comic books, poetry, and the keeping of **diaries and journals**—functioned as a means to transcend the reality of what was being experienced daily. In the final months of 1944, however, almost all the Jewish artists and intellectuals were transferred to extermination camps like Auschwitz. Among the 87,000 Terezín prisoners sent to their death, more than 83,000 were murdered. These included Hans Krása, the composer of *Brundibár*.

For many theater directors since the end of World War II, it impossible to divorce *Brundibár* from its context and present it as a purely aesthetic experience, even though it has been performed countless times and on all continents. For best effect, many consider that it is necessary to go beyond merely staging the opera; it is usually held that it is best also to give audiences a wider understanding of its history, the Holocaust context in which it was written and performed, and through this to reinforce Krása's original intention.

Further Reading

Karas, Joža. *Music in Terezín, 1941–1945*. New York: Beaufort Books, 1985.

BUDISAVLJEVIĆ, DIANA (1891–1978)

Diana Budisavljević, *née* Obexer, was born on January 15, 1891, in Innsbruck, Austria. In 1917 she met and fell in love with a Serbian medical student working as a surgical intern in Innsbruck, Julije Budisavljević, and the two married. In 1919 Dr. Budisavljević was appointed professor of surgery at the University of Zagreb, and they took up residence there.

When World War II broke out in 1939, Croatia was part of Yugoslavia. It had a population of approximately 3.78 million, of whom perhaps 40,000 were Jewish. It also had sizable minority populations of Muslims and Serbs. Most Croats were Roman Catholic. During the interwar years they sought an independent Croatia; to achieve this, nationalist leaders formed the Ustaše, a pro-Axis right-wing paramilitary political party. Soon after Yugoslavia joined the Axis alliance in March 1941, Ustaše leaders declared the creation of the Independent State of Croatia (*Nezavisna drzava Hrvatska*, or NDH).

The NDH governed most of modern Slovenia, Croatia, Bosnia-Herzegovina, and parts of Serbia, and in order to achieve a measure of homogeneity, its leaders implemented a policy of ethnic cleansing against Serbs, Jews, and Roma, setting up numerous concentration camps throughout the country.

Diana Budisavljević first learned about this policy in October 1941 from her Jewish seamstress, who told her of a camp holding children in a deserted castle at Loborgrad, north of Zagreb. Together with a few others, and capitalizing on her connections among Zagreb's social elite, she obtained permission to begin a relief campaign, which some nicknamed "Action Diana Budisavljević." With help from the local Jewish community—which until then had been supporting the inmates, and whose actions inspired Diana's own—her little operation began sending supplies of food, medicine, clothes, and money, first to Loborgrad and then to another nearby camp at Gornja Rijeka. This effort was to grow into arguably the biggest relief effort across Yugoslavia. Later, this would extend to obtaining permission for the removal of Serbian children from the Ustaše camps.

Much of the information we have about Diana's activities comes from a diary she kept between October 23, 1941, and August 13, 1945. When it was discovered and published in 2003, this rich resource comprised 388 entries written in German. It described the conditions of the children in the various camps she visited, their anxiety about their future, and how they suffered and died. She also recorded her meetings and discussions with some of those responsible for the conditions in which the children found themselves.

A powerful passage in the diary describes her visit to the women's camp at Stara Gradiška. In March 1942 she met a senior Red Cross nurse, Dragica Habazin, and formed an important bond with her that would help immensely in the coming months. When Diana and some of the Red Cross nurses entered Stara Gradiška, they were met, she wrote, with "something terrible inside." In the rooms there was "no furniture of any kind, only chamber pots, and sitting or lying down on the floor were impossibly thin little children. One could already see death in each one of their eyes. . . . The doctor said they were beyond help. But the transport leader said we should take every child who could be moved somehow. A choice was made. Those who could still stand on their own feet were taken, while those who were stumbling, who no longer had the strength to stand, were left behind."

At the beginning of July 1942, with help from a German officer, Diana was able to secure permission to take the children from Stara Gradiška, and with the assistance of the Croatian Ministry of Social Affairs, she relocated them into the care of families in Zagreb, as well as children-specific camps at Jastrebarsko and Sisak. In August 1942 she then moved several thousand children from other camps to families in Zagreb. Through her efforts, they were placed with families in Zagreb and rural communities.

Diana made sure to keep records of the children for whom she cared, with the hope that they might one day be returned to their families. A card-file of the children's names and details was made, which, by the end of the war, contained information on approximately 12,000 children. Diana was fortunate in having a small circle of helpers working to rescue the children. All risked their lives to help; indeed, on one occasion Diana herself became very ill, and the pressure she was under contributed to three nervous breakdowns.

The children she rescued were accommodated in various ways. Some, as shown previously, were housed with Croatian families, while others were taken in by the Catholic Church. Such assistance, however, was a double-edged sword. While the children's lives were saved, they were the victims of a process akin to **kidnapping** by another name. The NDH government permitted ordinary citizens to adopt the children only on the condition that they were raised as patriotic Roman Catholic Croatians, denying them any connections with their Serb, Jewish, or Roma origins—and thus the younger children were often lost forever to their parents and original culture.

It has been estimated that Diana's actions saved 15,536 children from Ustaše camps. From that total, 3,254 died either during the rescues or immediately after leaving the camp, exhausted by torture, hunger, and disease. Eleven members of her team lost their lives during the war.

After the **liberation** of Zagreb at the end of May 1945, security officers from Yugoslavia's Department for People's Protection (*Odjeljenje za zaštitu naroda*, or OZNA), acting on a request from the Ministry of Social Politics, visited Diana and demanded she turn over the files and photographs she had kept for the thousands of children who had been saved. Thus, she was prevented from maintaining her efforts to identify children. Her offer to continue helping was not accepted. As it turned out, the Yugoslav communist authorities did manage to locate many of the children's parents in subsequent investigations, but Diana's efforts during the war were largely written out of history—instead, the child-rescue operation was portrayed as a triumph achieved by the communist liberators.

After the war Diana never spoke in public about the operation. She and her husband lived quietly in Zagreb until 1972, when they moved back to Innsbruck, where she died on August 20, 1978, aged 87. Since then, she has been posthumously honored in Serbia and Croatia through several national awards; streets and parks in Belgrade, Zagreb, and other places have been named for her; and a memorial to the children of the Sisak concentration camp celebrates her efforts during the war. July 18, 2019, saw the world premiere of a documentary film about Diana. Entitled *Dianina Lista* (English title, *The Diary of Diana B.*), it was produced by Dana Budisavljević (no relation) and Miljenka Čogelja and earned several commendations and awards at various film festivals.

Further Reading

Lomović, Boško. *Heroine from Innsbruck: Diana Obexer Budisavljević*. Belgrade: Svet Knjige, 2014.

BULLENHUSER DAMM

Kurt Heissmeyer, an SS physician born on December 26, 1905, in Lower Saxony, was, like many Nazis, keen to utilize his position in order to advance his medical career and obtain a professorship. To achieve this, he needed to present a paper demonstrating original research, and in doing so, he developed a theory that injection of live tuberculosis bacilli into human subjects would act as a vaccine. He argued that racially inferior—that is, so-called subhuman—persons had lower resistance to diseases (such as tuberculosis) than those who were racially superior, so he requested Jewish subjects from concentration camps for his **medical experimentation** activities.

Heissmeyer's theory had previously been suggested by two Austrians researching tuberculosis, but it was unequivocally disproven internationally by eminent theorists. Heissmeyer, a general practitioner and not a specialist, was unaware that his hypothesis had been invalidated.

In spring 1944, through Heissmeyer's personal Nazi connections, permission to use prisoners from the Ravensbrück concentration camp was obtained from *Reichsführer-SS* Heinrich Himmler. Experiments took place at the Neuengamme concentration camp near Hamburg. Heissmeyer initially experimented on up to

100 Jewish and Slavic adult "subhuman" prisoners, but these trials failed to deliver the hoped-for results. To complete his trials, he then appropriated Jewish children for his tuberculosis experiments. Twenty Jewish children, 10 boys and 10 girls, all aged between 5 and 12, were accordingly transferred from Auschwitz to Neuengamme. Heissmeyer began his experiments just as Allied forces were crossing the Rhine.

As the already-weak children sickened, Heissmeyer removed their lymph glands and began injecting the tuberculosis bacteria into their lungs and bloodstreams. The children grew weaker and were confined to their barracks.

In March 1945, while the U.S. Third Army advanced into Germany, Heissmeyer sought advice as to what should be done with the sick and dying Jewish children. Oswald Pohl, the head of the SS Main Economic and Administrative Office, and Rudolph Hoess, the commandant of Auschwitz, then visited Neuengamme. Hoess decided the children should be euthanized by poison and gave the task to *SS-Obersturmführer* Arnold Strippel. Lacking poison, Strippel was forced to improvise.

In 1943 the Hamburg SS had taken over Bullenhuser Damm, a bombed-out school, and converted it into a satellite camp of Neuengamme. On April 20, 1945, when the British were less than three miles away, the 20 children, along with their two French physicians and two Dutch caretakers, were taken to this site and murdered by being hanged on hooks in the basement at Bullenhuser Damm. Strippel and other officers supervised the murders; following this, 18 Russian prisoners were also hanged. Strippel then loaded the corpses and returned to Neuengamme, where they were cremated. The war in Europe ended 17 days later.

Most of those involved in the murders were captured soon after the war ended. Some were executed in October 1946. Others escaped capture and punishment. One, Hans Petersen, fled to Denmark, where he served a short prison sentence in 1946 for his membership in the SS, and died in Sonderburg in December 1967. Another, Hans Klein, was not pursued; he became an instructor of forensic medicine at the University of Heidelberg.

After the massacre at Bullenhuser Damm, Arnold Strippel also went into hiding. In mid-December 1948, he was recognized in Frankfurt by a former Buchenwald torture victim. Police were summoned, and Strippel was arrested.

In Frankfurt, on May 31, 1949, Strippel was charged with murdering 21 Jewish prisoners at Buchenwald and of torturing others. On June 1, 1949, he was sentenced to 21 life terms plus an additional 10 years. He began his detention in the Butzbach prison, where he was given a privileged post in the prison hospital.

In October 1969 a new trial, lasting five months, began. The court held that while Strippel had participated in the murders of 21 Jews in Buchenwald, he had not actually fired any fatal shots. He was sentenced to time served in Butzbach and received 121,500 Deutschmarks by way of compensation. He moved to Frankfurt-Kalbach, where he worked as an accountant, purchased a home, and lived quietly until 1975, when he was accused of complicity in the murder of 41 inmates at Majdanek. Found guilty, he was ordered not to leave Germany.

On December 12, 1983, the Hamburg public prosecutor filed charges against Strippel for the murders of the children at Bullenhuser Damm and 22 Neuengamme inmates. After three years of additional legal wrangling, he was now deemed unfit to stand trial. He disappeared from public view and died on May 1, 1994, in Frankfurt-Kalbach.

On April 21, 1945, Kurt Heissmeyer, whose bogus experiments began the whole episode, fled the Hohenlychen sanatorium (where he had been hiding) and returned to Thuringia, where he worked in his father's medical practice. He eventually settled in Magdeburg in East Germany, where, for the next 18 years, he enjoyed a successful practice as the director of the country's only private tuberculosis clinic. His practice was so large that he was able to purchase homes for each of his three children, and he was recognized as one of Magdeburg's outstanding citizens.

Heissmeyer would have continued leading a prosperous life if in 1959 the West German magazine *Stern* had not published an article deploring the omission of Nazi crimes from the curricula of German schoolchildren—referring specifically to the murders of the children at Bullenhuser Damm. A retired economist from Nuremberg began researching the murders there and identified Heissmeyer's role. Four years later, after verification of his identity, he was arrested by the East German General Prosecutor's Office, charged with crimes against humanity, and imprisoned in Berlin. He initially denied the accusations but eventually led investigators to a box he had buried in the garden of his house in Hohenlychen, which contained documents and photographs relating to his experiments on children.

Heissmeyer's trial began on June 21, 1966. Found guilty, he was sentenced to life imprisonment. At his trial he stated, "I did not think that inmates of a camp had full value as human beings." When asked why he did not use guinea pigs, he responded, "For me there was no basic difference between human beings and guinea pigs." He then corrected himself: "Jews and guinea pigs." Unrepentant to the very end, on August 29, 1967, 14 months after being sentenced, Heissmeyer died of a heart attack.

Further Reading

Schwarberg, Günther. *The Murders at Bullenhuser Damm: The SS Doctor and the Children.* Bloomington: Indiana University Press, 1984.

C

CHÂTEAU DE LA HILLE

The Château de la Hille in Montégut-Plantaurel, near Toulouse in the Ariège region of France, is a castle built at the beginning of the 16th century. For four years during World War II, it served as a home run by the Swiss Association for War-Afflicted Children (from January 1, 1942, the name was changed to Child Relief of the Swiss Red Cross, or SRC) for Jewish refugee children.

After the *Kristallnacht* pogrom in Germany (November 9–10, 1938), Belgium accepted several hundred German and Austrian Jewish children as refugees, entrusted to the care of aid agencies in a program reminiscent of the **Kindertransport** initiative undertaken in the United Kingdom. Among them were about 100 boys and girls aged between 5 and 16 years, who were lodged in two homes in Brussels. When Germany invaded Belgium in May 1940, the children were able to escape at the last minute on a freight train, thanks to the intervention of the director of the girls' home.

After a six-day journey traveling through France along with tens of thousands of other refugees, the children arrived at the village of Seyre and were lodged in a large barn. When winter arrived, the *Secours aux Enfants*, part of the Swiss Red Cross, agreed to provide for them. In the meantime, arrangements were made in September 1940 to rent the Château at La Hille, which had been uninhabited for 20 years and was in a state of considerable disrepair. In May 1941 a new head was appointed to lead operations at the Château. Rösli Näf, a 30-year-old Swiss nurse, was assigned to direct the care and protection of the children as well as the adults also situated at the Château. Once it was cleaned up and rendered habitable, during which the older boys dug wells and latrines (among other activities), the children were able to move into the Château in June 1941.

Näf faced an extraordinary set of obstacles. There was barely any water supply and no electricity, so heating was going to be a problem in the winter. Näf had to organize the household and food, and laundry had to be washed and mended. Once organized, however, a daily routine was established, highly structured along educational lines that emphasized self-sufficiency.

In the summer of 1941, through the intervention of the American Friends Service Committee (Quakers), 20 of the youngest children were removed from the home and taken to the United States; two others were saved by relatives living in America.

On August 26, 1942, French police arrested 42 boys and girls over 15 years of age, together with some La Hille employees. They were taken secretly to Le Vernet internment camp, near Pamiers, from where they were to be deported to Auschwitz. Rösli Näf spent the next two days trying to locate them, eventually finding them at Le Vernet and arguing successfully for their release back into her care. The French authorities were hardly receptive to her entreaties until finally, with the support of the Swiss government, she threatened to end all Swiss Red Cross support to France. This secured the children's release.

As soon as the children were returned to La Hille, Näf immediately begged Swiss officials to let her take the children across the border to Switzerland, where they would be safe. When the Swiss refused to permit them entry, she decided her only choice was to help them escape, and she began organizing an escape route for the older girls and boys over the Pyrenees to Spain and the Alps to Switzerland, with assistance from the French underground and sympathetic Swiss citizens. Other older children were hidden among the local farming community. About a dozen teenagers joined the Resistance, and another dozen were caught during their attempts to flee and were killed at Auschwitz.

When Swiss Red Cross officials learned of Näf's activities in helping the children escape, she was dismissed on the grounds of having violated the Red Cross's neutrality principle, and in May 1943 she was recalled to Switzerland.

After the rescue of the teenagers from Le Vernet, they were able to return to the Château, though from this point there was ongoing concern as to what the future might hold. Older children began electing to take their fate into their own hands and started moving away. Twenty-five tried to reach Switzerland, and all but five were successful. Twelve sought to cross the Pyrenees; only five made it. Some of the young girls found sanctuary in a convent, while others of the teenage group joined the Resistance. One was killed by enemy bullets. In February 1943, when more and more deportations took place, four Jewish youths were arrested at La Hille; two of these four were later released and permitted to return to the Château, and the other two were deported.

In October 1943 a new director, Emma Ott, took over management at La Hille. By this time, most of the teenagers had already fled, and further escapes were always looming. Earlier, in May 1943, Anne-Marie im Hof-Piguet, a 26-year-old Swiss social worker, had joined the staff of the Château, and from then until her last rescue in May 1944, she was able to save 12 Jewish children by organizing and partly accompanying the illegal escape across the Swiss border. Once there, the children were picked up by im Hof-Piguet's father, the forest inspector Henri-Joseph Piguet, who took them to safety in Zurich.

By the fall of 1944, only nine of the older Jewish youths were still in the Château. In March 1945, Emma Ott left La Hille to become head of a maternity hospital in Montagnac; the home at La Hille was closed, and the remaining children were sent to other locations.

After the war, the efforts of those at La Hille were recalled in various ways. Rösli Näf and Anne-Marie im Hof-Piguet were recognized by Yad Vashem in Jerusalem as Righteous among the Nations for their efforts in saving the lives of Jewish children, while a commemorative stele was erected at the site on September 17, 2000, and a museum relating the history of the Château, situated at the entrance to the grounds, was inaugurated.

Overall, thanks to the efforts of their Swiss and French protectors, nearly 90 of the original 100 girls and boys sent from Belgium in 1940 survived the war and settled all over the world. Of the 10 children deported to Auschwitz, only one survived.

Further Reading

Im Hof-Piguet, Anne-Marie. *La Filiere in France Occupée, 1942–1944*. Yverdon-les-Bains: Éditions de la Thièle, 1985.
Reed, Walter W. *The Children of La Hille: Eluding Nazi Capture during World War II*. Syracuse, NY: Syracuse University Press, 2015.

CHEVRIER, FÉLIX (1884–1962)

Félix Chevrier was born in Épinal, a commune in northeastern France and the capital of the Vosges *département*, on August 25, 1884. He was the son of Del Chevrier, a laborer, and Julie-Cécile Granferry. Working in various jobs—horticultural laborer, water carrier, and mechanic—he became a union organizer before turning to journalism. In 1927 he cofounded a monthly newspaper, *Le Vosgien*, serving mainly as a newsletter for Vosges residents living in Paris. By 1939 he had become the official secretary to Marc Rucart, minister of public health in the government of Prime Minister Édouard Daladier.

In late 1939 Chevrier agreed to run a home for Jewish children under the auspices of the **Œuvre de Secours aux Enfants** (Children's Aid Society, or OSE), which had decided to open three houses to accommodate children in the Creuse region. Chevrier arrived at Chabannes in October 1939 to take up direction of one of these homes, an abandoned castle located near Saint-Pierre-de-Fursac. He prepared the home so that it could accommodate 80 children from Berlin, Warsaw, and Paris beginning in November 23, 1939.

Chevrier and those with whom he worked benefited from the support of members of the local community, who recognized the dangers faced by the children and who saw that taking care of them was a patriotic act at a time of national crisis. The children were, for the most part, welcomed by families in the region.

At Chabannes the children derived a sense of well-being, with efforts made to ensure that they enjoyed as close to a normal life as possible. A regular school timetable was created, during which physical education was compulsory. Some of the children attended local village schools, and Chevrier saw to it that Jewish religious traditions were upheld wherever feasible, such that Shabbat and religious holidays were regularly observed. By 1942, 102 Jewish children were lodged in Chabannes; during 1943, this rose to 120.

On April 13, 1942, Renée Paillassou, the principal of Chabannes primary school, was denounced by her best friend, who suspected her of showing sympathy for Jewish children. When she was summoned by the authorities, it was decided by the local town authorities, acting for the Nazis, that henceforth all Jewish students should be separated from non-Jewish children and concentrated only in state schools. This was just the beginning, however.

On August 26, 1942, French police arrived at Chabannes and arrested 12 Jewish boys of foreign origin, together with two teachers. Interceding on their behalf, a shocked Félix Chevrier managed to negotiate the release of six of the boys. The remaining six were deported, and of these, only two—Jerry Gerard and Wolfgang Blumenreich—survived the war.

From that point on, Chevrier decided that everything should be done to protect the children in his care. On September 1, 1942, the police returned and ordered Chevrier to hand over 10 girls and boys whose names were on a list they gave him. All had formerly been interned at Gurs and Rivesaltes camps, and Chevrier saw an opportunity to save their lives. Looking over the list, he identified a few spelling errors where certain names were concerned. He was thus able to report that four of children were not known to him at Chabannes, while the remaining six had left the home (though no one had seen them leave).

Just before another raid took place in the fall of 1943, Renée Paillassou's father, a retired policeman, was warned of its imminence. He told his daughter, and Renée rushed back to Chabannes on her bicycle and alerted Chevrier. He, in turn, organized the older children to flee into the forest, while the younger ones were hidden in the village. When the gendarmes arrived at Chabannes, they found the castle empty.

Toward the end of 1943, the OSE decided to close the home and disperse the children, with Félix Chevrier given the task of facilitating the operation. Throughout the entire period of his service to the children of Chabannes, he also provided services to the Resistance. Marcel Déninger ("Captain Durand"), an officer in the *Maquis*, was the husband of Chevrier's niece, Marcelle, and through this connection Chevrier was able to assist the Resistance while at the same time maintaining the facade of a law-abiding citizen.

During World War II, the Creuse region overall welcomed and gave refuge to nearly 3,000 Jews, including 1,000 children. In addition to Chabannes, the OSE had rented or bought other castles in which to house the Jewish children: these included Chaumont, near Mainsat, directed by Lotte Schwarz, and Le Masgelier, near Grand-Bourg, directed by Jacques and Hélène Bloch.

After the war Félix Chevrier was elected to office in a range of professional and special interest organizations. He was later honored for his wartime activities and awarded the Legion of Honor. He died in Champcueil, northern France, on November 20, 1962, and his ashes were scattered in the Garden of Remembrance of the Père-Lachaise Cemetery in Paris. On May 3, 1999, Yad Vashem posthumously recognized Félix Chevrier as one of the Righteous among the Nations for his efforts in saving the lives of Jewish children during the Holocaust.

Further Reading

Gossels, Lisa, and Dean Wetherell (producers). *The Children of Chabannes*. Good Egg Productions, 1999, at https://childrenofchabannes.org/.

CHILD EUTHANASIA

In August 1939, the Reich Committee for the Scientific Registration of Serious Hereditary and Congenitally Based Diseases was established in Germany. Its object was to remove from German society, through murder, children and young people who were incurably insane or physically handicapped.

On May 23, 1939, a request came from a German family for the mercy killing of their handicapped child, Gerhard Kretschmar, born that same year on February 29. His parents, who lived in Saxony, petitioned Adolf Hitler, asking for Gerhard to be "put to sleep" as he was born blind, mentally retarded, and lacking one leg and part of an arm. Hitler approved the request, and carbon monoxide gas was selected as the means of the baby boy's death.

This then served as the pretext for the initiation of a much larger "euthanasia" program. The program's original intention was to kill disabled infants and young children, and Dr. Karl Brandt, a medical doctor and SS officer who served as Adolf Hitler's personal physician, was placed in charge of the program's planning and execution along with Philipp Bouhler, head of the Reich Chancellery. They received a rare explicit authorization from Hitler, allowing them to grant "mercy deaths" to "incurable" patients. Before the program relating to children commenced, however, Hitler authorized its expansion to euthanize adults with disabilities as well.

Accordingly, Brandt and Bouhler organized what became known as Aktion T-4, from the address of the administrative offices in Berlin running the program, Tiergartenstrasse 4. Although starting as a program centering on children in August 1939, Hitler's preference to euthanize "life unworthy of life"—men, women, and children deemed mentally and physically disabled—was initiated to cover all categories in October 1939.

After that first child's death, others followed quickly, leading ultimately to the organized murder of up to 5,000 children in so-called special children's wards. Aktion T-4 covered two separate euthanasia programs: one dating back to spring 1939, dealing with infants and small children up to age three who had physical deformities; and a second that included mentally disabled older children and adults.

The child euthanasia program usually murdered its victims through lethal overdoses of medication. Adult patients, on the other hand, were removed from their home institutions and transferred to one of six designated killing centers throughout Germany, where they were murdered in specially designed gas chambers.

Planning the program meant that a departmental infrastructure and bureaucratic guidelines had to be established, and this was initiated in a directive from the Reich Minister of the Interior dated August 18, 1939. This specified the groups to be included in the program and was to apply not only to those children who had already been identified as incurably ill or handicapped but also to newborn babies suspected of a range of "congenital disorders" at birth.

Brandt would later develop another program involving forced abortions for women classed as "genetically defective," which likewise included those who were physically or mentally disabled.

On October 6, 1939, Hitler ordered Brandt to "relieve through death" those mentally ill individuals who could not "take any conscious part in life." He backdated his signature to September 1, 1939, to highlight the order's connection to the war; his logic was that the life of every dead soldier should be balanced by taking the life of a person "unworthy of life."

It now became the duty of doctors, nurses, and midwives to report to the appropriate health authorities if a child or newborn baby came across their purview with any of the designated conditions, so that further action (that is, their murder) could be undertaken. The registration of potential victims became a crucial determinant of whether a child was to be euthanized, in accordance with a stringent set of conditions. Under the prescribed format, three Nazi medical bureaucrats would receive the relevant registration forms, with comments made by the first two as to the nature of the case intended to assist the third in making his final determination. Only the reporting form was used in making the decision of life or death; the doctors did not examine the child in person or review previous records. Sometimes a child might not be condemned if the doctors concluded that he or she could grow up and be a productive member of society. These, however, were in the minority. The forms also included a clause in which those doing the reporting were required to indicate the child's race. This was so that Jewish children could be easily identified, and in these cases, death was mandatory.

As precedents were generated, the range of those to be included in the child euthanasia scheme was broadened. What began as an assault against children with psychological and physical handicaps was expanded such that those deemed to be "unfit for society"—those, for example, with behavioral problems—were also listed on registration forms, and many were subsequently assessed negatively and sent to euthanasia centers, where they were gassed.

Some children slated for compulsory euthanasia were even reprieved temporarily so that they could be "studied" as objects of medical or scientific research prior to being sent to their deaths.

The killing centers that were set up for children as specialized pediatric clinics were a precedent for much larger murder facilities catering to physically and mentally disabled adults. Once sent to these clinics, children received lethal injections or were sometimes simply starved to death. It is worth reflecting that children—whether Jewish or not—were the first and most vulnerable of Hitler's victims, as they remained throughout the war years and the Holocaust.

Further Reading

Aly, Götz, Peter Chroust, and Christian Pross. *Cleansing the Fatherland: Nazi Medicine and Racial Hygiene.* Baltimore: Johns Hopkins University Press, 1994.

Friedlander, Henry. *The Origins of Nazi Genocide: From Euthanasia to the Final Solution.* Chapel Hill: University of North Carolina Press, 1995.

CHILD SURVIVORS

Children who survived the Holocaust had lived through a dazzling array of experiences, dating from before the war and extending to the early years of the war itself, before becoming enmeshed in the very killing machinery of the Third Reich. Child survivors were victimized, deprived of an education, bullied, beaten, hidden, passed from place to place, smuggled over borders, starved, imprisoned in concentration camps, separated from their murdered parents, required to take care of smaller siblings, witnesses to atrocities, and, ultimately, liberated into a world devoid of direction or a future.

Of the millions of Jewish victims of the Holocaust, the figure of 1,500,000 children under the age of 18 is generally given as the best approximation of those who were lost. This translates into most European Jewish children alive in 1939. Only an estimated 150,000 survived. Some did so in hiding or with partisans in the forests. Some—a bare few—managed to come alive out of the concentration camps. The world into which they emerged bore little to no resemblance to the peaceful life they might have enjoyed before the war, if, indeed, they could remember it. A feature of many child survivors is that they were too young to have a memory of what "normal" life was before their Holocaust ordeal, and that, as a result, by the time of the **liberation**, much of their early life experience had been given over to the existential act of sheer survival. "Ordinary life" had never been part of their daily routine.

Thus, child survivors lost their early years, and in much of their subsequent life, they tried to catch up in the quest to find normality. The immediate aftermath of the war was preoccupied with issues relating to coping with loss, learning how to establish a new life, finding partners who might have some understanding of how best to appreciate what they went through, and then, perhaps, starting a family. For many, meeting these challenges meant confronting their Holocaust experience with silence about the events that had such a devastating impact on their first years. And in a world in which understanding of post-traumatic stress disorder (PTSD) and long-term counseling were yet to surface, child survivors often had to fend for themselves in these crucial areas.

In the aftermath of the Holocaust, efforts by various countries around the world—especially the United States, Israel, Latin America, and the British Commonwealth—saw large numbers of child survivors removed from displaced persons' camps and taken to new homes, often thousands of miles distant. Many were adopted by families who had little comprehension of what they had lived through, adding to the tribulations of the young survivors and contributing to their struggle to adapt to their new, post-Holocaust situation.

Of those born between 1928 and 1945—to offer a broad date range for the child survivor age cohort—many of the challenges were, in various ways, overcome. To the best of their ability they went on to raise families and establish careers, often in areas pertaining to the healing of others such as medicine, psychiatry, education, and the law. Others, who had been orphans with no homes of their own, sought their professional salvation in real estate or in creating businesses, while yet others, trying to bring creative color to a lost world they never knew, contributed to the arts as writers, artists, film makers, and poets.

Most importantly, perhaps, many child survivors were in the forefront of Holocaust memorialization, perhaps driven by a desire to provide a location for their grief and a monument to their lost families. There is no coincidence in the fact that the proliferation of Holocaust memorials and monuments came from the 1980s onwards, just as the child survivor population had reached the age when it could provide meaningful financial and institutional support to such ventures.

As the last eyewitnesses (and victims) of the Holocaust, child survivors are keenly aware of the important role they are able to play as memory keepers, but in addition to that, they also recognize that they have a responsibility to support each other in view of their shared traumatic experiences. This realization took a long time to emerge, as demonstrated by the gradual formation of what became the **World Federation of Jewish Child Survivors of the Holocaust and Descendants**. In this context, the members of child survivor organizations serve to help heal each other as well as passing on their legacy and relating what happened to them for future generations.

This is not to say that child survivors were always able to pick themselves up after the horrors of the Holocaust and then proceed as if nothing had happened. In traumatic circumstances that could last anywhere up to three, four, or five years, the dramatic disruption to the formation of young lives was, all too often, both devastating and long-lasting.

Still, their voices have been heard, and several important studies of the child survivor population—now, with time, diminishing—have been undertaken to help explain the issues and concerns that define survivorship among very young people. Moreover, they have generated a great deal of respect among those of the **Second Generation** and subsequent age cohorts, who have come to realize that the child survivors are the last remnants of those who experienced the Holocaust in their very flesh.

Further Reading

Cohen, Beth B. *Child Survivors of the Holocaust: The Youngest Remnant and the American Experience*. New Brunswick, NJ: Rutgers University Press, 2018.
Valent, Paul. *Child Survivors of the Holocaust*. Melbourne: William Heinemann, 1993.
World Federation of Jewish Child Survivors of the Holocaust and Descendants, at https://www.holocaustchild.org/.

CHILDREN AND FILM

When approaching an issue such as the Holocaust, the study of film can be useful in providing a window to achieving a deeper understanding of why it is that such extraordinary violence took place. Nonetheless, a few questions—common to all students of film and its relationship to historical phenomena—can be asked in the hope that deeper insight can be achieved: How useful was the film in developing an understanding of the causes and nature of the Holocaust? Was more learned about the Holocaust from the film than from other sources of information? Did it appear to have any biases? Do any specific scenes best describe the overall topic of the movie?

As a subject for motion pictures, the Holocaust presents the broadest range of themes possible, covering nothing less than the entirety of the human experience *in extremis*—social, political, cultural, economic, military, administrative, religious, gender, age, race, morality, and so on. Studying and critiquing film has become one of the largest and most popular contemporary ways of approaching the Holocaust.

Filmographies covering the Holocaust are immense in size and growing each year. For each film studied, however, the essential tools can remain the same. One must always be wary that the filmmakers do not fall into the trap of maudlin sentimentality, as this can detract from the impact a movie on the Holocaust can have on an audience—and, in particular, an uninformed or underinformed audience, such as many younger viewers today.

For the most part, however, it is simply not possible for filmmakers to recreate with complete accuracy everything that happened in any historical situation, so liberties must be taken—not with the truth so much as with representations of the truth. While filmmakers might have a commitment to telling the general outline of a story, in doing so they are often forced to select specific vignettes, themes, or exchanges in order best to convey the events depicted. The ambiguous caption "based on a true story" can lend credibility to even the most tenuous of movie tie-ins, but filmmakers seem generally content to employ the term if their movie has even the remotest grounding in authenticity. Indeed, even this term has been expanded to include the description "inspired by real events."

Of course, there is a danger here; those who would detract or deny the veracity of the history being portrayed could put forward that flaws in a movie generated by dramatic license negate the entire account. But filmmakers are, all too often, confined by the limits of their medium. An event relating to the Holocaust cannot be shown in all its shades and subtleties in the space of 90 or 120 minutes. As a result, filmmakers seek to interpret an incident or episode in accordance with the tools at hand. In this regard, the skills of the historian can meet those of the filmmaker in order to produce works that enhance understanding of the Holocaust.

The last three decades have seen a sharp increase in people's interest in the Holocaust, and motion pictures have been in the vanguard. Indeed, younger generations have probably learned more about the Holocaust through critical consumption of film than through any other medium. Audiences today, it might be concluded, are likely to glean much of their knowledge about the Holocaust through films, both before and after their formal education.

The most fundamental questions regarding filmic portrayals of historical issues can be addressed through viewing such movies: First, is the movie true to the historical reality (so far as it can be understood) upon which it is based? Second, is the movie useful in providing an understanding of what happened? And third, how effective can graphic depictions of the worst expressions of human depravity be for a new generation of viewers seeing such images for the first time?

Movies stemming from Holocaust themes play an important role in helping to provide a sense of "place" and "period" for viewers. They are not documentaries, and they should not try to be. This is one of the major concerns some people have with regard to any movies that take historical episodes as their theme; namely, that because films employ actors speaking contrived dialogue on movie sets that are recreations of what might have been, they have as little validity as if they were fiction. Yet an argument can be made that filmic portrayals of children's experiences during the Holocaust are often just as much an interpretation of historical realities as are other forms of analysis, such as historical writing. Thus, while movies can be a start, they are not (and cannot be) the only medium for generating a full grasp of what that awful event signified—or of what it represents for the future of the society in which viewers will be living once they leave the theater or turn off their television sets.

Although most films about the Holocaust focus on the experience of adults, some excellent movies have made children the main characters and viewed the horror from their perspective. In some cases, the focus has been on translating onto film the memoirs of those who were children; elsewhere, highly fictionalized accounts (even those rendered as fantasy) have been employed. A fundamental question arises, however: When films about the Holocaust featuring children are made, who is the intended audience? Arguments have been put forth—by educators, especially—that younger children should not be exposed to movies about the Holocaust (regardless of who the characters might be), given the fact that movies, as visual and aural stimuli, can be much more confronting for an audience than is literature, which relies more on imagination. And embedded within this contrast is the nature of the genre: Holocaust films can rarely claim "feel-good" status, and where children are concerned, they can often lead to traumatic aftermaths.

The Holocaust as a theme in motion pictures generated several important titles focusing on children between the 1950s and early 1990s. These include, but are not restricted to, such movies as *Forbidden Games* (René Clément, 1952); *The Diary of* **Anne Frank** (George Stevens, 1959); *Au Revoir Les Enfants* (Louis Malle, 1987); *Europa, Europa* (Agnieszka Holland, 1991); and **Korczak** (Andrzej Wajda, 1991).

Since then, interest in movies focusing on children during the Holocaust intensified, especially after the appearance in 1993 of the multi-award-winning *Schindler's List*, directed by Steven Spielberg. Since that time, the genre has seen an escalation of major movies, many of which have won critical and popular acclaim; these include **La Colline aux Mille Enfants** (Jean-Louis Lorenzi, 1997); *Life Is Beautiful* (Roberto Benigni, 1997); *The Devil's Arithmetic* (Donna Deitch, 1999); *Fateless* (Lajos Koltai, 2005); *The Boy in the Striped Pajamas* (Mark Herman, 2008); *Sarah's Key* (Gilles Paquet-Brenner, 2010); *La Rafle* (Roselyne Bosch, 2010); *Wunderkinder* (Markus Rosenmüller, 2011); *Run Boy Run* (Pepe Danquart, 2013); *The Book Thief* (Brian Percival, 2013); *Son of Saul* (László Nemes, 2015); and **Le Voyage de Fanny** (Lola Doillon, 2016).

Further Reading

Prorokova, Tatiana. "The Holocaust in Film: Witnessing the Extermination through the Eyes of Children." *Holocaust Studies* 23, no. 3 (2018), pp. 377–394.

CHILDREN'S CONCENTRATION CAMPS, CROATIA

The Independent State of Croatia (*Nezavisna drzava Hrvatska*, or NDH) was established as a result of the German-Italian invasion and occupation of Yugoslavia and the signing of the Treaties of Rome on May 18, 1941. Its territory covered much of modern Croatia and Bosnia-Herzegovina, as well as parts of modern Serbia and Slovenia. The NDH was run as a one-party state by the fascist Ustaše movement, led by Ante Pavelić, and targeted dissident Croats and Muslims as well as Serbs, Jews, and Roma as part of a large-scale campaign of genocide.

Enterprises owned by Croatia's Jews included large manufacturing and textile companies, banks, theaters, the chocolate enterprise now known as Kras, jewelry and watch store retailers, and tanneries. In 1941 the Ustaše rounded up Jews, Roma, Serbs, and other non-Catholic minorities, sending them to the Jasenovac concentration camp, one of the largest concentration camp complexes in Europe, established in August 1941. It was known to some as "the Auschwitz of the Balkans."

Between 1941 and 1945, the Ustaše established 22 concentration camps in Croatia. Among these Jasenovac was the largest, but two, Jastrebarsko and Sisak (a subcamp of Jasenovac), housed mainly Serbian, Jewish, and Roma children.

Sisak, officially called "the Shelter for Children Refugees," opened on August 3, 1942, following the Kozara Offensive (Operation WEST-BOSNIEN) by the Axis. Early in 1942, the Sisak synagogue had been looted and destroyed, and the building was turned into a worker's hall. Serb, Jewish, and Roma inhabitants of Sisak were tormented here by the Ustaše.

Sisak was under the direct control of Dr. Antun Najžer, a physician, and comprised several buildings riddled with filth and vermin. None of these buildings was suitable for housing children, infants, or babies, who had to lie on the floor with only a thin layer of straw and few clothes or blankets. Malnutrition and dysentery were rife.

The first group of 906 children arrived on August 3, 1942. The next day another 650 children came, while a third group of 1,272 arrived on August 6, 1942. During August and September 1942, Ustaše housed 3,971 children at Sisak whose parents had been selected for forced labor in Germany. From August 3, 1942, to February 8, 1943, a total of 6,693 Serb, Jewish, and Roma children were imprisoned at Sisak, which became infected with a typhus epidemic, causing the deaths of between 1,160 and 1,500 children.

Despite the actions of **Diana Budisavljević** (a humanitarian who led a major relief effort in Yugoslavia during World War II) and a tireless group of others, large numbers of children, up to 40 each day, died. Food parcels sent by the Red Cross were never passed on. Volunteers, working secretly with Yugoslavia's communist underground, rescued as many of the Serbian children as they could by finding homes for them with Croats, often as domestic servants or farm workers. The rescue effort relied on people working under code names in secret cells, coordinated from simple farms as well as aristocratic homes. Some 2,200 children were moved to Zagreb, while families from Sisak and surrounding villages sheltered 1,630 children taken from the camp.

After the war, survivors of concentration camps and forced labor in Germany returned and started searching for their children. Records kept at the Sisak camp, however, with information about each child, maintained by Diana Budisavljević, were confiscated by the Yugoslav Department for People's Protection (*Odjeljenje za zaštitu naroda*, or OZNA), the state security agency established in 1944. The public was not allowed to see these records. Thousands of children who had been in Sisak searched for their parents, as did their parents for the children; often, hopes were dashed on both sides.

Monuments were erected at the Reis saltworks and the Sisak Cultural Center for the children who died, but these were destroyed during the Balkan Wars of the early 1990s. The children's cemetery at the camp was landscaped in 1974 and a monument erected; it contains 2,000 children's graves but is now in a state of disrepair.

The Jastrebarsko concentration camp held Serb children who had been brought there from various locations across the NDH. It was established by the Ustaše and located in the town of Jastrebarsko, about 37 kilometers southwest of Zagreb. It operated from July 12, 1942, until October 1942.

The buildings set aside for the camp were a former castle that had been a children's home before the war; the nearby Franciscan monastery; and a former Italian barracks and stables. Preparations for the reception of the children were completed hastily by the Croatian Red Cross and local villagers. The camp opened on July 12, 1942, with administration provided by nuns of the Daughters of Charity of Saint Vincent de Paul working alongside members of the Ustaše Youth and female Ustaše.

In early July 1942, 16 Red Cross nurses were sent from Zagreb to the Stara Gradiška concentration camp to collect 650 children and bring them to Jastrebarsko. Only 566 children made it there alive; a second group of 770 children from Stara Gradiška followed on July 13–14, while a third group of 850 was transported from the concentration camp at Jablanac at the end of July 1942. On August 5, 1942, 800 more children arrived from Mlaka. The final group of 150 children, all boys, arrived from the nearby village of Gornja Reka on August 14, 1942. In total, 3,136 children aged between 1 and 14 entered the camp by August 14, 1942. It is estimated that anywhere up to 1,500 children died there, mainly from disease and malnutrition.

Children arrived at the camp in an emaciated, weak condition from other Ustaše camps. Some children were removed during antipartisan operations by German and NDH forces between April 1941 and June 1942. Their parents and older siblings had often been killed or sent to labor camps in other parts of Axis-occupied Europe, and their villages were burned to the ground.

Rather than killing the children outright, the Croatian government decided to re-educate these children along the lines of an Ustaše variant on the **Hitler Youth** and thereby turn them against their Serb parents as a way of placing pressure on the Yugoslav partisans. Preparations had not been made for their reception, however, with no accommodations having been set aside or food prepared. Such barracks as existed had no electricity or running water, and food initially consisted of little more than corn flour. The barracks were fenced with barbed wire, and the children slept on floors covered with straw. Only Serb children, from all over Croatia, were kept in the camp.

The children had to attend church for Catholic prayers and were required to greet others with the Ustaše greeting *Spremni* (Ready) or the Nazi salute. Those who failed to do so were punished with beatings or solitary confinement.

Over time, however, conditions improved, and the children were fed a variety of foods, including pumpkin soup, cucumbers, beets, and similar vegetables, and sometimes they received a little macaroni or beans, but very little bread. The Croatian Red Cross and others began to collect and distribute food to the children and to improve their situation, feeding them, decorating the walls, and treating their illnesses. At one point, 400 children were suffering from dysentery, 300 had measles, 200 had typhoid, 200 had diphtheria, and another 100 had mumps. Many were also suffering from scurvy due to the poor diet. Monthly mortality figures read as follows: July 1942, 153; August 1942, 216; September 1942, 67; and October 1942, 8. Five children died in the hospital in Zagreb.

The death rate of children at Jastrebarsko was much lower than that of children at Sisak for two reasons. Almost half those at Jastrebarsko were older children, more able to cope with the harsh conditions; and beginning at the end of July 1942, 26 local volunteers, along with several doctors and other medical personnel, began to intervene with the camp administration and Ustaše guards to improve the children's health.

Yugoslav partisans freed some 350 children from the main camp on August 26, 1942. Despite attempts by the nuns to hide the children, partisan troops broke into the buildings and rescued many children, with some partisans even finding a brother or sister there. They led away from the camp all the children who could walk. Some, however, were subsequently recaptured by the Ustaše and killed or returned to the camp.

The Ustaše understood that this partisan attack meant that Jastrebarsko and similar camps for children could not be maintained. In late October 1942, 500 of the remaining children were dispersed to families in the surrounding villages by the Catholic aid group, Caritas. A total of 1,637 boys and girls were taken in by families in Zagreb and villages surrounding Jastrebarsko. Another 113 children were relocated to Bosanska Gradiška, after which the Jastrebarsko camp was dismantled.

In 1968 the Jasenovac Memorial Museum was established, from which a comprehensive list of the names of individual victims of the Jasenovac concentration camp has been compiled and made available to the public.

Further Reading

Israeli, Raphael. *The Death Camps of Croatia: Visions and Revisions, 1941–1945.* New Brunswick, NJ: Transaction Publishers, 2013.

Megargee, Geoffrey P., and Joseph R. White (Eds.). *The United States Holocaust Memorial Museum Encyclopedia of Camps and Ghettos, 1933–1945*, vol. III, *Camps and Ghettos under European Regimes Aligned with Nazi Germany*. Bloomington: Indiana University Press, 2018.

CHILDREN'S LITERATURE OF THE HOLOCAUST

Over the past few decades, the library of Holocaust-related children's literature has grown substantially. There are children's books about the Holocaust for every age level, from picture books to novels. Numerous authors who were young people during the Holocaust—and lived to tell their tales—experienced situations that differed markedly from each other. Perhaps the most famous childhood account of Nazi persecution, *The Diary of a Young Girl* (1953), known popularly as *The Diary of* **Anne Frank**, deals with the experiences of Anne and her family in hiding, and perhaps for this reason, it strikes numerous chords in young readers; they can imagine themselves in a similar position more readily than if confronted with the utterly different world of the ghetto or concentration camp. *The Diary of Éva Heyman* (1988) and *The Diary of* **Dawid Rubinowicz** (1981), on the other hand, are simultaneously more pitiful and for this reason less attractive to young readers, although both have been compared to Anne Frank's diary owing to their being the diaries of children of about the same age and living at the same time. The reason for the pain is not the writing itself, but the events which each account depicts: Éva and Dawid witness physical persecution in the ghetto, arbitrary and often callous deaths, and debility of soul; and, like a Greek tragedy, we know the inevitability of their own deaths even as we read.

Such works do not fit into the usual category of what we might expect to call "children's literature of the Holocaust," given two facts: (a) they are **diaries and journals**, and (b) those who wrote them did not survive. In the normal run of events, owing to the nature of the times, the capacity for diary-keeping was substantially reduced, which is significant in that in "normal" times, this was a period in which keeping a diary was common. Likewise, in that these diaries were discovered after the war, and thus after their authors' deaths, we have another departure from all other literary accounts of childhood experiences during the Holocaust. The vast body of testimonies, memoirs, novels, and poetry about the Holocaust we have today come from after 1945, written either by those who survived or those who, for one reason or another, were never at risk. Though no less poignant, we must conclude that accounts such as that of Anne Frank come from a genre that is in fact atypical.

A far more extensive body of material for and about young people has come to us in the form of reminiscences. These tackle a variety of scenarios and cover a broad range of themes: from Ilse Koehn's recollections of the life of a **Mischling** in Nazi Germany (1977); to the fate of those who were **hidden children** or who were **passing** as Aryans in occupied Europe in order to survive, such as that from **Janina David** (1966) or Nechama Tec (1984); or memoirs of those who were not deported to concentration camps but, rather, lived in ghettos, such as that from **Janina Bauman** (1986). The classical tale of a child who was deported but lived to tell the tale is **Elie Wiesel's** *Night* (1960). Other books with a more specific focus accessible to young readers include Claudine Vegh's compilation of reminiscences from those who, as children, lost their parents and were raised as orphans during the Holocaust (1984) and poignant accounts of women who took Jewish orphan children under their wing and protected them from the fate intended by the Nazis, such as those from **Lena Küchler-Silberman** (1987) and **Sheva Glas-Wiener** (1981).

All these accounts have been composed by adults describing real events, but like most survivor accounts, they are rarely literary masterpieces. Indeed, for the most part they do not seek to be. Instead, they seek to tell their own story as best they can and, in so doing, bear witness to what happened to them as a legacy for future generations. They speak straight from the heart, and it is the hearts of young readers that are usually touched by works of this kind.

Alongside survivor literature written for and about children must be placed works of fiction that adopt the Holocaust as their motif. Some of these were written by survivors and are based to varying degrees on their own experiences; others are works of fiction written by authors who had no direct contact with the Holocaust.

In this regard, a remarkable approach was adopted by Jane Yolen, who won a National Jewish Book Award in 1988 with *The Devil's Arithmetic* (1990). Yolen's book begins with a young American girl, Hannah, telling her mother during Passover that "I'm tired of remembering." Reluctantly, she climbs into the family car in order to visit her grandparents' house, where the Passover meal will take place. At the high point of the evening, when Hannah, as the youngest child in the family, goes to the front door to symbolically welcome the prophet Elijah into the home, she suddenly finds herself cast back into the world of a Jewish *shtetl* in Poland in the 1940s. Soon, German soldiers have come to take the villagers away; only Hannah, having listened to her family's stories about the Holocaust, knows the truth about what the fate of the community will be. Using the device of time travel, Jane Yolen conveys a powerful message concerning the importance of remembrance for young readers who live safe lives remote from the dangers their grandparents experienced. *The Devil's Arithmetic* is a brilliantly imaginative approach that conveys both the spirit and the reality of the period to the generation of tomorrow.

Alongside books like *The Devil's Arithmetic*, some other works of fiction also demonstrate powerful storylines. *Friedrich*, by Hans Peter Richter (1970), tells the story of the relationship between a Jewish boy, Friedrich, and his unnamed best friend, a German non-Jew who relates Friedrich's story to us. Through the narrator's eyes, we see the encroachments on Jewish civil rights as the Nazis strengthen their grip over the lives of Germany's Jewish population. Ultimately, Friedrich dies, killed in an Allied air raid because his Jewishness has denied him the sanctuary of a public air raid shelter.

In a similar vein, two volumes by Claude Gutman, *The Empty House* (1991) and *Fighting Back* (1992), show us what it was like to be a teenager growing up Jewish in France during World War II. For most of the war, the orphan David is on the run, helped by good people he meets along the way. Having seen his parents deported and bearing guilt because his life has been spared at the expense of Claire, the girl he had come to love, David becomes obsessed by the idea of vengeance. The story has a powerful denouement set in the aftermath of the liberation, at a Holocaust survivors' gathering, when he again encounters his previously lost mother.

A similar work for young children is *When Hitler Stole Pink Rabbit* (1971) by Judith Kerr—herself a former child refugee from the Nazis who was forced to take only one toy with her as she and her family fled, via Switzerland, to Paris and then London before the war. The story relates how she had to leave behind her treasured pink rabbit, which was lost due to the ravages of the Holocaust. Told as a tale for children, the book became a best seller throughout the world and enabled young readers to derive a sense of meaning as to how intimate the Nazi destruction was even for children.

As might be imagined, much of the literature of the Holocaust embraces themes that focus on children in flight, living in the houses of strangers who have hidden them, or trying to hold body and soul together in forests or ghettos. Stories such as these expose young readers to the injustices that life can inflict on the innocent and, as with the story of *Friedrich*, show that we cannot always expect happy endings. But happy endings invariably do find their way into children's Holocaust fiction. The alternative would be too painful to bear in every case, and this form of storytelling would quickly lose its appeal as a genre if children were exposed to an unceasing diet of brutality ending in death.

Thus, in *I am David* (1965), Ann Holm has the fugitive David being reunited with his mother on the very last page of the book, after a search throughout Europe while knowing that at any moment "they" might catch up with him. In *Number the Stars* (1989) by Lois Lowry, young Annemarie Johanson of Copenhagen is the epitome of Christian goodness and bravery in offering to shelter her best friend Ellen from the Nazis. In *Hide and Seek* (1991) by Ida Voss, Rachel and her family live to see the liberation of Holland, having been hidden in friendly Dutch homes. Rachel's saddest moment, near the end of the book, is when she returns to school and finds how much classroom learning she has missed while the war has been in progress. Henryk Grynberg, who highlights the environment of destruction that torments the mind of a child constantly threatened by death, has his characters not only surviving but also liberated. His book, *Child of the Shadows* (1969), ends with the appearance of a Soviet soldier; the young narrator and his mother then emerge "into a land washed clean with shells"—the inference being that after the final days of the Third Reich, a newer, fresher world awaited in which the most detestable aspects had been physically expunged. Finally, in Hana Demetz's sad tale of life in wartime Czechoslovakia, *The House on Prague Street* (1980), we see that at war's end, not only do the trains again run on time, and that such delights as chocolate begin to reappear, but that a group of Auschwitz survivors return to Prague Street and live in the old house which for young Helene represents all that is solid and tranquil in otherwise turbulent surroundings.

The Boy in the Striped Pyjamas (2006), by Irish novelist John Boyne, is a fable of a child concentration camp prisoner who makes a weekly date with the son of the commandant. Controversial in some quarters owing to its use of Auschwitz as a backdrop for a parable, in some respects the book is equally—if not more—appropriate for adults who have at least an idea of what Auschwitz represented, and children reading this without any context could draw the wrong conclusions about the reality of the Holocaust. Nonetheless, the book became a bestseller and the subject of a highly successful motion picture (directed by Mark Herman) in 2008.

Children's fiction of the Holocaust can be evocative; it can be educational; it can even make for good reading. The nature of the subject matter it embraces, however, necessarily restricts it to a specific age group. If the fullest use is to be made of such literature, it must be able to be appreciated by a readership that is simultaneously mature and sensitive. The minimum age to expose children to Holocaust literature would, it is generally recognized, be about 12 or 13. This is not to say, however, that Holocaust-based fiction for very young children cannot be written or that any such attempts that have been made in the past have been unsuccessful. On the contrary, several quite outstanding works have been produced that provide very young children with both a story and a lesson.

Very young children, furthermore, can be exposed to the horrors of the Nazi Holocaust through the device of allegory. One of the finest examples of this has been produced by Eve Bunting, a prolific American writer of children's books. In her short work *Terrible Things: An Allegory of the Holocaust* (1989), Bunting skillfully shows the folly of doing nothing when faced with evil situations that do not affect one personally. Employing the metaphor of a small rabbit who watches while, one by one, the other creatures of the forest are taken away by the Terrible Things, Bunting provides a resource by which children can begin to approach the Holocaust period and even start, in a simple way, to understand why its recurrence must be prevented. Nowhere in the book do we see the words "Jew" or "Nazi" or any of the other realities of the actual events from the period 1933–1945; all the reader sees here are references to rabbits, birds, squirrels, porcupines, frogs, and fish. Such creatures are identifiable enough to young children to make an impact when the security of those who dwell in the forest is threatened by the Terrible Things, who come to capture everyone by means of their "terrible nets." This is an approach to the Holocaust that works for very young children.

The overall value of children's literature on the Holocaust—all types—is clearly tied to the ability of adults who will use it to assist children to make sense out of what happened in the Third Reich. It is an immensely rich resource and offers much more than simple story telling.

Further Reading

Kamenetsky, Christa. *Children's Literature in Hitler's Germany: The Cultural Policy of National Socialism.* Athens: Ohio University Press, 1984.

Lathey, Gillian. *The Impossible Legacy: Identity and Purpose in Autobiographical Children's Literature Set in the Third Reich and the Second World War*. Bern: Peter Lang, 1998.

Stephens, Elaine C., Jean E. Brown, and Janet E. Rubin. *Learning about the Holocaust: Literature and Other Resources for Young People*. Hamden, CT: Library Professional Publications, 1995.

THE CIGARETTE SELLERS OF THREE CROSSES SQUARE

The Cigarette Sellers of Three Crosses Square is the true account of a band of Jewish children, aged 7 to 16, who survived the Warsaw Ghetto. The author was Joseph Ziemian, a pseudonym for Józef Zysman, a lawyer who, before the war, defended unemployed workers facing eviction and fought for the rights of illegitimate children. In this regard he acted as a mentor for **Irena Sendler**, whose actions during the war saw her working closely with the **Żegota** organization in the overall rescue of vast numbers of Jewish children.

Written essentially for young adult readers, the book is part memoir and part reconstruction of the remarkable story of several Jewish children who eked out a precarious existence selling cigarettes, newspapers, and anything else worth hawking to Poles and Germans while hiding the fact that they were Jewish.

Three Crosses Square was in the heart of a Warsaw district taken over by the German authorities as a center of operations. A nearby youth welfare building had become a barracks for SS troops; another was the location of a German police station; and a third housed an allied Hungarian force. Not far away, the Gestapo maintained an office.

Joseph Ziemian, a commander of the Jewish Fighting Organization (Żydowska Organizacja Bojowa, or ŻOB), was a Jew **passing** as a non-Jew on the Aryan side of the wall. He had a watching brief for street children who escaped from the ghetto, and, while in possession of a false identity card that gave him freedom of movement, he one day encountered two of the children by accident at a soup kitchen in central Warsaw. This meeting was to lead him into a world in which several Jewish children were surviving together by begging and selling items such as cigarettes to Germans and Poles.

After the ghetto had been established in 1940, some of the older children would sneak out to obtain additional food for their hungry families by various means to supplement their meager rations. They would beg on the Aryan side, after which they would engage in **smuggling** activities by bringing back into the ghetto what they had managed to obtain. Over time, and with no one left in the ghetto to whom they were responsible, they remained on the Aryan side of the wall. Most were orphans; all hid their Jewish identities and slept on the streets, in cemeteries, or (rarely) with friendly Polish families.

The background to the cigarette sellers was to be found in the true-life story of Irving (Ignacy) Milchberg, born in 1927, who had taken the Polish name Henrik Rozowski but was known by the nickname Bull. Within the ghetto, he and his family had managed to make ends meet until the Germans began their roundup of

Jews for the first deportation to Treblinka in the summer of 1942. Escaping custody three times, he obtained a false work permit from some forced laborers working at the Ostbahn rail yards and began smuggling food and goods into and out of the ghetto. One day, Bull noticed a group of four Jewish children. They soon found themselves under his care, with the Ostbahn laborers helping as well—until they were themselves deported. For a year and a half, Bull and the other children lived a hand-to-mouth existence under conditions of extraordinary stress and fear of exposure, arrest, and possible deportation. Among Bull's friends were other street children who went by names such as Toothy, Hoppy, Conky, Baldy, Whitey, Carrot Top, Frenchy, and Chopper.

Bull, for his part, also smuggled small arms into the ghetto, adding these to the cache used by the Jewish Fighting Organization in the Warsaw Ghetto Uprising of April and May 1943.

By 1942, Ziemian had befriended members of the amorphous group, which numbered anywhere between 14 and 25, including at least five girls, often the sole survivors of their families. Having welcomed them into the group, Ziemian was able to provide them with false identity papers like his own. How they remained undetected by the Nazis is a feature of the book.

Ziemian shows, moreover, that the story was not one of unimpeded success. Some boys, such as Frenchy, disappeared when picked up by an SS man and handed over to the Gestapo. Fearing that Frenchy, if he was still alive, might expose them, the cigarette sellers scattered and went their own ways until the **liberation** of Warsaw by the Soviet Army in January 1945. By the end of the war, all but three of the original group were still alive. As an act of remembrance, Ziemian, who did not use anyone's last name for reasons of privacy, named the three who had died. Most of the survivors moved to Israel, the United States, or Canada, and as **child survivors**, all were successful in later life.

After the war, Ziemian recorded the story of the cigarette sellers based on notes he had taken coupled with exceptional skills of recall. His account was published in 1963 as *Papierosiarze z Placu Trzech Krzyży* and then translated into English as *The Cigarette Sellers of Three Crosses Square*, published in London by Vallentine Mitchell in 1970. Soon after its English publication, the book was awarded a literary prize by the World Jewish Congress in New York. Since then, it has appeared in Polish, Romanian, Hebrew, and Yiddish editions, and a dramatized version has been broadcast in Israel.

Born in 1922, Joseph Ziemian died in 1971, aged 49. Irving Milchberg, known as Bull, died in Toronto in January 2014, aged 86. One of the remarkable features of the whole story is that at the time he took the cigarette sellers under his wing, Ziemian was only five years older than Bull, the oldest of the children.

Further Reading

Ziemian, Joseph. *The Cigarette Sellers of Three Crosses Square*. London: Vallentine Mitchell, 1970.

CIRCUMCISION

Circumcision is the surgical removal of the foreskin of the penis. The Biblical commandment to circumcise male children was given to Abraham in the Torah (Genesis 17:1–14; Leviticus 12:3). As a Jew, Jesus was circumcised on the eighth day after his birth, in keeping with Jewish tradition; as the first male followers of Jesus were Jews, the early Christian Church argued that circumcision was compulsory for converts (though this is no longer the case today). Circumcision is practiced by Jews and Muslims, which are both Abrahamic religions.

The covenant of *brit milah* (circumcision) is a Jewish religious ceremony performed on the eighth day of a baby boy's life, and the operation is delayed only upon the doctor's advice. The operation is performed by the circumcisor (*Mohel*) in the presence of the child's father, the *Sandek* (godfather, often the grandfather), and a religious quorum of 10 men (*minyan*). It is a celebration witnessed by family, friends, and community members. The child is usually named in the blessings that follow the procedure. The ritual is an ancient practice that has been carried out by Jewish parents for more than 3,000 years. It is symbolic of the Jewish boy entering the covenant between God and the Jewish people, though it is not an initiation rite; a baby boy will be Jewish regardless of whether he is circumcised. Such is the importance of *brit milah* that circumcision can take place on the Sabbath or a holy day, even though drawing blood is not usually allowed on these days for other reasons under Jewish law. Often, Jews with only a tentative connection to Judaism will have their sons circumcised. Even during the bleakest days of Nazi persecution, Jews strove to observe the practice.

In countries that do not circumcise, the wider population has often been hostile toward those who do. It was extremely rare, for example, for a non-Jewish Pole during the 1930s to have been circumcised. Consequently, when German police were unsure if a male was Jewish or not because he did not fit the stereotypical appearance of a Jew, they would commonly check men taken in raids, who would be forced to expose themselves. This was a widely reported occurrence generating intense fear for Jews in hiding or **passing** among the non-Jewish population. For boys attempting to hide their Jewish identity, using a public restroom or participating in sports could lead to their discovery. In desperation, to avoid being identified as Jews because of their circumcision, some parents would even dress their sons as girls—a situation that would have to last for the duration of the war to avoid detection.

The persecution of Jews under the Nazi regime made circumcision an existential threat, making no difference whether the person had lost his foreskin for religious reasons or because of a medical condition. Every circumcised boy and man at that time was in danger of being denounced and therefore had to hide his penis or undergo complicated surgery reversing the circumcision. This dilemma is illustrated clearly in a remarkable memoir from one such boy who was passing as an Aryan, Solomon Perel (*Europa, Europa*, 1990). To avoid detection, there were often occasions when prewar medical certificates of circumcision were falsified.

In occupied Poland, Żegota, the Polish Council to Aid Jews, helped with "uncircumization" procedures. Dr. Feliks Kanabus, a successful non-Jewish surgeon, performed about 70 circumcision-reversal operations; most were effective, and in one case a German medical board was deceived by his skills. After becoming a well-respected surgeon in a pediatric hospital, Kanabus admitted Jewish children who had escaped from the ghetto, devising fictitious charts enabling them to stay there until a refuge could be found. Later, he began helping his Jewish medical colleagues leave the ghetto. Among his many activities on behalf of Jews, Kanabus performed cosmetic operations on "Jewish-looking" refugees, as well as the circumcision-reversal procedures already mentioned, with the help of his wife, Irena, who acted as his assistant. In risking their lives to help Jews, Feliks and Irena Kanabus were guided by humanitarian motives that overrode considerations of personal safety or economic hardship. On September 21, 1965, Dr. Feliks Kanabus was recognized by Yad Vashem as one of the Righteous among the Nations; Irena Kanabus was similarly recognized on October 18, 1995.

Further Reading

Bartoszewski, Władysław, and Zofia Lewin. *The Samaritans: Heroes of the Holocaust.* New York: Twayne Publishers, 1970.

Yad Vashem. Kanabus Family, at http://db.yadvashem.org/righteous/family.html?language=en&itemId=4043969.

COHN, MARIANNE (1922–1944)

Marianne Cohn saved Jewish children during World War II as a member of the French-Jewish resistance, and she lost her life doing so.

Born on September 17, 1922, in Mannheim, Germany, she was eldest child of Dr. Alfred and Grete Cohn, *née* Radt. The family was Jewish, though not religiously observant. In 1929 they moved from Mannheim to Berlin, and in 1934, after the Nazi seizure of power the previous year, to Barcelona in Spain. With the onset of the Spanish Civil War in 1936, they moved again in 1938, this time settling in France.

When World War II started, Marianne's parents, as German nationals, were detained at the Gurs internment camp, and Marianne and her younger sister, Lisa, were sent to a farm run by the **Éclaireurs Israélites de France** (the Jewish Scouts, or EIF) at Moissac, in southern France. Marianne lived and worked there for the next three years, helping to take care of recently arrived refugee children and learning how to engage in resistance work under the tutelage of Édouard Simon, who ran the home, and his friend Simon Lévitte. This work was an important element of the *Mouvement de la Jeunesse Sioniste* (Zionist Youth Movement, or MJS), which had been founded in May 1942 by Lévitte and Jules ("Dika") Jefroykin. Using the EIF home at Moissac as a base, Lévitte organized training programs to ensure the protection of those housed there. Soon instrumental in Lévitte's forging operations in and around Moissac, Marianne quickly became his coordinating secretary. The false documentation center, which Lévitte entrusted to Otto ("Toto") Giniewski, became Marianne's training ground; when this shifted to Grenoble, she followed.

Here, she assisted in providing food, shelter, and medical care to Jewish refugees. This was just the beginning, and soon she would find herself in the position of smuggling Jewish children out of France.

Convoys of children would often leave Limoges (where many Jewish refugees were concentrated) in order to reach Lyon. From there they would be conveyed to Aix-les-Bains or Annecy, where they were handed over to **Georges Loinger**, assisted by young Jewish helpers such as **Mila Racine**. During the summer of 1943, Marianne, then still learning her craft as a *passeur*, was arrested by Vichy police with another MJS operative (originally from the Netherlands), Jacques Klausner ("Marcel"). As a novice rescuer, it was almost inevitable that Marianne would be found out. She was threatened with deportation and imprisoned in Nice for three months, and her ordeal served to alert her as to the trials she could face in the future if she was to continue her acts of defiance. It was during this period that she wrote a poem, "*Je trahirai demain*" ("I Shall Betray Tomorrow"). In its English translation, this immortal statement of rebellion and loyalty in the face of persecution read as follows:

> *I shall betray tomorrow, not today.*
> *Today, pull out my fingernails,*
> *I shall not betray.*
> *You do not know the limits of my courage,*
> *I, I do.*
> *You are five hands, harsh and full of rings,*
> *Wearing hob-nailed boots.*
> *I shall betray tomorrow, not today.*
> *I need the night to make up my mind.*
> *I need at least one night,*
> *To disown, to abjure, to betray.*
> *To disown my friends,*
> *To abjure bread and wine,*
> *To betray life,*
> *To die.*
> *I shall betray tomorrow, not today.*
> *The file is under the window-pane.*
> *The file is not for the window-bars,*
> *The file is not for the executioner,*
> *The file is for my own wrists.*
> *Today, I have nothing to say,*
> *I shall betray tomorrow.*

At the end of the war one of the children saved by Marianne Cohn passed the poem to the head of the MJS. It is a testimony of courage and one of the great poems of the French Resistance.

In 1943 Marianne was living in Grenoble. Volunteer *passeurs*, who escorted Jewish children to Switzerland, undertook hazardous missions under constant risk of detection by Nazis or French collaborators. When Mila Racine was captured on

October 21, 1943, Marianne was sent by the MJS to replace her. Using the false identity of Marie Colin, she then undertook nine further transfers of children, taking groups of about 30 into Switzerland on each occasion.

In January 1944 Marianne began working with a Roman Catholic resister, Rolande Birgy, with whom she ferried groups of up to 20 children across the southern border into Switzerland. Rolande, who had earlier teamed with Mila Racine, was known as the "Blue Beret" in resistance circles. In 1984 she was recognized as one of the Righteous among the Nations by Yad Vashem.

By the start of 1944, Marianne had taken hundreds of children to Switzerland, but on the evening of May 31, 1944, a German patrol arrested her near Annemasse, just 200 meters from the border, while escorting a group of 28 children ranging in age from 4 to 15. She was held at the local Gestapo jail, known as the Prison de Pax. The Vichy-appointed mayor of Annemasse, **Jean Deffaugt**, who sympathized with the Resistance (and was later also recognized as one of the Righteous), intervened on behalf of the children. The younger ones were sent to local orphanages, while Marianne and the older children were paroled to work in Annemasse during the day and returned, under guard, to the prison at night.

This worked for a short time, but the Resistance knew that Marianne was in extreme danger; not only this, but the whole escape operation was in jeopardy. A plan was arranged to rescue her, but she refused to leave the children, fearing reprisals.

Resistance leaders then sent a message to the Gestapo, threatening to kill its members if any of the detainees were harmed. The Gestapo began their interrogation, nevertheless. On July 3, 1944, a special squad was sent to Annemasse from Lyon with the assignment of removing six of the prisoners, including Marianne. In her defiance, she refused to hide behind her alias and revealed her identity; for her rebelliousness, she was tortured horribly. She did not, however, speak—other than to say that she had no regrets for her actions.

On the night of July 7–8, 1944, only three weeks before the liberation of Annemasse, she was taken to nearby Ville-la-Grand and murdered along with the other five prisoners; it is recorded that the Gestapo continually hit them with shovels and kicked them until they were dead. They were buried hastily, and their mutilated bodies were discovered after the war. The 28 children imprisoned with Marianne were all saved and released as a result of the liberation in August.

When Marianne Cohn was murdered, she was just 22 years old.

Further Reading

Bartrop, Paul R., and Samantha J. Lakin. *Heroines of Vichy France: Rescuing French Jews during the Holocaust*. Santa Barbara, CA: Praeger, 2019.

COMITÉ DE DÉFENSE DES JUIFS

Belgium was occupied by Nazi Germany from May 28, 1940, until the Allied liberation in September 1944. In November 1941 the Germans created the *Association des Juifs en Belgique* (Association of Belgian Jews, or AJB), a Jewish-run Council to administer the Jewish population. All Jews had to register (only about half, however, did so). The AJB provided social services to Belgium's Jews and prevailed upon Jews to turn up for deportation when summoned.

From May 27, 1942, Jews were required to wear the yellow star in public, and after August 4, 1942, deportations began. The first were stateless Jews who left Mechelen (Malines) transit camp for Auschwitz. In September 1942 armed German units, relying on paid informants, raided homes to steal valuables. At the same time, Jews with Belgian citizenship were deported for the first time, prompting opposition from the wider Belgian population. By the end of the occupation, more than 40 percent of all Jews in Belgium were in hiding; many were hidden with assistance from the non-Jewish population, particularly Catholic priests and nuns.

In September 1942 the *Comité de Défense des Juifs* (Committee for the Protection of Jews, or CDJ) was founded by the Jewish communist Hertz Jospa and his wife, Have Groisman (**Yvonne Jospa**), in the house of Chaim and Fela Perelman. The Perelmans had turned their home into a temporary refuge for Jews on the run; they saw themselves as the managers of an underground network designed to rescue Jewish children and adults from deportation and death. The CDJ became an organization of the Belgian Resistance, affiliated to the *Front de l'Indépendance*.

Chaim Perelman recruited Yvonne Jospa as a social worker in the child placement section, with another operative, Ida Sterno, assisting. At Perelman's instigation, the mayor of the town of Uccle, Jean Hérinckx, wrote a letter to the German authorities on behalf of the mayors of the Brussels metropolitan region, denouncing anti-Jewish measures such as the wearing of the yellow star. As late as September 1943, Perelman contacted the responsible officer in the Ministry for Provisions asking for additional food for Jews awaiting deportation who were interned in the Dossin Barracks. He begged for food from the Wijgaerts family, who operated a big food chain in Brussels, for Jews in hiding. Furthermore, the printing firm of A. Wolf in Liège provided Perelman with numerous false stamps. In Antwerp, Alphonse Goethals, in charge of provisions, also responded to Perelman's appeal for ration card stamps, offering 1,500 stamp pages per month out of the 8,000 pages that he produced.

When the Germans forbade Jewish children from attending public schools, Fela Perelman appealed to Hérinckx, as well as other officials in the Brussels municipality, to set up a special school for Jewish children under the name of *Nos Petits* ("Our Little Ones"). This request was granted. Hérinckx also arranged for a special tram to take the children to and from school. Fela ("Denise Dumont") interviewed candidate teachers willing to serve at *Nos Petits* and recruited **Jeanne Daman**, who became the school principal and Fela's chief helper. Fela and Jeanne helped find safe sheltering places for the children with the help from the *Office de la Naissance et de l'Enfance* (National Office of Children, or ONE). This occurred even before the creation of the CDJ. Later, Fela helped find additional women as escorts for the **hidden children**, providing their hosts with payment and food ration cards where necessary.

With the formation of the CDJ, Fela Perelman also helped by placing Jewish women as maids in non-Jewish homes. Noemi Perelman, her daughter (born in 1936), was placed in a foster home in 1941, a year ahead of the deportations, while the Perelman home itself served as a refuge for Jews on the run hoping to cross into either Switzerland or Spain.

Maurice Heiber and his wife, Estera, were also founders of the CDJ, though Maurice Heiber also maintained a role in the AJB for a time. Heiber administered the special children's department of the CDJ, having prior experience with running orphanages through his work with the Jewish orphanage in Brussels. The main day-to-day work was carried out by four professional social workers—Yvonne Jospa and Ida Sterno, who were Jewish, and **Andrée Geulen** (later **Geulen-Herscovici**) and Suzanne Moons-Lepetit, who were not. These four women traveled throughout Belgium, searching out addresses and permanent homes for the children. They looked to religious institutions, children's homes and boarding schools, as well as individuals who could help. The social workers had to provide new identities, papers, money, and ration cards, as well as food and clothing for the children. Meetings between parents and their children were organized in a neutral venue so the adults would not know where the children were sheltered.

The CDJ had about 30 members in its children's section alone who formed an effective committee and came from all political and religious backgrounds, overcoming their divergent views to unite for the sake of saving Jewish children. The CDJ succeeded in saving about 3,000 of the 5,000 children, who became known as *enfants cachés* (hidden children).

On one occasion, Jewish children had been placed by the CDJ in a suburb of Brussels. Learning that the Gestapo was about to undertake a large and methodical search for the children, teams of young women from the CDJ were immediately dispatched with the task of removing the children and taking them to safety. On another occasion, 15 girls who had been placed in a convent near Ghent were pulled out in a hurry when their presence was inadvertently disclosed by one of the nuns. In May 1943, however, when another group of 15 Jewish children under the tutelage of the AJB "disappeared" while in hiding, Maurice Heiber and his wife, Estera, were arrested by the Gestapo. He was imprisoned in the Mechelen-Malines transit camp but released through the intervention of senior members of the Belgian civilian administration.

The price paid for all such activities was high, and many other members of the CDJ, together with their associates, were arrested by the Nazi and Belgian collaborationist authorities.

Intelligence about the fate of Jews who had been deported also served to galvanize the rescue activities on behalf of children. In early 1943, the *Front de l'Indépendance* sent Victor Martin, a professor of economics at the Catholic University of Louvain, to gather information on the fate of deported Belgian Jews using the cover of a research post he held at the University of Cologne. Martin visited Auschwitz and witnessed the crematoria. Arrested by the Germans, he escaped and was able to report his findings to the CDJ in May 1943.

In September 20, 1943, Maurice Heiber explained to Yvonne Nèvejean, director of the ONE, that by strictly following the Belgian laws and the German ordinances, the AJB endangered children more than it protected them. Nèvejean replied that ONE would support Heiber on this issue, but on September 30, 1943, Heiber's worst fears were confirmed when the 80 children of a home in Wezembeek-Oppem were arrested and transferred to Mechelen. It was only through the intercession of Queen Elisabeth the Queen Mother—later recognized as one of the Righteous among the Nations for her work in saving Jewish lives—that the children were freed.

Maurice and Estera Heiber used the AJB's official register of all Belgian Jews to contact families and obtain their agreement to save their children through the CJD's own network, and as a result, thousands of Belgian Jewish children escaped deportation.

Estera Heiber ("Mrs. Pascale") developed a system for coding information about children in care, which was necessary to avoid the Gestapo's prying eyes. She created four notebooks: the first included the names and a reference code; the second, this reference code and the false identity of the children; the third had the code and the places where they were hiding; and the fourth had the code and their real addresses. Only three people held these notebooks: Estera and Maurice Heiber and Yvonne Jospa. Other notebooks existed that were used for the accounting of sums paid to the people hiding the refugees. These notebooks assisted the return of the children to their parents, or to close family when the parents had been deported and not returned. After the war, the work of the CDJ continued, as four orphanages were established for children whose parents had not survived.

Further Reading

Gross, Alan G., and Ray D. Dearin. *Chaim Perelman*. Albany: State University of New York Press, 2003.

Paldiel, Mordecai. *Saving One's Own: Jewish Rescuers during the Holocaust*. Philadelphia: Jewish Publication Society, 2017.

D

DAMAN, JEANNE (1918–1986)

Jeanne Daman, a preschool teacher, taught children at a Jewish school in Belgium during the Nazi occupation. After seeing what the Germans were doing to the children, she risked her life to save her students and their families and, in doing so, saved upward of 2,000 children overall.

She was born in Belgium into a Roman Catholic family on November 14, 1918. In her early 20s, she became a schoolteacher. After Germany occupied Belgium in May 1940, the classroom curriculum was organized to fit Nazi propaganda requirements. New antisemitic laws and regulations were introduced, including the banning of Jewish children from public schools.

Jeanne's teaching was affected. She resigned from public school teaching because she diarized that she could not teach what she wanted to, and she would not teach what the Nazis wanted her to teach. She recounted later that her parents agreed with her resignation. (Her uncle lost his life as a political prisoner at Mauthausen, and her cousin was incarcerated for two years in Ravensbrück). Jeanne took on secretarial work instead, and as she spoke German, the Nazis paid no attention to her. In short, she felt "safe."

In 1942 the Jewish community was forced to establish its own kindergartens, after Jewish children were forbidden to attend school alongside non-Jews. Fela Perelman ("Denise Dumont"), who organized rescue efforts for Jewish children at the time, therefore required qualified and experienced teachers for the new schools to cater for the youngsters who were excluded, and on the recommendation on the director-general of educational services in Brussels, Perelman asked Jeanne, then 21, to join the staff of her private Jewish school, *Nos Petits* ("Our Little Ones"), which had some 325 children.

Jeanne was a Catholic and had no previous contact with Judaism or the Jewish world, but she had grown up with a strong sense of right and wrong. Her family heard that, because of a Nazi roundup, a small child left alone at home fell through a window to the street below and was killed. For Jeanne, her involvement was based on compassion for the children affected. She accepted the offer.

In time, she identified an increasing absence of students. More families were deported; each day saw absentees among the children, as it turned out that the families were rounded up. Other children became instant orphans and were placed into homes when their parents were taken away while they were at school.

Jeanne became the headmistress of *Nos Petits* at the age of 23. As the occupation continued, the attitudes of the *Nos Petits* staff toward their students changed. Jeanne wrote later that her own attitude was altered after an incident at the height of the Nazi raids in which Gestapo agents arrived at the school. They identified three children whose mothers, they said, had asked them to pick up and take their children to them. Jeanne knew what this visit meant but could not react because she had 60 other children in the school that day. Dressing the children herself, she delayed until the very last moment when the Nazis would take them away. The children's parents were hiding; the Nazis used this ruse to get them out in the open, and it worked. All were captured.

This experience was to change her life. Jeanne felt she should do something; she wanted to strike back. Mothers who now foresaw the worst for their children approached the school for assistance.

Jeanne commenced covert endeavors to rescue the children, to find shelter and hiding places for them. She began helping them by locating safe places where they could hide, and when she was successful, children were placed with kindly non-Jewish Belgian families.

Soon the Jewish school had to be closed in order to prevent the Nazis from recognizing the Jewish children. Over time it became necessary to find money to make monthly payments to Belgian families providing shelter, and Jeanne saw to it that the children were given new names and identities. Each child would repeat these details, with Jeanne emphasizing to them the importance of never making a mistake. Contact was made with the Œuvre Nationale de l'Enfance (National Office of Children, or ONE), mostly in the person of Nelly Lameere, Mme. Volon (an assistant of Yvonne Nèvejean, director of the children's chain of vacation homes), and Jean Hérinckx (mayor of Uccle), with whom there was daily contact. Thanks to their cooperation, Jeanne was able to move the children to safety.

After the Jewish school closed, Fela Perelman asked Jeanne to continue her rescue efforts. Many more children suddenly had become orphans, and someone was needed to go with them to their new clandestine refuges. Jeanne often led them and always remained in touch after their new locations had been secured. She trekked all over Belgium; for example, she visited a priest, Father Rausch in Felenne, just north of the French border, who took in 50 children.

As the Nazi hunts became more frequent, Fela and Jeanne cared for adults who required refuge. They created a system in which Jewish women became maids in Belgian elite households. Jeanne guided them to their future employers, having delivered them false identity papers and ration cards, mostly provided by Fela Perelman's husband, Chaim. Jeanne also kept these women informed about their children, who were hiding elsewhere. She also helped rescue many Jewish men by finding false papers for them.

Fela Perelman introduced Jeanne to Albert Domb of the Jewish underground. Domb asked Jeanne to help the Resistance find Belgians who were denouncing Jews to the Gestapo, looking for their locations so that they could be found and eliminated. Forced to adopt a new identity, she became a social worker with the *Secours d'Hiver* (Winter Help, the German-imposed welfare organization). Her new connections and her uniform made it easier for her to carry out that role.

Toward the end of the war, Jeanne also became involved with the MRB (*Mouvement Royal Belge*), which dealt with illegal operations prior to the liberation. For this work she transported arms on her bicycle. As an intelligence agent, she was active in the Brussels corps of the *Armée Belge des Partisans* (Belgian Partisan Army).

After the war, she assisted in returning the hidden children to their families and finding relatives for Jewish orphans. She also helped with the special care of those children who had survived deportation to Nazi concentration camps.

In 1946 she moved to the United States, where she raised funds for Israel through the United Jewish Appeal. On June 28, 1952, she married Aldo Domenic Scaglione, an Italian immigrant who had been involved with the Italian resistance.

On February 2, 1971, Yad Vashem recognized Jeanne Daman as one of the Righteous among the Nations, crediting her with saving the lives of as many as 2,000 children. In 1980 she was awarded the *Entr'aide* medal through the Belgian Jewish community, under the patronage of the King of Belgium. Jeanne Daman died in June 1986 in California.

Further Reading

Yad Vashem. Jeanne Daman-Scaglione (Belgium), at https://www.yadvashem.org/yv/en/exhibitions/righteous-women/daman.asp.

DAVID, JANINA (b.1930)

Janina David (Dawidowicz) was born on March 19, 1930, in Kalisz, Poland. After surviving the Holocaust, she wrote a series of three books that tell, from the viewpoint of a child, the story of her middle-class family's journey to their death at the hands of the Nazis, her survival in wartime Poland, and her postwar experiences.

Janina was an only child who lived with her parents in a remote Polish town. Until 1937, when the family business—a flour mill—burned down, Janina was able to take her summer holidays abroad. After the loss of the mill, she spent her summers in the woods surrounding the town, where children came on holidays, picked mushrooms and berries, and sat in tree branches exchanging stories. Janina was considered a delicate child and was made to eat large bowls of semolina; she recalled in her first book, *A Square of Sky*, that the annoyance of having to eat semolina was the only jarring note in an otherwise cozy, loving family life.

With the outbreak of war in September 1939, the family moved to Warsaw, which had a huge Jewish population compared to anywhere else in Poland and where the family could retreat to a "safety in numbers" environment. Janina's writing of this first period of the war showed a child who was relatively detached, watching as typhus, hunger, and bombing gradually destroyed the people. She wrote that her family's life continued in overcrowded apartments or hiding places until, a year after arriving in Warsaw, they were all on the verge of starvation, sharing a small room in the Warsaw Ghetto.

During the first years of the German occupation, the primary danger for ghetto inhabitants was death from starvation. There were daily hunts for food in the ghetto streets, and Janina wrote that refugees from the distant parts of Poland were losing the fight and growing thinner and more desperate every day.

In the long run, however, survival depended on avoiding deportation. As a volunteer ghetto policeman, Janina's father lasted longer than most, but in the end, he was taken to a concentration camp. When it became clear in 1943 that none of the family was likely to survive, Janina, now a 13-year-old, was smuggled out of the ghetto to live with a German-Polish family. The mother of this family was a Polish woman, married to a German husband, and they had two young sons. Janina was explained to curious visitors as being a child from the German's first marriage. For Janina, this involved suppressing her Jewish origins and **passing** as a Christian by adopting the family's Catholicism.

From her hiding place one morning, she saw columns of smoke rising over the ghetto; the uprising had begun. Shortly thereafter, her existence as a Jew was discovered, and her presence became even more hazardous and risky for the German-Polish family shielding her, so she was moved to a different location.

To avoid detection, she was placed with false identity papers into the care of a courageous Mother Superior in a convent; then she was sent to a second (and safer) convent school. The nuns risked their lives to hide her, and Janina lived in constant fear of being discovered or denounced. In this second convent school, accompanied mostly by Polish Catholic children who were orphans, Janina managed to survive the rest of the war. Her survival was remarkable as nearly every relative and friend from the first nine years of her life had perished.

With the end of the war, Janina returned to the empty apartment in Kalisz. She waited day after day, for almost a year, for her mother's return. In the summer of 1946, she was recognized on the street by a man who was in Majdanek with her father, and from him she understood that she would never see her parents again. She left Poland in 1946 and moved to Paris, where she spent two years in an international orphanage. Her postwar wanderings between 1946 and 1948 are described in her book *Light over the Water*.

On the eve of her 18th birthday, she migrated to Australia. For a short time, she worked in a factory, but then she completed school and studied at the University of Melbourne, gaining a bachelor of arts degree and acquiring Australian citizenship. In 1958 she moved to London, where she served as a hospital social worker.

In 1959 she commenced writing her life story in her three-volume autobiography, *A Square of Sky*, *A Touch of Earth*, and *Light over the Water*. *A Square of Sky* was first published in German as *Ein Stück Himmel* in 1982. It recorded Janina's recollections of the events around her as seen through the eyes of a lonely child, very scared but willing herself to survive. Being forced to reconcile herself to the death of her parents, she wrote without self-pity or bitterness. In their English version, *A Square of Sky* and *A Touch of Earth* were first written and published as two separate books, but they were later reissued as a single volume.

Further Reading

David, Janina. *A Square of Sky: A Jewish Childhood in Wartime Poland*. London: Hutchinson, 1964.

David, Janina. *A Touch of Earth: A Wartime Childhood*. London: Hutchinson, 1966.

DECEPTIONS

When deceptions during the Holocaust are discussed, they are most often couched in terms of how the Nazis deceived their victims. Euphemisms such as "deportation," "the East," "resettlement," and so on were intended to lull Jews into a false sense of security as to their fate, right up to the final deception that told them they were entering "showers" for the purpose of "delousing."

Another form of deception, however, lay with the Jews themselves—in particular, the urgent need to deceive the Nazis in order to stay one step ahead of death. While various forms were employed, some stand out for their sheer ingenuity and audacity.

Pierre Bouty operated one such scheme. He and his wife, Marguerite, operated the Les Fougères Préventorium, a health-care home for children in Brantôme (Dordogne, France), which commenced operations progressively throughout the period 1935–1936 to help children recover from disease and surgery. It was known particularly as an institution for patients infected but recovering from tuberculosis.

When the south of France was invaded by Germany in 1942 and arrests of Jews became more frequent, different underground networks approached Bouty to take in children needing shelter. He immediately accepted, and he and Marguerite began to accept Jewish children. Hiding them as "patients" in need of lengthy periods of "convalescence," they were able to save dozens of Jewish children and British soldiers, even asking the man who farmed the estate on which the Préventorium was located to raise Dutch cows so that the children never lacked milk. And though the Préventorium was centrally located and surrounded by German troops, the deception was never revealed.

Pierre and Marguerite Bouty never asked for any compensation for their efforts. They spoke to no one else about their wartime activities, and after the **liberation**, they did not speak about the children they had saved. Pierre Bouty was known merely to have said that he "only did his duty" as a human being caring for children in need. On August 6, 2007, Yad Vashem recognized Pierre and Marguerite Bouty as Righteous among the Nations.

Marie-Antoinette Gout was a nurse in Epinal, capital of the *département* of Vosges, in the occupied zone. She was well known to the Jewish community as a kind friend who was always prepared to help Jews in trouble. In May 1942 she was asked by a local Jewish resident, Madame Hecker, for her help in smuggling her two daughters, Norah, 16, and Josette, 18, to relatives in unoccupied (or Vichy) France. Responding positively, Marie-Antoinette managed to obtain false papers for the girls and five other young Jews, and then she began to consider how to smuggle them across the demarcation line.

The method she developed and then implemented was as imaginative as it was daring. In her capacity as a nurse, she said she was accompanying a group of tuberculosis patients whom she was taking to help in their recovery and convalescence in the Alps. To ensure the deception would be believable, she explained to the children how they were to behave en route, behaving like sick children and engaging in appropriate coughing fits whenever they approached German or French checkpoints, or at other times of inspection. She dressed the Hecker girls, Josette and Norah, in clothing that made them look younger. Once the train on which they were traveling reached Lyon, the children were received by waiting relatives and dispersed.

Denounced by an informer, Marie-Antoinette Gout was arrested, taken to the prison in Nancy, and deported to Ravensbrück for the duration of the war. Upon her return to France, she explained her actions as being motivated by "humanitarian and patriotic sentiments." Receiving several decorations from the French government, including the Legion of Honor and the Croix de Guerre, she was recognized by Yad Vashem in Jerusalem on May 3, 1973, as one of the Righteous among the Nations.

Deception also took place in other ways, often through masquerading Jewish children into other guises. The vulnerability of boys, for example, was exposed through the German demand to see their **circumcision**, a sure way to identify a Jewish male. In the case of a Jewish mother and son in Poland whom we know as Larissa and Sasha, this was avoided through Larissa's inspired decision to trade a valuable piece of jewelry for Aryan papers covering a mother and daughter. Larissa, a widow, and Sasha, who was aged nine when the war broke out in 1939, saw little other option than that of deceiving the Nazis as to who they really were. Thus, to save Sasha's life, Larissa transformed him into Sala, a teenage girl. She then trained Sasha to be a girl, altering his clothing, hair, the way he used his voice, his walk, his mannerisms, and practically all other elements of his public persona—notably, how to behave like a Polish girl in wartime. Hidden in plain sight thus, Sasha thereupon spent the next three-and-a-half years impersonating a girl whom everyone knew as Sala.

The deception worked. With the end of the war, mother and newly restored son began adjusting to a new normality, prior to reentering life. Sasha, now a young teenager, resumed his male identity, met a girl named Mila, and eventually married. Their daughter, Anita Selzer, brought the story of Sala/Sasha to a broad audience in 2018.

While hiding in plain sight through physical transformation was one form of deception, another was through simply recasting an identity and **passing** in non-Jewish society. The case of the Polish Mendelsohn family is instructive in this regard. Robert Melson's (Mendelsohn) mother, Nina, managed to obtain false identity papers to disguise herself, her husband (Willy), and her son for the duration of the war. Their papers did not simply mean they could pass among the regular Polish population, however; they became transformed into the Zamojskis, an aristocratic Polish family comprising the Count and Countess Zamojski and their son, Count Bobi, who had been born in 1937.

As an aristocrat with unblemished pedigree and German language skills, "Count Willy" not only entertained leading Nazis in his grand home in Kraków but also managed to create for himself a highly profitable career in business. "Count Bobi," aged only eight when the war ended, had to navigate between being Jewish and being Catholic, know how to behave like a boy of noble birth, and not give the game away through some innocent childish gaffe. Ultimately, the deception was successful: the "Zamojskis" saved not only themselves but also an uncle and three Jewish women along the way.

Overall, the number and type of deceptions employed by Jews and non-Jews to save the lives of Jewish children was varied and limited only by the human imagination. Ingenuity, boldness, and, in the Jewish vernacular, chutzpah were the inescapable characteristics of such performances whenever they appeared.

Further Reading

Melson, Robert. *False Papers: Deception and Survival in the Holocaust.* Champaign: University of Illinois Press, 2000.

Pike, Robert. *Defying Vichy: Blood, Fear and French Resistance.* Stroud, UK: The History Press, 2018.

Selzer, Anita. *I am Sasha.* Melbourne: Penguin Books Random House, 2018.

DEFFAUGT, JEAN (1896–1970)

Jean François Deffaugt was born on May 31, 1896, in Verchaix, a commune in the Haute-Savoie region of southeastern France. He began his working life as an adult in Lorraine before settling in Annemasse, close to the border between France and Switzerland, in 1935.

After the defeat of France in 1940, he saw to the welfare of evacuees from the north, and eventually over 12,000 French men and women from the occupied area were housed in a reception center established by Deffaugt in Annemasse in what was, at that time, his own private initiative. Noticed for this patriotic voluntary action by the authorities, he was chosen by the Special Delegation established by the Vichy Regime and appointed deputy mayor of Annemasse. When the mayor fled, Deffaugt replaced him and became mayor in his own right in 1942.

In early 1943 Deffaugt was approached by **Georges Loinger**, a Jewish resistance fighter and member of the OSE, to set up a Jewish children's conduit that would enable them to move to a safe refuge in Switzerland, and with the assistance of Colonel Georges Groussard and other members of the Gilbert resistance network, he was put in touch with smugglers able to serve as *passeurs* to help the children. In this way, Daffaugt was responsible for sending numerous fugitives into Switzerland from Annemasse.

By May 1944 Deffaugt thus had a reputation for standing up on behalf of those oppressed by Vichy authorities and the German occupiers. On October 21, 1943, one of the *passeurs*, **Mila Racine**, was conducting a convoy that included 30 children from Nice, accompanied by another Jewish resister, Roland Epstein. This was a difficult group. It comprised children, an older couple, a young mother with a baby, and another couple with a small child. Without warning, they were intercepted by Germans with police dogs at Saint-Julien-en-Genevois. Gunshots rang out; one woman was killed and another wounded. Mila, Roland, and the children were taken to Annemasse and incarcerated in the Prison de Pax, right across from Gestapo headquarters.

Suffering continued Nazi torture, Mila divulged nothing as the Gestapo sought information regarding the smuggling operations. Jean Deffaugt managed to visit the prison and arranged with the Nazis to allow some of the children, including a baby of 14 months, to be freed and placed in a nearby children's home. Through the underground movement, he also managed to provide Mila with an escape plan. This was not something she could accept, however, as she had an instinctive feeling that the children would be punished—or worse—if she was to escape.

The Pax Prison in which Mila Racine was held was first created during the Italian occupation of Annemasse in June 1943. Established in a warehouse opposite the hotel, it took little time for the prison to develop a reputation as a place of terror. With an appalling level of hygiene, seemingly always overcrowded, and suffering stifling extremes of heat, after the arrival of the Germans in September 1943, the prison became even more congested. It became a place of detention, torture, and summary executions, feared by all. Deffaugt petitioned the German authorities to improve conditions, and the impression he made on the Gestapo commander was such that he gave Deffaugt a permit allowing him access to the prison to visit all those held there. In this way, before each visit, he collected food, medicines, blankets, and other vital necessities, and the prisoners were also able to use him as a conduit for the receipt and delivery of mail.

After the arrest of Mila Racine, moreover, his good offices were needed more than ever. Late in the afternoon of Wednesday, May 31, 1944, Mila's replacement, **Marianne Cohn**, took charge in the nearby city of Annecy a group of 28 Jewish children (according to some accounts, 32; the exact number varies according to witness statements) ranging in age from 4 to 15 years. When the truck conveying them was only 200 meters from the border, it was stopped by a German patrol. The children and Marianne were interrogated; some were beaten, and all were taken to the German customs office in Annemasse, where they were handed over to the Gestapo at the Hotel de Pax.

The leader of the Resistance, Emmanuel Racine ("Mola," Mila's brother), contacted Deffaugt, seeking his intervention with the Germans as a means to mitigate whatever fate they had in mind for the convoy. Deffaugt, in turn, managed to obtain the provisional release of an initial group of 17 of the younger children (aged 4 to 11), who were sent to local orphanages. The 11 older children and adolescents (five boys and six girls) were to remain in prison, though paroled to work in the kitchen at the Hôtel de France in Annemasse during the day; they would leave the prison at 10:30 each morning and return, under guard, at night. Deffaugt was also successful in acting as a go-between for Marianne and her network, with both he and his assistant, Ernest Balthazard, risking their lives to smuggle messages into and out of the prison.

Owing to his previous contacts with the Resistance, he knew that Marianne was one of Emmanuel Racine's operatives, and he recognized that he would have to offer whatever help he could. First, the children had to be protected, and with that objective secured, he and Racine concluded that Marianne had to be helped to escape. Offered the opportunity, however, she, like Mila Racine before her, declined, saying that "these children were entrusted to me; I have no right abandoning them." She concluded that she could not leave the children and that it was her duty to stay.

While they were in the prison, moreover, the captives were forced to rely on the goodwill of Jean Deffaugt and the people of Annemasse for feeding and upkeep. He and his assistant Ernest Balthazard searched for donations from all over town. Deffaugt never received any money for the prisoners' sustenance from Vichy authorities; indeed, when later he presented the government with an account for 52,000 francs, he was told, "It was not for you to feed the prisoners; you took this initiative, too bad for you."

A few days before the liberation of Annemasse, the Gestapo in Lyon went to the town to collect and murder Marianne Cohn, whose mutilated remains were later found in a mass grave with five other resistance fighters.

Deffaugt, however, managed to obtain the release of the children after the French Forces of the Interior conquered the region. He then sent the children on a truck to Switzerland. All had been saved as a result of Marianne Cohn's bravery and Jean Deffaugt's persistence. After the war he kept in touch with the children, and even 20 years later, he was receiving mail from them in other parts of France, in Britain, and in Israel. On February 25, 1966, he was recognized by Yad Vashem in Jerusalem as one of the Righteous among the Nations for his work in saving Jewish lives. Moreover, the work undertaken so willingly by Deffaugt in trying to save Marianne (and, earlier, Mila), and the success he had in saving the children, were not isolated events. It was well known that he saved other Jewish children during the war years.

After the **liberation** Jean Deffaugt remained mayor of Annemasse until 1947, continuing as a municipal councilor from 1947 to 1959 and again from 1965 to his death, aged 74, on July 1, 1970. He was appointed a *Chevalier de Légion d'honneur*, and on February 25, 1966, Yad Vashem recognized him as one of the Righteous among the Nations.

Further Reading

Bartrop, Paul R., and Samantha J. Lakin. *Heroines of Vichy France: Rescuing French Jews during the Holocaust.* Santa Barbara, CA: Praeger, 2019.

Paldiel, Mordecai. *The Path of the Righteous: Gentile Rescuers of Jews during the Holocaust.* Hoboken, NJ: KTAV, 1993.

DIARIES AND JOURNALS

A diary is a personal record, arranged by date, relating the writer's experiences, thoughts, or feelings on events they have typically either experienced or witnessed. In most cases a diary will outline what has happened over the course of a day or other period. As such, a diary is for the most part an intimate and confidential chronicle intended to remain private, and in this sense, it differs from an appointment book, which simply lists what a person will be doing or has done each day. Sometimes the term *journal* is employed as a synonym for diary.

The generations that lived and died during the Holocaust, whether as victims or perpetrators, old or young, were confirmed diary writers. At a time when more people were literate than at any other period in history up to that point, keeping a diary was somewhat natural, even expected. During the Holocaust, children were foremost among those keeping diaries, and their impressions provide an important window to how Nazi persecution was seen at "ground level" by those writing without the inhibitions often associated with adults. Given this, it might be said that diaries written by children are among the most important of Holocaust primary sources—particularly as they illustrate not only what happened to the victims but also how they coped on a day-to-day level.

Indeed, several the children featured in the current volume, such as **Yitskhok Rudashevski**, **Mary Berg**, **Éva Heyman**, **Helga Weiss**, **Pavel Wiener**, **Anne Frank**, **Dawid Sierakowiak**, **Dawid Rubinowicz**, and **Moshe Flinker**, left diaries that provide important insights into various aspects of the Holocaust experience.

The diaries of children provide us with insights as to both their innermost thoughts and their observations of daily life. Yet writing was far from an easy task. Depending on where they were located, the very act of finding paper on which to write was one of the first tasks presenting difficulties. Pens and ink were often just as difficult to acquire. In the ghettos or concentration camps, writing materials were often as good as nonexistent, as were quiet spaces in which to compose diary entries unimpeded. Further, as diaries are by their very nature confidential records, the question arose as to where the writing could be hidden from the prying eyes of the Gestapo, kapos, ghetto police, or other authority figures who literally held the power of life and death in their hands.

Probably the most celebrated diary from this period is that of **Anne Frank**. In many ways, however, Anne was not actually representative of most Jewish children during the Holocaust. While large numbers did, certainly, survive for various periods in hiding or **passing** as non-Jews, most did not—and were exposed to the full force of the Nazi antisemitic rampage. Because she was in hiding, Anne did not experience what most Jewish children caught in the Nazi net experienced. Her diary and the story of hope it delivers has served, however, to inspire vast numbers of children, and with the privileging of Anne's story, the external, awful reality of how most Jewish children lived and died has been avoided for many.

It is impossible to compose a standard profile of those who kept diaries during the Holocaust. They came from every background of youth, class, religious observance, and geographic location. Their wartime circumstances varied enormously. Yet while each diary expresses the specificity of its author's experience, when considered as a genre, these diaries offer an important way to approach the Holocaust as seen through the eyes of those most vulnerable to Nazi (and adult) depredations.

Ghetto diaries comprise most of the journals kept by Jewish children during the Holocaust. Writing during the interminable days in which they waited for their fathers to return home from forced labor or for their mothers to return with some food, writing not only provided them with a vehicle to break the monotony but also enabled them to express their anger, frustrations, and fears. The writers would often pour out their sense of helplessness in the face of the terrors they had to face daily. Sometimes we see the steady deterioration of the young writers, as physical suffering is coupled with mourning, increasing starvation, and overall deprivation.

On occasion, we also see the diary come to a sudden stop, with no explanation as to why. Sadly, in view of what current generations know, the reason is all too obvious.

Through their diaries, children could explore (though not always find) meaning in what they were experiencing and witnessing. While they learned quickly that writing presented them with a coping strategy, they were also able to explore their inner selves. Such introspection is often painful to read, as diary writers confide their own worsening psychological and/or physical condition.

The very act of writing diaries was an act of resistance. Children knew this and were aware that if they were caught, it would, in most cases, mean instant death. Yet the act also provided them with a sense of empowerment, even if that should only be within the universe of their own creation. What remains is little short of astounding. Under the circumstances they faced, they were able to provide future generations with a glimpse into the horror of the Holocaust, their writing unconstrained by adult formality, caution, or fear of humiliation. The children wrote for themselves—but through the inheritance they have left, they have also written for us.

Further Reading

Holliday, Laurel. *Children in the Holocaust and World War II: Their Secret Diaries*. New York: Pocket Books, 1995.

DUNERA BOYS

In September 1941 an Australian Department of the Army document detailed the occupations of German and Austrian internees who had been sent from the United Kingdom and were now held in Australian internment camps. A figure of 105 was given for young German Jewish internees under 19 years of age who were "Not Considered of Use" to the war effort, with an additional 62 "Considered of Use." These youths had been transferred from the United Kingdom in 1940 on board a military transport ship, the *Dunera*. Most were **Kindertransport** boys who had arrived in the United Kingdom from Nazi Germany and Austria prior to the outbreak of war and identified as enemy aliens owing to the nationality on their documents.

In the dark days of early summer 1940, the British government ordered that all males of enemy nationality aged between 16 and 60 should be taken into custody and interned as a security measure. In early July several thousand were concentrated at ports of embarkation for a possible evacuation, as a call went out from the British government to Canada and Australia to take some of these people off Britain's hands.

On July 10, 1940, *Dunera* left Liverpool bound for Melbourne and Sydney carrying 2,732 internees of all ages. Most were Jewish refugees; mixed in with them were also 251 German prisoners of war, several dozen Nazi sympathizers, and 200 Italians. There were 141 in the guard detachment and ship's crew.

The story of the voyage has been often told; instances are recorded of the most appalling injustices and mistreatment perpetrated by the guards on board the ship. A military inquiry later found proof of beatings, looting of property, torture, and numerous forms of intimidation.

Upon their arrival in Melbourne on September 3, 1940, some 500 were disembarked and sent to internment camps at Tatura in northern Victoria; the rest, numbering about 2,000, arrived in Sydney four days later and were taken by train to a camp at Hay, in the far west of New South Wales. The Australian government's position was that they would be housed, fed, and guarded, but that they would remain the responsibility of the British government.

Within the camps, welfare organizations organized schools for the boys. The subjects available, often taught by some of the leading professors and teachers of pre-Nazi Germany—also internees—ensured that those enrolled received a first-rate education to which they might not otherwise have had access were they not interned.

For the *Dunera* boys, the purpose of such endeavors, in the form of matriculation into the University of Melbourne, was ready-made. Negotiations were conducted to accept interned students under the university's External Studies scheme, with permission granted for others to sit for the School Leaving examination leading to matriculation. Boys able to provide evidence that they possessed the necessary prerequisites to sit for the examinations were given the opportunity to do so. Where original documentation from Germany had either been left in Britain or lost on the voyage out, sworn testimonies from the camp's teaching staff were enough. The university made the necessary approaches to the army for its approval, while faculty members from the university also lent their support. At the end of 1941, seven students sat for matriculation into the University of Melbourne, and 40 others sat for the School Leaving examinations.

As a result of the entry of Japan into the war in December 1941 and the consequent threat to Australia in February 1942, the situation for everyone from the *Dunera*, including those who arrived underage, changed dramatically. With every available man now required to contribute to the war effort, agricultural labor quickly became scarce, and certain of the internees, under special conditions, were permitted to volunteer for fruit harvesting duty in the farms around Tatura. This acted as a precedent for a more general enlistment into an army labor corps, resulting, in April 1942, in the formation of the Eighth Employment Company.

Most of those who had arrived on the *Dunera* had been released by the end of 1942. By the end of the war, at least 50 *Dunera* boys had obtained degrees from the University of Melbourne. The war service of those in the Eighth Employment Company forced a government rethink on the permanency of their migration. By November 1945 some 785 former *Dunera* men—no longer boys—were still in Australia, the rest having returned to Britain or transmigrated elsewhere. Of those left in Australia, 417 were in civilian employment, and 368 were still in the army. The government's position was that they should now be offered the prospect of remaining and becoming Australian citizens.

The youths sent to Australia on the *Dunera* were presented with a golden opportunity to receive an education at the very moment when the prospects of doing so would have seemed at their most remote. They were, after all, of enemy alien nationality, prisoners of both the British and Australian military, and separated from family and friends by 19,000 kilometers of distance. They arrived in poor spirits, with few possessions. They had little going for them, their fate in the hands of others.

Many, of course, would never again get to see their parents or other family members left behind in Germany, Austria, and Czechoslovakia. The break with Europe was often total, with the boys shoved into a new life—boys no longer, but young men looking toward a future they unquestionably could not have envisaged when they left Europe as *Kindertransport* youths in 1938 and 1939.

Further Reading

Bartrop, Paul R., with Gabrielle Eisen (Eds.). *The Dunera Affair: A Documentary Resource Book*. Melbourne: Schwartz and Wilkinson, 1990.

Pearl, Cyril. *The Dunera Scandal: Deported by Mistake*. Sydney: Angus and Robertson, 1983.

E

ÉCLAIREURS ISRAÉLITES DE FRANCE

The Jewish Scouts (*Éclaireurs Israélites de France*, or EIF) was a prewar **Jewish youth movement** that evolved into a rescue and resistance organization during World War II. Such activity was especially pronounced through the activities of one of its groups, *La Sixiéme* ("the Sixth"). While the EIF was neither religious nor Zionist by its nature, its idea of sending young Jews to the countryside was like the pioneering ideals of the Zionist movement who sought to prepare Jewish youth for life in Palestine.

The EIF, founded as far back as 1923, was one of the first to go into action in the unoccupied zone after the armistice with Germany in June 1940. An organization that integrated both native-born and foreign-born Jewish youth, the EIF showed how united action on behalf of Jewish children facing Nazi persecution could be directed through hiding them and smuggling them across the border. In its first acts of defiance, however, it could not altogether act entirely clandestinely: it was, after all, already a well-known element within French society.

To best appreciate this, it is necessary to explore the origins of the EIF before the fall of France in 1940; it will then quickly become apparent that its history is inextricably intertwined with the life of its founder.

Robert Gamzon was born on June 30, 1905, in Lyon, the son of Lazare Gamzon, a mining engineer from Lithuania, and Esther Naomi Gamzon *née* Lévy, the daughter of France's onetime chief rabbi, Alfred Lévy. As a boy, during a stay in the Massif Central in southern France, Gamzon came across a camp of Protestant Scouts. The ideals of Scouting interested him, and he became keen to create a similar movement for young Jews. In 1923, at the age of 17, he founded the Jewish branch of the Scouting movement, which he called the *Éclaireurs Israélites de France*. On May 27, 1923, the first group took their oath in the synagogue at Versailles, in the presence of Chief Rabbi Maurice Liber.

Gamzon's idea was to utilize Scouting to instill a Jewish consciousness among French Jewish youth as a counter to the temptation of assimilation. At the same time, the movement would encourage the integration of recently arrived Jewish immigrants into wider French society. By 1935 there were 3,000 members in Paris, with groups in Strasbourg, Mulhouse, Lyon, and Marseille; in North Africa, there were EIF groups in Tunis, Algiers, Oran, and Casablanca.

In line with its founding aims, by 1926 Gamzon opened the movement to all Jewish children, regardless of their background. He was the main architect behind how the movement developed, including the unification of EIF religious practices in 1932 to encompass a "common minimum" of observance, including Shabbat and the maintenance of Jewish dietary laws.

In 1933, with the help of a close associate, Léo Cohn, Gamzon transformed the EIF again: he launched the idea of a return to manual work and a career orientation that encouraged skilled work and agricultural labor.

Gamzon had earlier married a fellow Scout leader, Denise Lévy, in Paris in 1930. With the onset of war in September 1939, she succeeded in opening three (and, eventually, five) houses receiving EIF children evacuated from urban centers. These homes also extended to young foreign Jews at a time when their status counted against them. Thus, the centers of Villefranche de Rouergue and Saint Affrique (Aveyron), Saint Céré (Lot), Beaulieu sur Dordogne (Corrèze), and Moissac (Tarn), where the national EIF secretariat was located, were all established. Activities included a training farm, and a carpentry workshop was opened in Paris.

After the armistice in June 1940, the EIF hastened to reinforce its organizational arrangements, appointing paid commissioners devoted to the movement's operations. Traveling throughout France to revive EIF activities, in short order, some 26 groups were created in the southern zone, catering to over 2,000 young Jews. With the approval of the Vichy authorities, Gamzon began setting up children's homes, workshops, welfare centers, and training farms for refugee children, including one in Lautrec in the Tarn. Denise Gamzon was appointed as deputy director, training the new cohort of EIF leaders and assistants.

Robert Gamzon was a regular visitor to Vichy, where he sought assistance from every quarter. Through various sources he was able to learn of likely raids on EIF homes and was able to hide young Jews (particularly those most targeted, of foreign background) and provide them with false papers.

In Moissac, Simon Lévitte of the *Mouvement de la jeunesse sioniste* created a documentation center; from here, he distributed not only fake documents but also teaching materials of benefit to the EIF in the form of songs and correspondence courses. In addition, a traveling library was created.

On November 29, 1941, the *Union Générale des Israélites de France* (General Union of French Jews, or UGIF) was created, at Vichy insistence and on orders from the Germans, to consolidate all Jewish organizations in France into a single unit and dissolve existing bodies. This included the EIF. The UGIF was far from an independent body and was frequently forced to yield to German and Vichy French demands. In January 1942 Robert Gamzon was appointed to its executive board; by joining, he reasoned, it would be better to be inside the system so as to be able to monitor developments. At the same time, the now-banned executive of the EIF agreed that from this point on, it would commit the movement to clandestine activity for the sake of those within its responsibility—thus, when deportations of Jews to "the East" commenced in 1942, the Scouts played a major part in placing and hiding hundreds of children with French families.

In his role as a director of UGIF, Gamzon went to Paris in May 1943 to help to coordinate the various covert networks in the capital and to organize underground actions there, culminating in the establishment of an EIF Jewish partisan unit in the Tarn district of southwestern France in December 1943. Those who joined were mainly young people who had been Scouts or had participated in Gamzon's workshops. Gamzon attached his partisan unit to the *Armée Juive* (Jewish Army); by doing so, he helped unite all of France's Jewish underground militias.

Overall, the EIF's activities during World War II can summarized as follows: maintaining the Scouting movement and establishing new groups throughout Vichy France as well as North Africa; establishing children's homes for Jewish children of foreign background who had been separated from their parents; establishing training groups in agricultural work for possible resettlement in Palestine; creating the means to hide young Jews at risk; sometimes, when necessary, to arrange for them to be smuggled out of the country; and, finally, establishing the EIF underground combat unit in 1944.

Further Reading

Bartrop, Paul R., and Samantha J. Lakin. *Heroines of Vichy France: Rescuing French Jews during the Holocaust*. Santa Barbara, CA: Praeger, 2019.

EDELWEISS PIRATES

The Edelweiss Pirates (*Edelweisspiraten*) were groups of German youths who opposed Nazi rule and were especially resistant to the way in which the **Hitler Youth** movement had taken over the lives of young people in Nazi Germany.

It is perhaps an exaggeration to refer to the Edelweiss Pirates as a "movement," but whatever organization existed can be said to have emerged sometime during the second half of the 1930s, after the Nazi state had made membership of the Hitler Youth compulsory in 1936. The Pirates was more like a loose association of several movements that developed in response to the regime's policy of regimenting youth so that leisure activities and other freedoms were now denied. They rejected the quasi-military lines of the Hitler Youth; they maintained their freedom to express their thoughts; and the free mingling of the sexes, forbidden in the Hitler Youth and **League of German Girls**, was encouraged.

For the most part, Edelweiss Pirates were aged between approximately 14 and 17 and were disaffected by the strictures imposed by the Nazi education system no less than the likelihood of impressment into the Nazi organizations or conscription for military service as they got older. It was these antiauthority, nonconformist young people who formed Edelweiss Pirate groups of 10 to 15 boys and girls, attracted by a freer way of life outside of the suffocating rules and regulations of the Nazi regime. Mostly from working-class backgrounds, in the evenings and weekends, they would meet in cafés or parks, prior to defying the Nazi ban on nonsanctioned hiking or camping, where they would speak openly, sing songs banned by the regime, dance, and engage in relationships the government would have considered unacceptable. At night they would sleep in barns or tents.

During the later 1930s, the authorities considered the Edelweiss Pirates to be an irritating group of ill-informed, ill-disciplined adolescents who were highly antagonistic to the Hitler Youth movement, and they engaged in street violence against them. The Pirates had different names in different places and existed in most German cities (particularly in the western regions). They shared, however, the same fundamental antiestablishment beliefs and attitudes.

With the outbreak of war, Nazi tolerance was exhausted. It was assumed by the regime that because of the Pirates' antigovernment views, they would support Britain; hence, the rumor was circulated that some Pirate groups collected Allied propaganda leaflets and posted them through mailboxes, in what was a clear case of sedition. As children of the working class, they refused to be cowed by the Nazis into an unacceptable degree of conformity.

The war saw increased levels of anti-government activity, leading to more and more repression from the Gestapo. Individuals arrested were sometimes sent to youth concentration camps, and as Germany suffered from Allied bombing between 1942 and 1945, the conflicts between the Edelweiss Pirates and the Nazi authorities intensified. In Cologne, for example, Edelweiss Pirates offered shelter to German Army deserters and escapees from concentration and labor camps. Pirate graffiti became a problem for the regime, and no matter how often or how quickly it was removed, anti-Nazi slogans returned after a few days. Pirate groups were also known to make armed raids on military depots and sabotage war production.

With the increase in such activities, punishments became more extreme. On October 25, 1944, SS chief Heinrich Himmler ordered a crackdown on the Edelweiss Pirates, and in November, 13 young people from Cologne (not all of whom were Pirates) were hanged in public.

Yet this was an extreme response, late in the war. A more standard punishment in earlier times was for an arrested Pirate's head to be shaved as a mark of public humiliation. It was really Himmler who took repression up several notches, ordering Reinhard Heydrich (before his assassination in June 1942) to crack down on all youths who seemed to be failing in their total obedience to the state. He declared that detainment in work camps was an inappropriate punishment and that, rather, those caught should instead be sent to concentration camps for a period of two to three years. Here, they would be beaten constantly and worked until they dropped. It did not matter if they were boys or girls. Once released, they would never be permitted to return to school, thus condemning them to a working life of manual labor. Under this new approach, patrols were sent out to look for Pirate members. Those caught could not only be imprisoned but also sent to reform schools or psychiatric hospitals in addition to labor and concentration camps. In a single day of raids in December 1942, the Düsseldorf Gestapo made more than 1,000 arrests.

Nevertheless, government repression never managed to break the spirit of most groups. A subculture that rejected the norms of Nazi society, the Edelweiss Pirates were often just as unyielding when it came to the Allied occupation at the end of the war. While some offered themselves to the Allied occupiers, they were for the most part rejected on the ground that they were too closely connected to the Nazi past (even in opposition). Neither pro-British nor pro-American, the Edelweiss Pirates were cast in the role of social outcasts, their movement not permitted to function alongside other, newly created youth groups. In the eastern sector, the Soviet Union refused to permit the Edelweiss Pirates to exist at all.

The Edelweiss Pirates was one of the largest groups in Germany to reject Nazi youth policies. Loosely organized, their existence demonstrated that anti-Nazi opposition existed at the grassroots level while remaining true to their own codes of moral conduct.

Further Reading

Peukert, Detlev J. K. *Inside Nazi Germany: Conformity, Opposition and Racism in Everyday Life*. London: B. T. Batsford, 1987.

EDUCATION IN THE THIRD REICH

Believing that youth held the future of Germany in their hands, Adolf Hitler maintained very strong opinions on education. Schools were used to indoctrinate children with National Socialist ideology, with Nazi beliefs intruding directly into the school curriculum. All German schools, at every level, were Nazified very soon after Hitler came to power in early 1933. Textbooks were rewritten and curricula were altered, sometimes drastically. All teachers had to join the National Socialist Teachers' League, which vetted them for political and racial suitability. Teachers were compelled to attend summer seminars for intensive training in National Socialist principles, with an emphasis on Hitler's racial doctrines. Students were encouraged to inform the authorities if teachers did not support Nazi ideas.

The role of schools and universities became one of indoctrinating children into the racial ideas of Nazism, to make them loyal to Hitler, to train girls to be good Aryan wives and mothers, and to prepare boys to be effective soldiers.

School curricula were altered to reflect Nazi ideology and priorities. History classes, which were frequently fictionalized, were useful only insofar as they highlighted past German victories. Academic subjects were downgraded, with subjects such as chemistry and mathematics devalued. Geography became geopolitics, the study of the fatherland being fundamental. Biology became transformed into "race science" (*Rassenkunde*) and was compulsory. Complementing this, the study of eugenics was added to the curriculum, such that "racial awareness" saw children reminded constantly of their racial duties to the "national community" (*Volksgemeinschaft*), of which all formed part. Children were taught about breeding and hereditary disease.

Physical fitness training was made compulsory for all, as was youth labor service. Students were supposed to attend twice-weekly fitness and indoctrination classes, and some schools had at least five one-hour sessions of physical education every week. Health education and physical training were given a racial emphasis, with boys required to learn boxing and other martial sports. All this was intended to breed an esprit de corps in which boys (and girls, for whom the study of home economics was compulsory) would see and know their place within the Aryan master race.

Jewish children, by contrast, were ritually humiliated in the classroom. Heads and noses were assessed with tape measures, while eye colors and hair texture were checked against government approved charts of "Nordic" categories. With Jews viewed as the worst variety of "sub-human" (*Untermensch*), by 1938 Jewish children were banned from attending public schools altogether. As if to underscore the nature of state education preferences, moreover, religious education in all schools was also dropped.

In order to accommodate the new curriculum, all existing textbooks had to be withdrawn and new ones written. History and biology were priorities. Biology textbooks, for instance, emphasized Hitler's views on race and heredity, with additional teaching materials produced when needed. Alongside the new geopolitical curriculum, geography textbooks taught concepts such as living space (*Lebensraum*) and blood and soil (*Blut und boden*). New textbooks were also introduced in mathematics, with specially crafted exercises designed to expose students to Nazi ideology. One such question cited frequently by observers required students to calculate how much it would cost the state to keep a mentally ill person alive in an asylum for a fixed sum over a specified period. Another question asked children to provide an answer to the following mathematical problem: "An airplane flies at the rate of 240 kilometers per hour to a place at a distance of 210 kilometers in order to drop bombs. When may it be expected to return if the dropping of bombs takes 7.5 minutes?" (The answer was one hour and 52.5 minutes.)

The teaching profession was transformed completely by the Nazi state. As early as 1933, all Jewish teachers were dismissed from German schools and universities. Any other teacher who did not support the Nazi Party was fired. By 1936 over 32 percent of teachers were Party members, but for many it was a survival measure that did not necessarily connote adherence to Nazi ideals—though there were certainly plenty who did. Teachers were classified as civil servants and thus subject to Nazi racial legislation, and all teachers took an oath to "be loyal and obedient to Adolf Hitler." Later, it was a requirement that teaching positions would only be awarded to men who had served in the SA, the Labor Service, or the **Hitler Youth**.

By 1938 most elementary school teachers had received special indoctrination in a compulsory one-month training course, the intention being that they would then teach what they had learned. Notwithstanding changes to the curriculum and textbooks, the relationship between teacher and student also changed. Upon entering the classroom, the teacher would greet his (mostly his) students with the "Hitler salute" and "Heil Hitler!" It was required that the students would stand and respond accordingly, further reinforcing the inclusive nature of Nazi ideology even in the classroom.

As Nazi Germany was a misogynistic society, education for girls was reduced as a state priority. By 1937, grammar-school education for girls was abolished, and they were also forbidden from learning Latin—a requirement for university entrance. As one of the objectives of the government was to reduce the number of women in higher education, only 11 percent of university places were reserved for girls, and as a result, the number of female students in higher education fell from just over 17,000 in 1932–1933 to under 6,000 by 1939. Correspondingly, the government also ordered a reduction in the number of women employed as teachers.

Instead, the Education Ministry did its best to steer women into domestic education, an ideal underscored by Hitler's creation of the National Socialist Women's League (*NS-Frauenschaft*), headed by Gertrud Scholtz-Klink. As the private sphere of women became inextricably bound up with masculinist Nazi ideology, the state sought strict control over female reproduction, with women's bodies providing the means for engineering racial purity. Scholtz-Klink's view was that education of girls thus had to emphasize that, in every way, "the mission of woman is to minister in the home and in her profession to the needs of life from the first to last moment of man's existence." There was little room in this scheme for girls to enjoy an education that could lead to a career or profession outside the home.

In accordance with Nazi ideology, young Germans in the Third Reich were educated in a highly physical and anti-intellectual environment. The teaching profession as it had been before 1933 was effectively destroyed, replaced by an edifice that was an arm both of propaganda and of sociocultural engineering. It was to form the bedrock of the racial state, founded on principles of ethnic hierarchy, eugenics, and, ultimately, the destruction of "lesser races," with the Jews in the forefront.

Further Reading

Blackburn, Gilmer W. *Education in the Third Reich: Race and History in Nazi Textbooks*. Albany: State University of New York Press, 1984.

ELLI: COMING OF AGE IN THE HOLOCAUST

Elli: Coming of Age in the Holocaust is a personal account of Holocaust survival by Livia E. Bitton Jackson, born Elli L. Friedmann to Laura and Markus Friedman in Somorja (Šamorín), in what had been Czechoslovakia prior to 1938, when Hungarian troops occupied the town. Born on February 28, 1931, she was 13 years old when, in the spring of 1944, she, her mother, father, aunt, and 16-year-old brother, Bubi, were imprisoned in a Hungarian ghetto in Nagymagyar (Zlaté Klasy).

Not long after this, they were deported to Auschwitz. Elli and her mother stayed there for 10 days, and then, in June 1944, they were transferred, along with 500 other women, to the forced labor camp of Płaszów, near Kraków. After seven weeks there, they were returned to Auschwitz. In August 1944 they were taken from Auschwitz to a factory in the German city of Augsburg, where they were put to work on an assembly line producing precision guidance instruments for fighter aircraft. They remained there until April 1945.

In her memoir, Elli recalled how she and her mother (indeed, all the prisoners they encountered) suffered numerous physical and psychological hardships. Most of this took the form of beatings, rapes, murders, and hard labor. Elli survived partly because of her keen instincts and resourcefulness, but the book shows at least one way she had no control over her fate when she realized that the Germans were putting bromide in the prisoners' food. She noted that she missed her menstrual period, which, for this 14-year-old, was proof enough that the Nazis were attempting to sterilize the women. Either they ate the food they were given, or they starved. Beyond this, Elli noted, the Nazis worked on the women in other ways as well. The longer she was imprisoned, the more Elli learned from older prisoners of Nazi **medical experimentation**, of gassing of prisoners, and of children (such as herself) being shot, tortured, or burned alive.

Although she received much of this as secondhand information, Elli's memoir provides us with enough information regarding her own experiences to show that her hold on life was always precarious. Working at hard labor, she received no protection from the sun in summer or from the cold in winter. The arduous daily work in which she was engaged was long and caused numerous injuries to the women alongside of her. And there was always the threat of beatings from those ruling the prisoners.

At the very end of the war, Elli and her mother were taken to Mühldorf, a subsidiary camp of Dachau, where they had a reunion with Elli's older brother, Bubi. As the Allies got closer, the three surviving members of the family were taken by trains deeper into Germany. During the trip, Bubi was shot but survived. On April 28, 1945, Elli, her mother, and her brother were liberated by American forces. Elli was then 14, fatherless, a displaced person, and dreadfully weak.

After the **liberation**, the little family of three returned to their hometown of Šamorín, and Elli hoped that her father would be waiting for them there. It was there that they found out he was dead. Bubi went to the United States to study in New York on a scholarship visa; Elli was given the opportunity to travel with him but preferred to remain in Czechoslovakia with her mother. They stayed in Šamorín until 1951, when they finally left to join Bubi in the United States. After arriving in New York, Elli resumed her education, eventually enrolling for a degree at New York University. She then earned a PhD in Hebrew Culture and Jewish History from the same institution and became a professor of history at City University of New York (CUNY).

In 1980 she wrote *Elli: Coming of Age in the Holocaust*. As in many personal testimonies of this nature, much of the book is written in the present tense—always an indication of the intimacy and immediacy of the author's recollections. We read of her anguished life in the camps and the anxiety she felt over the fate of her family. We also read of her own painful experiences, as well as her determination to support her mother and brother in their efforts to stay alive. We see shocking descriptions of how low humans can fall in this most extreme of environments, as well as the heroism that can surface at surprising times. *Elli* won the Christopher Award, the Eleanor Roosevelt Humanitarian Award, and the Jewish Heritage Award. In 1997 Elli adapted the book for young readers, retitling it *I Have Lived a Thousand Years: Growing Up in the Holocaust*. In 1998 she again won the Christopher Award, this time for the adaptation of her earlier work.

In 1977 Livia E. Bitton Jackson moved to Israel but continued teaching at CUNY for 37 years. Now retired, she lives in Israel with her husband, children, and grandchildren.

Further Reading

Bitton Jackson, Livia E. *Elli: Coming of Age in the Holocaust.* New York: Times Books, 1980.

ERRÁZURIZ, MARÍA (1893–1972)

María Errázuriz was a Chilean woman who worked with the French Resistance during the Nazi occupation in World War II, saving Jewish children at considerable risk to her own life.

Born in Santiago into an aristocratic Catholic family in 1893, she was the daughter of Agustín Edwards Ross, who served as president of the Chilean Senate between 1893 and 1895. At a young age, she married an aspiring diplomat, Guillermo Errázuriz Vergara, who was a nephew of renowned artist José Tomás Errázuriz and a member of an elite family from central Chile. The young couple moved to Paris, where Guillermo had been sent to take up a diplomatic post. In 1922, however, he committed suicide. With Paris now her home, María remained in France from this point on and stayed after the Germans arrived in 1940.

During the occupation Mariá, who was a social worker by profession, volunteered as a nurse at the Rothschild Jewish hospital. After 1942 one of the hospital's primary aims was to conceal as many Jews as possible from the Nazis, and María would often risk her life to rescue Jewish children who had been separated from their parents. Some of the hospital buildings had been enclosed to become a *de facto* internment camp, where patients who recovered were detained prior to being sent to the transit camp at Drancy and then deported to Auschwitz.

Another social worker, Claire Heymann, who was Jewish, organized several escapes with María, who used her wealth to assist in helping those in distress. Claire had been at the Rothschild Hospital as a social worker since March 1932 and is considered an unsung hero for organizing the escape network from the hospital throughout the war. Along with others, these two supplied false papers for Jewish children, arranging for them to be sent to friendly non-Jewish families for sanctuary. To the children in their care, they were known universally as "Auntie Claire" and "Auntie Marie." In February 1943, María participated in a celebrated escape and transfer (organized by Claire) of 16 children from the Rothschild orphanage to safe houses and convents in Paris and the province of Touraine.

In 1944 Mariá was arrested by the French collaborationist police as a resister. Handed over to the Gestapo for interrogation, she was tortured repeatedly as her persecutors sought knowledge of the whereabouts of French Resistance fighters and of Jews who were in hiding. It was reported later that she had been subjected to the so-called ice bath torture, where her head was held under ice water until she nearly drowned. She never broke and was eventually released, owing to her background as a Chilean national and through the intervention on her behalf of the Spanish ambassador in Paris.

On September 2, 1953, the French government awarded María Errazuríz the Legion of Honor for bravery and her contributions to the Resistance during the war. In 1960 she returned to Chile and married her second husband, the French writer Jacques Feydeau. In 1972, at the age of 79, María Errazuríz died, but on October 27, 2005, she was recognized posthumously by Yad Vashem in Jerusalem as one of the Righteous among the Nations. Present at the ceremony were her granddaughters Barbara, Solange, and María Victoria.

Further Reading

Bartrop, Paul R. *Resisting the Holocaust: Upstanders, Partisans, and Survivors*. Santa Barbara, CA: ABC-CLIO, 2016.

F

FLINKER, MOSHE (1926–1944)

Moshe Ze'ev (Maurice Wolf) Flinker was born in The Hague, Netherlands, on October 9, 1926. His parents were Mindel Flinker and her husband Eliezer Noah Flinker, a Polish Jew who had migrated to the Netherlands where he became a businessman. The family kept an Orthodox home. In 1940, in the wake of the German occupation, the Flinker family fled Holland for Belgium, living as non-Jews with the help of false identity papers. Moshe was unable to attend school owing to Nazi race laws, and to avoid boredom, he began writing a diary, which lasted from November 1942 to September 1943. In it, he described his difficulties, fears, and hopes. He wrote confidently that God would save him and his family and redeem the Jewish people. The family was denounced in April 1944, however, and Moshe and his parents were sent to Auschwitz and murdered there.

Moshe began his diary in Hebrew, describing his problems, concerns, and aspirations. Seeing himself as a political leader in a future Jewish State in Palestine, he recorded his belief in God's ultimate redemptive power. By this time, he was already fluent in many languages: Dutch, Hebrew, Yiddish, French, English, German, and classical Latin and Greek. He began studying Arabic in order to help achieve his goal of becoming a leader in a future Israel, on the basis that those already resident there spoke Arabic and that arriving Jews would have to live in peace with their Arab neighbors. He was conscious of the fact that both Arabs and Jews were descendants of the biblical patriarch Abraham and that, as a result, they were kindred peoples.

Moshe recorded his family's struggles under Nazi occupation, grappling with the question of why the Jewish people suffered, and where was God—what did their suffering mean, and why was God not preventing it? He wanted to comprehend Nazi persecution in the light of Jewish history, turning to prayers and scripture and incorporating them into his own text, making his diary itself into a kind of prayer.

In April 1944 the Flinker family was denounced by a Belgian Jewish collaborator. Moshe Flinker, his mother Mindel, and his sisters, Esther Malka and Leah, were arrested at their home and deported to the Belgian transit camp at Malines/Mechelen. His father, warned by a neighbor, contacted Moshe's four other siblings and stopped them from going home, arranging for them to find refuge at the **Tiefenbrunner Orphanage** of Brussels, created by Belgium's occupation government near Antwerp and directed by a young Orthodox rabbi, Yona Tiefenbrunner.

Two weeks later, Moshe's father was caught and sent to Malines, where he found the remainder of his family. All were deported to Auschwitz-Birkenau in May 1944.

Moshe's mother, Mindel, was murdered on arrival. His sisters, Esther Malka and Leah, remained in the women's camp.

Moshe and his father stayed at Auschwitz for several months, after which they were transferred to Echterdingen, a labor camp of Natzweiler-Struthof, where they both contracted typhus. From there, they were sent to Bergen-Belsen, where they both died in January 1945.

Esther Malka and Leah survived Auschwitz-Birkenau and were reunited with their four siblings in Brussels after the liberation. When the sisters returned to Brussels at war's end, they found Moshe's diary in the basement of their old apartment building. Written in Hebrew, the diary was first published under the title *Hana'ar Moshe: Yoman shel Moshe Flinker* in 1958; it was translated into English and published later as *Young Moshe's Diary: The Spiritual Torment of a Jewish Boy in Nazi Europe*.

Further Reading

Flinker, Moshe. *Young Moshe's Diary: The Spiritual Torment of a Jewish Boy in Nazi Europe*. Jerusalem: Yad Vashem, 1965.

FRANK, ANNE (1929–1945)

Anneliese Marie Frank, known as Anne, was a German-born Dutch-Jewish diarist who left a poignant diary of the Holocaust. Her rise to prominence only came after her death, at the age of 15, through the postwar publication of the diary under the title *The Diary of a Young Girl*. This work has become one of the iconic books of the Holocaust, taught in schools around the world and the subject of several movies, plays, expanded editions, and academic studies.

Anne Frank was born on June 12, 1929, in Frankfurt, Germany, to Otto and Edith Frank. They already had one other daughter, three-year-old Margot. In 1933, when the Nazi Party came to power in Germany, Otto Frank decided to relocate his family to Amsterdam in the Netherlands, where he had business and personal contacts. By March 1934, the entire Frank family was living there; it was here that Anne, then aged four and a half, was to live for most of the rest of her life.

Between 1934 and 1940, Anne enjoyed a comfortable life with her family. Her father was on the road to becoming a successful a food producer, having started Pectacon, a food wholesale company to complement his existing business, Opekta, a pectin and spice company founded in 1928. Anne attended a Montessori school, and Margot went to public school. Life seemed to be comfortable and safe.

Things changed dramatically, however, when, on May 10, 1940, Germany invaded the Netherlands. The ensuing Battle of the Netherlands lasted from then until the government surrendered on May 14, following which the Germans completed a full occupation of the country. The Franks, like all other Jews, were henceforth subjected to intensifying antisemitic persecution. By the fall of 1941, Jewish children were removed from their schools and only able to attend specifically designated Jewish places of instruction, while Jewish adults were

denied the opportunity to own businesses. In April 1941 Otto Frank acted to circumvent the anti-Jewish laws by transferring control of Opekta and Pectacon to one of his trusted non-Jewish associates, Johannes Kleiman, and had all assets of the company transferred to Gies and Company, headed by Jan Gies, husband of **Miep Gies**.

The major turning point for the Frank family came on July 5, 1942, however, when Margot Frank received a notice that she was to report to a labor camp for national service. Perceiving the likelihood that this could mean a permanent separation, Otto Frank made the decision that his family would have to go into hiding. This was earlier than originally planned; Otto and Edith Frank had already proposed that they would go into hiding on July 16, 1942. With the help of a few key friends and neighbors, the Franks moved into a small attic annex at 263 Prinsengracht Street on July 6, 1942, directly above the Opekta offices. This hiding place became known as the *Achterhuis*, referred to in Anne's diary as the Secret Annex. They were soon joined by another Jewish family, Auguste and Hermann van Pels and their son Peter, as well as another Jewish acquaintance, Fritz Pfeffer. Together, these eight people lived in hiding until they were discovered by the police on August 4, 1944.

Photograph of Anne Frank in 1940, attending her Montessori School in Amsterdam. Anne Frank was a German-born Dutch-Jewish girl who left a poignant diary of the Holocaust. During her family's two years in hiding, in an attic above her father's factory, Anne kept a diary that detailed their secret life. Anne died in Bergen-Belsen in 1945, but her diary was published after the war under the title *The Diary of a Young Girl*. (Unknown photographer; Collectie Anne Frank Stichting Amsterdam)

During their two years in hiding, Anne kept a diary that detailed the families' secret life—lived mostly at night—as well as her own adolescent viewpoints of the situation in which she found herself. She reflected on her relationships with the members of her family and the differences in each of their personalities and noted the tensions that intruded upon the various people in the two small rooms in which they were cramped together. Most of Anne's time in the Secret Annex was spent reading, studying, and writing her diary entries. She described events as she saw them and as they took place, but she also used the diary to confide her feelings, beliefs, and ambitions. With time, she extended the range of topics about

which she wrote, such as human nature, her own sexuality, and her belief in God. She also noted her level of understanding as to the situation in which the families found themselves and observed that their security could only be maintained with cooperation and respect. Anne's writing, moreover, expressed hope that the Allies would liberate Europe before the Secret Annex was discovered.

Anne continued writing regularly until her last entry, dated August 1, 1944. On the morning of August 4, 1944, the *Achterhuis* was stormed by a group of German police—some said as the result of denunciation. On August 8, 1944, the Frank and van Pels families, along with Pfeffer, were moved to the transit camp at Westerbork. Then, on September 3, 1944, they were deported from there to Auschwitz, where they arrived three days later. Anne's mother, Edith, died in the camp. In October or November 1944, Anne and Margot were transferred to Bergen-Belsen in Germany, where they died—it is generally presumed by typhus—sometime in February or March 1945. (Dutch authorities have set March 31 as their official date of death, but this is disputed.) Otto Frank survived to be liberated from Auschwitz in January 1945 and returned to Amsterdam in June 1945. Here, he found that Anne's diary had been saved by Miep Gies.

Amazed by his daughter's compelling account of life in hiding, he decided that it should become a public document—something Anne had foreseen herself. Anticipating her own survival, she wrote and rewrote parts of the diary for public consumption, and with her thoughts uppermost in mind, Otto Frank spent the next two years preparing the manuscript for publication. His efforts led to its publication in Dutch in 1947. It became a runaway success, and by 1952 there were editions in English, German, and French. The diary was subsequently translated into more than 60 languages. *The Diary of a Young Girl* (often rendered as *The Diary of Anne Frank*) was adapted into a successful play by Frances Goodrich and Albert Hackett and a multi–Academy Award winning movie of the same title in 1959 directed by George Stevens and starring Millie Perkins in the title role. This would be the first of several movies with Anne Frank as the theme.

Despite its success in bookstores and popular culture, controversy has also surrounded the diary. Literary rights were disputed between several publishers, Otto Frank, and others. Some commentators have expressed concern at the way in which Anne's life has become commercialized, and yet others have disputed whether it can truly be called an expression of the realities of the Holocaust.

It is in the area of education, however, where the diary has arguably had the greatest impact, and in countless school districts around the world, the study of Anne's diary is compulsory as a testament to human strength in the face of unrestrained oppression. Indeed, the girl Anne Frank has to some degree been cast into the background, replaced by Anne Frank, the image of hope in a dark and troubled world.

Anne Frank's diary is unquestionably the best-known document of the Holocaust and continues to inspire many across the globe, while another example of the Frank family's experience, the building where they hid, is now the home of the **Anne Frank House**, an international organization aimed at educating the world's youth to reject racism and discrimination. Although she died in 1945, Anne

denied the opportunity to own businesses. In April 1941 Otto Frank acted to circumvent the anti-Jewish laws by transferring control of Opekta and Pectacon to one of his trusted non-Jewish associates, Johannes Kleiman, and had all assets of the company transferred to Gies and Company, headed by Jan Gies, husband of **Miep Gies**.

The major turning point for the Frank family came on July 5, 1942, however, when Margot Frank received a notice that she was to report to a labor camp for national service. Perceiving the likelihood that this could mean a permanent separation, Otto Frank made the decision that his family would have to go into hiding. This was earlier than originally planned; Otto and Edith Frank had already proposed that they would go into hiding on July 16, 1942. With the help of a few key friends and neighbors, the Franks moved into a small attic annex at 263 Prinsengracht Street on July 6, 1942, directly above the Opekta offices. This hiding place became known as the *Achterhuis*, referred to in Anne's diary as the Secret Annex. They were soon joined by another Jewish family, Auguste and Hermann van Pels and their son Peter, as well as another Jewish acquaintance, Fritz Pfeffer. Together, these eight people lived in hiding until they were discovered by the police on August 4, 1944.

Photograph of Anne Frank in 1940, attending her Montessori School in Amsterdam. Anne Frank was a German-born Dutch-Jewish girl who left a poignant diary of the Holocaust. During her family's two years in hiding, in an attic above her father's factory, Anne kept a diary that detailed their secret life. Anne died in Bergen-Belsen in 1945, but her diary was published after the war under the title *The Diary of a Young Girl*. (Unknown photographer; Collectie Anne Frank Stichting Amsterdam)

During their two years in hiding, Anne kept a diary that detailed the families' secret life—lived mostly at night—as well as her own adolescent viewpoints of the situation in which she found herself. She reflected on her relationships with the members of her family and the differences in each of their personalities and noted the tensions that intruded upon the various people in the two small rooms in which they were cramped together. Most of Anne's time in the Secret Annex was spent reading, studying, and writing her diary entries. She described events as she saw them and as they took place, but she also used the diary to confide her feelings, beliefs, and ambitions. With time, she extended the range of topics about

which she wrote, such as human nature, her own sexuality, and her belief in God. She also noted her level of understanding as to the situation in which the families found themselves and observed that their security could only be maintained with cooperation and respect. Anne's writing, moreover, expressed hope that the Allies would liberate Europe before the Secret Annex was discovered.

Anne continued writing regularly until her last entry, dated August 1, 1944. On the morning of August 4, 1944, the *Achterhuis* was stormed by a group of German police—some said as the result of denunciation. On August 8, 1944, the Frank and van Pels families, along with Pfeffer, were moved to the transit camp at Westerbork. Then, on September 3, 1944, they were deported from there to Auschwitz, where they arrived three days later. Anne's mother, Edith, died in the camp. In October or November 1944, Anne and Margot were transferred to Bergen-Belsen in Germany, where they died—it is generally presumed by typhus—sometime in February or March 1945. (Dutch authorities have set March 31 as their official date of death, but this is disputed.) Otto Frank survived to be liberated from Auschwitz in January 1945 and returned to Amsterdam in June 1945. Here, he found that Anne's diary had been saved by Miep Gies.

Amazed by his daughter's compelling account of life in hiding, he decided that it should become a public document—something Anne had foreseen herself. Anticipating her own survival, she wrote and rewrote parts of the diary for public consumption, and with her thoughts uppermost in mind, Otto Frank spent the next two years preparing the manuscript for publication. His efforts led to its publication in Dutch in 1947. It became a runaway success, and by 1952 there were editions in English, German, and French. The diary was subsequently translated into more than 60 languages. *The Diary of a Young Girl* (often rendered as *The Diary of Anne Frank*) was adapted into a successful play by Frances Goodrich and Albert Hackett and a multi–Academy Award winning movie of the same title in 1959 directed by George Stevens and starring Millie Perkins in the title role. This would be the first of several movies with Anne Frank as the theme.

Despite its success in bookstores and popular culture, controversy has also surrounded the diary. Literary rights were disputed between several publishers, Otto Frank, and others. Some commentators have expressed concern at the way in which Anne's life has become commercialized, and yet others have disputed whether it can truly be called an expression of the realities of the Holocaust.

It is in the area of education, however, where the diary has arguably had the greatest impact, and in countless school districts around the world, the study of Anne's diary is compulsory as a testament to human strength in the face of unrestrained oppression. Indeed, the girl Anne Frank has to some degree been cast into the background, replaced by Anne Frank, the image of hope in a dark and troubled world.

Anne Frank's diary is unquestionably the best-known document of the Holocaust and continues to inspire many across the globe, while another example of the Frank family's experience, the building where they hid, is now the home of the **Anne Frank House**, an international organization aimed at educating the world's youth to reject racism and discrimination. Although she died in 1945, Anne

denied the opportunity to own businesses. In April 1941 Otto Frank acted to circumvent the anti-Jewish laws by transferring control of Opekta and Pectacon to one of his trusted non-Jewish associates, Johannes Kleiman, and had all assets of the company transferred to Gies and Company, headed by Jan Gies, husband of **Miep Gies**.

The major turning point for the Frank family came on July 5, 1942, however, when Margot Frank received a notice that she was to report to a labor camp for national service. Perceiving the likelihood that this could mean a permanent separation, Otto Frank made the decision that his family would have to go into hiding. This was earlier than originally planned; Otto and Edith Frank had already proposed that they would go into hiding on July 16, 1942. With the help of a few key friends and neighbors, the Franks moved into a small attic annex at 263 Prinsengracht Street on July 6, 1942, directly above the Opekta offices. This hiding place became known as the *Achterhuis*, referred to in Anne's diary as the Secret Annex. They were soon joined by another Jewish family, Auguste and Hermann van Pels and their son Peter, as well as another Jewish acquaintance, Fritz Pfeffer. Together, these eight people lived in hiding until they were discovered by the police on August 4, 1944.

Photograph of Anne Frank in 1940, attending her Montessori School in Amsterdam. Anne Frank was a German-born Dutch-Jewish girl who left a poignant diary of the Holocaust. During her family's two years in hiding, in an attic above her father's factory, Anne kept a diary that detailed their secret life. Anne died in Bergen-Belsen in 1945, but her diary was published after the war under the title *The Diary of a Young Girl*. (Unknown photographer; Collectie Anne Frank Stichting Amsterdam)

During their two years in hiding, Anne kept a diary that detailed the families' secret life—lived mostly at night—as well as her own adolescent viewpoints of the situation in which she found herself. She reflected on her relationships with the members of her family and the differences in each of their personalities and noted the tensions that intruded upon the various people in the two small rooms in which they were cramped together. Most of Anne's time in the Secret Annex was spent reading, studying, and writing her diary entries. She described events as she saw them and as they took place, but she also used the diary to confide her feelings, beliefs, and ambitions. With time, she extended the range of topics about

which she wrote, such as human nature, her own sexuality, and her belief in God. She also noted her level of understanding as to the situation in which the families found themselves and observed that their security could only be maintained with cooperation and respect. Anne's writing, moreover, expressed hope that the Allies would liberate Europe before the Secret Annex was discovered.

Anne continued writing regularly until her last entry, dated August 1, 1944. On the morning of August 4, 1944, the *Achterhuis* was stormed by a group of German police—some said as the result of denunciation. On August 8, 1944, the Frank and van Pels families, along with Pfeffer, were moved to the transit camp at Westerbork. Then, on September 3, 1944, they were deported from there to Auschwitz, where they arrived three days later. Anne's mother, Edith, died in the camp. In October or November 1944, Anne and Margot were transferred to Bergen-Belsen in Germany, where they died—it is generally presumed by typhus—sometime in February or March 1945. (Dutch authorities have set March 31 as their official date of death, but this is disputed.) Otto Frank survived to be liberated from Auschwitz in January 1945 and returned to Amsterdam in June 1945. Here, he found that Anne's diary had been saved by Miep Gies.

Amazed by his daughter's compelling account of life in hiding, he decided that it should become a public document—something Anne had foreseen herself. Anticipating her own survival, she wrote and rewrote parts of the diary for public consumption, and with her thoughts uppermost in mind, Otto Frank spent the next two years preparing the manuscript for publication. His efforts led to its publication in Dutch in 1947. It became a runaway success, and by 1952 there were editions in English, German, and French. The diary was subsequently translated into more than 60 languages. *The Diary of a Young Girl* (often rendered as *The Diary of Anne Frank*) was adapted into a successful play by Frances Goodrich and Albert Hackett and a multi–Academy Award winning movie of the same title in 1959 directed by George Stevens and starring Millie Perkins in the title role. This would be the first of several movies with Anne Frank as the theme.

Despite its success in bookstores and popular culture, controversy has also surrounded the diary. Literary rights were disputed between several publishers, Otto Frank, and others. Some commentators have expressed concern at the way in which Anne's life has become commercialized, and yet others have disputed whether it can truly be called an expression of the realities of the Holocaust.

It is in the area of education, however, where the diary has arguably had the greatest impact, and in countless school districts around the world, the study of Anne's diary is compulsory as a testament to human strength in the face of unrestrained oppression. Indeed, the girl Anne Frank has to some degree been cast into the background, replaced by Anne Frank, the image of hope in a dark and troubled world.

Anne Frank's diary is unquestionably the best-known document of the Holocaust and continues to inspire many across the globe, while another example of the Frank family's experience, the building where they hid, is now the home of the **Anne Frank House**, an international organization aimed at educating the world's youth to reject racism and discrimination. Although she died in 1945, Anne

Frank's words continue to educate, inspire, and prompt millions to remember the tragedies of World War II.

Further Reading

Barnouw, David, and Gerrold Van Der Stroom (Eds.). *The Diary of Anne Frank: The Critical Edition*. New York: Doubleday, 1989.
Enzer, Hyman A., and Sandra Solotaroff-Enzer (Eds.). *Anne Frank: Reflections on Her Life and Legacy*. Urbana: University of Illinois Press, 2000.
Frank, Anne. *The Diary of a Young Girl*. New York: Doubleday, 2003.
Gies, Miep. *Anne Frank Remembered*. New York: Simon and Schuster, 1987.
Lee, Carol Ann. *The Hidden Life of Otto Frank*. New York: HarperCollins, 2003.
Muller, Melissa. *Anne Frank: The Biography*. New York: Metropolitan Books, 1998.
Rittner, Carol (Ed.). *Anne Frank in the World: Essays and Reflections*. Armonk, NY: M. E. Sharpe, 1997.

FREIER, RECHA (1892–1984)

Recha Freier, *née* Schweitzer, was born on October 29, 1892, into a religiously observant Jewish family in the seaside town of Norden, in northern Germany. Her parents, both teachers, were Bertha (*née* Levy) and Menashe Schweitzer. In 1897 the Schweitzer family relocated to Silesia. Recha was homeschooled by her parents for some years before attending school in the town of Glogau. It was here that she encountered personal slights about her being Jewish; her response was to become an enthusiastic Zionist.

Recha then attended a private gymnasium in Breslau (Wrocław), completing her studies in record time. In 1912 she received permission to enter higher studies and passed her examinations at universities in Breslau and Munich. In 1919 she married Rabbi Dr. Moritz Freier, and by 1925 they had moved to Berlin. Over the next few years, they raised a family of four children, while Recha also taught high school.

Considering the family's options for the future, Recha realized that employment for her children was going to be difficult as Jewish teenagers were being eased out of education for the professions. In 1932 her husband asked her to help five Jewish teenage boys find employment. After being rebuffed at every turn, she had the idea to send the boys to Palestine, where they could be trained as farmers and become agricultural pioneers. By October of that year, an initial group had left Berlin in a scheme that was the nucleus of what became the Youth Aliyah immigration scheme to Palestine.

On January 30, 1933—the same day that Adolf Hitler was appointed chancellor of Germany—Recha Freier created the Committee for the Assistance of Jewish Youth (*Hilfskomitee für Jüdische Jugend*). It would soon change its name to Youth Aliyah. The program was recognized by the World Zionist Congress, but it needed both money and an accepting organization receptive to the idea in Palestine. Recha contacted the then-director of the Social Service Bureau of the

Va'ad Leumi (National Council) in Palestine, Henrietta Szold, who had founded Hadassah, the Women's Zionist Organization of America. She was, however, reluctant to take on any new projects, worried about the inability of the organized Jewish community in Palestine to provide for young Jews already there. She rejected the proposal.

The ascent to power of the Nazis soon convinced her that Jewish lives could be in danger, and this turned her around. She eventually accepted the role Recha offered her to take care of the teenagers after their arrival in Palestine, and Henrietta Szold thus become the director of Youth Aliyah's Jerusalem office under the control of the Jewish Agency. Because of this Jerusalem connection, she is often wrongly assumed to be the founder of Youth Aliyah.

Recha Freier continued to run things in Germany, but she experienced significant opposition from a Jewish community worried about drawing too much attention to itself. Moreover, parents feared an uncertain separation of indeterminate duration from their children at this time of considerable instability.

After the Nazi takeover of Austria in March 1938, Recha turned her attention to saving the young Jews of Austria. Later that year, as a result of the November pogrom known as *Kristallnacht*, she attempted to have German and Austrian Jewish men and youths released from concentration camps. To do so, and without authority, she appropriated 100 exit permits issued by the Nazis and given to the Jewish representative body—the Reich Association of Jews in Germany—and filled in the names of Jews then in concentration camps. While the men were released and made their way to Palestine, Recha was expelled from the board and as director of Youth Aliyah in Germany for what were deemed to be illegal activities.

Before the outbreak of war in September 1939, Recha was responsible for saving at least 7,000 German and Austrian Jewish children by arranging their transport both to Palestine and to European countries willing to accept them in transit. A total of 5,012 children were taken to Palestine alone. In the middle of 1940 she left Germany, crossing the border into Yugoslavia illegally with the help of professional people movers. En route, she also arranged transit for up to 120 young Jews who went to Palestine. She herself remained in Zagreb with her 11-year-old daughter for several months until reaching Palestine in March 1941.

Upon her arrival in Jerusalem, she sought the opportunity to continue her work of rescuing Jewish youth from Nazi Germany, but her ongoing dispute with Henrietta Szold over control of Youth Aliyah prevented this. Szold informed her that there was no position for her in the running of the Youth Aliyah in Palestine, and Recha was forced to withdraw from the organization she had created.

Yet even this was not to stifle her resolve to take care of Germany's Jewish youth. In 1943 she founded the Agricultural Training Center for Israeli children, the aim of which was to provide a decent education for children from impoverished families—many of whom had come to Palestine as refugees.

The remarkable story of Youth Aliyah from this point proceeded without Recha's involvement. With over 7,000 youths taken to Palestine and elsewhere before the war, between 1945 and 1948, an additional 15,000, most of them young survivors of the Holocaust, were taken to Palestine. Since then, Youth Aliyah has been responsible for hundreds of thousands of successful migration success stories.

In addition to her activities on behalf of Jewish youth, Recha Freier gave vent to her cultural passions, establishing the Israel Composer's Fund in 1958, and in 1966, she and composer Roman Haubenstock-Ramati founded the Testimonium music festival, designed to support composers setting major Jewish themes to music. She herself wrote or arranged the libretti for many of the Testimonium works.

It was only after Henrietta Szold's death in 1945 that Recha's achievements in establishing Youth Aliyah were recognized. In her later years, she occasionally felt bitter about how the feud with Szold had led to her being written out of the historical record. Recognition only came in 1975, when, at the age of 83, she received an honorary doctorate from the Hebrew University of Jerusalem, and in 1981, when she received the Israel Prize from Prime Minister Menachem Begin for her outstanding contribution to the people and State of Israel.

Recha Freier died in Jerusalem on April 2, 1984, aged 91.

Further Reading

Amkraut, Brian. *Between Home and Homeland: Youth Aliyah from Nazi Germany*. Tuscaloosa: University of Alabama Press, 2006.

G

GAREL NETWORK

At the end of 1942, Dr. Joseph Weill, medical director of the *Œuvre de Secours aux Enfants* (Children's Aid Society, or OSE), concluded that Jewish children grouped in orphanages had little protection if Germans or Vichy police came looking for them. In response, he felt that there could be little other alternative than to arrange for them to be dispersed out to friendly families, preferably in the countryside. Weill introduced a former soldier, Georges Garel, to a small group of resisters he had gathered at Lyon, to whom he presented his plan to form clandestine networks for concealing children with non-Jewish families and in friendly institutions. This, in short course, would evolve into what became known as the *Circuit Garel*, or Garel Network.

Georges Garel ("Gasquet," *né* Grigori Garfinkel) was born on March 1, 1909, in Vilna (Vilnius), then in the Russian Empire. In 1912 his family moved to Kiev, and in 1924, they moved to Berlin. In 1926, aged 17, Garel migrated to Paris. After obtaining French citizenship in 1934, he undertook officer training at the *Préparation Militaire Supérieure* military college, and on August 30, 1939, he was mobilized as a lieutenant of artillery and fought until France's capitulation in the summer of 1940. In December 1942 Joseph Weill gave Garel his assignment to look after Jewish children under 16 years of age. His brief was to disperse them out to non-Jewish environments, give them Aryan identities, and, wherever possible, have their well-being taken care of by non-Jews.

Charles Lederman, an administrative delegate with the OSE stationed at the Rivesaltes internment camp between April and November 1941, had a specific interest in taking care of adolescents over the age of 15. He opened an office of the OSE in Lyon and founded the *Union des juifs pour la résistance et l'entraide* (Union of Jews for Resistance and Mutual Aid, or UJRE). This resistance organization managed to save about 180 Jewish children. In mid-August 1942, Lederman met with Jules-Géraude Saliège, Archbishop of Toulouse, to whom he pointed out the existence of the camps, the kidnappings, and the deportations that were being carried out against the Jews of France. This shocked Saliège and steeled his resolve to try to find a way to help the Jews.

On the recommendation of Lederman and Father de Lubac, a Jesuit priest, Saliège received Georges Garel in December 1942 and provided him with a letter of introduction allowing him to contact several Catholic charities. Through such contacts, nearly 300 children could be hidden quickly—though being hidden was not enough in and of itself. The children still had to be monitored and have their maintenance guaranteed. Social workers involved in Garel's network therefore undertook to check regularly on the children's welfare, provide them with moral and material support, and ensure they remained healthy and safe. Where possible, they would also bring the children news or letters from their parents. More than a dozen Catholic and Protestant organizations would eventually lend their assistance; during 1943 several of the priests, on Saliège's authority, were involved in helping Jews through providing false baptism certificates in their parishes. At its fullest extent, the network covered 30 *départements* across four regions of France.

By the summer of 1943, the *Circuit Garel* was organized along the following lines: the central-eastern region, directed from Garel's base in Lyon and protecting 350 children, covered the *départments* of Rhône, Ain, Loire, Haute-Loire, Puy-de-Dôme, Cantal, and Allier; the southeast region, with 400 children, covered the Drôme, Ardèche, Isère, Haute-Savoie, Basses-Alpes, and Hautes-Alpes; the central region, with 450 children, covered Haute-Vienne, Creuse, Corrèze, Dordogne, and the Indre; and the southwest region, directed from Toulouse with 400 children, covered the Haute-Garonne, the Hautes-et-Basses-Pyrenees, the Tarn, the Tarn-et-Garonne, Lot, Lot-et-Garonne, Gers, Herault, Aveyron, and Lozère. Garel, assisted by **Andrée Salomon**, took charge of the entire operation.

A highly secret system consisting of coded registers, individual records, and three lists—placed in different locations—allowed those authorized to find all the information concerning the double names of children, parents, and host institutions, the better to enable both parents and children to be reunited after the **liberation**. In cases where children were identifiably "Jewish" by their foreign accent, their attachment to dietary laws, or other features, they were handed across to people movers (*passeurs*) working with Resistance organizations to assist them in crossing the Swiss border or the Pyrenees into Spain. Given this consideration, Garel also ensured that false papers and ration cards were created and kept up to date.

Between January 1943 and the autumn of 1944, the *Circuit Garel* is estimated to have saved the lives of nearly 1,500 children. For its part, however, the network lost some 30 of its own operatives, whether through capture, execution, or deportation (from which only four returned).

One of those in the Garel Network was **Georges Loinger**, recruited by Garel in January 1943 to organize a means whereby secure border crossings to Switzerland could take place for several hundred Jewish children in and around Annemasse, in Haute-Savoie. With this, the transformation of the OSE was complete; it would henceforth move from assisting and housing children in need to smuggling them across borders to safeguard their very lives. Throughout the period 1943–1944, Loinger managed the successful passage of about 350 children.

In 1943 Georges Garel married Lily Tager ("Élisabeth-Jeanne Tissier") in Lyon, and they had seven children. He was appointed director general of the OSE-France in 1944, and in 1948, under peacetime conditions, he resumed his post as an engineer with the *Compagnie Électro-Mécanique* (CEM), a French electrical engineering manufacturer. He remained here until 1974, at the same time continuing as a member of the board of the OSE. In this capacity he was president between 1951 and 1978. He died of a heart attack in Paris on January 9, 1979.

Further Reading

Garel, Georges, with Katy Hazan. *Le sauvetage des enfants juifs par l'OSE*. Paris: Le Manuscrit, 2012.

GARNETHILL HOSTEL

When unaccompanied children from Germany, Austria, and Czechoslovakia were put on **Kindertransport** trains between 1938 and 1939 to send them to safety, an estimated 70 percent were Jewish. Some 8 percent of these were cared for in Scotland during the war years. These unaccompanied children had initially come from comfortable middle-class families, and many did not speak English. They were lodged in institutional homes in Scotland such as Garnethill Hostel.

The first Jews arrived in Scotland the late 17th century, and at its highest point, after World War II, the Jewish community boasted close to 20,000 members, with 15,000 calling Glasgow home. Garnethill Synagogue, Scotland's first purpose-built place of Jewish worship, was constructed in 1879. The congregation took an early role in the rescue of Nazi-era refugees; the minutes of its general meeting of December 11, 1938 recommended that every male seat holder of the congregation agree to contribute a minimum sum of one shilling and sixpence per week for the Appeal Committee of the Council for German Jewry and that a committee of 12 be formed to supervise the collection of contributions. The *Jewish Echo* of February 24, 1939, reported on the active preparation of the new hostel, noting that rapid strides were being made in the redecoration and reconstruction of the house at 125 Hill Street, which would become Glasgow's first hostel for German Jewish refugee children. With 15 rooms, each of them large, well-lit, and solidly built, the hostel was expected to accommodate 30 boys between the ages of 12 and 16 and a small household staff.

The Garnethill Boys' Hostel was operated by the congregation from 1939 to 1948 in a house adjoining the synagogue. The hostel's register lists over 175 individuals who were admitted across that period. Some of the refugees stayed only a few days or weeks, others longer. A number came and went more than once. For each individual, the register provides columns for name, date of birth, date of arrival, occupation, nationality, prior address, and date of departure and destination.

The care and nurture of these refugee children was working class in its character and content. Residential facilities such as that at Garnethill lacked many necessities, space, and any comforts, a situation exacerbated by wartime. Nurtured by caregivers with lower educational expectations, today those who were children at the time frequently express their struggle to complete even their basic schooling. The point at which compulsory schooling ended brought an end to their full-time education—but the general deterioration in standards was not restricted only to refugee children. Air raids and blackouts, the loss of trained teachers and caregivers, and the general shortage of resources or suitable premises made it difficult for all Scottish minors to obtain access to a good education. Between 1939 and 1945, hundreds of thousands of children were living without education or basic school services, including free milk and health care.

The Physical Training and Recreation Act 1937 encouraged physical exercise, outdoor pursuits, and membership of youth clubs such as the Boy Scouts. These all tended to promote the ideals of the rural outdoor life. The refugee children joined an array of youth groups, including Maccabi Clubs for sports and the Scouts or Zionist groups for rural excursions and outdoor pursuits.

Lodging at the hostel was temporary for many of the refugee children. An excerpt from the registry of the Garnethill Hostel covering the period 1939–1948 indicated that of the 75 percent of residents who listed their country of origin, 42 percent were from Germany; 14 percent were from Austria; and the remainder were from Poland, Russia, Romania, Hungary, and Czechoslovakia. Many residents went on to lodge with families, both Jewish and non-Jewish, and to other hostels in Scotland, as well as England, the United States, Canada, and Palestine.

Additional hostels for Jewish refugees in Scotland included a Quaker hostel for women and girls, located on the other side of the synagogue in Renfrew Street, from 1940 to 1942 (this accommodated 15 people at a time, mostly adults); Whittingehame House, the former home of Arthur Balfour in East Lothian, which served as a farm training school for refugee teenagers from 1939 to 1942 (it was run on the model of the Hachshara Kibbutz and on Youth Aliyah philosophy); and Polton House, near Dalkeith in Midlothian, which also promoted a rural lifestyle through agricultural training in a rural setting. Other hostels were at Birkenward, Skelmorlie in Ayrshire, Ernespie House (Castle Douglas), and the Priory in Selkirk. No admission registers have been found for these three other hostels.

On May 1, 2018, the Scottish Jewish Archives Centre (SJAC) and Garnethill Synagogue Preservation Trust received a grant of £296,900 from the National Lottery for their Scottish Jewish Heritage Centre project based in Glasgow's Garnethill Synagogue. It was expected that this would serve as Scotland's first Jewish and Holocaust era Study Center to open up public access to the SJAC's unique collections on this period, with resources for education, research, tourists, and community groups. A public display would detail the history and experience of refugees and survivors from the Nazi regime who found sanctuary and a chance to build a new life in Scotland. The display would highlight how Scottish society, churches, trade unions, and others rallied to support refugees, and it would also highlight the contributions many of the refugees went on to make to Scottish cultural, medical, educational, and business life in their adopted homeland.

Further Reading

Williams, Frances. *The Forgotten Kindertransportees: The Scottish Experience*. London: Bloomsbury, 2013.

GERLIER, PIERRE-MARIE (1880–1965)

Pierre-Marie Gerlier was a French Roman Catholic Cardinal who served as Archbishop of Lyon and Primate of All Gaul, with his base in Lyon. He used his authority to save and protect Jewish children in Vichy France from 1941 onward.

GERLIER, PIERRE-MARIE (1880–1965)

Born on January 14, 1880, in Versailles, his initial training was as a lawyer before he found his calling and became a priest. In World War I, he served as an officer in the French Army, and he was wounded and captured by the Germans. He was ordained on July 29, 1921. On May 14, 1929, he was appointed Bishop of Tarbes and Lourdes before becoming Archbishop of Lyon on July 30, 1937. On December 13 of that year, he was elevated to cardinal.

Living in Lyon meant that Gerlier found himself under the collaborationist regime at Vichy during World War II. He supported the government of Marshal Philippe Pétain and encouraged Catholics to support him. He was, however, opposed to the government's anti-Jewish policies and condemned the deportation of Jews to the euphemistically named "East."

Together with Marc Boegner, the head of the Protestant church in France, Gerlier was honorary president of *Amitié Chrétienne*, a Christian ecumenical group established in 1941 that linked Catholics and Protestants with Jewish welfare organizations trying to save Jews. In this capacity, he at one point threatened to excommunicate anyone who bought property unjustly seized from Jewish families. Moreover, he asked that Roman Catholic religious institutions take Jewish children into hiding and instructed Catholic villagers across southern and eastern France to hide Jewish children of parents who were in French concentration camps or who had been deported to Germany. In early 1943 he intervened with the Gestapo to obtain the release of Jean-Marie Soutou, an *Amitié Chrétienne* leader who was arrested, imprisoned, and interrogated on suspicion of hiding Jews.

Just outside the city of Lyon, an internment camp had been established at Vénissieux. Its several buildings were guarded by 15-foot-high walls and Vietnamese troops directed by French officers. Conditions were appalling, and volunteer workers of *Amitié Chrétienne* took on the thankless and difficult job of drawing up lists for deportation. They had to deal with 1,300 cases, including orphaned children for whom foster homes had to be found. In July 1942, the Vichy government had undertaken to deliver to the SS so-called stateless Jews from Germany, Austria, Poland, Czechoslovakia, the Soviet Union, and Danzig. These people had to be found somewhere, and *Amitié Chrétienne* took on the thankless task of screening who should go and who should stay.

On August 26, 1942, 1,016 Jews from the region were arrested and interned at Vénissieux. Other roundups took place across the night of August 27–28. With the large number of new arrivals, it took no time for the camp administration to be swamped.

Clearly, circumstances had to change, and some measure of organization had to be brought into play. A screening commission was established within the camp to identify who would or would not be deported, operating from a recently-issued directive stipulating that orphans would be exempt. Gilbert Lesage, a Quaker charity worker, had already learned on August 16 that large-scale roundups had been planned, and he decided to warn as many Jewish and other rescue organizations as could be contacted.

In desperation, they swung into action. Leading representatives of several relief organizations spent a stormy night presenting possible scenarios to camp officials to find ways of identifying those who could be exempted from deportation. Through their efforts they managed to save 160 adults, 80 of whom were rearrested the next day. They also saved 108 children under the age of 15 and a few older teenagers.

The children who had been screened for departure left the camp on Saturday, August 29, after the police chief learned that the Vichy authorities had given new instructions concerning the children. The plan was that they be sent to the camp at Rivesaltes prior to being transported to Drancy. Eventually, they would be deported to "the East."

Two of the priests who had been involved in the screening at Vénissieux, Father Pierre Chaillet and Father **Alexandre Glasberg**, informed Cardinal Gerlier of the danger to which the children were exposed. On August 30, 1942, the authorities pressured the leaders of *Amitié Chrétienne* to hand over the 108 Jewish children; it was suspected that they had illegally removed the children from the camp at Venissieux. Without hesitation, Gerlier gave his support to the rescuers, insisting that the children be dispersed immediately and placed in various church institutions. It was thus at his order that they were saved.

On January 17, 1965, Cardinal Gerlier died from a heart attack in Lyon at age 85. On July 15, 1981, for his efforts in saving Jewish children during World War II, he was posthumously recognized by Yad Vashem as one of the Righteous among the Nations.

Further Reading

Georges, Olivier. *Pierre-Marie Gerlier, le cardinal militant*. Paris: Desclée de Brouwer, 2014.

GETTER, MATYLDA (1870–1968)

Mother Matylda Getter was a Polish Catholic nun, the superior of the Warsaw Province of the Congregation of the Franciscan Sisters of the Family of Mary (*Congregatio Sororum Franciscalium Familiae Mariae*, or CSFFM, frequently shortened to the Family of Mary) in pre–World War II Warsaw. During the war she worked alongside of **Irena Sendler** and **Żegota**, of the Polish underground movement's Council to Aid Jews. Through her contacts, Getter was responsible for saving the lives of hundreds of Jewish children from the Warsaw Ghetto.

Matylda Getter was born on February 25, 1870, and attended school in Warsaw. Little is recorded of her early years, other than that she entered the convent when aged 17. In 1936 she was chosen as mother superior of the Warsaw province with her headquarters located at 53 Hożej Street, Warsaw. When Germany invaded Poland in September 1939, she was nearing 70 years of age.

Before the outbreak of war, the Franciscan Sisters of the Family of Mary were one of the largest active religious orders in Poland, running nurseries, orphanages, general schools, boarding schools, hospitals, and clinics. The original mother house was in Lwów (now Lviv) with other locations in Poznań, and Warsaw. Mother Matylda received several national awards for her achievements in educational and social work, having established many facilities for children in Anin,

Białołęka, Chotomów, Międzylesie, Płudy, Sejny, and Wilno (Vilna, Vilnius), among other locations.

After the onset of increasingly draconian measures against Jews in the Warsaw Ghetto and other places, by 1942 Mother Matylda declared that she would attempt to save every Jewish child she could. In her capacity as Mother Superior, she organized all children's homes and orphanages under her jurisdiction to hide Jewish children; in Warsaw the task was made a little easier as the convent wall abutted the ghetto itself.

She also contacted the workers of Centos (the National Society for the Care of Orphans), an organization that ran schools and provided food, clothing, and shelter. It arranged care for abandoned Jewish children and orphans in the Warsaw Ghetto. Many of the children for which it cared, after being smuggled out of the ghetto, were sent directly to Mother Matylda's institutions. The help was far from passive, however; she led a broad campaign to find and then hide Jewish children from the ghetto. Her directive was simple and unmistakable: "If anyone comes to our courtyard and asks for help, we cannot refuse in the name of Christ."

The strategies employed to safeguard the children were varied but focused on making them as undetectably Jewish as possible. Consequently, they were given new names and new birth certificates with signatures and the seal of a parish. Fake baptism certificates were generated, though most of the children were baptized formally while under the Family of Mary's care—not to convert them, but to enable them to survive. They were taught how to pray as Catholics. During inspections the Germans would often order the children to pray, listening carefully for any signs of hesitation or unfamiliarity as to Catholic liturgy. The sisters, consequently, instructed the children thoroughly and then incorporated the prayers into the everyday life at orphanages and schools, rendering the Jewish children undetectable from the others. After the liberation, Mother Matylda made sure that, wherever possible, all reverted to Judaism.

Mother Matylda's efforts grew to involve a giant secret network scattered across Poland, and, working alongside of Żegota, rescue activities even reached Ukraine. Those who could live **passing** as non-Jews were hidden in the orphanages, but those who looked more identifiably Jewish (in accordance with Nazi stereotypes) were smuggled further east, where it was believed they would be safer. Within Poland, Mother Matylda risked her life and the lives of her sisters by taking the children into her orphanages and hiring adults to care for them. Żegota's children's department, led by Irena Sendler, smuggled children out of the ghetto in large numbers, but the problem was always going to be one of where they could be hidden. Thus, Żegota, Irena Sendler, and Mother Matylda worked together as a rescue chain, rather than individually.

It is unclear how many Jewish children were saved due to the activities of Mother Matylda and the institutions of the Family of Mary during the Holocaust. An estimate of about 500 children and some 250 adults is the most likely approximation. In the orphanage at Płudy alone, for instance, some 40 Jewish girls found refuge, with all surviving the war. Mother Matylda always considered it her duty to save those in trouble. She never demanded payment for her services, and after the war, she did not talk much about her rescue activities.

Mother Matylda Getter died in Płudy on August 8, 1968, aged 98. On January 17, 1985, Yad Vashem recognized her as one of the Righteous among the Nations, and in subsequent years, another six sisters from the Congregation of the Franciscan Sisters of the Family of Mary were similarly recognized. On Wednesday, August 8, 2018, on the 50th anniversary of her death, a cornerstone was laid for the construction of a new Museum for the Rescue of Jewish Children, to be constructed in the courtyard and in the convent cellars of the mother house at 53 Hożej Street. At the same time, at Warsaw's Powązki Cemetery, a new tombstone was unveiled at Mother Matylda's gravesite.

Further Reading

Paldiel, Mordecai. *Sheltering the Jews: Stories of Holocaust Rescuers.* Minneapolis: Fortress Press, 1996.

GEULEN-HERSCOVICI, ANDRÉE (b.1921)

Andrée Geulen-Herscovici is a Belgian rescuer who helped hide Jewish children during the Nazi occupation of Belgium between 1942 and 1944.

Born Andrée Geulen on September 6, 1921, she studied to become a teacher, and at the age of 18, she began teaching at a local school. In May 1940, with the German invasion and occupation of Belgium, anti-Jewish laws were introduced throughout the country. The first time Andrée, then aged 20, encountered Jewish persecution was when some of her students arrived at school wearing a compulsory yellow star. Like many other Belgians, until then she had not paid much attention to the Nazis' persecution of the Jews. Once faced with the reality confronting her students, however, she decided to act by ordering all her students to wear aprons to school, covering the yellow stars.

Then, when teaching at a school in Brussels in 1942, the Gestapo arrived to arrest her Jewish pupils. After meeting Ida Sterno, a member of the secret Jewish rescue organization, the **Comité de Defense des Juifs** (Jewish Defense Committee, or CDJ), Andrée decided to join. There were decided benefits for the children by her doing so: as a non-Jew, she could accompany them to their hiding places in a way that was safer than if adult Jews were to do so. She was given a code name, Claude Fournier, and moved into the Gaty de Gamont School, a boarding school where she was teaching. The school by that stage was deeply involved in hiding Jewish children, largely at the initiative of the headmistress, Odile Ovart. One of Andrée's tasks was to persuade Jewish parents to part from their children so that they could be taken to hiding places, after which she would transfer the children to welcoming non-Jewish families who would hide them.

In May 1943, however, the school was raided in the middle of the night. The students were woken up and dragged out of bed to have their identities checked. The Jewish children were isolated immediately, and the teachers, including Andrée, were interrogated. She managed to evade arrest, and after the Nazis had left, she visited the homes of all the Jewish children she knew, warning their parents of the imminent danger and telling them not to return their children to the school because it was now unsafe. Tragically, Odile Ovart and her husband were arrested and deported to a German concentration camp, where they later died.

The incident did not deter Andrée from continuing her illegal work, however, and she expanded her resistance activities. She secured an apartment under an assumed name, sharing it with Ida Sterno, who was now also in hiding. Andrée became one of the leading points of contact for the CDJ, taking dozens—perhaps hundreds—of Jewish children from their homes and placing them with Christian families, monasteries, and churches. She visited almost all of them regularly, providing them with food, clothing, and other essentials. She maintained close contact with a number of rescue organizations through secret post office boxes and kept coded records of the original names and places of refuge for hundreds of children. Thus, she was able to ensure that they could be returned to their families or relatives when the war ended. She also committed to memory each of the children's names, original addresses, and other details, in case the records were lost or discovered.

In May 1944 the Germans arrested Ida Sterno and imprisoned her in the Malines/Mechelen transit camp. She was saved from deportation only because of the liberation of Belgium by the Allies in September 1944, but during her incarceration, she was visited by Andrée—now herself in hiding—under an assumed name. The two women continued their rescue activities right through to the end of the war.

Andrée's work was not finished, however, and upon liberation she kept busy working in a reverse direction: to bring the children back from the families that had shielded them and return them to their parents or relatives. Tragically, however, some had no families to which they could return.

All in all, perhaps up to 1,000 children were rescued as a result of Andrée's work; she married after the war and became known as Geulen-Herscovici. On August 2, 1989, she was recognized by Israel's Yad Vashem as one of the Righteous among the Nations for her wartime work of rescue. On April 18, 2007, she returned to Yad Vashem for the Children Hidden in Belgium during the Shoah International Conference. At a special ceremony during the conference, she was awarded honorary citizenship of the State of Israel.

Further Reading

Paldiel, Mordecai. *The Righteous Among the Nations: Rescuers of Jews during the Holocaust.* New York: Harper, 2007.

Yad Vashem, at https://www.yadvashem.org/righteous/stories/geulen-herscovici.html. "Geulen's List: Andrée Geulen-Hersovici."

GEVE, THOMAS (b.1929)

Thomas Geve is a Jewish engineer, author, and Holocaust survivor. Born Stefan Cohn on October 27, 1929, in Züllchow (żelechowa), a suburb of Stettin

(Szczecin), he lived in Beuthen before his family moved to Berlin in 1939. His father was able to obtain a permit to migrate to Britain, but young Stefan and his mother were unable to join him, so they were forced to remain in Berlin.

When Jewish schools were closed by the Nazis, and Stefan was forced out of public education, he had to go to work before he was even a teenager; for part of that time, he labored as a gravedigger at the Jewish cemetery at Weissensee in Berlin while his mother worked as a seamstress in a factory producing German Army uniforms. Walking the streets of Berlin, the tall, strongly built boy seemed to revel in ignoring the increasing danger faced by the Jews, and he had many scrapes with the authorities that did little to diminish his enthusiasm for life.

In June 1943, however, fate caught up with the mother and son, and they were deported to Auschwitz. At the infamous ramp, where incoming Jews were separated into those who would work and those who would be killed, Stefan went to the side for slave labor and was assigned to a bricklaying commando. His mother was murdered. Stefan displayed curiosity regarding his surroundings at Auschwitz, seeking to learn as much as he could about the camp environment—how it was developing, what changes were made, and how this might affect him and his comrades. He learned the appropriate techniques of "organizing" (*organisieren*), procuring items in other than strictly legal ways (perhaps approximating the general idea of scrounging). Organizing was not regarded as stealing, as such activities were always directed against the SS and the camp itself and never against other prisoners. At the same time, Stefan was always searching for an older guardian or protector, as well as other youngsters such as himself, following the principle of safety in numbers.

He survived at Auschwitz almost until the very end of its existence, but with the approach of the Red Army in January 1945, he was evacuated on a death march—first to the camp at Gross-Rosen before moving on to Buchenwald. In April 1945, after the inmates rose and took control of the camp, it was finally liberated by units of the U.S. Army. He later recalled the moment of liberation as being "between three and four o'clock, the date 11 April 1945. We waited in suspense and with unprecedented tension." After hearing shouts from the main camp, he and his comrades "rushed out to investigate," only to see that the Nazis were gone. "I lifted my eyes and searched for the pyramid-shaped roof on the main watch-tower that stood out from beyond the main camp. The crooked cross of Fascism had gone. Fluttering from the symbolic flagpole was something white. The moment we had so anxiously been longing for had come."

At the time of the camp's liberation, Stefan, now 15, was in a poor physical state. Remaining in Block 29 for approximately a month while he regained his strength, he turned to drawing in order to pass the time. "Organizing" what he referred to as "a few stumps of colored pencils," he set down on paper a record of camp life in 79 drawings depicting his observations of Auschwitz, the death march, Buchenwald camp, and its liberation. He made sketches of prisoners, of the American soldiers, and of the camp gate with the white bedsheet that replaced the Nazi flag. Each of these small drawings, the size of a postcard, not only documented his personal observations; they acted as a form of therapy to assist him regain his emotional well-being as his physical strength was returning.

After a period of further convalescence, he was transferred to an orphanage in Switzerland, after which he was reunited with his father in Britain. In 1950 he migrated to Israel, where he undertook military service and then, settling in Haifa, began work as a construction engineer.

In 1958 he wrote a personal account of his life under the Nazis, *Youth in Chains*, which was first published in Jerusalem and subsequently republished and translated into six other languages. It told the story from his birth until the time he was liberated in May 1945. A second work, published first in German (and then in English in 1987), recounted his experiences after the war. *Guns and Barbed Wire: A Child Survives the Holocaust*, reproduced 17 of Thomas Geve's (as he now called himself) color drawings from the time of his liberation. Since that time, his experiences have also been covered in two documentaries, in which his story—and his drawings—are exhibited and explained for younger audiences.

Further Reading

Geve, Thomas. *Youth in Chains*. Jerusalem: Rubin Mass, 1958.

GIES, MIEP (1909–2010)

Miep Gies was an Austrian-born Dutch citizen who helped hide **Anne Frank** and her family, along with several other Jews, in Amsterdam between 1942 and 1944.

She was born Hermine Santruschitz on February 15, 1909, in Vienna. In 1920 she was sent to Leiden in the Netherlands to escape the unrest and food shortages of post–World War I Austria and was taken in as a foster child by the Nieuwenburg family. As a girl she was given the nickname "Miep."

In 1933 she went to work for Otto Frank, a German Jewish businessman who had fled Germany with his family to escape the Nazis. Soon thereafter, she met Jan Gies, a bookkeeper. They grew fond of the Frank family, with whom they developed a close friendship.

In 1941 German occupation officials in the Netherlands insisted that Miep join a Nazi women's association. When she refused, her passport was canceled, and she was ordered to be deported to her native Austria within 90 days. By way of response and in haste, Jan Gies married her on July 16, 1941, so she could obtain Dutch citizenship and thereby avoid deportation. Then, as German occupation officials and Dutch collaborators began to persecute Jews and deport them to unknown destinations in "the East," Jan and Miep decided to keep the Frank family safe. In July 1942, after some consideration as to method, they hid the Franks, along with several other Jews, in a small second-story apartment above Opekta, Otto Frank's spice company located at Amsterdam's Prinsengracht 263.

At considerable risk to her own safety, Miep supplied the Franks with food and medicine. The hiding place was only a short distance from Miep and Jan's home, and Miep continued to work in the office below the apartment in order to prevent unwanted intrusion from anyone seeking access to the second floor. Throughout the period in which the Franks were in hiding, Opekta had to continue operating in order to protect the family, as any change in routine could have led the Gestapo to investigate. Therefore, Miep and those around her kept things running smoothly to maintain the charade that there was nothing untoward.

On August 4, 1944, as Miep worked at her desk, a police official walked into the office, pointed a gun at her, and demanded that she show him the secret room. Somebody had tipped the police off about the Franks. Within minutes, the Franks and other people hiding in the second-floor apartment were arrested and taken away. Miep escaped only because the police officer had been a native of Vienna and understood her situation. The Franks were eventually sent to death camps.

Miep saved and hid Anne Frank's diary, the whereabouts of which she kept secret until the end of the war. In 1945 Otto Frank, who had survived Auschwitz, returned to Amsterdam and was reunited with Miep and Jan Gies. It was then that he learned of Anne's death at Bergen-Belsen. Determined to let the world know about his family's ordeal, in 1947 he permitted the diary's publication.

Miep hid the Frank family for more than two years. Although devastated by their arrest, she had enough presence of mind to ensure that she was not picked up at the same time, which enabled her to continue her work as a resister.

After the war, Miep developed into something of a celebrity, a status she eschewed. She always held that she did not do anything remarkable and preferred to consider that she did what anyone in the same position should have done. In her view, although risking arrest every day for two years, what she did was simply her human duty. She developed her ideas around this theme in her memoir, *Anne Frank Remembered: The Story of the Woman Who Helped to Hide the Frank Family*. In 1947, when she and Jan moved to a new home at Jekerstraat 65, they allowed Otto Frank to move in with them.

Miep Gies received many honors recognizing her efforts to save Jewish lives during the Holocaust. In 1994 she was awarded the Order of Merit of the Federal Republic of Germany, and in 1995 she was recognized as one of the Righteous among the Nations by Yad Vashem. In 1997 she was knighted in the Order of Orange-Nassau by Queen Beatrix of the Netherlands; on July 30, 2009, she received the Grand Decoration of Honor for Services to the Republic of Austria.

On January 11, 2010, just short of her 101st birthday, Miep Gies died after a fall in a nursing home in Hoorn, a town outside of Amsterdam.

Further Reading

Gies, Miep. *Anne Frank Remembered*. New York: Simon and Schuster, 1987.
Muller, Melissa. *Anne Frank: The Biography*. New York: Metropolitan Books, 1998.

GLAS-WIENER, SHEVA (1916–1986)

Sheva Glas-Wiener was a Polish Jewish teacher who tended for two years to her group of orphans in Marysin orphanage, which formed part of the Łódź ghetto. Although they were all deported, the teacher and a few of her children survived.

Many years later Glas-Wiener wrote up the stories of the children she had taken care of in a memoir, *Children of the Ghetto*.

Sheva Glas-Wiener was born in Radoszyce, Poland, on June 26, 1916, graduated as a teacher in Łódź in 1938, and taught in a primary school. The Germans occupied Łódź in 1939, and in May 1940, they sealed off the ghetto from the outside world. Jews in the ghetto were forced to produce goods for the German war effort, in return for which they were given skimpy rations and free accommodation in Baluty, the worst slum part of downtown. As a result, many died of starvation, cold, and exposure. Numerous men were deported, leaving their families without support, while orphaned children roamed the streets, begging for food and help.

In mid-1940 the Jewish welfare society organized homes for some of the thousands of children who had nowhere else to go. The Children's Colony of Marysin was set up in a place where railway workers and their families once lived. The orphanage had a school, cultural center, library, pharmacy, and a sports club. It housed about 1,600 children, who were divided into 50 groups according to sex and age. Marysin was included in the Łódź ghetto because the only road to the Jewish Cemetery ran through the village.

Between 1940 and 1942, Sheva worked as a teacher in the Marysin orphanage school, teaching 32 girls aged from 7 to 15. The background of the children varied greatly: some came from the Baluty slums; others were from wealthy middle class or professional foreign families who had been deported to Łódź from Berlin, Vienna, Paris, and Prague. The only differences within the groups was the quality of their clothes. Their fate as Jews taught the children to bond, and they all experienced hardship and hunger. Sheva wrote that the slum children taught the middle-class children how to survive.

She also documented the lives of the children she taught, writing about how one child saved food from their meager rations to give to their mother, and that when the food was stolen and eaten by another hungry child, the mother died of hunger. Sheva considered the friendships between the children that developed in the orphanage, reporting how one child gave blood so her very sick friend could survive, and then the donor, herself weakened from the blood donation, died from anemia. She wrote how two older children fell in love and tried to marry and live a more normal life. Her stories detailed how the human spirit responded to the tragedy of everyday life in the orphanage. The stories of the children are not dark and sad—the children themselves have energy and hope. Locked up in the Marysin orphanage, they were unaware of the mass atrocities being committed to their fellow Jews outside the walls.

During the summer of 1942, the Germans emptied all the ghetto hospitals and sent the sick to the extermination camp at Chełmno, 60 miles from Łódź. They then started to deport all 16,000 residents from Łódź to Chełmno.

In August and September 1942, during *Allgemeine Gehspere* (*Wielka Szpera*, or General Curfew), most of the Marysin orphanage children were deported to their deaths. Sheva and a few children, however, survived the Auschwitz and Stutthof concentration camps.

Close to the end of war, Sheva was driven off with the last of the Stutthof survivors to a cargo ship already loaded with a vast quantity of explosives, and then, in the middle of the Baltic Sea, the vessel was set afire. By a miracle, a handful survived, Sheva Glas-Wiener among them.

Sheva migrated to Australia in 1950, married, and had a son. She first published her stories of the lives of the children as a book in Yiddish in 1974; the book was then translated by the author and Shirley Young and published in English in 1983. Her testimony contained many stories of heroism, sharing, mutual assistance, and solicitude against a background of poverty, hunger, and death of the children under her care.

Sheva Glas-Wiener died in Melbourne on September 26, 1986, aged 70.

Further Reading

Glas-Wiener, Sheva. *Children of the Ghetto*. Fitzroy, Victoria: Globe Press, 1983.

GLASBERG, ALEXANDRE (1902-1981)

Father Alexandre Glasberg was a French Catholic priest who saved the lives of Jews (particularly children) during the Holocaust.

Alexandre was born to a Jewish family in Zhitmomir, Ukraine, in 1902, and his parents had him and his brother, Vila (later to be known as Victor Vermont), baptized when they were children. In 1921 Glasberg went to Vienna to escape anti-Jewish pogroms in the aftermath of the Russian Revolution, and while there, he undertook religious studies. In 1933 he moved to France, where he entered the seminary of Moulins prior to being ordained in 1938. He was appointed vicar of the parish of Notre-Dame de Saint-Alban, a poor suburb of Lyon, whose pastor, Father Laurent Remilleux, was a pioneer in providing welfare and relief to refugees.

After the Nazis occupied France in 1940, Glasberg was appointed by Cardinal **Pierre-Marie Gerlier** of Lyon as delegate to the Committee to Aid Refugees, and from there he began playing an active role in the French Resistance. He started by hiding political refugees from the Nazis but extended this to working with the OSE, a Jewish organization dedicated to rescuing Jewish children.

In early 1942, alongside of Father Pierre Chaillet, Jean-Marie Soutou, and a young student, Germaine Ribière, he founded the resistance group *Amitié Chrétienne* ("Christian Friendship"), whose purpose was to help Jews and other victims of Nazism from being interned in French camps. He created a network of five absorption centers stretching throughout southern France and established shelters to take in hundreds of Jews who had been released from French internment camps.

In the summer of 1942, with the start of large-scale arrests of Jews in southern France, Glasberg began forging the identities of those he was trying to rescue and stepped up the pace of his activities. He actively participated in the rescue of 180 Jewish children held in the camp at Vénissieux, near Lyon, while moving others through various safe houses. He also worked with Jewish rescue associations and made sure that the Jewish children living in his shelters were not pressured into converting to Catholicism.

In December 1942 he was forced to go into hiding after French police and the Gestapo tried to arrest him. Soon thereafter, in early 1943, a fictitious position was created for him by Pierre-Marie Théas, Bishop of Montauban, under the false name of Father Elie Corvin. He was appointed pastor of the Honor-de-Cos in the hamlet of Léribosc, in the department of Tarn-et-Garonne. During this period, he was an active member of the Resistance, occupying a position within the Departmental Liberation Committee chaired by Paul Guiral.

While he was in hiding, his brother, Vila, took charge of rescue activities, but on August 16, 1943, the Gestapo, mistaking Vila for Father Alexandre, arrested, deported, and murdered him. Father Glasberg continued to evade the Gestapo and survived the war in hiding.

After 1945 Glasberg helped facilitate the emigration of Holocaust survivors to Palestine, participating in the activities of *Aliyah Bet*, the illegal campaign helping Jews migrate from Europe to what was then still Mandate Palestine under British control. He was closely involved with the ship *Exodus 1947*, a celebrated case in which some 4,515 Jewish refugees and displaced persons forced their way into Palestine under the guns of Britain's Royal Navy. Glasberg and Rose Warfman, *née* Gluck, a survivor of Auschwitz and member of the French Resistance, made false identity papers for the passengers, the easier to facilitate their arrival in Palestine upon landing.

After the establishment of the State of Israel on May 14, 1948, Glasberg also worked with the Israeli intelligence organization Mossad in assisting the migration process. Beyond this, he used his position as a Catholic priest in order to enable Israeli soldiers to maintain communication through East and West Jerusalem during the War of Independence and was one of those responsible for purchasing weapons in Czechoslovakia and facilitating their transit through Corsica to Israel. In 1951 he participated in the airlift organized by the Mossad to evacuate Iraqi Jews, Operation EZRA AND NEHEMIAH, and assisted in the mass emigration of Jews from Morocco and Egypt.

Father Alexandre Glasberg died in France in 1981. In 2004, he and his brother Vila were both recognized as Righteous among the Nations by Yad Vashem. An argument was put by many observers at the time that if they had still been alive, the brothers would probably have preferred to have been identified as Jews rather than those "among the nations." It was acknowledged, however, that because the status of "righteous" is only awarded to non-Jews, they could not have been recognized for their work by Yad Vashem if that had happened.

Further Reading

Lazare, Lucien. *The Mission of Abbé Glasberg in the French Resistance during WWII*. Oegstgeest, Netherlands: Amsterdam Publishers, 2016.

GUNDEN, LOIS (1915-2005)

Lois Mary Gunden was an American Mennonite and professor of French who helped rescue and shelter war orphans—including Jewish children—in France during World War II. In 2013, Israel's Yad Vashem posthumously recognized her as one of the Righteous among the Nations for her work and sacrifice. She was only the fourth American to have been so recognized.

Lois was born on February 25, 1915, in Flanagan, Illinois, into a Mennonite family. She graduated from Goshen College in 1936 and received a master's degree in French from Peabody College in 1939. That same year, she secured a position teaching French at Goshen College. In 1941, at the age of 26, Lois joined the Mennonite Central Committee, which was dedicated to saving Jewish children and child refugees in France. Her tasks also included overseeing a food distribution program in several outlying villages.

She embarked on the S.S. *Excambion* in New York on October 4, 1941, and after arriving in Lyon became affiliated with *Secours Mennonite aux Enfants* (Mennonite Children's Rescue) and began work establishing a rescue mission and orphanage along France's southern coast. She had not been involved with overseas relief work before and had never been to Europe.

The Mennonite Church had secured a large 20-room summer home on the shores of the Mediterranean, the Ville St. Christophe refugee children's home in Canet-Plage (now Canet-en-Roussillon), just 30 miles north of the Spanish border. On October 22, 1941, Lois began her rescue work, keeping a diary that described her activities. (This was later to form the base upon which she wrote a short memoir, published in 1945.) She began her work caring for 60 children, ranging from toddlers to teenagers. She took in several young Spanish refugees as well as Jewish children who had been imprisoned with their families at Rivesaltes internment camp administered by the collaborationist Vichy French government. Many of the children were severely malnourished, and Lois and the other workers at the home, many of whom were refugees themselves, patiently nursed the children back to health.

Despite great personal peril, during 1942 Lois smuggled several dozen Jewish children out of Rivesaltes, often only after pleading with their parents to release the children to her care. Her efforts were helped by connections with the American Friends Service Committee, a Quaker aid organization, and the OSE. The children in her charge later remarked that Lois was kind, compassionate, and fiercely determined to save as many children as she could. Lois was also sometimes ingenious in her attempts to shield her young refugees.

When the Germans were engaged in deporting Jews during August, September, and early October 1942, children under the age of 16 not already being held in the camps with one or both parents were not always apprehended, particularly if French officials knew they could already meet their quota for the scheduled transports. It was upon such a realization that Lois saw the absolute importance of moving as many Jewish children out of the camps and into the Ville St. Christophe children's home as possible—and protecting them from deportation once there.

On at least one occasion, as she recorded in her diary, she had a close encounter with the local police that she managed to navigate successfully. When French police arrived at the safe house to arrest three Jewish children, she refused to allow to them to search Ville St. Christophe. She repeatedly stalled for time, praying that the police would eventually give up and move on. In the end, they never returned, and the three children were saved.

In November 1942 the Germans occupied southern France, and even though she was now an enemy alien, Lois continued to run her home for children. She and others created an operating plan so that existing staff could continue to care for the children. The staff moved the children several months later, when German occupiers requisitioned the villa. Two months later, in January 1943, Lois was arrested and detained by the Germans. Escorted by police to Mont-Dore on January 27, 1943, she and other Americans captured in southern France were held in a hotel for several weeks before their transfer to Baden-Baden, Germany, as part of the official North American Diplomatic Group, where they were held in a resort hotel complex for more than a year. After complex negotiations for a prisoner exchange, they arrived in New York City on the *Gripsholm* on March 15, 1944.

Returning to Indiana and her teaching post at Goshen College in the fall of 1944, she subsequently began graduate work at Indiana University, and she earned a PhD in French literature in 1958. That same year, she married a widower, Ernest Clemens. Without children of her own, she gained a stepdaughter through her marriage to Clemens. The couple moved to Pennsylvania, where Lois taught at Temple University from 1965 to 1975 and North Penn High School in Lansdale, Pennsylvania.

Lois Gunden Clemens remained actively engaged in Mennonite church activities, ministering for the church and editing a national Mennonite publication covering women's missionary services. She authored a book entitled *Women Liberated* and sat on the board of overseers for Goshen College. She died in Lansdale, Pennsylvania, on August 27, 2005. On February 27, 2013, Yad Vashem recognized Lois Gunden posthumously as one of the Righteous among the Nations for her activities in rescuing Jewish children during the Holocaust. Her niece accepted the honor on her behalf in July 2013.

Further Reading

Yad Vashem. Women of Valor: Stories of Women Who Rescued Jews during the Holocaust, at http://www.yadvashem.org/yv/en/exhibitions/righteous-women/gunden.asp.

H

HAINING, JANE (1897–1944)

Jane Haining, known as the "Scottish Angel of Auschwitz," was a Church of Scotland missionary who, in 1932, was posted to Budapest as matron of a girls' home, preaching to Hungarian Jews. When war came to Hungary in March 1944, she refused to leave the 400 Jewish girls in her school, whom the Nazis found her protecting. On April 25, 1944, she was arrested on a contrived charge of "suspicion of espionage on behalf of England," as well as working among Jews, visiting British prisoners of war, and listening to the BBC. She was deported to Auschwitz, where she died on July 17, 1944, aged 47.

Jane Mathison Haining was born at Lochenhead Farm in Dunscore, Dumfriesshire, Scotland on June 6, 1897. She was the fifth child of Thomas Haining, a farmer, and his first wife, Jane Mathison. She grew up as a member of the Evangelical Craig church in Dunscore, was educated at the village school, and won a scholarship to Dumfries Academy in 1909. She trained at the commercial college of Glasgow Athenaeum and worked for 10 years as secretary to a spinning factory in Paisley. She lived in Pollokshields in Glasgow and attended Queen's Park West United Free Church.

In 1932, at the age of 35, she volunteered for service as a missionary at the Scottish Mission School in Budapest. The mission had been set up in 1841, with its key mandate being to evangelize to Hungarian Jews. A school was established in 1846. Jane liked Budapest and Hungary and soon became fluent in Hungarian. She had direct care for 50 of the school's 400 pupils.

Jane was vacationing in Cornwall in 1939 when World War II broke out, and she returned to Budapest immediately. By 1940, faced with the worsening war situation, the Scottish missionaries were ordered by their church to return home. Jane refused to leave; she believed that her charges would need her now more than ever. She wrote that if these children needed her in days of sunshine, "how much more do they need me in days of darkness."

From the very beginning of the war, Jewish refugees from Nazi-occupied European countries began arriving in Hungary. Despite Hungary's own toxic antisemitism, in 1941 it was a safer refuge for Jews compared to its neighbors. Jane regarded the Scottish Mission home as a sanctuary for her students. As early as 1938, when four Jewish child refugees from Austria had arrived at the school, Jane wrote: "What a ghastly feeling it must be to know that no one wants you and to feel that your neighbors literally grudge you your daily bread." According to one colleague, she would rise at 5:00 a.m. on market days to find food for the home and would carry the heavy bags back herself. She is reported to have cut up her leather suitcase to repair the girls' shoes. Many years later, one former student that "we understood even as third-graders, that we are protected here, we are not harmed, we are protected, and we are equals. We could see, we could understand this, because they behaved accordingly."

On March 19, 1944, German forces invaded Hungary, and the SS immediately began arranging for the country's Jews to be deported to Auschwitz. Once again Jane was ordered by the church to leave Hungary and return to Scotland, and once again she refused. On March 31, 1944 a range of anti-Jewish restrictions was introduced, one of which required that by April 5, Jews over the age of six would be required to wear a yellow star. Jane was distressed at having to sew these on her students' clothes.

She was arrested in April 1944 and detained by the Gestapo, accused, among other things, of working among Jews and listening to the BBC. She admitted all the charges except those of political activity. She was detained at Főutca prison in Buda and then moved to a holding camp in Kistarcsa. She was sent to Auschwitz in May 1944, where she was tattooed as prisoner 79467 and forced into hard labor. She sent a last postcard on July 15, 1944. In that card she wrote that she was "here on the way to heaven."

Jane Haining died at Auschwitz on July 17, 1944, aged 47, of "cachexia following intestinal catarrh"—though it is thought that she might have been gassed. She is one of 10 Scots (including three women) thought to have died in the Nazi extermination camps.

On January 27, 1997, Yad Vashem recognized Jane Haining as one of the Righteous among the Nations, and in 2010 the British government named her a British Hero of the Holocaust.

In 2016, Jane's personal effects were discovered in the attic space of the Church of Scotland's head office in George Street, Edinburgh. These included more than 70 photographs of the Jewish girls she had risked her life trying to save and several documents outlining efforts attempting to secure her release. One of these was a typed report from 1945 that Bishop László Ravasz of the Reformed Church in Hungary wrote to the Synod in Hungary about how he unsuccessfully tried to intervene with Hungarian authorities to procure Jane's release from prison before she was sent to Auschwitz. The items were placed in the National Library of Scotland.

Among the memorials to Jane Haining are two stained-glass windows in Queen's Park Govanhill Parish Church of Scotland in Glasgow, where she worshipped; a plaque in the little Kirk of Dunscore; and two plaques in the Scottish mission in Budapest. A memorial cairn to Jane now stands between Dunscore Kirk and the village graveyard, made possible by public donation. Arguably her major memorial was the naming, in 2010, of a section of the main riverside road on the Pest side between the Chain and Elizabeth bridges as the "Jane Haining Embankment."

Further Reading

Brown, Gordon. *Wartime Courage: Stories of Extraordinary Courage by Exceptional Men and Women in World War Two*. London: Bloomsbury, 2008.

Miller, Mary. *Jane Haining: A Life of Love and Courage*. Edinburgh: Birlinn, 2019.

HANA'S SUITCASE

Hana Brady was a Czechoslovak Jewish girl murdered on October 23, 1944, at Auschwitz. Her story became known when a suitcase bearing her name and birthdate were sent to a Japanese Holocaust Center in Tokyo. The center director, Fumiko Ishioka, made many attempts to learn about its owner.

Hana Brady was born Hanička Bradyová on May 16, 1931, in Prague to Markéta (*née* Dubsky) and Karel Brady. Her family lived in Nové Město in the Moravian region of Czechoslovakia. She had a happy life until Germany's occupation of the country on March 15, 1939, when the family became subjected to the Nuremberg Laws. As the months passed, Hana and her older brother George (Jiří) could no longer go to the movies, play in the park, or skate on the lake. By 1940, when Hana was in third grade, she and George were no longer allowed to go to school. They were the only Jewish children in the district, and under the new arrangements, her friends become afraid to associate with her. Forced to wear a yellow star, she henceforth remained at home.

Hana and George watched in 1941 as first their mother was arrested and taken to Ravensbrück and then, within months, their father was also arrested. They never saw either of their parents again. They had an aunt, Hedda, who was married to Ludvik, a non-Jew, and the two children went to live with them. There they received letters from their father. On April 30, 1942 the children were sent a notice that they were to report to a deportation center, and on May 14, 1942, when Hana was just 11 years old, both children were sent to **Theresienstadt**, where they were housed separately. Within a year the children's grandmother arrived in Theresienstadt but died of starvation and illness within three months of her arrival. In October 1944, Hana and George were deported to Auschwitz; whereas George survived by working as a laborer, Hana was sent to the gas chambers a few hours after her arrival on October 23, 1944.

In 1998 an anonymous donor endowed the Tokyo Holocaust Education Resource Center in Japan, dedicated to teaching Japanese children about the Holocaust and thereby contribute to global tolerance and understanding. At a Children's Forum on the Holocaust held in 1999, 200 students from schools in the Tokyo area met with Yaffa Eliach, a Holocaust survivor. She told them that children have the power to create peace in the future. Fumiko Ishioka then formed a dozen or so students aged 8 to 18 into a group called Small Wings, which met monthly, published a newsletter, and worked under Fumiko's guidance.

Fumiko sought to teach the children using physical objects they could see and touch. She wrote to Holocaust museums seeking a loan of artifacts but was turned down on the basis that her museum was too small and too far away. In the fall of 1999, she visited the Auschwitz Museum in Poland, which sent her a package containing a child's sock and shoe, a child's sweater, and a Zyklon-B gas canister, contained in a suitcase. The suitcase was big, brown, battered about the edges, with a polka-dot patterned lining. Across the front of the case was the name Hanna (sic) Brady, date of birth May 16, 1931, and the word *Waisenkind*, the German word for orphan. The suitcase was the only object linked to a name held by the Center. The Small Wings worked out that Hana had been 13 when she was sent to Auschwitz. They wanted to know more, but the Auschwitz Museum knew nothing else about Hana. Fumiko wrote to Yad Vashem in Jerusalem; it was unable to assist but referred her to the U.S. Holocaust Memorial Museum in Washington, D.C., which also had nothing. Then the Auschwitz Museum wrote to Fumiko informing her that Hana had been sent to Auschwitz from Theresienstadt.

Fumiko undertook further research about Theresienstadt and learned that while Jews had been sent from there to Auschwitz, the inmates had set up classes to teach the children how to paint and draw. She learned that some 4,500 drawings had survived the war and hoped that some of these might have included drawings from Hana. She wrote to the Terezín Ghetto Museum, which sent her photographs of five of Hana's paintings.

The newsletter of the Small Wings then solicited letters, poems, and paintings from Japanese school children who visited the Tokyo Holocaust Center. From this, Fumiko received enough material from visiting children to set up an exhibition called "The Holocaust through Children's Eyes." Visitors were most interested in the suitcase and wondered what Hana had looked like. Fumiko wrote to back to the Terezín Ghetto Museum seeking more information. Receiving no response, she decided to visit Theresienstadt herself, arriving on July 11, 2000. She only had a day set aside for the visit and had not made any appointments ahead. It was a public holiday and the Museum was closed. But Fumiko found a woman named Ludmila working in the archives and asked for information on Hana Brady. Ludmila located a book detailing the 90,000 Jews who had been transferred from Theresienstadt to Auschwitz and found Hana's name and that of her brother George. Hana's name was marked as one who never returned, but George's was on a list of inmates indicating that he had survived, together with a Kurt Kotuoc, whom Ludmila knew to be a child survivor. Ludmila referred her to the Prague Jewish Museum, and in Prague the Jewish Museum located Kurt Kotuoc, who was working as an art historian. Not only did he remember George Brady, but he had contact details from him in Canada.

On Fumiko's return to Tokyo, she sent a parcel and letter to George Brady in Canada, telling him that his little sister was being honored at the Center. George then wrote to Fumiko, enclosing copies of his photographs of Hana. He also told Fumiko about the life Hana had in her hometown of Nove Mesto, about her family, and how she loved to ski and dance. He also told Fumiko about his Canadian family. After this, George visited Fumiko in Tokyo with his daughter Lara. He told Hana's story and looked at her suitcase, while the Small Wings group presented him with their pictures and poems.

The suitcase still sits in a glass cabinet at the Tokyo Holocaust Center. While visitors knew beforehand that it was from Auschwitz, they now know who Hana was, that she came from Czechoslovakia, what she looked like, and what happened to her. In February 2004 it was discovered by Lara Brady, George's daughter, that the suitcase was in fact not the original, but a replica. The real suitcase, on loan, was destroyed by neo-Nazi arsonists in 1984, who set fire to a warehouse where it was stored in Birmingham, in the United Kingdom.

The story of Hana Brady, and how her suitcase led Fumiko to Toronto, was printed in the *Canadian Jewish News*. It was then the subject of a CBC radio documentary. Karen M. Levine, producer of that documentary, wrote the story as a nonfiction children's book published in 2002. It became a best seller and was translated into some 40 languages.

A play based on the book was written by Emil Sher and made into a documentary film, *Inside Hana's Suitcase*, directed by Larry Weinstein; this premiered in Canada on April 30, 2009. In 2011, a Hebrew version of the play was staged by the Nephesh Theater in Holon, Israel.

In 2012, a 10th Anniversary Edition of *Hana's Suitcase* was released, featuring 60 pages of bonus material, including updates from the author, from Hana's brother George, and from Fumiko Ishioka. It also included some of the many letters, tributes, poems, art, and photographs sent in by children who have cared about Hana's story. Nobel Laureate Archbishop Desmond Tutu wrote the foreword.

Further Reading

Levine, Karen. *Hana's Suitcase* (Anniversary Edition). Sydney: Allen and Unwin, 2014.

HART, KITTY (b.1926)

Kitty Hart was born on December 1, 1926 in Bielsko (Bielitz), a Polish town bordering Germany and Czechoslovakia. From the age of 12, she and her family were on the run from the Nazis. Kitty and her mother Lola survived six prisons and camps, including Auschwitz, as well as forced labor at I. G. Farben's rubber plant in Bittersfeld and at Phillips's electronics factory near Breslau (Wrocław).

Kitty Hart (*née* Felix) was born to Karol Felix and his wife, Lola. Kitty had a brother, Robert, who was five years older than her. Karol Felix had studied law in Vienna and in World War I had served as a captain in the Austro-Hungarian Army. On his father's death, Karol and his sister took over the family farm and agricultural supply business. Lola had studied English in London at Bedford College and returned to Poland to teach advanced English to children.

Bielsko was part of Austria-Hungary, and most of its residents were German speakers. The Felix family spoke German at home; Kitty did not speak Polish until she began school, while she learned English from her mother. Kitty was very fit and competed in skiing, swimming, gymnastics, and athletics. She and Robert would hike in the mountains in summer and ski in winter. The family was prosperous, middle class, and nonobservant, only attending synagogue occasionally.

HART, KITTY (b.1926)

Initially Kitty went to a Jewish primary school, and later she studied at the Convent School of Notre Dame, a prestigious private all-girls school that, although not Jewish, was mostly attended by Jews. Kitty only attended for one year, after which the war broke out. She was initially oblivious to antisemitism. During her year at Notre Dame, a girl joining her school said that she and her family were expelled from Germany for being Jews, and shortly after this, Kitty and her Jewish swimming team were stoned during a competition.

In late August 1939, while on vacation in the mountains with her mother, she was called home, and her father put Kitty and Lola on board a train to Lublin. Two days later, Karol and Robert joined them, having boarded one of the last trains east before Germany's invasion of Poland on September 1, 1939.

In time, all Jews in Lublin were relocated to a ghetto in a single area of the city. In the winter of 1940–1941, the family endeavored to escape to Russia, arriving at the border only to find that it had closed 24 hours earlier. Trying to cross the frozen river by sleigh they were shot at, so they returned to the Polish side.

Karol Felix was able to obtain false passports, birth certificates, and identity cards, and the family split up to increase their chances of survival. With these documents, Kitty and Lola were smuggled onto a train of Polish forced laborers bound for Germany. They were sent to Bittersfeld to work at I. G. Farben's rubber and munitions factory.

On March 13, 1943, Kitty, Lola, and 12 other women suspected of being Jewish were betrayed and taken by the Gestapo. Three days later they were charged with endangering the security of the Third Reich and unlawfully entering Germany with false papers; all were sentenced to death by firing squad. Camp guards conducted a mock execution, firing shots into the air, and the victims were then told their sentences had been commuted to life imprisonment at Auschwitz.

Kitty and Lola were transferred to a prison in Dresden, and then, on April 2, 1943, they arrived at Auschwitz. Kitty's family had now been on the run since she was 12. She wrote later that at Auschwitz, the obedient prisoner who stuck to the rules only lived for three to six weeks; camp food could not maintain life for longer. Kitty and her mother, however, managed to survive for almost two years. They found jobs working with dead prisoners, which was less physically demanding than jobs beyond the wire. For inmates, working outside was a death sentence.

For eight months Kitty was lucky enough to work with a group of inmates sorting through the possessions of prisoners deported by train to Auschwitz. In that place, known as "Canada," she regained her strength and her health after a bout of typhus, because she had access to food and water. Kitty and Lola took items from the looted possessions; these and other items were traded with other prisoners.

Kitty sorted through men's jackets; each jacket had to be searched for loot—gold, jewelry, money. Any inmate caught with valuable items would be punished with death. Currency found was of no value to prisoners, who used it as toilet paper. Inmates ate from decomposing piles of food that littered the place, even though this was forbidden.

Kitty's witnessing of the mass murders put her life at risk. Her work close to the four crematoria and gas chambers meant that she saw mass killing from April to November 1944, at the peak of the murders. She wrote later that her brain could not accept what she was watching. Among those who died, she learned afterward, were 30 members of her own family.

In August 1944 rumors circulated that Auschwitz was to be evacuated. Lola was selected as one of 100 prisoners to be removed from the camp. Lola, who had been working in the camp hospital, saw the camp commandant, Franz Hössler, walking; she pleaded that her daughter be allowed to leave the camp with her. Lola was in her 50s; there were no other women of that age, and she spoke respectful, formal German. Hössler obliged. Lola's conversation probably saved Kitty's life.

On November 11, 1944, Kitty and Lola, with several hundred other prisoners, were taken to Gross-Rosen concentration camp, near Breslau, then in eastern Germany. Every day, the prisoners were marched to a nearby town to work in the Philips electronics factory. On February 18, 1945, in response to Allied advances, Kitty, Lola, and the others were forced to trek on a two-week death march over the Sudeten Mountains, without food or shelter. After the march, the prisoners were put on open coal trucks and taken 1,000 kilometers across Europe to work in an underground factory in Porta Westfalica in northwestern Germany. Only about 200 of the original 10,000 prisoners who had set out from Gross-Rosen, including Kitty and her mother, survived the journey.

Sometime in March 1945, Kitty and Lola were sent to the Bergen-Belsen concentration camp. There they were abandoned in a locked cattle truck and left to die; many suffocated. The prisoners took turns breathing through a crack in the floor. Suddenly the door was pulled open by three German soldiers, and the survivors were taken to a nearby subcamp for women located outside Salzwedel, capable of holding more than 1,000 female prisoners. Eventually over 3,000 women were held there, both Jews and non-Jews. In the second week of April 1945, the SS guards disappeared, and on April 14, the camp was liberated by American troops.

Kitty and Lola began working as translators for the British Army. Later, they helped with the Quaker Relief Team in a displaced persons camp, outside Braunschweig. Here they found that they were the only survivors of their family. Karol Felix had been murdered by the Gestapo. Robert Felix died during the fighting in the Soviet Union. Kitty's grandmother was murdered at Bełzec.

Their work for the British Army earned Kitty and Lola special permits to live in Britain, and they started a new life in Birmingham. Kitty married Rudi Hart, and had two sons. Besides her work for Holocaust survivors and victims, Kitty became a nurse at the Birmingham Royal Orthopedic Hospital, after which she qualified as a radiologist. Later she helped her husband set up his own upholstery business. For more than 50 years, Kitty committed herself to fostering an understanding of the Holocaust through her writing, talking to school groups and public meetings, and through documentaries.

Further Reading

Hart, Kitty. *I Am Alive*. London: Transworld Publishers, 1962.
Hart, Kitty. *Return to Auschwitz: The Remarkable Story of the Girl Who Survived the Holocaust*. London: Atheneum, 1983.

HELGA'S DIARY

Helga Weiss was born in Prague on November 10, 1929, as Helga Hošková-Weissová. Her father, Otto, a talented musician, had served and been wounded in World War I and went on to work in the Czechoslovakian state bank. Her mother, Irena, was a seamstress by trade. After Germany's invasion of March 1939, the family experienced the imposition of Nazi antisemitic measures: as a Jewish girl, she was forbidden from attending regular school, and her father was thrown out of state employment. When not yet aged 10, Helga began keeping a record of what she saw happening around her, as well as drawing and painting various scenes of daily life.

On December 10, 1941, soon after Helga's 12th birthday, she and her parents were sent to the Terezín ghetto, known in German as **Theresienstadt**. Allowed a maximum of 50 kilograms of luggage to take with them, they packed their clothes and personal items. Helga took with her two small dolls, a sketch pad, watercolors, and crayons. Once at Theresienstadt, the family was split up, with Otto sent to the men's barracks and Helga and Irena remaining together. Later, Helga was relocated to a *Kinderheim* (children's home), where she roomed with girls of her own age. Together, they managed to reclaim a semblance of social life in which they enjoyed some of the features of daily existence they had left behind. And although Helga and her parents were separated, they managed to see each other and exchange notes from time to time.

Soon after her arrival at Terezín, Helga drew a picture, which she smuggled to her father. His advice upon receiving the gift was that she should from this point on "draw what you see." She then began to record life as she witnessed it. Her pictures showed various aspects of daily activity: food queues; women and girls in the washroom; a sick girl; a bread cart; people on stretchers; and other scenes. Her drawings, like those of many other children at Terezín, became a testament of what everyday life was like for Jews in the ghetto. For the next three years, Helga documented her experiences in both written form through the diary and through her paintings.

On October 4, 1944, now aged 15, Helga and Irena were deported to Auschwitz. Just before she left, she managed to smuggle her diary, together with other papers and some drawings, to her Uncle Josef, who worked in the Terezín records department. He hid the materials by bricking them into a wall. Here they remained until after the war, when Uncle Josef reclaimed them.

At Auschwitz, during the process known as selection—which might have been conducted by Dr. **Josef Mengele**—Helga learned through whispers that the older she could portray herself, the greater would be the possibility of staying alive. She pulled off the deception, and she also claimed successfully that her mother was younger than she was in actuality. They thus both managed to obtain entry to the camp rather than being murdered on arrival, an achievement not matched by most children and their mothers sent to Auschwitz.

Ten days after arriving at Auschwitz, Helga and Irena were transferred to Freiberg, a labor camp near Dresden. They worked there as slave labor for five months, but near the end of the war, they were moved on—in a hellish journey lasting 16 days—to the camp at Mauthausen, in Austria. Here they remained until the camp was liberated by U.S. forces on May 5, 1945.

After the war, Helga continued working on her Terezín diary, recording from memory everything that happened after it had been hidden and she had been deported to Auschwitz. Later, the notebooks the diary comprised were found at the bottom of a drawer and were handed across to Venetia Butterfield, a British publisher who had learned about the diary's existence in 2010 when Helga came to London for a concert to commemorate Terezín. Reconstructed from these original notebooks, the diary was then published by Norton in the United States in 2013 as *Helga's Diary: A Young Girl's Account of Life in a Concentration Camp*. The book contains an introduction by noted American writer Francine Prose and a detailed, frank interview between translator Neil Bermel and Helga, then in her mid-80s. It is also illustrated with several of Helga's drawings and paintings from her time in Terezín.

A total of 15,000 children from Czechoslovakia and other places were taken to Terezín. Most were deported to Auschwitz, and no more than 100 are known to have survived the Holocaust. Helga was one of this tiny number who managed to live to tell the tale of what had happened—not only by speaking about her experience (which she did in later life) but also through her contemporary observations in the diary and her paintings and drawings. The result is a vivid and unique firsthand historical document about the Holocaust written by a true expert.

Further Reading

Weiss, Helga. *Helga's Diary: A Young Girl's Account of Life in a Concentration Camp*. New York: Norton, 2013.

HEYMAN, ÉVA (1931–1944)

Éva Heyman was a Hungarian Jewish girl who kept a diary during the Holocaust and died in Auschwitz at age 13. Although her diary only covered a short period, from the first entry on February 13, 1944 (her 13th birthday), to the final entry on May 30, 1944, the entries detail the atrocities experienced by her family and their stress under the Nazi occupation.

Éva was born on February 13, 1931, in Oradea, Romania, to Agnes (*née* Racz) and Bela Heyman, who were both architects. Oradea, which had been part of Romania since 1919, was renamed Nagyvárad and transferred to Hungary in 1940.

In early 1944 Éva was living with her grandparents, as she had for most of her life; her parents had divorced, and her mother had remarried a Jewish writer and publicist, Bela Zsolt. Éva began her diary shortly before German forces entered Hungary on March 19, 1944, and the restrictions on Jews became even more severe. Éva called her diary "my best friend" and spilled out her fears into it. One of the rare diaries written by a young person in this part of Europe during the war, Éva's diary showed that she anticipated her likely fate under German occupation, as her friend Marta and her Polish family had been deported and killed. She also knew that roundups of Jews had already begun in Budapest, and many killings, including those of children, had occurred. On March 28, 1944, she wrote in her diary that she did not want to die because she "had hardly lived." Her diary recorded the eviction of Jews from their homes, her own experiences of oppression, including the forced wearing of the yellow star, the speedy seizure of private possessions, the departure of the family's Christian cook and friend Mariska Szabó, and the arrest of her father.

On May 1, 1944, the family was told they would be moved into a ghetto in the Jewish district of Nagyvárad, which occurred on May 4, 1944. Éva described this as a demeaning and upsetting move. She diarized that everything was forbidden, and that punishments included death. The family remained in the ghetto for one month. Éva continued to confide to her diary her growing fear that she would be murdered like her friend Marta.

May 15, 1944, marked the start of the deportation of Hungarian Jewry. On May 30, 1944, Éva made her last diary entry. She passed her diary to Mariska Szabó when she visited Éva in the ghetto on May 30, 1944.

Éva and her grandparents were arrested and deported to Auschwitz on June 2, 1944. Her grandparents died there, and Éva was transferred to Birkenau on June 6, 1944. Here, her cousin, Marcia Kecskeméti, died in her arms. At the age of 13, Éva was herself gassed on October 17, 1944. Evidence suggests that Dr. **Josef Mengele** personally pushed Éva onto a truck to be sent to the gas chamber.

Éva's mother and stepfather had escaped to the Oradea typhus hospital and were sent from there to Budapest, prior to being placed onto a special train for Switzerland organized by Rezső Kasztner in December 1944. After the end of the war, Agnes Zsolt came back to search for her daughter, only to receive the details of how she had been killed. She was given Éva's secret diary by Mariska Szabó. After this, completely grief-stricken, Agnes Zsolt succumbed to a downward spiral of self-destructiveness and despair and committed suicide.

The diary was originally published in Hungarian in 1947, then in Hebrew as *Yomanah shel Evah Hayman* (*The Diary of Éva Heyman*) in 1964. It first appeared in English as *The Diary of Eva Heyman* in 1974 before a revised edition was published in 1988. In 2012, a research center for Jewish history was opened at the University of Oradea (Nagyvárad) that was named after Éva Heyman, and in 2015 the city dedicated a statue in memory of the children of the town who were murdered in the Holocaust. In 2017 a theatrical performance entitled *Eva Heyman: **Anne Frank** of Transylvania* was staged in Romania based on Éva's story.

On May 2, 2019, the *Eva.Stories* project was launched, visually depicting extracts from the diary on Instagram. Produced with a multimillion-dollar budget, 400 staff and actors, and elaborate sets, including tanks and train carriages, the stream of dozens of mini-stories was aired throughout Yom Hashoah (Holocaust

Remembrance Day) and described the story by picturing Éva as recording her days on a smartphone. The portrayal of the diary featured hashtags, internet jargon, and emojis as employed by a 21st-century teenager.

The attempt to represent the diary using Instagram generated considerable controversy, with critics arguing that Instagram's short, flashy videos trivialized the Holocaust. In response, its creators, Mati Kochavi, an Israeli hi-tech billionaire who is from a family of Holocaust victims and survivors, and his daughter, Maya, said that they produced the Instagram version to refresh what they saw as fading memories of the Holocaust, and to tell the story to future generations that will never get to meet those personally impacted by the experience. They argued, further, that the videos make the story easy to digest and share, especially considering the shorter attention spans of social media users.

Further Reading

Boas, Jacob (Ed.). *We Are Witnesses: Five Diaries of Teenagers Who Died in the Holocaust.* New York: Henry Holt, 1995.
Heyman, Éva. *The Diary of Éva Heyman.* New York: Shapolsky, 1988.

HIDDEN CHILDREN

Nazi racial ideology saw Jews as "subhumans" (*Untermenschen*) who should be eradicated. This included children, even infants. Considering this, some Jewish children stayed alive by being hidden, their identities concealed or kept away from the outside world.

There were several ways of concealing children. Some were secreted with a parent in a hidden space, such as a farmhouse barn or a secret attic. To hide in this way, the child and parent needed the active assistance of a non-Jewish helper to supply their food and other needs. Some children were placed in convents, where they survived by **passing** as Catholic children. The child would have to learn, and be word perfect with, Catholic rituals and prayers: to know how to recite them, to follow the Mass, narrate the Rosary, and follow Catholic practices.

Sometimes a child was hidden with a non-Jewish family and raised as part of the family unit. Often these were young children or babies, and the host family might explain the new child as a relative from elsewhere whose home had been destroyed. Some of these fostering arrangements were negotiated by the OSE as part of their activities in France.

The risk to all who helped hide Jewish children was enormous, and if they were denounced, it was possible that all helpers might be murdered in retribution. Hidden children feared raids, denunciations, and betrayals, and if caught, many were destined to die in concentration camps.

A few older children survived on their own or in small groups by hiding in cellars and sewers, on farms, and in forests. Like other children in hiding, they had false names and papers, and they had to fend for themselves. Hidden children had to cope daily with fear, difficulties, and danger. Any careless words or the curiosity of prying neighbors could lead to denunciation, discovery, and death; and without parental support, the child might be dependent on the care of strangers.

The everyday feelings of hidden children differed, depending on whether they could attend school and socialize with others their own age or had to be physically concealed. Those who could not play outside found life in hiding repressive and all too often filled with pain, torment, and boredom. Reading, playing, and creative expression could help to fill seemingly endless hours and temporarily divert the child's attention from his or her desperate situation. For some, the writing of **diaries and journals** served as an outlet for this.

After the war, like almost all **child survivors**, hidden children only rarely regained their parents, who generally had been murdered by the Nazis. Often a young child had grown to love the foster family, and many such families were traumatized by the removal of the child after the war by a family survivor or Jewish organization. Many hidden children who survived did not speak after the war about their experiences because they were emotionally still in hiding years later. And compounding their distress was that they were often not recognized as "legitimate" among Holocaust survivors, who told them that they had not suffered as much as survivors of camps and ghettos. In certain instances, because of this, some were not entitled to reparations from the German government in the years that followed.

In 1980 the First International Hidden Child Gathering took place, coterminous with the appearance of a documentary about the rescue of over 4,000 children in Belgium during the Holocaust, *As If It Were Yesterday* (*Comme si c'était hier*), produced by filmmaker Myriam Abramowicz. This first conference enabled the hidden child survivors to express themselves without having to justify how their childhood was shaped.

In 2014 the German government, through the Claims Conference, made an extra restitution payment of €2,500 to each hidden child over and above any other restitution for Holocaust experiences to which they were entitled. This recognized that any physical or emotional trauma suffered by a child would be greater than that suffered by an adult in similar circumstances, because the child would not yet have developed full mature coping skills. The amount being paid, though a recognition, was nonetheless in reality only a small token payment.

The Hidden Child Foundation, a partner organization supported by the Anti-Defamation League, is based in New York. Established in 1991, it keeps in close contact with a worldwide membership, and it liaises between the U.S. government and hidden child survivor groups. It provides cultural and social programs for those living in the New York area while honoring all rescuers, including those recognized as Righteous among the Nations, on International Rescuers' Day. The Foundation advocates for all members, including those of the **Second Generation** (and beyond) who need financial, psychological, or social assistance, as well as providing a Speakers' Bureau for all audiences. The Foundation publishes that its mission is to educate all people about the consequences of bigotry and hatred in the hope that no one will ever again suffer the atrocities and injustices endured by those who lived through the Holocaust.

Further Reading

Krell, Robert. *Child Holocaust Survivors—Memories and Reflections.* Victoria, BC: Trafford Publishing, 2007.
Moskovitz, Sarah. *Love Despite Hate: Child Survivors of the Holocaust and Their Adult Lives.* New York: Schocken Books, 1983.
Valent, Paul. *Child Survivors of the Holocaust.* Melbourne: William Heinemann, 1993.

HIRSCH, ALFRED (FREDY) (1916–1944)

Alfred (Fredy) Hirsch was a Jewish athlete born in Aachen, Germany. In 1935 he fled from Germany to Czechoslovakia, but after the Nazis occupied Prague in 1938, he was sent to **Theresienstadt** (Terezín), before being deported to Auschwitz. In both camps he took care of children's education, and the regimen he introduced—demanding strict hygiene, exercise, and discipline—lowered their mortality rates.

Alfred Hirsch was born on February 11, 1916, the second son of Heinrich and Olga Hirsch. His older brother, Paul, was born in 1914. Heinrich Hirsch, a butcher, died when Fredy was 10 years old, after which Olga remarried. The boys attended the Aachener Couven-Gymnasium. At 15 years old, Fredy was already giving lectures, and he left school in March 1931 to lead the Aachen **Jewish youth movement**. In 1932 he helped found the Aachen branch of the German Jewish Scouting Association (*Jüdischer Pfadfinderbund Deutschland*, or JPD), an organization affiliated with *Maccabee Hatziar*, a Zionist sporting association.

In 1933 he moved to Frankfurt and led a Scout group there. Pursued by rumors that he was gay—though not accused of inappropriate behavior or misconduct—he moved to Dresden in 1934 to work as a sports instructor for *Maccabee Hatziar*.

In 1935, the Nuremberg Laws were enacted, and Paragraph 175 of the German Criminal Code outlawing homosexuality was expanded. Now 19 years old, Fredy fled to Prague, where he was active in *Maccabee Hatzair* and the Zionist *Hechalutz* organization, having convinced the chairman of *Maccabee Hatziar* in Czechoslovakia that his homosexuality did not impact his work. He ran summer camps to prepare young Jews to migrate to Palestine.

From October 1936 to April 1939, Fredy and his partner, Jan Mautner (a medical student from Olomouc), lived together in Brno, where they published the Maccabee newspaper. Sponsored by the Zionist World Federation, Fredy set up local youth and adult physical education groups. He managed the 1937 Maccabee Games for Czechoslovakia held in Žilina with 1,600 participants. After Brno refused him a residence permit and threatened to expel him, he returned to Prague. Working at the Zionist Youth Aliyah School run by Egon (Gonda) Redlich, he prepared young Jews seeking to immigrate to Palestine, training them in horticulture, agriculture, and basic military training. Until 1940 he organized an annual Czech camp where youth exercised and learned Hebrew. Fredy Hirsch viewed physical education as essential to promoting well-being and a Zionist consciousness.

After the German occupation of the Czech lands during 1938 and 1939, Fredy continued to prepare young Jews for emigration. In October 1939, 18 boys he had trained escaped to Denmark, from where they migrated to Palestine in 1940. Fredy drew lots as to who would accompany them; he lost and remained in Prague, where Jan Mautner joined him.

After the Nazis banned Czech Jews from public spaces, Fredy organized a playground at Hagibor, Prague, to enable Jewish children to exercise. Fredy and Jan Mautner ran soccer matches, athletic competitions, study groups, and theatrical performances there. As Fredy spoke Czech poorly, he taught the classes in Hebrew. **Dita Kraus** was one of Fredy's students.

In late 1941 the Nazis began deporting Czech Jews, first to the Łódź ghetto. Fredy helped those being deported to prepare the 50 kilograms of luggage they were permitted to take with them.

On December 4, 1941, Fredy was himself transported to Theresienstadt. Working under Gonda Redlich, he became the deputy leader of the Youth Services Department. Jan Mautner was deported to Theresienstadt in early 1942.

At Theresienstadt, children lived separately from adults. Fredy maintained their self-esteem through discipline, regular exercise, and strict hygiene as a means to maximize their chances of survival. Together with Redlich, he educated the children (despite this being prohibited), teaching Hebrew, English, mathematics, history, and geography. They arranged separate barracks and slightly better conditions for the children. While occasionally they were able to remove children from transports taking them to extermination camps, more than 99 percent of the children at Theresienstadt were eventually deported.

Children aged 14 and older had to work; Fredy got them jobs in the vegetable gardens to improve their health and prepare them for life in Palestine, at the same time negotiating space for a play area inside the camp.

On August 24, 1943, 1,200 children from the Białystok ghetto arrived at Theresienstadt. The **Białystok Children** were separated from the rest of the camp by a barbed-wire fence and kept strictly segregated from the general population. Fredy, however, jumped the fence; he was arrested, brought to the commandant's office, beaten, and deported to Auschwitz with other Jews on September 8, 1943.

On arrival at Auschwitz, this group received privileged treatment. They lived in a separate block (BIIb), known as the Theresienstadt family camp. Tattooed, they avoided selection on arrival, retained their civilian clothes, and did not have their heads shaved. Families could write to relatives at Theresienstadt and even to friends in neutral countries to convey that "deportation to the East" did not necessarily mean death.

Fredy Hirsch was appointed as kapo of the family camp because the SS respected his leadership. He refused to use violence against other prisoners and asked to be released from this position so he could manage the children. Replaced by Arno Böhm, a German criminal, Fredy persuaded Böhm to allocate a barracks, Block 31, for children younger than 14. Fredy then oversaw Block 31 as the *Blockältester* (block elder). Each morning, counselors would bring those aged between 8 and 14, who lived with their parents, to the children's block. Children spent the day at Block 31, where they were taught German, history, music, and Judaism. There were only 12 books and few supplies, so teachers taught from memory. A children's opera, **Brundibár**, was performed. The walls of Block 31 were decorated with

Disney characters and other images by Dina Gottliebová. Block 31 was so orderly that it was shown off to the SS, who visited frequently and helped organize better food for the children.

Fredy also convinced the Germans to hold roll call inside the barracks, so the children were spared the hours-long ordeal of standing outside in all weather. After another transport arrived in December 1943, there were about 700 children in the family camp; Jan Mautner was also on this transport.

Arno Böhm later allocated Fredy a second barracks for children aged three to eight so that the older children could prepare a performance of Snow White. The play was performed on January 23, 1944, with many SS officers attending.

Fredy's strict hygiene regime required the children washed daily, even in the frigid winter of 1943–1944, and there were regular inspections for lice. Further, his discipline code ensured that there were no acts of violence or theft in the barracks. Under Fredy's management, the mortality rate for the children was nearly zero, compared to the overall mortality of about 25 percent of residents in the family camp during the first six months. On February 11, 1944, his 28th birthday, the children threw him a surprise party, and in the same month, a delegation from the Reich Security Main Office and the German Red Cross visited the family camp and reported favorably.

Over time, the Auschwitz resistance movement had drawn the conclusion that most arrivals were murdered within six months of their arrival. For Fredy's transport, this meant around March 8, 1944, and the resistance saw Fredy as a natural leader for an uprising. This was to mark his death-knell. According to some accounts, he committed suicide by taking pills on March 8 in order not to have to witness the deaths of his children; an alternate view is that he was poisoned by Jewish doctors who would have been killed if an uprising had broken out.

In 1996 a monument was placed on the wall of the former school building at Terezín; Fredy's face is carved in stone alongside the text "In memoriam Fredy Hirsch: Gratefully, Children of Terezín, Birkenau BIIb." On the centenary of his birth in 2016, the gymnasium he attended in Aachen renamed the cafeteria "the Fredy-Hirsch-AG." He was the subject of a documentary in 2016, *Heaven in Auschwitz*, which included accounts from 13 survivors of Theresienstadt and Auschwitz, and he was also featured in the 2017 Israeli documentary *Dear Fredy*, by Rubi Gat.

Further Reading

Adler, H. G. *Theresienstadt 1941–1945: The Face of a Coerced Community*. Cambridge: Cambridge University Press, 1955.

Keren, Nili. "The Family Camp." In Michael Berenbaum and Yisrael Gutman (Eds.), *Anatomy of the Auschwitz Death Camp*. Bloomington: Indiana University Press, 1998, pp. 428–440.

Redlich, Egon. *The Terezin Diary of Gonda Redlich*. Lexington: University Press of Kentucky, 1992.

HITLER YOUTH

The Hitler Youth (*Hitlerjugend*) was an organization established by Adolf Hitler to indoctrinate German boys into the ideology of the Nazi Party. Young people were a dynamic yet malleable force that Hitler believed could be a powerful influence in moving German unity forward.

The Hitler Youth was founded in 1926. While it complemented the female **League of German Girls** (*Bund Deutscher Mädel*), it formed a more important element of Nazi society due to the strict military regimentation it demanded and the socialization it fostered for boys into Nazi ways of thinking and behaving.

Given that the encouragement of youth was viewed as the way to the future, the Nazis placed a priority on integrating all youth activities into the structure of the new German order, and by 1935 the Hitler Youth movement was a huge institution, embracing nearly 60 percent of all German boys. On July 1, 1936, membership became compulsory when the organization became an official state agency. Parents found guilty of trying to keep their children from joining the Hitler Youth or the League of German Girls were subject to heavy prison sentences.

The Hitler Youth organization comprised various grades based on age. From the ages of 6 to 10, a boy served a sort of apprenticeship for the Hitler Youth as

Adolf Hitler with a group of adoring Hitler Youth boys who have come to meet their Führer. The Hitler Youth (*Hitlerjugend*) was a Nazi organization established in 1926 with the aim of indoctrinating German boys into the ideology of the Nazi Party. Over time, it became a vast organization, and grew even bigger after March 1939, when the government issued a law conscripting all boys into the Hitler Youth on the same basis as they were drafted into the Army. (Library of Congress)

a *Pimpf* ("youngster"). Each boy was given a book in which would be recorded his progress through the entire Nazi youth movement, including his ideological growth. On December 1, 1936, with the implementation of the Law on the Hitler Youth, it became mandatory for all boys to register with the authorities in the year he turned 10. His background would be investigated to determine that he was racially "pure." If he qualified for inclusion, he entered the *Deutsches Jungvolk* (German Young People). At 14, he joined the Hitler Youth, with much ceremony that marked a new stage in life, and was asked to make a statement of faith in Hitler and the future of Germany. He would remain with the Hitler Youth until he was 18, when he became eligible to join the Nazi Party. He would then undertake compulsory Labor Service, prior to joining the army until the age of 21.

The Hitler Youth became a vast organization. By the end of 1938, it numbered 7,728,259, and although this did not represent the total population in the appropriate age category, it was nonetheless a huge body of potential recruits. In March 1939 the government issued a law conscripting all boys into the Hitler Youth on the same basis as they were drafted into the army.

The Hitler Youth was organized on paramilitary lines like the SA (*Sturmabteilung*, or Storm Troopers), and youths approaching adulthood received systematic training not only in camping, sports, and Nazi ideology but also in soldiering. Boys in the Hitler Youth were taught all the principles of the Nazi Party, including Aryan superiority and antisemitism. The qualities of dedication, comradeship, and obedience were elevated and rewarded. The organization indoctrinated its members with the full range of Nazi ideologies and developed a cult of physical fitness, service to the state, leadership, and militarism. The leader of the movement from the very start of the Third Reich until 1943 was Baldur von Schirach, who managed all the country's youth programs. Later convicted at Nuremberg for his antisemitic activities, he was sentenced to 20 years' imprisonment prior to his release and retirement to a quiet life in southern Germany.

During the war years, members of the Hitler Youth were pressed into service to substitute for men who had been called up to the military. They worked in local fire brigades and helped clear rubble in cities affected by Allied bombing. Hitler Youth members also worked on the railroads, in antiaircraft defense activities, and with the postal service.

By 1943 ideas began to circulate for a Waffen-SS combat division made up of Hitler Youth members born in 1926, and Adolf Hitler approved the plan in February 1943. This saw active service as the 12th SS-Panzer-Division Hitlerjugend during and after the Allied invasion of Normandy in June 1944, with considerable loss of life. On October 18, 1944, the *Volkssturm*, a Home Guard force, was established, and all males between the ages of 16 and 60 not currently serving were conscripted. By 1945, during the Battle of Berlin, 12-year-old Hitler Youth members were being drafted to supplement the army's huge losses, and these young fighters were themselves decimated by advancing Soviet troops.

To emphasize the ideological nature of the Hitler Youth—always masked as comradeship and service to the state—a boy's schooling in the movement could lead to one of three elite educational institutions, all of which were designed to produce the very finest and most committed Nazis.

The first of these were the Adolf Hitler schools. Instruction began with the most promising children taken from the *Jungvolk* at the age of 12 and given six years of intensive training for leadership in the Party and in the public services. There were 10 such schools founded after 1937, in which students lived in dormitories under conditions of military discipline. Upon graduation, after having been thoroughly indoctrinated, they were eligible for entrance to university.

The second of these elite training institutions were the National Political Institutes of Education (Napolas), the purpose of which was to cultivate the same martial spirit found in earlier Prussian military academies. While courage and a sense of duty were paramount, students were also indoctrinated with additional training in Nazism beyond what they had learned when they were younger. Administration of these schools was under the direct supervision of the SS, which supplied the teaching staff. The first three Napolas were established in 1933; by the outbreak of the war, this had grown to 31, including three for women.

The final tier of political education saw the Order Castles (*Ordensburgen*), located at the very pinnacle of Nazi Germany's education system. These provided for those who would have attended university and were trained to be Germany's future leaders. Taken together, the Adolf Hitler schools, Napolas, and Order Castles catered to an entire generation of 11- to 25-year-olds who were meant to be the next generals, admirals, senior Party administrators, and Party politicians.

On October 10, 1945, after Germany's defeat and surrender, the Hitler Youth—together with other Nazi Party organizations—was designated an unconstitutional organization and dissolved by *Kontrollratsgesetz Nr. 2* under Section 86 of the German Criminal Code administered by the Allied Control Council.

Further Reading

Koch, H. W. *The Hitler Youth: Origins and Development 1922–45*. London: Macdonald and Jane's, 1975.

Rempel, Gerhard. *Hitler's Children: The Hitler Youth and the SS*. Chapel Hill: University of North Carolina Press, 1989.

HÜBENER, HELMUTH (1925–1942)

Helmuth Hübener, a youthful opponent of National Socialism, was executed for his anti-Nazi stance at the age of 17—one of the youngest opponents of the Third Reich to be judicially sentenced to death and executed as a result.

Born on January 8, 1925, Helmuth came from a religious family in Hamburg and was a member of the Church of Jesus Christ of Latter-day Saints (LDS, or Mormons). He had been a Boy Scout, but at the age of 10, when the Nazis banned the Scouting movement in 1935, he joined the Hitler Youth. Three years later, when the *Kristallnacht* pogrom occurred in November 1938, he broke with the Hitler Youth on the grounds that its violence against Jews was unacceptable.

Helmuth's stance went against LDS policy. In 1937 the World LDS President, Heber Grant, visited Germany from the United States and counseled members not to react negatively toward the Nazi regime. In the aftermath of the *Kristallnacht*, Grant arranged for all non-German Mormon missionaries to be evacuated from the Third Reich, leaving dissidents like Helmuth Hübener dangerously exposed. Local branch president Arthur Zander, for example, was an enthusiastic Nazi who, in 1938, posted notices on LDS churches stating, "Jews not welcome." In Helmuth's own congregation, Jews were barred from attending services. Helmuth came to be viewed as a young troublemaker by some other LDS members.

In 1941 Helmuth finished school and entered as a trainee at the Hamburg Social Authority. His circle of contacts widened, and as he learned more about the world outside, he was exposed to the BBC by a radio at the home of a friend. In the summer of 1941, he learned that his older brother Gerhard, at that time serving in the German Army, had a shortwave radio, which enabled private listening sessions at home. Listening to the BBC, of course, was a crime, and Helmuth, armed with "new" information, began to write leaflets opposing the government. He drew attention to the regime's criminal activities regarding human rights—the Jews in particular. He wrote about how the war was destroying Germany, with defeat inevitable, and distributed copies within his neighborhood.

As 1941 unfolded, Helmuth drew two of his fellow LDS members—Karl-Heinz Schnibbe and Rudi Wobbe—into his project, together with Gerhard Düwer, whom he had met at work. The more they learned, the more horrified they became, particularly concerning the situation (as they understood it) facing the Jews. Together, they listened to BBC radio and worked on the leaflets and then began distributing the 60 or so pieces Helmuth had produced.

On February 5, 1942, less than a month after turning 17, Helmuth Hübener was arrested by the Gestapo. Heinrich Mohn, a Nazi with whom he worked, saw him trying to translate his pamphlets into French and denounced him. On February 15, 1942, acting on orders from the Gestapo, the LDS excommunicated him. Over the next few months he was brutally interrogated and tortured in Gestapo prisons in Hamburg and Berlin before finally being brought before Judge Otto Georg Thierack of the People's Court (*Volksgerichtshof*) in Berlin on August 11, 1942.

Helmuth's performance during the trial would have been remarkable for anyone standing in such a situation; for a 17-year-old, it was phenomenal. Tried as an adult despite his age, and having been deprived of his civil rights, he was found guilty of conspiracy to commit high treason and advancing the cause of the enemy. Karl-Heinz Schnibbe and Rudi Wobbe were also found guilty and given sentences of 5 and 10 years at hard labor, respectively. Helmuth, as the ringleader of the group, received the death penalty. Witnesses said that after the sentence was read, he turned to Thierack and shouted, "You have sentenced me to death for telling the truth. My time is now—but your time will come!"

Appeals for clemency proved fruitless; it was to be two months from the time of sentencing to the execution. When his death appeared imminent, he wrote several letters of farewell to family and friends. In one of them he wrote: "My Father in Heaven knows that I have done nothing wrong." On another, penned the day of his execution, he stated: "I know that God lives, and He will be the Just Judge in this matter."

On October 27, 1942, the Nazi Ministry of Justice upheld the verdict and sentence. Helmuth was told of the Ministry's decision at 1:05 p.m. on the scheduled day of execution, and at 8:13 pm, in Berlin's Plötzensee prison, he was beheaded by guillotine. He was the youngest person ever to be sentenced by the People's Court and executed for conspiracy to commit treason against the Nazi regime.

In 1946 Helmuth Hübener was posthumously reinstated in the LDS Church, ordained an elder, and, on January 7, 1948, rebaptized. Since then, he has been honored many times as a hero of the resistance against Hitler, and an exhibit focusing on his resistance, trial, and execution is situated in the former guillotine chamber at Plötzensee prison.

Further Reading

Nelson, David Conley. *Moroni and the Swastika: Mormons in Nazi Germany*. Norman: University of Oklahoma Press, 2015.

HULST, JOHAN VAN (1911–2018)

Johan (sometimes, Jan) van Hulst was the principal of the Pedagogical Academy in Amsterdam, and he was personally involved in saving the lives of hundreds of Jewish children. Born in Amsterdam on January 28, 1911, he studied psychology and pedagogy at the *Vrije Universiteit Amsterdam*.

A strictly Calvinist (*Gereformeerd*) Protestant, van Hulst worked as a teacher in several Dutch cities before becoming principal of the Pedagogical Academy—an office he was to hold between 1942 and 1960. He was at the same time a patriot and a pedagogue opposed to any watering down of children's education. Thus, he and most other faculty members rebelled in the early summer of 1942 when Jan van Dam, secretary-general of the Nazi-controlled Ministry of Education, tried to force the Academy to close by withholding its government subsidy. Preferring to keep the doors open, they continued to teach despite government pressure and with little to no money.

In response, the then-principal resigned, and on September 1, van Hulst became the new principal of the *Hervormde Kweekschool te Amsterdam* (Reformed Teacher Training College). This now came into play as a crucial location for the saving of Jewish children, as it was situated at 27 Plantage Middenlaan, only two buildings away from a Jewish crèche from where, beginning in January 1943, children were being smuggled out and hidden at addresses outside Amsterdam.

Much of this activity was orchestrated by one of the leaders of the Nazi-imposed Jewish Council (*Joodse Raad*), **Walter Süskind**; an administrator with the *Hollandsche Schouwburg* (Dutch Theater), Felix Halverstad; and the director of the crèche, Henriette Henriques Pimentel. Together, they created a means for Jewish children to be rescued. They would be brought secretly to the *Hervormde Kweekschool* and, with van Hulst's assistance, passed through the garden and into the theater. The children would be moved from the crèche over the low fence and temporarily hidden in one of the classrooms until they were collected by rescuers, who would then take them to safe places outside of the city.

In this way, the organizations involved managed to smuggle at least 100 Jewish children through van Hulst's school. On his own initiative, he helped save another hundred, who were taken away by his students.

On the morning of June 19, 1943, however, it seemed as though van Hulst's operation was about to collapse. An inspector from the Ministry of Education, Mr. Fieringa, had been sent to the college to oversee the matriculation exams and, seeing the children, asked whether they were Jewish. Conceding that they were, van Hulst was terrified as to what might happen next, but Fieringa simply shook his hand and wished him well with the caution, "In God's name, be careful."

When the Nazis ordered that the crèche should be cleared out in late September 1943, the principal, Virrie (Virginia) Cohen—the daughter of David Cohen, president of the *Joodse Raad*—went to van Hulst and told him that the children were about to be taken away. Faced with the agonizing task of choosing only some who could be rescued, van Hulst took a dozen of the children, aged between 5 and 12, to safety.

After this, it seemed as though van Hulst's options to do more had come to an end, but he continued to find ways to help people in hiding and managed to keep the college open until the end of the war. With just three weeks left before the Netherlands was liberated, he was forced to go into hiding. Upon later reflection, he asserted that he had no regrets but would have preferred to have saved more children than he did.

Johan van Hulst was to have a successful life after the **liberation**, becoming a politician with the Christian Historical Union (CHU), a political party that merged into the Christian Democratic Appeal (CDA). He served as a senator between July 3, 1956, and June 10, 1981, and as Senate leader of the CHU from December 10, 1968 until June 8, 1977. When the CDA was formed, he became Senate leader there until June 10, 1981. He was also a member of the European Parliament between 1961 and 1968. Throughout this time, he remained a professor of pedagogy (and, later, emeritus professor) at the *Vrije Universiteit*.

In view of his work in facilitating the rescue of literally hundreds of Jewish children during the Holocaust, Yad Vashem recognized him as one of the Righteous among the Nations on March 8, 1972.

Johan van Hulst died on March 22, 2018, at the age of 107. In his honor, the Netherlands Senate honored him at its plenary session of April 17, 2018.

Further Reading

Paldiel, Mordecai. *The Path of the Righteous: Gentile Rescuers of Jews during the Holocaust.* Hoboken, NJ: KTAV, 1993.

INFANTICIDE

The relationship between infanticide and the Holocaust—indeed, of any genocide—was intimate. The most frequent justifications given by the Nazi perpetrators related to three possibilities: first, the general need to destroy all members of the Jewish "race"; second, the specific need to kill the children of the current generation in order to ensure that future generations would not be born and, as leading Nazis repeated on numerous occasions, seek revenge against the German people at a later time; and third, the economic value of the state not having to feed what were regarded as "useless eaters."

The Nazi regime also considered that the elimination of non-Jewish infants with physical or psychological handicaps was an ideal to be pursued in a **child euthanasia** campaign. This was part of the so-called T-4 operation that was intended to remove "defective" genes from German society.

These notions fit in well with ideological views stemming from Social Darwinism, and to these could be added the forcible separation of children from their families in countries occupied by Germany during World War II. This would later be recognized as genocide, in which the intention was to destroy an identifiable group either physically, through killing, or by removing children from their families and thus depriving them of their ethnic, racial, religious, or national identity into the future. Such destruction was wrought with ferocious single-mindedness against children and infants.

As the Holocaust therefore had a focused biological—that is, racial or ethnic—dimension, there was all too often little way out for newborn babies and infants, whose lives were often forfeit through their very existence.

During the Holocaust, Jewish children were targeted during the period's most destructive phase, in Eastern Europe during 1941–1943. General estimates run to a death toll of over 1,000,000 Jewish children under the age of 14 killed either when they arrived in killing centers at places like Auschwitz; immediately after birth or in institutions; during forced labor and in Nazi **medical experimentation** processes; or during reprisal operations by the Nazis against civilian populations. The images of starving, dying, and dead children in the Warsaw Ghetto and other places that we see today are stark examples of the reality of death and suffering on what was clearly a genocidal scale.

In Nazi Germany, of course, race-thinking elevated Aryan youth to a higher status than in other societies on account of their minds not having been "corrupted" by "decadent," Western ways. Consequently, for those accepted into the inner echelons of the Nazi Party as **Hitler Youth** members, they received substantial authority relative to those who were not members. However, for those children from a racial or ethnic background viewed as incompatible with the Nazi regime, the future was bleak. During the war years, this future could be very short, and violent death became commonplace. As noted, however, it could also be slow and excruciating, such as through enforced starvation. Only Aryan families could be accepted for the Nazi future, and Jewish family groups were deported to their deaths in the euphemistically named "East." There was thus little standing in the way of wholesale destruction of entire cohorts of children during the period of the Third Reich.

Small children were extremely vulnerable. Newborn infants were often among the first to be killed, as they were the least likely to resist, and their deaths were employed to destabilize and demoralize the adult populations prior to them being targeted for more widespread destruction. At death camps like Auschwitz, children were usually killed at birth. Women who arrived in concentration camps pregnant were forced to abandon their babies, often after SS doctors—in particular, Dr. **Josef Mengele**—took great care to see to it that professional medical procedures were adopted in facilitating the birth. In cases where German Aryan women successfully gave birth in the camps, their babies would be taken away from them and placed either up for adoption or sent to orphanages. Jewish women, on the other hand, had their babies removed and killed, often in front of them.

At the very end of the war, in rare circumstances, babies were permitted to live. Some survived owing to the imminence of the war ending and a desire on the part of camp commandants or guards to use these babies as bargaining chips in negotiations with the Allies in return for their own lives. But these were exceptions to an otherwise unrelieved regime of terror and murder.

Further Reading

Chalmers, Beverley. *Birth, Sex and Abuse: Women's Voices under Nazi Rule*. Surbiton, UK: Grosvenor House, 2015.

JEWISH YOUTH MOVEMENTS

Jewish youth movements, particularly in Eastern Europe during the interwar period, saw substantial growth as the expansion of state education and a decline in traditional religious observance found young people seeking their own solutions to social and national problems.

The growth of Jewish youth organizations in Eastern Europe between the two world wars mirrored broader trends elsewhere in Europe. Zionist and socialist student organizations in Germany and Poland, among other places, spawned youth movements, and in Poland Scouting played an important role in showing young people that their views were worthy of attention.

All had different motivations and sprang from various origins, whether religious, social, cultural, or political. As the Nazis began persecuting Jews throughout Europe, members of the Jewish youth movements took a leading role in resistance activities and in assisting their fellow Jews.

When discussing Jewish youth movements, however, it is important that clarity be given to defining what is meant by the term. In the first place, how can "youth" be described? And second, what is meant when reference is made to a "movement?" A short definition of both would have it that when discussing a youth movement, we are talking about a sizable (though not necessarily large) grouping of individuals aged anywhere between 10 and 18, sometimes informal in nature, that focuses on specific political or social issues. During the Nazi period, these issues became transformed into actions that were much more activist in character.

The political youth movements sought to prepare their members for passage into the adult expressions of their respective organizations. Most movements maintained separate activities only for younger boys and girls; as they got older, little distinction was made between the sexes when it came to the various activities in which they engaged. Religious youth movements, however, retained separation between the sexes.

In Eastern Europe, many of the youth movements were Zionist in nature. Among the first of these was *Hashomer Hatzair*, as early as 1915. This combined both Zionism and radical socialism in its ideology. *Dror* was like *Hashomer Hatzair*, though its members generally came from poorer backgrounds. Other movements included *Gordonia, Ha-No'ar ha-Tsiyyoni*, and *Akiva*, all of which shared some sort of Zionist or Jewish cultural foundation. *Betar* was the youth wing of the Zionist Revisionist political movement.

Another important influence was the Scouting movement established in the United Kingdom by Lieutenant-General Sir (later Lord) Robert Baden-Powell, whose book *Scouting for Boys* (1908) enjoyed enormous success and was translated into Polish in 1911. From Baden-Powell, young Jews took the idea of quasi-military discipline and structure, intended to inculcate values such as obedience, self-sacrifice, and group solidarity. The movement also carried a nationalistic strain within it that was embraced in several growing Jewish youth movements.

Many were aligned to, or part of, specific settlement initiatives in Palestine, and a significant part of their energy was devoted to preparing young members for *Aliyah* (migration). Thus, many members participated in agricultural training programs prior to emigration. It has been estimated that immediately prior to World War II, there were some 100,000 young Jews involved in the various youth movements in Poland.

Poland was thus the main center of Zionist youth movement activity. In Germany and other centers, youth movements were also active, but here their origin was not so much political as it was inspired by the structures and values of non-Jewish German movements such as the pre–World War I *Wandervogel* movement. Jewish youth and adults had their own *Wandervogel* body, the *"Blau-Weiss"* ("blue-white") group, which eventually became a Zionist youth movement. In Germany, *Hashomer Hatzair* existed, influenced by the *Wandervogel*.

Beyond Poland and Germany, practically the only active Jewish youth movements were Zionist, and not all took their lead from these two countries alone. *Betar*, for example, originated in Latvia in 1925 and only emerged in Poland later. Yet Poland took a lead that many other countries followed. A key exception to this was Czechoslovakia, where the *El-Al Blau Weiss* movement operated under the influence of the older and larger German organization.

The viability of all the youth movements, regardless of their location, was influenced by such factors as location, gender, and age divisions. In certain countries, their operational effectiveness was often constrained by the oppressive political regimes within which they had to operate, leading to situations in which they were forced to carry out their activities clandestinely.

During the war years, when Jewish communal life was all but destroyed, youth movements throughout Europe resisted Nazi attempts at annihilation in various ways. In Poland and elsewhere, there was little option for rescue through emigration to Palestine (or, indeed, anywhere else), and for the youth movements the possibility of rescue was thus of secondary importance to that of armed resistance. Everywhere, it seemed, this was led by members of *Hashomer Hatzair* or other Zionist youth organizations, from Poland in 1939 and Lithuania in 1941, right through to Hungary in 1944.

In Western Europe (and Hungary), on the other hand, efforts were primarily concentrated on the quest to rescue Jews. Much of this was centered on France, where the EIF and especially its "Sixth Bureau" (*La Sixième*), engaged in supplying Jewish children with forged identity papers, placing them in safe homes, or **smuggling** them out of France into Switzerland or Spain. Some also took part in the battles to liberate France.

In December 1941, in Lyon, it was decided to establish a single organization that would incorporate all the Zionist youth movements in France. A meeting in Montpellier in May 1942 resolved to set up a clandestine underground—the *Mouvement de la Jeunesse Sioniste* (Zionist Youth Movement, or MJS)—that would focus on rescue activities. Members smuggled Jews out of camps in the southern zone and found hiding places for them, as well as producing false identity documents. In late 1942 the movement transferred its center of operations to Grenoble, where it organized groups of children and smuggled them across the border into Switzerland. At other times during the war, efforts were made to smuggle fighters from France, through Spain, and on to Palestine, from where they would resume the fight against Nazism and at the same time become the nucleus of a fighting force for a future Jewish state.

In all youth movements, other forms of resistance were also undertaken, notably, activities such as organizing and running study courses, seminars, workshops, and other educational programs. Youth movements from France to Belgium to Poland also published a vigorous underground press, producing newspapers, leaflets, and posters. In Warsaw, the youth movements set up a courier network of *Kashariyot*, girls (some as young as 15) and young women to transport documents, papers, money, and weapons across borders and keep a news presence between ghettos.

Even though the Nazis outlawed Jewish youth movements and their activities from the outset, the movements continued in secret. In France, Jewish youth movements were involved in armed resistance and rescue activities; in Hungary, they saved thousands through forged identity documents. In Warsaw, Vilna, and other places, youth movements took up arms and carried out uprisings. In other places, Jewish youth escaped to the forests and either joined partisan groups or formed their own. Leaders of the Jewish youth movements, wherever they were located, arrived at the realization early that survival under the Nazis was unlikely and that their only chance was resistance of some kind, whether armed or through rescue initiatives.

Further Reading

Cohen, Asher, and Yehoyakim Cochavi (Eds.). *Zionist Youth Movements during the Shoah.* New York: Peter Lang, 1995.

JOFFO, JOSEPH (1931–2018)

Joseph Joffo was a schoolboy whose family was forced to flee Paris when, in 1942, the German occupiers of northern France demanded that Jews wear a yellow star to mark them out from the rest of the French population. Together with his brother Maurice, Joseph went from being a Parisian schoolboy to a refugee in the French countryside, to the two of them acting as students passing as Catholic in a rural military school. At the end of the war in 1944, Maurice and Joseph returned to Paris to work in the family hair salon. In the early 1970s, Joseph commenced writing his childhood memoirs, which were published in 1973 as *Un sac de billes* (*A Bag of Marbles*).

Joseph Joffo was the youngest of seven children of Rouman and Anna Joffo. At the age of seven, Rouman had fled Russia to avoid pogroms, and Anna also came from Russia. Joseph was born in Paris in the 18th arrondissement on April 2, 1931. The family hairdressing shop, "Joffo-Coiffure," was in rue de Clignancourt; the Joffo family lived in an apartment over the shop. Joffo left school at 14, having completed his primary education, and started working with his brothers in the family business.

The family's life in Paris was very happy, until the German invasion in 1940. When the wearing of a yellow star became compulsory on June 7, 1942, the Joffo family escaped from Paris to Vichy France in the south. Joseph, reluctant to identify himself as "different," swapped his yellow star with Zérati, a school friend, in exchange for a bag of marbles.

Realizing that traveling together as a family would attract attention, Rouman sent his two elder sons, Henri and Albert, ahead to Nice, warning them to deny their faith or risk death. The boys arrived safely in the border town of Menton, which was occupied by the Italians. Rouman Joffo then gave 10-year-old Joseph and his 12-year-old brother Maurice 5,000 francs each and instructed them how to escape from Nazi-occupied Paris by foot, train, and bus to join their older brothers in Menton. The boys crossed the Demarcation Line at night with the help of a local boy, Raymond. They spent four months in Menton with Henri and Albert before leaving for Nice, where their parents were waiting.

In the summer of 1942, the family remained in Nice. At that time, it was under Italian occupation, which was fortuitous as the Italians were not antisemitic as were both the French and the German occupiers. The boys returned to school in September 1942 and spent an uninterrupted year there.

On September 8, 1943, Marshal Pietro Badoglio signed the Italian capitulation while southern Italy continued the war on the side of the Allies. The Italian occupation zone was then invaded by the Germans, who had already maintained a presence at Vichy since November 1942.

With the surrender of the Italians and the arrival of the Germans, roundups of Jews began. Joseph and Maurice fled to *Moisson Nouvelle*, a camp for boys run by the Vichy government. They were safe here for a while and made many friends, but a ride with a truck driver named Ferdinand into Nice inadvertently led them into a Nazi trap. The boys were taken to the Hôtel Excelsior, the local Nazi headquarters.

The boys claimed to be Catholic but could not prove it. Warned of the situation by the parish priest of the Saint-Pierre d'Arène Church in Nice, Bishop Paul Rémond drafted two baptismal certificates and two certificates of solemn communion for Joseph and Maurice. He also wrote a letter in which he demanded their release. The boys were freed a month later, but their father had been arrested and was transported from Drancy to Auschwitz on November 20, 1943.

Joseph and Maurice traveled north to join their sister, but it was risky for them to stay, so they joined their older brothers and their mother Anna in the small Alpine resort of Aix-les-Bains in southern France. They spent the rest of the war in nearby Rumilly. Maurice worked at the Hôtel de Commerce, a location that supported the

Resistance. Joseph lived in the home of a bookseller, who was a staunch supporter of Marshal Philippe Pétain. In exchange for room and board, Joseph delivered newspapers and worked as a courier. His host family, although collaborators, did not know that he was Jewish. Rumilly was liberated on August 19, 1944.

The boys returned on an overcrowded train to Paris shortly after peace was announced. They reunited with their family (though without their murdered father) in the Joffo hair salon. After the war Joseph thanked Bishop Rémond (later recognized by Yad Vashem in Jerusalem as one of the Righteous among the Nations) for saving his life.

By the late 1960s, Joseph Joffo was a highly successful hairdresser whose clients included François Mitterrand and Jacques Chirac, together with actors such as Alain Delon and Jean-Paul Belmondo. Joffo opened a dozen salons in Paris. Around 1970 he began writing an autobiographical novel, *A Bag of Marbles*, recounting his experiences under the occupation. In this book he told of his flight with Maurice to the free zone in Vichy France and described in detail his stays in Aix-les-Bains and Rumilly.

The book was initially rejected by four publishers before being accepted by Éditions Jean-Claude Lattès, but Joffo was required to engage an editor to sharpen the text. The book was published in 1973; a phenomenal best seller, it was made into a major film two years later. The book has since been translated into about 20 languages, with a Chinese edition published in 2012. To date, in its various editions, it has sold over 20 million copies. *A Bag of Marbles* is regularly incorporated into European school curricula for children studying the history of the Holocaust.

Joseph Joffo died at age 87 on December 6, 2018, at a hospital in Saint-Laurent-du-Var, Alpes-Maritimes, after a short illness.

Further Reading

Joffo, Joseph. *A Bag of Marbles*. Chicago: University of Chicago Press, 2000.

JONAS, REGINA (1902–1944)

Regina Jonas was a woman unique anywhere on the globe: during the 1930s she was the first (and, to that point, only) female rabbi, anywhere. She was born in Berlin on August 3, 1902, the daughter of Wolf and Sara Jonas, and grew up in the Scheunenviertel, a poor, mostly Jewish neighborhood. Her father was a merchant; when Regina was 11, he died of tuberculosis, leaving her mother to take care of herself; her son, Abraham; and Regina.

During high school, Regina's passions for Jewish history, Bible, and Hebrew saw her develop an interest in what at the time was unthinkable for a girl: she wanted to become a rabbi. She spoke about it often with her fellow students and studied hard in order to be able to teach. She enrolled in Berlin's *Hochschule für die Wissenschaft des Judentums* (Higher Institute for Jewish Studies) and took courses designed for liberal student rabbis.

Several people supported her along the way, leading Orthodox rabbis among them. She was even tutored in a weekly *shiur* (study session) by Rabbi Max Weyl until his deportation to **Theresienstadt** during World War II. In 1924 she graduated as an "Academic Teacher of Religion" along with her fellow female students. She then became the only woman who hoped to go one step further and be ordained a rabbi.

The thesis that followed would, in the normal run of events, have been required as one of the important steps leading to ordination. Supervised by Professor Eduard Baneth, who was responsible for rabbinic ordination, her thesis was entitled, "Can a Woman Be a Rabbi According to Halachic Sources?" Submitted in June 1930, this was the first known attempt to find a basis in Jewish religious law that would allow for female ordination. Her conclusion was that there was no prohibition *in law* holding women back from being ordained.

Her work received a grade of "good," which should have paved the way for ordination. Shortly after the thesis had been passed, however, Professor Baneth died, and his conservative successor, Rabbi Hanoch Albeck, refused to ordain her because she was a woman. The result saw Regina graduate as a teacher of religion—but only that.

After the Nazis came to power in early 1933, there was an increased demand for Jewish religious teachers. Jewish children were forced out of public schools and into Jewish establishments, and "Miss Jonas" worked hard to impart both Jewish knowledge and *Ahavat Yisroel* (a love of the Jewish people) to her pupils.

Throughout the years following, she continued to pursue ordination until finally, in 1935, Rabbi Max Dienemann agreed. On December 27, 1935, she became Rabbinerin Regina Jonas. She began working as a chaplain in various Jewish organizations, though as a woman she was denied a pulpit by congregations across Germany. The spiritual head of German Jewry, Rabbi Leo Baeck, endorsed her ordination after the fact, though he refused to assist in the process leading her to the rabbinate on the ground that a female rabbi, at that time in German Jewish history, would have caused massive and unnecessary complications within the Jewish community.

In the years that followed, Regina threw herself into pastoral work. Although she did not have her own pulpit, she spent long hours visiting the sick in Berlin's Jewish Hospital and cared especially for elderly Jews whom circumstances—whether through age or finances—had left in a precarious position. With the onset of war, she became a roving rabbi, ministering to Jewish communities in towns that no longer had one.

In 1941 she led special services in lieu of regular worship, such activity no longer being viable in smaller communities from where large-scale emigration had taken place. Her messages were always positive, emphasizing the need to remain true to Judaism and a Jewish identity despite the horrors taking place outside.

On November 6, 1942, Regina and her mother were deported to Theresienstadt. Two days beforehand, she was forced to fill out a declaration listing all her property; this was then confiscated by the state.

At Theresienstadt she continued working. Here, as well as counseling older Jews, she spent a lot of her time and energy preaching to children about the glory of being Jewish and the privilege of doing God's work. Her work with children, in fact, represented her commitment to a Jewish future, despite the trials facing the Jewish people at that time. She helped the renowned Austrian Jewish psychoanalyst Viktor Frankl in establishing a department of mental hygiene to prevent suicide attempts.

Working without a break for two years, she lectured, preached, counseled, and gave hope constantly to those around her. Being a "woman rabbi" was never a concern to her; being a rabbi, *per se*, was. She was aware of her unique status but considered that to be only temporary; her hope was that she would be the harbinger of more to follow.

On October 12, 1944, time ran out. Rabbi Regina and her mother were deported to Auschwitz and probably killed that day or the next. There is no certainty, however; it could even have been as late as December of that year.

Among her papers, found in 1991 by Dr. Katharina von Kellenbach from St. Mary's College of Maryland, was a sermon that could have been her epitaph: "May all our work be a blessing for Israel's future (and the future of humanity). . . . Upright 'Jewish men' and 'brave, noble women' were always the sustainers of our people. May we be found worthy by God to be numbered in the circle of these women and men. . . . The reward of a mitzvah is the recognition of the great deed by God."

Further Reading

Klaphek, Elisa. *Fraulein Rabbiner Jonas: The Story of the First Woman Rabbi*. San Francisco: Jossey-Bass, 2004.

Silverman, Emily Leah. *Edith Stein and Regina Jonas: Religious Visionaries in the Time of the Death Camp*. London: Routledge, 2014.

JOSPA, YVONNE (1919–2000)

Yvonne Jospa was a founder, with her husband, Jewish communist Hertz Jospa, of a Belgian resistance organization known as the ***Comité de Défense des Juifs*** (Committee for the Protection of Jews, or CDJ). Born in Romania in 1910 as Have Groisman, the third of four girls, she came from a background that was traditionalist in its adherence to Judaism. Her father was one of three judges in their hometown, and her mother was actively involved in the work of the local Jewish school.

Yvonne Jospa—a *nom de guerre* in the Belgian resistance—attended school in Kishinev (Chișinău) before moving to Belgium to study social work at the University of Liège. In 1933 she married Hertz Jospa, a pharmaceutical chemist. Right after their wedding, Yvonne and Hertz joined the Communist Party of Belgium, and in 1934 they became Belgian citizens. Prior to the outbreak of World War II, they worked with child refugees from the Spanish Civil War and organized the passage through Belgium of Romanian antifascist volunteers going to Spain to fight with the International Brigades.

During 1935 and 1936, Yvonne also took care of Jewish refugees from Germany and Austria. After the *Kristallnacht* pogrom of November 9–10, 1938, her work intensified dramatically. She would often shield illegal immigrants in her house, prior to smuggling them out of the country.

On May 10, 1940, Nazi Germany invaded Belgium, which capitulated on May 28. At this point, Yvonne stopped work in order to devote herself fully to social and relief matters. As one who was Jewish, communist, and anti-Nazi, she knew she was in extreme peril if her activities led to her being arrested, and as a result, she and Hertz moved around constantly with false names and papers. In September 1942 they established the CDJ, with Yvonne as head of the branch working to rescue Jewish children. Through her efforts, over 3,000 Jewish children were saved from deportation by placing them with sympathetic non-Jewish Belgian families.

The means by which the CDJ operated was simple. Committee workers would separate the children from their parents to make it easier to hide them, with two subcommittees in play—one for adults and one for children. For the adults, the committee's problems were twofold: finding places to stay and providing them with subsistence. Children presented other difficulties. They would be farmed out to carefully chosen Belgian families, but those who took them in had to be people the parents did not know; moreover, the parents could not know the family's name or where their children had been sent.

Overseeing the children's committee required considerable organizational skills. A staff of 16 volunteers worked tirelessly to ensure the operation's success, and it is to Yvonne's credit that no one was arrested for harboring Jewish children. The committee maintained three sets of documents: in the first were the real names of the children; in the second were the children's places of sanctuary and their false names; and the third was a coded book that connected the two, and for security, the three sets were kept separate.

Survival, however, came at a price. In order to save the children, the children had to live as Belgians, abandon their Jewish identity, and assume new names and identities—even going to school as Belgians. Friendly priests prepared false baptism certificates so the children could be registered in their new schools, and parents and children were able to maintain contact through the introduction of an underground mail system. Ration cards and stamps for Jewish children in hiding were organized through partisans stealing documents.

In June 1943 Hertz was arrested, caught meeting with a courier who was identified as Jewish. He was deported as a political resister, not as a Jew, which saved him from being sent to Auschwitz. After a period of detention in Belgium, in May 1944 he was deported to Buchenwald. Yvonne lost contact with him and thought he had died, but he returned on May 8, 1945, after the camp was liberated. When he returned, he was but a shadow of what he had been prior to his arrest; he was emotionally and physically exhausted and very sick. It took a long period of convalescence for him to return to health.

When peace and **liberation** came, there were inevitable problems of reintegration for the children and their parents—some of whom had not seen each other for years. In certain cases, rescuing families did not want to give the children back; in others, where parents did not return, there were serious discussions within the Jewish community regarding the children's future. Some Zionists held that they should be moved to Palestine; Yvonne's position was that they should not be moved out of Belgium until they were old enough to decide their own future. Ultimately, a series of compromises saw some moved overseas, and some remained in Belgium.

All the members of Yvonne's family who remained in Romania were murdered during the Holocaust. A sister who was with her in Belgium survived. No one, however, other than those with whom she had the closest contact during the war, knew of her accomplishments on behalf of Jewish children. In 1964 she co-founded the *Union des Anciens Résistants Juifs de Belgique* (Union of Former Belgium Jewish Resistance Members) for the community of resisters she had played such an important part in facilitating. She remained honorary chairperson of this organization until her death in Brussels in 2000.

Further Reading

Bartrop, Paul R. *Resisting the Holocaust: Upstanders, Partisans, and Survivors*. Santa Barbara, CA: ABC-CLIO, 2016.

Vromen, Suzanne. *Hidden Children of the Holocaust: Belgian Nuns and Their Daring Rescue of Young Jews from the Nazis*. Oxford: Oxford University Press, 2008.

K

KERKHOFS, LOUIS-JOSEPH (1878–1962)

Louis-Joseph Kerkhofs was the bishop of Liège during World War II, and he used his significant authority to encourage the priests in his diocese to assist in saving the lives of Jews. His stance inspired many people and religious institutions around Liège to help, and a large number of rescues resulted from his intervention. He worked closely with Albert van den Berg, a lawyer in Liège, to save over 300 Jewish children.

Louis-Joseph Kerkhofs was born in Val-Meer, Belgium, on February 15, 1878. He studied at Peer, Hasselt, and Rome and was ordained on September 22, 1900. In 1901 he was appointed professor of philosophy at the seminary of Sint-Truiden and in 1917 became professor of dogmatic theology at the major seminary of Liège, of which he became the director in 1922. In December 1924 he was appointed Coadjutor Bishop of Liège, receiving his episcopal consecration on February 11, 1925.

Between January 15 and March 2, 1933, Mariette Beco, an adolescent girl living in Banneaux, Liège, spoke of her vision of a Lady in White, the "Virgin of the Poor," who said she had come to relieve suffering. Kerkhofs convened a canonical commission to investigate, and following its favorable report in 1942, the veneration of the Virgin Mary as "Virgin of the Poor" was authorized and approved by the Holy See.

During World War II, Belgium was occupied by Nazi Germany. By the end of May 1941, a decree was issued requiring that Jews had to register all their possessions, and Jews were banned from supervising workplaces. In August 1941 a night curfew was instituted for Jews between 8:00 p.m. and 7:00 a.m., and they were only permitted to live in Antwerp, Brussels, Charleroi, and Liège. In November 1941 mixed marriages were banned; in December 1941 Jewish children were expelled from public schools, and Jewish students were forbidden from attending universities. On May 27, 1942, all Jews over six years old were forced to wear the Star of David.

On August 4, the first convoy of Jews left the Mechelen/Malines transit camp for Auschwitz. The months of August, September, and October 1942 then became known as the "hundred days of deportation," and the period from November 1942 to August 1944 saw the arrest and deportation of many more Jews, including those who had escaped previous roundups.

During the war Monsignor Kerkhofs undertook various initiatives to protect Jews from deportation. He sheltered the chief rabbi, Solomon Ullmann, at his own home and hid the rabbi of Liège, Joseph Lepkifker, and his family in a convent, where they stayed until the **liberation**. In this rescue operation, Kerkhofs worked closely with Fathers Emile Boufflette and Joseph Peeters, who was executed by the Germans.

As a result of Kerkhofs's appeal to the priests under his jurisdiction, the Banneux monastery protected many fleeing Jews. Other monasteries and Catholic seminaries spontaneously followed suit, including the Benedictine monks in Liège, in Charneux and in Val Dieu, the Holy Heart of Maria in Ter Hulpe, and other religious institutions.

In September 1942, in the middle of the deportations of Jews from Liège, Albert van den Berg, a lawyer from the city, was tasked by Monsignor Kerkhofs with organizing the rescue of Jewish children. Kerkhofs actively supported the illegal rescue organizations that brought Jewish children to Catholic institutions and holiday camps.

With the help of his secretary, Pierre Coune, van den Berg worked with Monsignor Kerkhofs to place 300 Jewish children and adults in refuges in Banneux. On the authority of Kerkhofs, van den Berg created and ran a network that arranged hiding places for Jewish children and adults in some 20 monasteries throughout the country, with other children hidden in private homes. Van den Berg's network looked after the costs of hiding the children. False identity papers, together with food coupons, were acquired for the **hidden children**.

Van den Berg was arrested when such papers were found on him but was found innocent of the separate charge of "aiding Jews" thanks to his lawyer, who argued in his defense that there was no prohibition in Belgian law against helping Jews. On July 27, 1943, the German military court sentenced van den Berg to five months' imprisonment. Two weeks before he was due to be released, on September 29, 1943, he was sent to the Vught concentration camp in the Netherlands. On March 1, 1944, he was transferred to the Neuengamme camp in Germany, from where he never returned. Allegedly he died in 1945 while attending to a suffering comrade, but the circumstances of his death have not been established with certainty.

Tensions between church and occupier culminated in March 1943 when the Germans declared that Belgians born between 1920 and 1924 must go to compulsory labor in Germany. Further, the Germans removed church bells for use in the German war industry. On March 15, 1943, the Belgian bishops answered with a pastoral letter condemning the compulsory labor roundups. It was read in all pulpits, attacking the sanctions taken against Belgians who refused to work and the confiscation of the church bells. Nothing was said about the deportation of the Jews. However, Belgian help was effective to the extent that almost half the Jewish population was spared during the occupation.

Louis-Joseph Kerkhofs served as the 88th bishop of Liège from 1927 to 1961. On December 8, 1961, he was elected as emeritus bishop, and shortly before the opening of the Second Vatican Council, he received the honorary title of Archbishop of Serre. He died in Liège on December 31, 1962.

A commemorative plaque marking the actions of Monsignor Kerkhofs during World War II is affixed on a wall of St. Paul cathedral in Liège. In 1981 Monsignor Kerkhofs was recognized as one of the Righteous among the Nations by Yad

Vashem in Jerusalem, while Albert Van den Berg, in turn, was similarly recognized on July 19, 1995.

Further Reading

Paldiel, Mordecai. *Sheltering the Jews: Stories of Holocaust Rescuers.* Minneapolis: Fortress Press, 1996.

Vromen, Suzanne. *Hidden Children of the Holocaust: Belgian Nuns and Their Daring Rescue of Young Jews from the Nazis.* Oxford: Oxford University Press, 2008.

KERTÉSZ, IMRE (1929–2016)

Imre Kertész was born on November 9, 1929, into the secular middle-class family of László Kertész and his wife, Aranka, in Budapest, Hungary. His parents separated when he was five, and he was sent to a boarding school. In 1940 he was relocated to a special class designated specifically for Jewish students.

On June 30, 1944, Kertész, then aged 14, was deported with other Hungarian Jews to Auschwitz. Upon arrival at the camp, during the initial "selection," he lied about his age and called himself a worker rather than a schoolboy, in the hope that he would appear more useful to camp officials. This ensured his survival in the immediate term. He was later sent to Buchenwald and was eventually liberated by American troops. By a quirk of Nazi record-keeping, the Buchenwald register noted the death on February 18, 1945 of "prisoner 64921, Imre Kertész." After the liberation, Kertész returned to Budapest, where he graduated from high school in 1948. He then turned to writing as a profession.

His first novel, a semiautobiographical account of his life during the Holocaust, was *Fatelessness* (1975). The hero is a teenage boy who has grown to adulthood living with the terrible experiences of the Nazi death camp in which he was imprisoned and who finds himself incapable of reverting to his previous lifestyle. The book's documentary style was a new literary approach to the literature of the Holocaust and was a clear outgrowth of Kertész's experiences as a boy in Auschwitz and Buchenwald. Following *Fatelessness*, Kertész's *Fiasco* (1988) and *Kaddish for an Unborn Child* (1990) formed the second and third parts of what became a Holocaust trilogy.

In 2002 Kertész was awarded the Nobel Prize for Literature as a recognition of his work in bringing to light the trauma of the individual when faced with the horrors of the state. It was only after he received this award that *Fatelessness* was brought to a broader audience. Kertész maintained that choosing to become a writer was his way of refusing to collaborate with dictatorship and that his writing was the result of having experienced both fascism and communism in Hungary. A common theme running through his writing centers on Auschwitz, which he considered to be a culminating point of Western civilization. Derived from this is the proposition in *Fatelessness* that it is evil, not good, that is explicable: evil is simply the result of making decisions, whereas good has no logic to it. And, post-Auschwitz, good is still out of the ordinary.

In 2005 he wrote the screenplay for a new movie based on *Fatelessness*, to be called *Fateless* (*Sorstalanság*), directed by Lajos Koltai. Reviewers considering both the film and the book noted that the former was more autobiographical than the novel on which it was based. It tells the story of a 14-year-old boy, György Köves (played by Marcell Nagy), who is sent to Auschwitz and Buchenwald. Here, the camp environment forces him find ways to survive, learning along the way what his priorities are and where he fits into the bigger picture of life and death. It is a powerful, moving, and startling film, and Kertész's screenplay asks questions of what the essence of survival means. His rendering of his childhood experience was not an attempt to aestheticize the Holocaust. Rather, it represented his conviction that there were aspects of the experience itself that could be described as beautiful—particularly after his postwar return to "normal" life and the incredulity of those who did not experience the camps and had little understanding of what he went through. He even feels almost nostalgic for the camaraderie he experienced there in that other world.

Imre Kertész accepted his Nobel Prize for Literature on October 10, 2002, in Stockholm, awarded "for his literary work, advocating an individual's vulnerable experience against the barbaric arbitrariness of history." He died at his home in Budapest, aged 86, on Thursday, March 31, 2016, after a long illness suffering from Parkinson's disease.

Further Reading

Vasvári, Louise O., and Steven Tötösy de Zepetnek (Eds.). *Imre Kertész and Holocaust Literature*. West Lafayette, IN: Purdue University Press, 2005.

KIDNAPPING

During and after the German invasion of Poland, many Nazis were shocked when they encountered Polish children who exhibited what they perceived to be Aryan or "Nordic" physical characteristics. It was general accepted that such children were biologically Germans who had been Polonized through acculturation.

In order to "rescue" the genes, therefore, a number of schemes were initiated to remove these children from their families—wherever they could be found—and have them placed with German families and raised as Germans. If attempts to Germanize them failed, or after further research they were found to be racially "unworthy," they would be killed. It is estimated that anywhere between 50,000 and 200,000 Polish children were removed from their families to be Germanized during the German occupation, with at least 10,000 murdered when they were deemed to be "unfit."

The **Lebensborn** program, another initiative designed to increase the Aryan population, saw the kidnapping and transfer of Polish children, mostly orphans, to families in Germany. Elsewhere in Europe the Nazis also engaged in kidnapping children. These included children from Yugoslavia, Russia, Ukraine, Czechoslovakia, Romania, Estonia, Latvia, and Norway. Some of these children were orphans, but large numbers were simply stolen from their parents. Such kidnappings were authorized at the highest level, with *Reichsführer-SS* Heinrich Himmler consulting with Adolf Hitler about his ideas on several occasions.

Himmler gave orders for the SS to kidnap up to 200,000 blond, blue-eyed Polish children from their homes or as they walked to school, to be transferred to Nazi families and brought up as Germans. By 1942, the term *Lebensborn* had become a code word for the kidnapping of Polish and other children who met these idealized Nazi racial characteristics.

These developments were not new. As early as November 25, 1939, Himmler had seen an SS position paper arguing for Polish children who were deemed to be "racially valuable" not to be deported out of the German-occupied areas but, rather, to be raised in Germany itself as ethnically German.

Then, in May 1940, two further documents called for children who had been chosen using racial criteria "to be abducted and Germanized." The selection of such children, aged between 6 and 10, would take place annually. Those chosen would be taken to Germany, given new names, and Germanized. Overall, thousands of children were accordingly transferred to the *Lebensborn* centers. In the southern Polish county of Zamość, for example, as Germany sought the forcible removal of the entire Polish population between November 1942 and March 1943 prior to the settlement of ethnic Germans in the region, some 30,000 children were taken. Of these, 4,454 were chosen for Germanization; they were given German names, forbidden to speak Polish, and reeducated in SS or other Nazi institutions, where many died of hunger or disease.

Beyond Poland, other children, sometimes in large numbers, were also kidnapped and removed to the Reich. These were taken from the Soviet Union as well as Western and Southeastern Europe. Of course, it was far less likely—and ideologically impossible—for Jewish children to be taken, though thousands of Polish, Ukrainian, and Russian children were. Where France was concerned, Hitler spoke of the prospect of an annual quota of racially desirable children who could be taken from France's "Germanic" population, presumably from Alsace and Lorraine. Other forced kidnappings also took place, such as in the aftermath of the massacre of Czech villagers at Lidice, in early June 1942. The adult male population of the village was wiped out, but 91 children were considered racially acceptable for Germanization and sent to Germany.

By 1945, British, American, and Soviet forces uncovered evidence of child kidnapping in the *Lebensborn* homes they captured. The fate of hundreds of these **child survivors** was from this point on less certain than it had been while they were in the homes. Many who had been living with German families had no awareness of their past and no birth families to which they could return. The authorities were frequently unaware of where they had come from originally, and so they could not even repatriate them to their native countries.

Some children suffered emotional trauma when they were removed from their adoptive German families and returned to their biological parents, and in certain cases, German foster families refused to give back the children they had raised as their own during the war years. Sometimes, the children themselves refused to return to their birth families, knowing no other reality than the German family they had known since they had memories.

It is nearly impossible to know how many children were kidnapped in the occupied countries. In 1946, it was estimated that up to 250,000 children were kidnapped from across Europe and sent to Germany, with no more than 15 percent located after the war and returned to their families.

Further Reading

Koehl, Robert L. *RKFDV: German Resettlement and Population Policy 1939–1945.* Cambridge, MA: Harvard University Press, 1957.

Lukas, Richard C. *Did the Children Cry? Hitler's War against Jewish and Polish Children, 1939–1945.* New York: Hippocrene Books, 2001.

KINDERTRANSPORT

Kindertransport ("the transport of children") was the informal term used to describe the British government's program intended to temporarily resettle mainly Jewish children from Germany, Austria, Czechoslovakia, and Poland between December 1938 and September 1939.

Arguably an answer to the Evian Conference of July 1938, some individuals in Britain decided to respond upon realizing that if every Jew in Germany could not be saved, then at least an effort should be made on behalf of the children. The response was the *Kindertransport*, organized in the immediate aftermath of the *Kristallnacht* pogrom of November 9–10, 1938. With this, the British government approved a measure (the Refugee Children Movement) to allow the entry of Jewish refugees ranging in age from infancy to 17, on the proviso that they had a place to stay and landing money of £50 to enable them eventually to return home. On December 2, 1938, the first group of Jewish children arrived in Britain. They were the advance guard of what became some 10,000 children rescued in roughly nine months.

Much of the preliminary work was done by Jewish relief organizations, who planned to rescue the children. For the most part, Jewish children were relocated between December 1938 and September 1939, resettled in hostels, foster homes, and farms.

On November 15, 1938, in the immediate aftermath of *Kristallnacht*, Jewish leaders in Britain appealed directly to Prime Minister Neville Chamberlain for help in rescuing Jewish children. Specifically, they asked that immigration requirements be altered so that unaccompanied Jewish children might be allowed to enter on a temporary basis. In short order, Parliament took up the issue and agreed to the request, deciding not to set a limit on the number of children to be admitted. Various Jewish relief agencies swung into action, as did the World Jewish Relief Fund, which worked with British officials to identify children to be moved and planning for their transport and resettlement.

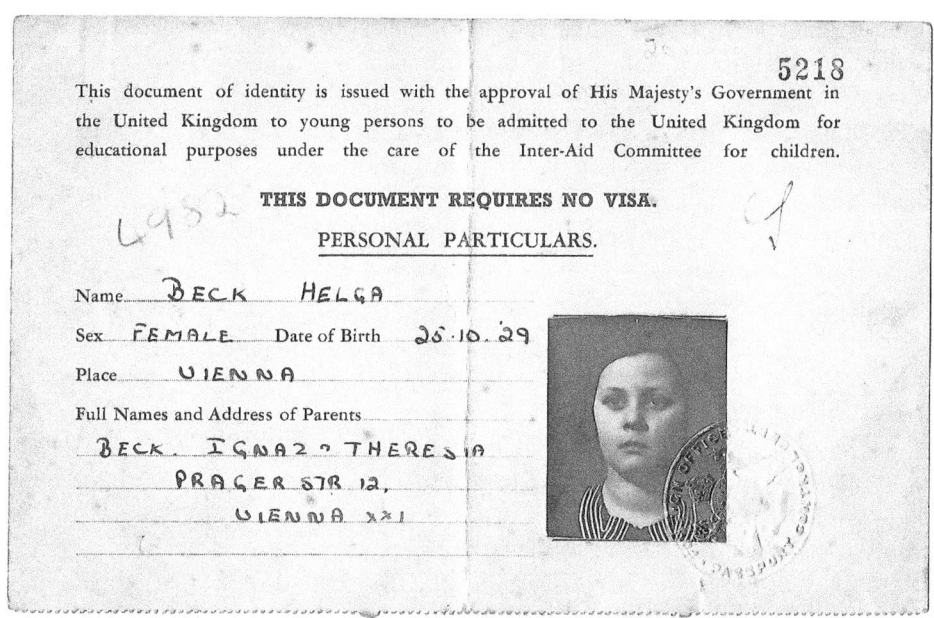

An identity document issued in 1939 for a 10-year-old Austrian Jewish girl traveling to the United Kingdom. *Kindertransport* was the German name given to rescue campaign, conducted largely from Britain, that took thousands of mainly Jewish children to safety during 1938 and 1939. It helped 10,000 children to leave Germany, Austria, Czechoslovakia, and Poland between December 1938 and September 1939. (Courtesy of Neil/HuddyHuddy)

Once word was received of the British offer, Jewish community organizations in Germany and Austria worked to identify the best ways to send the children to safety. Parents would send letters through bodies such as the U.S.-based Hebrew Immigrant Aid Society (HIAS) to sponsors in Britain; some of these sponsors were Jewish, though many were not.

Within days of the public announcement of the *Kindertransport* program, some 500 British households offered to take in a child (and, sometimes, more than one). Children were sent by train to the Netherlands or Belgium and then by boat to Harwich in southeast England, where they were handed across to waiting families. The children left their homes without valuables, a maximum of 10 marks (the figure set by German authorities for all émigrés), and one small suitcase. None was accompanied by parents; a few were babies carried by other children. Most were marked with a name tag on their clothes for the purpose of identification.

The first *Kindertransport* left Berlin on December 1, 1938, bringing 196 children from a Jewish orphanage burned by the Nazis during the *Kristallnacht* pogrom on November 9. It arrived in Harwich the following day.

Most transports left by train from Vienna, Berlin, Prague, and other major cities. Hundreds of children who did not go straight to Britain remained in Belgium and Holland, safe for the time being. On one occasion, a Dutch social worker, Geertruida Wijsmuller-Meijer, went to Vienna to see Adolf Eichmann in person, demanding that he permit children to leave for the United Kingdom immediately. After suffering many indignities at the hands of the Gestapo, she was granted permission to take 600 children out of Austria, and the first *Kindertransport* from Vienna was able to proceed.

In Britain a number of hostels were administered by members of *Habonim*, a Zionist **Jewish youth movement**, to house the children. Many other children spent time with English families and in hostels organized through local Jewish communities (such as **Garnethill Hostel** in Glasgow).

Later, after the Germans invaded Czechoslovakia, the program was expanded to include Czech Jewish children, in an initiative that lay directly at the feet of a British Jew acting in a private capacity, **Nicholas Winton**, later knighted for his services in rescuing the children. Several groups also came from Poland, especially during the summer of 1939.

The *Kindertransport* program effectively ended in September 1939 when Germany attacked Poland, though one last transport for Britain left from the Dutch port of Ijmuiden on May 14, 1940, one day before Holland surrendered. The 80 children on board had been brought by earlier transports to what was expected to be safety in the Netherlands. Despite the remarkable figure of around 10,000 children who were saved and resettled in Britain, there is room for speculation to suggest that had the program commenced earlier, that number would certainly have been much larger. It took the November pogrom of 1938, however, for Jewish parents in Germany and Austria to realize the urgency of the situation facing their families.

With the end of the war in 1945, many *Kindertransport* children attempted to reunite with their loved ones. Although some were successful, it was a sad fact that many were unable to do so, as their families had perished in the Holocaust or had been killed in combat or other wartime tragedies.

In 1989 the *Kindertransport* Association was created, dedicated to helping unite survivors with family members and sponsoring reunions to share memories and insights into their common ordeal. Today, the Association raises money for children in need, is involved in numerous educational endeavors, and publishes a quarterly journal.

Further Reading

Byers, Ann. *Saving Children from the Holocaust: The Kindertransport*. Buchanan, NY: Enslow Publishers, 2011.

Samuels, Diane. *Kindertransport*. London: Nick Hern Books, 2010.

KOR, EVA MOZES (1934–2019)

Eva Mozes was born in Romania. At the age of 10, she and her **twin** sister Miriam were subjected to **medical experimentation** on twins undertaken by Dr. **Josef Mengele** at Auschwitz.

Eva and Miriam were born on January 31, 1934, in the village of Port (located in Sălaj County), Romania, to farmers Alexander and Jaffa Mozes, who were the only

Jewish residents in the area. The twins had two siblings, Edit and Aliz. In 1940 Hungarian troops occupied their village, and in 1944, after the German invasion of Hungary, the family was deported to Auschwitz. Upon arrival, a selection took place, and the twins were taken away by an SS officer. Their parents and siblings were never seen again.

The twins were selected to be part of a group of children used in experiments under Mengele's direction. Approximately 1,500 sets of twins were subjected to these experiments, with most dying as a result.

Each Monday, Wednesday, and Friday the Nazi doctors placed Eva and Miriam, together with other twins, naked in a room for six to eight hours, measured their bodies and compared these measurements to previous charts. Every Tuesday, Thursday, and Saturday, they were taken to a laboratory where both arms were ligatured to restrict blood flow. Blood was taken from the left arm, and no fewer than five injections were given in the right arm. Neither twin knew what was contained in the injections. After one visit Eva became very ill with a very high fever, and her legs and arms were swollen and painful. When Mengele checked her fever, she was taken immediately to the camp hospital. Although she almost died and could no longer walk, she could crawl on the floor to reach a water tap. Meanwhile Miriam continued to receive her injections. After two weeks, Eva's fever broke, and she returned to Miriam. The twins spent 10 months in the camp until their rescue by Soviet troops on January 12, 1945.

Upon their **liberation**, only some 180 children, mostly twins, were found alive. They were sent to an orphanage in Katowice, Poland. In a nearby displaced person's camp, Eva and Miriam located Rosalita Csengeri, a friend of their mother, who also had twin daughters abused by Mengele in his experiments. Csengeri took care of Eva and Miriam and helped them return to Romania.

Eva and Miriam then lived in Cluj, Romania, with their Aunt Irena. There they went to school and recuperated. In 1950, now aged 16, they received permission from the communist government to leave Romania and migrate to Haifa, Israel. Eva attended an agricultural school, and Miriam studied drafting. Both girls served in the Israeli Army. Eva became a nurse and attained the rank of sergeant major in the Army Engineering Corps.

In 1960, Eva married Michael Kor, an American citizen and a fellow Holocaust survivor, and joined him in the United States. In 1965, she became a U.S. citizen, while Miriam remained in Israel. Eva and Michael had two children, Rina and Alex, and the family moved to Terre Haute, Indiana, where Eva settled into domestic and professional life raising a family and working in real estate.

Eva suffered numerous miscarriages as a result of her treatment in the camp. When she did have a child, she developed cancer and contracted tuberculosis. Miriam had kidney problems due to her organs never having had the chance to develop fully. Eva donated one of her kidneys to Miriam, but she died in 1993 of kidney cancer.

In 1978, after NBC's miniseries *Holocaust* aired, Eva and Miriam, who was still living in Israel, began locating other survivors of Mengele's experiments. In 1984 they founded the organization CANDLES ("Children of Auschwitz Nazi Deadly Lab Experiments Survivors") and through this program located 122 other survivors.

Taking things further, in 1984 Eva founded the CANDLES Holocaust Museum and Education Center in Terre Haute, intended to educate the public about eugenics, the Holocaust, and the power of forgiveness. Holocaust education, the story of the Mengele twins, and personal forgiveness became the foundation of CANDLES.

Eva received international attention when she publicly forgave the Nazis for what had been done to her. She spoke all over the world, wrote an autobiography, and appeared in multiple documentaries, sharing her story whenever possible. Her rationale for embracing forgiveness was that people can overcome hardship and tragedy, but forgiveness can help them to heal. This story was later explored in the 2006 documentary *Forgiving Dr. Mengele* (produced and directed by Bob Hercules and Cheri Pugh). She authored or coauthored six books and took part in numerous memorial services and projects.

In April 2015 Eva Kor testified in Germany in the trial of former Nazi Oskar Gröning, at which time she thanked him for his willingness, at the age of 93, to affirm the events of seven decades earlier. On January 23, 2016, she became the focus of a British documentary, *The Girl Who Forgave the Nazis* (dir. Steve Humphries), which explored her meeting with Gröning.

The recipient of many awards for her advocacy of peace and reconciliation, Eva Mozes Kor remained active throughout the first two decades of the 20th century by giving lectures and guided tours across university campuses in the United States and elsewhere. She returned to Auschwitz on numerous occasions, often accompanied by friends and community members.

On July 4, 2019, Eva Kor died in Kraków while escorting a CANDLES group visiting Auschwitz. She was 85 years old.

Further Reading

Kor, Eva Mozes, and Lisa Rojnay Buccieri. *Surviving the Angel of Death: The Story of a Mengele Twin in Auschwitz*. Terre Haute, IN: Tanglewood, 2009.

Kor, Eva Mozes, and Mary Wright. *Echoes from Auschwitz: Dr. Mengele's Twins. The Story of Eva and Miriam Mozes*. Terre Haute, IN: Candles, Inc., 1995.

KORCZAK, JANUSZ (1878–1942)

Janusz Korczak (born Henryk Goldszmit), was born in Warsaw July 22, 1878 (some accounts say 1879) to the assimilated Jewish family of Józef Goldszmit and his wife Cecylia née Gębicka. He was an author, pediatrician, and pedagogue who sacrificed himself in 1942 in order to accompany the children in his orphanage to the gas chambers of Treblinka.

Korczak's father was a prominent Warsaw lawyer; when he died on April 25, 1896, the family was left without a source of income, so at the age of 18, Korczak became the sole breadwinner for his mother, sister, and grandmother.

In 1898 he first used the name Janusz Korczak as a pen name in a writing competition. Between that year and 1904, he studied medicine at the University of Warsaw and wrote for several Polish newspapers. Upon graduation he became a pediatrician and worked at the Children's Hospital, and then he set out to minister to the sick and underprivileged, even refusing at times well-paying offers from wealthy patients. While studying in Berlin in 1907–1908, he met a Polish Jewish educator, Stefania "Stefa" Wilczyńska; the two would have a close working relationship for the rest of their lives.

During the Russo-Japanese War of 1904–1905, he served as a doctor in the Russian Army, and in 1911 he became the director of *Dom Sierot*, an orphanage of his own design for Jewish children in Warsaw. He appointed Stefa to work with him as his deputy director and house mother. About 100 children lived in the orphanage, where he established what he termed a "republic for children," with its own parliament, a court of law, and a newspaper. When World War I broke out, he rejoined the army, serving in field hospitals until Russia's withdrawal from the war in 1917. Building on the precedent established with the Jewish orphanage, in 1919 he created an orphanage for Polish children, also in Warsaw. These homes were highly innovative in their approach to child welfare, not only because of their hygienic surroundings and a devoted staff but also, more significantly, due to their giving children an important role in administering the institution.

Korczak served again as a military doctor in the Polish Army with the rank of major during the Polish-Soviet War of 1919–1920. After his war service, he resumed his medical practice in Warsaw.

During the 1930s he was a popular radio broadcaster, answering educational questions and promoting the rights of children to a broad audience, especially in his program, *The Old Doctor's Talk*. In conjunction with the program, he also published a children's newspaper. In 1933 he was awarded the Silver Cross of Polonia

Statue entitled "Janusz Korczak and the Children" by sculptor Boris Saktsier, situated within the memorial square. Janusz Korczak was an author, pediatrician, and pedagogue who sacrificed himself in 1942, refusing to abandon the children of his Warsaw orphanage and accompanying them to the gas chambers of Treblinka. At Yad Vashem in Jerusalem, a special memorial has been dedicated to his memory. (Courtesy of Berthold Werner)

Restituta, prior to traveling to British Mandate Palestine in 1934 and 1936, where he stayed in kibbutz Ein Harod and closely observed the educational system there.

It was as a writer that Korczak had the broadest effect during his lifetime. Not only attuned to the physical needs of children, Korczak was at home in their imaginative world as a children's author. He wrote over 20 books, many of them about children's rights and the child's life experience in the adult world. Such books included *King Matt the First*, *The Bankruptcy of Little Jack*, *How to Love the Child*, *The Child's Right to Respect*, and *Rules for Living*.

When Germany invaded Poland in September 1939, Korczak was prepared to volunteer once more for duty in the Polish Army, but he was precluded by his age; instead, he remained with the children at the orphanage in Warsaw. In 1940 he and the orphans were forced into the newly created Warsaw Ghetto, just when the number of children had increased given that whole families had been killed during the German invasion. By the start of 1940, there were about 150 children in the orphanage.

The daily routine under the restrictions of ghetto life remained as close to "normal" as Korczak could make it. The children continued to play their part in the running the orphanage as before, to which Korczak added amusements and diversions such as plays and concerts that were open to the public. Every Saturday Korczak would tell the children a story they had chosen for themselves.

The greatest concern facing Korczak and Stefa always related to their ability to obtain enough food for the children. With the onset of starvation in the ghetto, Korczak went from door to door begging for food, warm clothes, and medicines. He was offered several opportunities to leave the ghetto and obtain refuge of the other side of the wall, but repeatedly rebuffed all approaches, saying that he could not abandon the children—despite being in poor health and burdened with deep foreboding about the future.

On August 5, 1942, during a period of intensified roundups, it became the turn of the orphans to feel the full force of the Holocaust. Heavily armed troops arrived to collect the 192 orphans (some accounts give 196) and 12 staff members to take them to the *Umschlagplatz* (deportation point to the death camps) prior to their dispatch to Treblinka. Again, Korczak was presented with the chance to save his life: the Polish underground organization **Żegota** offered to take him over to the Aryan side of the city, but once more he declined, saying that he could not abandon his children.

Eyewitness reports wrote that as they left, they were dressed in their best clothes, holding each other by the hand, with each carrying a blue knapsack and a favorite book or toy. Korczak led the procession through the ghetto. When the group reached the *Umschlagplatz*, Korczak, together with Stefa and the children, saw the awaiting train. Even here he was given one final chance to save his life, but he refused, insisting on remaining to the end with his children. He, Stefa, and the children then boarded the train that would take them to Treblinka, where, upon arrival, all were gassed to death.

The life, work, and death of Dr. Janusz Korczak has since become an important symbol of devotion to the lives of others, even at great personal expense. He has become a role model as an educator for decency, with a legacy much loved throughout the world.

Further Reading

Cohen, Adir. *The Gate of Light: Janusz Korczak, the Educator and Writer Who Overcame the Holocaust*. Madison, NJ: Fairleigh Dickinson University Press, 1994.

Lifton, Betty Jean. *The King of Children: The Life and Death of Janusz Korczak*. New York: Collins, 1988.

KRAUS, DITA (b.1929)

Dita Kraus, *neé* Polachova, was born in Prague on July 12, 1929, where she was raised in a happy, loving, secular Jewish home. An only child of scholarly parents—her father was a lawyer—her home was filled with German, Czech, and French books, and reading became an integral part of her life. The secular nature of the family meant that she did not even know she was Jewish until she was eight, when she was in second grade at school.

Then, when she was nine, the Nazi invasion of Prague in March 1939 forced the family to move. Within a month her father lost his job, the family's apartment was confiscated, and they went to live with Dita's grandparents. In 1941 they were again evicted and now had to live in a single room in an apartment shared with another Jewish family.

At age 13, in November 1942, Dita and her parents were sent to the concentration camp/ghetto at **Theresienstadt** (Terezín). Dita and her mother stayed for just over a year. Like many other children, Dita busied herself through the creation of drawings and artworks, some of which have survived.

In December 1943 Dita and her mother were deported to Auschwitz, and the number 73305 was tattooed on Dita's arm. The compound in which they were located, known as Family Camp BIIb, contained a children's block, Block 31, overseen by the notorious "Angel of Death," Dr. **Joseph Mengele**.

Now aged 14, Dita met **Fredy Hirsch**, a young, inspirational Zionist educator who ran the children's block and organized a school for children in the BIIb family camp. It was his idea to convince the Nazi authorities to allow one block to be set aside for children. Hirsch, aged 27, was already known to Dita from her childhood in Prague, where he was her sports instructor. He was also successful in persuading the camp administration to have young people aged between 14 and 16 designated as "assistants" at a time when the Nazis defined children as only those aged up to 14 years. It was this ruse that allowed Dita to remain in the children's block.

One of the tasks set by Fredy Hirsch was for Dita and a boy of around the same age to become "librarians" in the children's block. There was only a tiny collection of eight tattered books there: these included the Czech-language version of *A Short History of the World*, by H. G. Wells; an atlas; something by Sigmund Freud; and a book of short stories by Czech writer Karel Capek. The library was used by those teaching the alphabet to the younger children.

The library had to be kept a secret from the Nazis, and one of Dita's tasks was to care for the books and hide them. These random volumes had been found among the luggage of Jews arriving at Auschwitz, and a few more came into the collection the same way. Dita managed to keep and maintain her little library across 1943 and 1944. These books, she was to say later, enabled her to maintain her humanity in her darkest days, even though in March 1944, half of those living at the children's block were murdered.

Fredy Hirsch also lost his life on March 8, 1944, when the mass murder of the children seemed imminent. After learning of this, he was found in a coma from an overdose, possibly of painkillers or sleeping pills. His death was shrouded in mystery, but it was believed that Jewish doctors, fearful for his safety in the event of a revolt, had drugged him to keep him away from harm, but misjudged the dose. Fredy Hirsch was much beloved by the children, and his death was a shock—especially for Dita, who looked up to him as an older brother if not a father figure.

In July 1944, Dita and her mother were among 1,000 women still able to work, sent by Mengele to a forced labor camp in Hamburg. From there, they were sent to Bergen-Belsen, where they were liberated by British troops in April 1945. At Belsen, Dita, like tens of thousands of others, contracted typhus, as did her mother, who became ill on June 27, 1945, after the **liberation**. She died two days later. Dita's father Hans had earlier died of starvation at Auschwitz, aged 44. Dita, now an orphan, was not yet 16.

Returning to Prague, she was, to the best of her knowledge, the only survivor of her family; she had no home and practically no possessions. A few weeks after her return, however, she met up with Otto (né Ota) Kraus, a writer she had known of (but never met) as one of the instructors in the children's block at Auschwitz. They started writing to each other, and in 1947 they were married. In 1949 they moved to Israel with their young son, Peter-Martin, and commenced a new life. Eventually they had two more children, Michaela (born 1951) and Ronny (born 1957). Ota Kraus died on October 5, 2000, but Dita still lives to this day in Netanya, surrounded by grandchildren and great-grandchildren.

Further Reading

Iturbe, Antonio. *The Librarian of Auschwitz*. New York: Henry Holt, 2012.

KRAUS, GILBERT (1898–1975) AND ELEANOR (1905–1989)

Gilbert (Gil) and Eleanor Kraus were an American-born Jewish couple from Philadelphia who helped rescue 50 Jewish children from Austria and Germany in late 1939.

Gil was born in 1898 and became a successful lawyer. He married Eleanor, who was born in 1905, and they had two children. With the intensification of anti-Jewish measures in Austria following the German annexation of that country in March 1938, Gil and Eleanor, distressed by what they were learning through the American press and by speaking with Jewish friends, decided that they had to do something to save Jewish children. This would not be an easy task. At the time, the U.S. government had strict immigration quotas that prevented Jews from Germany and Austria migrating to America. Moreover, antisemitic circles in the United States made it difficult to rally support for their cause.

Nevertheless, early in the winter of 1938, Gilbert Kraus, encouraged by Lewis Levine, president of Brith Sholom (a Jewish fraternal organization in which he was active), worked out a scheme that would satisfy both American and German regulations and officials in order to enable Gil and Eleanor to travel to Germany, select 50 children in need of rescue, bring them back across to the United States, and resettle them with American families in and around Philadelphia. They sought to convince American families to sign affidavits sponsoring the children, after which visas could be secured for the children under the guise that they would be attending a summer camp in the United States. Once the children were safely in America, it was hoped that the U.S. government would permit them to stay after their visas had expired.

The plan was viewed as quixotic by some in the Jewish community once it began to be discussed behind closed doors, however, as it was considered that the plan was not only bound to fail but could also generate further antisemitism in the local area.

Undaunted, Gil and Eleanor began to lobby both the U.S. government and the German and Austrian embassies. Where the U.S. regulations were concerned, they discovered that many visas previously issued to Jews seeking to emigrate had never been used. With this realization, they successfully persuaded the U.S. State Department to allow these unused visas to be reissued for the benefit of 50 children whose parents were willing to allow the Krauses to transport their children to United States.

A few months later, Gil and Eleanor, along with Levine and several others, traveled to Vienna, Austria. There they painstakingly worked with Jewish leaders and selected 25 boys and 25 girls who would return with them to the United States. The children were not orphans, but their parents were prepared to hand them over for safekeeping while they worked on procuring visas for themselves that would lead to their own migration. The Krauses personally interviewed each child and his or her family before deciding which ones would make the best candidates. In one sense the rescue scheme followed the same ideals as the British **Kindertransport** scheme.

With the voyage to America made, Gil, Eleanor, and the 50 children landed in New York on June 3, 1939. They were housed initially in a location resembling a summer camp in Pennsylvania and were then placed with sponsoring families. The Krauses themselves took in two of the children. Although most of the children would never see their families again as a result of the Holocaust, some were able to have at least one if not both parents join them later to be reunited as a family.

The Krauses rarely spoke of the actions they undertook in 1938–1939, even to family members, and it was not until after Eleanor's death in 1989 that the full story about their rescue mission became known to their children and grandchildren.

Eleanor had kept a detailed diary and journal in which she had recorded many details—including documents and photographs—relating to the rescue mission.

The story was not brought to the public's attention until 2013, when a journalist and writer, Steven Pressman, wrote, produced, and directed a documentary film chronicling the event. Entitled *50 Children: The Rescue Mission of Mr. and Mrs. Kraus*, it was first shown by HBO on Yom Hashoah (Holocaust Memorial Day) on April 8, 2013. In 2014, Pressman (who had married one of Gil and Eleanor's granddaughters) published a book under the same title. Both the film and the book used passages from Eleanor's journal, as well as photos, documents, and interviews with more than a dozen of the surviving children, to tell the story of the Krauses and their rescue mission.

It is believed that the Kraus mission brought the largest single group of unaccompanied children to the United States during the period of the Third Reich. The Krauses had planned on another rescue mission, but the outbreak of war in Europe in September 1939 prevented it from being carried out.

Further Reading

Pressman, Steven. *50 Children: One Ordinary American Couple's Extraordinary Rescue Mission into the Heart of Nazi Germany*. New York: HarperCollins, 2014.

KÜCHLER-SILBERMAN, LENA (1910–1987)

Lena Küchler was born in January 1910 in Wielczka, near Kraków, Poland. She attended a Hebrew-language high school in Kraków and then studied at the University of Kraków, graduating in philosophy. She taught at a Jewish school in Bielsko and lectured at a teacher training academy. After the Jews of Bielsko, including her parents, were deported to Bełżec in June 1942, Küchler and her sister Fela made their way to Warsaw, where both assumed Aryan identities and began **passing** in wider society. Bleaching her hair blond and posing as a Catholic, Lena worked on a farm and in the city as a governess to two girls. Her own daughter died of malnutrition during the war, and her husband abandoned her.

Prior to this, earlier in 1942, Lena found a live baby boy lying on top of the corpse of his mother. She smuggled him out of the ghetto and found him a refuge in a monastery, even though the monks initially refused to accept a child with a **circumcision**.

At the end of the war Lena went to Kraków to live with her brother, an army colonel, and commenced working on her doctorate. Meanwhile, she went to the Jewish Refugee Center in Kraków to look for her missing sister, Fela, only to learn that Fela had been tortured to death by the Gestapo three days prior to the **liberation**. At the Refugee Center, Lena was appalled at the plight of around 100 children housed there: some had been liberated from concentration camps, whereas others had been wandering the streets of Kraków or Warsaw or had been dropped off by priests and families that had protected the children during the war but were no longer willing or able to feed them. Nobody wanted the children; they were sick, starving, unloved, filthy, and frightened.

The older refugees were too troubled to help these hardened, terrified children. Lena found only one person, a woman named Bella, who was willing to help with the continuous task of washing and feeding the children. In Poland reintegration assistance was in short supply, but Lena pressured various authorities for at least a minimum of help.

She abandoned work on her doctorate and started to care for the 100 children. Initially she brought food from home, but then, through her brother's army connections, she managed to obtain a quantity of sugar on the black market, which she then bartered for food and supplies for the children. She also aimed to provide physical and emotional rehabilitation for a group of children who had often been forced to live in closets or forests, as well as for the many who had seen their parents murdered. She chose to take them to the country town of Zakopane so there would be time and space to recuperate and gain an education, despite warnings of antisemitism in rural Poland. The owners of a onetime mountain resort agreed to take in the children.

There was, however, a lot of prejudice against Jews after the war. The teachers at the local school did not want the Jewish orphans to enroll as students, and although the occupying Soviet authorities pressured the teachers to take them in, local children beat up on the orphans as they went to and from school and in the schoolyard. Eventually the Jewish children were too scared to attend school and were taught instead at the orphanage. Even that was not enough for the local inhabitants, who prepared to set fire to the resort to get rid of the Jewish children. Zakopane's Communist Safety and Security office refused to take responsibility for the safety of the orphanage.

In March 1946 Lena managed to obtain 50 Greek passports for the children through the Jewish Orthodox organization Vaad Hatzali. Late one night, following up on this, she told the children they were going on a trip but that they were not to tell anybody. Next morning, they were driven out in three large, tarpaulin-covered trucks and went to Berlin, though many of the children were scared to get on board because they reminded them of the trucks that had taken them from their homes to concentration camps. From Berlin the children went to Czechoslovakia, where they stayed for a time with nuns in a convent in Prague, after which they went to France, where they stayed for two years and were taught French and Hebrew. Almost all the children migrated to Israel from France in early 1949, where they were taken care of by the Kvutzal Stiller community.

Lena also moved to Israel, where she settled in Tel Aviv, studied psychology in an academy for kindergarten and school trainee teachers, worked as an educational superintendent, and later set up an educational services center. She remarried, and in 1957 she and her husband had a daughter, Shira. She published five books (translated into numerous languages), the most well-known of which is *My Hundred Children*, which became a bestseller. In 1987 a movie was made of her rescue actions with the children, entitled *Lena: My 100 Children*. Directed by Edwin Sherin, it starred Linda Lavin in the title role.

Lena Küchler-Silberman kept in touch with her adopted children even after they had grown up. She retired in 1972 and died in Israel in 1987, aged 77.

Further Reading

Küchler-Silberman, Lena. *One Hundred Children*. New York: Doubleday, 1961.

KULSKI, JULIAN EUGENIUSZ (b.1929)

Julian Eugeniusz Kulski was born in Warsaw on March 3, 1929, into the Protestant family of Julian Spitosław Kulski and his wife, Eugenia. His father was the deputy mayor of Warsaw prior to World War II and served as mayor during the war itself. During the invasion of Poland, Julian Spitosław Kulski actively led a defense of the city together with Stefan Starzyński, who had served as Warsaw's mayor before the war, and refused to leave during the German attack on the city.

Julian Eugeniusz Kulski was only 10 years old when the war began. He had been active in the Polish Boy Scouts (*Związek Harcerstwa Polskiego*, or ZHP). During the German occupation between 1939 and 1945, the ZHP became underground resistance fighters, establishing the *Szare Szeregi* (Grey Ranks) on September 27, 1939, in Warsaw under the leadership of the Supreme Scouting Council. They actively resisted and fought German occupation in Warsaw all the way through to January 18, 1945, and contributed to the resistance operations of the Polish underground, working under the auspices of the Government Delegation of the Republic of Poland to the Country and the Home Army Headquarters. It was said that by the end of the war some of its members were among the Home Army's best-trained troops.

Julian was active in the youth division of the Grey Ranks. His leader was Ludwik Berger ("Goliath"). Youths aged 12 to 14 did not normally take part in combat but performed auxiliary services such as traffic regulation, communication, and rescue. In 1941, Julian took the soldier's oath and adopted the codename "Chojnacki," joining the Union of Armed Struggle (*Związek Walki Zbrojnej*, or ZWZ), Poland's underground army. This existed from November 13, 1939, until February 14, 1942, when it was reconstituted as the Home Army (*Armia Krajowa*, or AK).

In 1942 Julian was arrested by the Gestapo and imprisoned in the Pawiak prison, which had become part of the Nazi concentration camp system. He did not reveal information under interrogation, and in due course, he was released. He then left Warsaw for a short time but returned in time to witness the Warsaw Ghetto Uprising of April 19 through May 16, 1943. At that time, he was just 14 years of age.

After the death of his guardian and commander, Ludwik Berger, Julian adopted Berger's codename, Goliath. Then he moved to AK 9 Company and fought with the Polish Home Army in its two-month-long battle against the German Army in the Warsaw Uprising between August 1, 1944, and October 3, 1944. For his exploits and courage in battle, he was awarded the Cross of Valor. After the failure of the uprising, Julian, not yet 16 years of age, was imprisoned in the Stalag XI-A Altengrabow prison camp. After Poland's liberation and the release of prisoners, he was placed in the care of Allied troops in May 1945.

Shortly after the end of the war, Julian wrote up his diary, an intimate and harrowing account of Poland's agony under the Nazis, in an attempt to record the events through which he had lived. Writing of his experiences provided him with the catharsis that would make it possible for him to return to daily life in the postwar world.

After World War II, Julian relocated to the United Kingdom, where he studied architecture at Oxford University between 1947 and 1948. He earned a bachelor's (1953) and master's (1954) degree in architecture from Yale University; and then began a PhD in city planning at Warsaw Institute Technology. He earned his degree in 1966. His father, Julian Spitosław Kulski, remained in Warsaw, where he died at age 76.

Today Julian Eugeniusz Kulski is a fellow of the American Institute of Architects, a professor of Urban and Regional Planning, and works extensively in developing countries throughout the world as a consultant architect for several United Nations agencies. He lives in northern Virginia.

Thirty-three years after the events, he translated his journal into English, and his book, along with more than 150 photographs (many previously unpublished), was published in New York in 1979.

Further Reading

Kulski, Julian Eugeniusz. *Dying, We Live*. New York: Holt, Rinehart and Winston, 1979.

L

LA COLLINE AUX MILLE ENFANTS

La Colline aux Mille Enfants (*The Hill of a Thousand Children*), directed by Jean-Louis Lorenzi in 1997, is a French film dramatizing the story of Pastor **André Trocmé** and the villagers of **Le Chambon-sur-Lignon**, France, during World War II. Set in occupied France in the fall of 1941, the film recounts the story of Pastor Jean Fontaine (Patrick Raynal) and his wife Martha (Ottavia Piccolo). As more and more Jewish children arrive in the village of Le Chambon, Pastor Fontaine and Martha work every day and through the night to help with the stream of refugees.

While dealing with the German occupation of France during World War II, the film specifically relates to the rescue of hundreds of Jewish children at that time. Attempts are made to consider why the people of this region were so well disposed toward those they were shielding, and reference is made to the historic memory pervading the community, whose Protestant population suffered after the revocation of the Edict of Nantes in 1685. The memory is recalled in the film of how the Protestants of that time, just like the Jews during the war, were driven into hiding and that, as a result, how the population sympathizes with the plight of the Jews. From the pulpit, Pastor Fontaine passionately presses those in his church to remember this history and to work together to provide sanctuary for Jewish children.

We see individual Jewish stories as a way to understand the broader picture: of Clara (Jip Wijngaarden), the first Jewish refugee among the hundreds who will follow her; of Myriam (Wioletta Michalczuk), a Jewish teenager originally from Poland; and of David (Ruben Honigmann), a little boy from Berlin who tries to retain his Jewish identity through keeping kosher and remembering his prayers. We see also how the children are hidden in plain sight through being dispersed in rural areas surrounding the village, where they are concealed from the eyes of prying French collaborators or occupying Germans.

The film shows how the provision of sanctuary worked at ground level, when, for example, French teacher Jean Lescot (Lucien Darget), in class with his students, is assaulted by gendarmes looking for Jewish children in the school. Lescot, denying that there are any Jews, is struck by a policeman in front of his pupils in a most humiliating manner, before leaving with the threat that he is being watched. Neither the teacher nor the other pupils ever give away the Jewish children in the school.

La Colline aux Mille Enfants is a study in the pressures faced by all the citizens in the village, from the pastor through to those in whose homes the children have been given refuge. It is filled with high suspense, drama, and tragedy, and viewers are provided with an inkling into the courage of the people of Le Chambon during this most trying of times. Pastor Fontaine's fundamental message was that the people should engage in resistance against the policies of the German occupation and the Vichy regime, but as a pacifist his idea did not embrace resistance through violence, but, rather, through spiritual struggle and defiance. We see the degree to which all involved are faced with complex choices, particularly over whether the use of violence is ever justified. In an important moment in the film, Clara, an outspoken teenager, confronts the Pastor by telling him that his pacifism is useless and that she is going instead to join the partisans.

The film shows that what happened at Le Chambon was multifaceted and thoroughly human. The older children are confronted by their awakening sexuality, and the character of Myriam becomes a coming-of-age study as she falls in love with Marc (Philippe Lefebvre), a young teacher of mathematics at the school. Marc, in turn, while committing himself to Myriam, is taken by the Germans as a hostage after a Resistance action and is executed.

The personification of evil—and collaboration—is represented in the film by an incoming police commissioner, Robert Vitrac (Jean-François Garreaud). Himself a Protestant ("You're one of us," Fontaine tells him at one point when seeking clemency for Marc), Vitrac is an Inspector Javert–type figure who brooks no opposition and is relentless in his pursuit of Jews and those who defend them. Through this figure, the movie adds another layer to the complexities of resistance and collaboration during the Vichy period, and the circumstances of Vitrac's ultimate departure from the movie only serve to add to the intricacies of appreciating daily life under the Vichy regime.

Once the Germans arrive in force in November 1942, however, the contrasts between black and white are much easier to appreciate. Under the Germans, the threats become much more pronounced, with the threat of roundups intensifying. In a climactic scene toward the end of the movie, a major German operation is launched throughout the village to flush out all Jewish children; with the word spreading from house to house that the Germans are on their way (all that is needed in a knock on the door followed by "They're here"), the children—hundreds, it seems—know what to do. The scene that follows, with streams of children emerging from buildings throughout the village, converging, and then all running to a prearranged hiding place, is a moment of high drama.

Eventually, the children are moved to an ultimate refuge in Switzerland, taken clandestinely by *passeurs* working with various Jewish and Christian child welfare agencies. Prior this, however, one further dilemma arises for Myriam: inspired by Pastor Fontaine and the goodness she has experienced during her time in the village, she asks Fontaine to help her become a Protestant. This is not something he is prepared to do; only after she has discussed it with her parents, later, will he consider it. The audience, aware of the situation facing returning Jewish adults, is left wondering whether that discussion will ever take place.

Released widely in France to positive critical reviews in 1997, *La Colline aux Mille Enfants* won the International Emmy Award from the United States for 1996.

Further Reading

Grose, Peter. *A Good Place to Hide: How One French Community Saved Thousands of People during World War II*. New York: Pegasus Books, 2015.

Hallie, Philip. *Lest Innocent Blood Be Shed: The Story of the Village of Le Chambon, and How Goodness Happened There*. New York: Harper Perennial, 1994.

Moorehead, Caroline. *Village of Secrets: Defying the Nazis in Vichy France*. New York: HarperCollins, 2014.

LAPID-ANDRIESSE, MIRJAM (b.1933)

Mirjam Lapid-Andriesse was born in the eastern Netherlands city of Deventer on April 17, 1933. She was the youngest of four children, two boys and two girls. She grew up in Deventer and Utrecht in a family committed to Zionism. She was later to recall that as a little girl, she was jealous of her older sister and brothers who could participate in the meetings of a **Jewish youth movement** in the family living room.

Soon after the German invasion of the Netherlands in May 1940, Nazi antisemitic measures began to be introduced to the Jews of Holland. Mirjam recalls that the children were unable to go to the swimming pool or the cinema, had to hand over their bicycles and were forbidden from attending public schools. As a result, she missed three years of regular schooling.

By early 1942 most Jews had been forced into ghettos, and as many as 15,000 were rounded up and sent to forced labor camps in the Netherlands and Germany. Most of the remaining Jews in the country were concentrated in one large ghetto in Amsterdam, which is where Mirjam and her family, taken from their home in Utrecht, were sent in April 1943 when Mirjam was 10 years old. Deportations from Amsterdam had already begun in the summer of 1942, mainly to Auschwitz and Sobibór, so Mirjam's family were in one sense fortunate to have been held back for so long.

In June 1943, however, they were taken by train to the transit camp at Westerbork. From here, they were sent to Bergen-Belsen. Mirjam's elder brother did not suffer this fate: already he had joined the Dutch resistance. He would eventually be caught, however, and sent to Dachau. All would ultimately survive, save Mirjam's father Herman, who died from starvation and exhaustion on February 24, 1945, just six weeks before the **liberation**.

At the beginning of April 1945, with the war all but over, it seemed only a matter of time before Bergen Belsen would be liberated. Although the camp was hopelessly overcrowded and left largely alone by the Nazis, SS units decided to move as many prisoners out of the camp as possible in the short time they had left. As a result, some 7,500 sick, dying Jewish inmates were loaded onto three transport trains, all bound for **Theresienstadt**.

The first train left the camp on April 6; reaching Theresienstadt, the prisoners were liberated by Soviet troops a few days later. The second train left on April 7, but only made it as far as Magdeburg before it was stopped, and the prisoners were freed by units from the U.S. Army. On April 9, the remaining 2,500 prisoners, including Mirjam, were loaded onto a third train. Her mother had recently been gravely ill with typhus and was initially forbidden from joining the train because she was unable to walk the seven kilometers to the train. Miryam's brother and sister lifted her up, however, and between them managed to drag her along to the station. She became sicker during the day-long train ride to Theresienstadt, however, and fell into a coma. It was the day before Mirjam's 12th birthday; the next morning she received a birthday present: her mother was still alive.

As it turned out, the train did not arrive at Theresienstadt. With so many railroad tracks destroyed as a result of incessant Allied bombing, a circuitous route had to be charted to the northeast in hopes of finding a way through to the south. This led to the train wandering aimlessly through eastern Germany for the next two weeks in search of a way through, essentially disappearing. Conditions on board were dreadful. Many people were already sick with typhus while in Belsen, and with little in the way of food, water, or sanitation, many of those on board—at least 600, by some estimates—died. The ages of the passengers ranged widely, from infants to some over 70. On April 17, Mirjam celebrated her 12th birthday on what became known as "the Lost Train."

On April 23, the train was forced to stop in the little German town of Tröbitz, located near Dresden. Soon, Soviet troops arrived to provide whatever assistance they could to those still alive, including Mirjam and her family. Since that day, Mirjam has continued to celebrate her second birthday on April 23. They were held at Tröbitz for the next two months, recuperating while arrangements were made for their repatriation to the Netherlands. Mirjam returned to Utrecht with her mother and two older siblings.

In 1953, aged 20, Mirjam moved to Israel. Eventually her entire family relocated there as well. She married, settled at Kibbutz Tzora, and raised five children, all of whom became officers in the Israel Defense Forces.

Further Reading

Polak, Joseph A. "The Lost Transport." *Commentary*, September 1995, at https://www.commentarymagazine.com/articles/the-lost-transport/.

Siret, Mal. "Child Holocaust Witness Reveals Lucky Escape Aboard the Lost Train." BBC News, August 6, 2019, at https://www.bbc.com/news/world-europe-49233817.

LE CHAMBON-SUR-LIGNON

Le Chambon-sur-Lignon is a small Protestant town 88 kilometers southwest of Lyon, on the Vivarais Plateau in the Haute-Loire region of the Auvergne, a hilly region of south-central France. Since the 1600s the residents of Le Chambon have been mainly Huguenot Protestants. As Huguenots they had been persecuted by the Catholic authorities from the sixteenth to the eighteenth centuries, and, as such, they provided shelter to fellow Protestants fleeing persecution and discrimination.

The memory of their own suffering as a religious minority made the residents of Le Chambon suspicious of despotic regimes. In 1914, the village hosted Alsatian refugees, and, between 1936 and 1940, Republicans fleeing the civil war in Spain.

During World War II, most residents of Le Chambon refused to cooperate with the Vichy government or take an oath to Marshal Pétain; church bells were not rung in his honor. After the Vichy government was established in June 1940, Pastor **André Trocmé**, a staunch pacifist, engaged in a peaceful civil disobedience campaign. While he and others like him were the principal catalysts of nonviolent rescue activity, the effort involved many others, including Protestant pastors in nearby parishes as well as Catholics, American Quakers, Jews, Swiss Protestants, Evangelicals, students of various faiths, and nonbelievers.

In the winter of 1940, an organized rescue effort on behalf of Jews began; Pastor Trocmé contacted the American Friends Service Committee (Quakers) in Marseille to assist in providing relief supplies to the 30,000 foreign Jews held in internment camps in southern France. In December 1940 CIMADE, a Protestant refugee-relief organization, was present in internment camps such as Gurs, Rivesaltes, and Les Milles in the south of France, as well as opening refugee centers, such as the *Côteau fleuri* near Le Chambon.

Burns Chalmers, a leading American Quaker, then told Pastor Trocmé that while the Quakers might be able to get internees released from the camps, he knew that no one was prepared to offer them shelter. Trocmé assured Chalmers that Le Chambon would take them in. Chalmers was able to negotiate the release of many Jews, especially children, from some of the camps in the south. In addition to those who arrived as a result of this organized rescue effort, Jews and others also arrived as individuals or in small groups. Among them were Spanish Republicans who had fled internment camps, anti-Nazi Germans, and many young Frenchmen seeking to avoid deportation to Germany for forced labor. Also sheltered were members of the French Resistance, which became active in the region in 1942.

The refugee Jews were mostly foreign-born and not French citizens; a majority were children. They were dispersed among small isolated villages and farms in the mountainous region surrounding Le Chambon. The OSE played an important role in escorting children to Le Chambon and placing them in private homes, boarding houses, and refugee homes funded specifically to shelter them. The Quakers, American Congregationalists, Swiss Red Cross, and even national governments like Sweden gave money to fund these homes, in which the children received food, clothing, and false identity documents, as well as attending school. In order to maintain an appearance of normalcy and to conceal the presence of Jews in the communities, they frequently attended Protestant religious services, while Pastor Trocmé encouraged them to continue their Jewish observances.

In a public sermon on August 16, 1942, Trocmé protested the mass roundup of Jews in Paris at the Vélodrome d'Hiver in July 1942, stating that the church must seek God's forgiveness for its cowardice.

Whenever villagers learned of impending visits from Vichy police or German troops, they moved the refugees deeper into the country. Once the soldiers left, the villagers would go out to where the refugees were hiding and sing a song, signaling that it was safe for those hiding to come home.

Some refugees were helped to cross the border to the safety of neutral Switzerland, following paths pioneered by persecuted Huguenots centuries earlier. CIMADE was especially active in finding escape routes to Switzerland, with a common underground route leading from Le Chambon to Annemasse, close to the Swiss border, from where *passeurs* would convey the children across the frontier and to safety.

When the Germans invaded France's southern zone in November 1942, the situation for Jews worsened, and the people of Le Chambon acted to protect thousands of children and adults in open defiance of the authorities. The unity of the local population compelled the Vichy establishment to proceed with caution. On February 13, 1943, however, French police arrested Pastor Trocmé and another minister, Pastor Édouard Theis, as well as the headmaster of the local primary school, Roger Darcissac. They were interned at a camp in Saint-Paul d'Eyjeaux, near Limoges. After 28 days they were released, at which point they simply resumed their rescue activities. In late 1943 rumors of rearrest sent them into hiding, and Magda Trocmé took over leading the rescues. By the summer of 1943 the Gestapo offered a reward for André Trocmé's capture, but no one betrayed him during the 10 months in which he was hiding.

On June 29, 1943, the Gestapo raided a local secondary school and arrested 18 students. Five were identified as Jews and were sent to Auschwitz, where they were murdered. The Gestapo also arrested their teacher, Daniel Trocmé, Pastor Trocmé's cousin, and deported him to Majdanek concentration camp, where the SS murdered him. Roger Le Forestier, Le Chambon's physician, who helped Jews obtain false documents, was he arrested and subsequently shot by the Gestapo on August 20, 1944, in Montluc prison in Lyon.

The plateau on which Le Chambon-sur-Lignon is situated was liberated by the Free French First Armored Division on September 2–3, 1944. It has been estimated that certainly hundreds, but more likely thousands of Jewish children were rescued by the people of Le Chambon during World War II.

In 1990 Le Chambon became the first entire community to be recognized as Righteous among the Nations by Yad Vashem in Jerusalem, and two trees dedicated to the village were planted in the Garden of the Righteous there. In addition, Pastor Trocmé and his wife Magda were both honored individually, on January 5, 1971 and May 14, 1984, respectively.

Further Reading

Grose, Peter. *A Good Place to Hide: How One French Community Saved Thousands of People during World War II*. New York: Pegasus Books, 2015.

Hallie, Philip. *Lest Innocent Blood Be Shed: The Story of the Village of Le Chambon, and How Goodness Happened There*. New York: HarperPerennial, 1994.

Moorehead, Caroline. *Village of Secrets: Defying the Nazis in Vichy France*. New York: HarperCollins, 2014.

LE VOYAGE DE FANNY

Le Voyage de Fanny (*Fanny's Journey*), directed by Lola Doillon, is a fictionalized 2016 movie about a group of Jewish children who flee Nazi-occupied France during the Holocaust, escaping to Switzerland through the heavily guarded frontier area facing Geneva.

It is based on the true-life story of Fanny Ben-Ami, a German-born Jewish girl born in Baden-Baden in 1930. Her Russian-born parents left for Paris in 1933 to flee the Nazis when Fanny was three. In late August 1939, just before war was declared, her father was arrested, and Fanny and her sisters were sent by their mother to the Château de Chaumont in central France, a home run by the OSE. In this safe environment, the children were content until, in 1943, the village priest reported the presence of Jewish children to the authorities. The children were then sent, just in time, to other hiding places. Fanny and her sisters were split up at this time, though they were reunited in Mégève in the Haute-Savoie, where they lived in an OSE hostel. It was intended that this would be temporary, with a plan set in motion to send the sisters and a group of other children, aged from four to 17, to the Swiss border under the protection of a 17-year-old boy. The group comprised 28 children, all desperately trying to avoid deportation. When the young guide suddenly abandoned them, 13-year-old Fanny took over. She was to head by train to the border town of Annemasse, from where they would meet their *passeur* (people mover). But they never reached Annemasse because the bridge at Annecy was bombed. After a series of hazardous experiences, the children ultimately did reach Switzerland and safety.

Lola Doillon's movie adaptation of Fanny Ben-Ami's story was inspired by Ben-Ami's memoir, published in French in 2011 after first appearing in Hebrew in 1986. Seen through the eyes of the nine (not 28) children fleeing the Nazis and Vichy police, the movie's narrative shows poignantly how the younger children barely understand what is going on as they move from one scenario to another. Fanny (Léonie Souchaud), together with her little sisters Erika (Fantine Harduin) and Georgette (Juliane Lepoureau) and the other children, develop a shared sense of solidarity in the face of their common plight. Learning to work together, they grow more confident in their relationships with each other, as well as in their abilities to stand up for themselves.

This begins early in the film, when Madame Forman (Cécile de France), a social worker with the OSE, begins the process of leading the children to safety. She obtains false passports for the children and instructs them as to their new names and family histories. Just as all are about to board a train heading towards the Swiss border, Vichy police appear at the station. To distract their attention, Mme Forman pretends to fall into a faint; the children are left alone, and she and the children get separated. Fanny, having been instructed by Mme Forman to lead the little group, must now, like a young (and female) Moses, lead the children of Israel to salvation. The film ends with a shot of the real Fanny, a senior citizen who now lives in Israel, and an epilogue to her story.

The cast—many of whom were non-professionals acting in their first roles—show great acting skills. It was said that director Dillion screened up to 10,000 children before finding the cast that was just right for what she wanted to achieve. She was successful. *Le Voyage de Fanny* was selected as a feature in a number of Film Festivals around the world and won several awards.

For Fanny Ben-Ami—who was a special guest at many of these same Festivals—the experience of bringing the children through from Vichy France to safety in Switzerland was just one part of her wartime experience. The more traumatic elements came after the war. During her time in exile in Switzerland, she was motivated to not lose hope for the future by the vision of a reunion with her parents after the war. This, however, would not take place. Both parents, who had been deported after their daughters' safety had been secured, died at Auschwitz and Majdanek.

Further Reading

Ben-Ami, Fanny. *Le Journal de Fanny: L'histoire vraie d'une jeune fille au destin hors du commun.* Paris: Éditions de Seuil, 2011.

LEAGUE OF GERMAN GIRLS

The League of German Girls (*Bund Deutscher Mädel*, or BDM) was the female division of the German youth movement during the Nazi period. This complemented the male **Hitler Youth** (*Hitlerjugend*), its role being to indoctrinate girls into the beliefs and ideals of Nazism. Although an important socializing agency among young females, it nonetheless did not rank on an equal footing with its male counterpart in the misogynistic Nazi state.

The BDM was formed in 1930, prior to the Nazi accession to office, and was structured on parallel lines to the Hitler Youth. At first, the League consisted of two sections: the *Jungmädel*, or Young Girls League, for girls ages 10 to 14, and the League itself for girls aged 14 to 18. In 1938 a third section was introduced, and girls became eligible for entry to the *Glaube und Schönheit* (Faith and Beauty) organization, where they were taught domestic science and received advanced training in preparation for marriage. This was voluntary and open to young women between the ages of 17 and 21.

On December 1, 1936, with the implementation of the Law on the Hitler Youth, it became mandatory for all girls aged 10 to 14 to be in the *Jungmädel* and for girls aged 14 to 18 to be in the BDM. They had to be "racially" German, German citizens, and free of hereditary diseases.

BDM teaching emphasized that the singular role of women in the Third Reich was to bear and raise children. With this in mind, it focused on ensuring that girls would know their place in the Nazi state: they would be dedicated to Nazi ideals, dutiful housewives paying an appropriate level of deference to their husbands, and would grow up with an unquestioned understanding of the intended role of women in the Third Reich to become mothers, ensuring the continuation of the Aryan race. All activities were designed to prepare the girls for marriage and motherhood, and while **education in the Third Reich** devalued scholarly pursuits for girls and women, they were exposed to classes in history, biology, and geography, underscoring Nazi ideology. Other activities, popular among many girls, included singing, theater, arts and crafts, and other cultural pursuits.

Like boys in the Hitler Youth, girls in the BDM were required to serve a year of compulsory national labor service. For many, this translated to working in agriculture, in line with the Nazi notion of "Blood and Soil" in which farm life was viewed as noble activity contrasted with the corruption of the cities. National service could also involve domestic work helping large families with several children, though it was generally considered that the Reich Labor Service for young women (*Reichsarbeitsdienst der weiblichen Jugend*) would be better served on the land.

This also reinforced the Nazi ideals of health and physical fitness, service to the state, and working together for the "People's Community" (*Volksgemeinschaft*). Given this, sport in the BDM was highly regarded; it was seen as a vehicle for creating healthy girls capable of producing large numbers of babies. Sports such as swimming, gymnastics, and running formed an important part of BDM activities, as were team sports that encouraged working together for the greater good of the group. To underscore the political nature of the BDM, girls were required to attend Nazi Party meetings and rallies alongside their brothers from the Hitler Youth.

As the girls got older and approached marriageable age, the Faith and Beauty organization of the BDM focused on cooking, sewing, education, and national political life. Here, they could pursue their interests in art and sculpture, clothing design and sewing, general home economics, and music. Because membership of Faith and Beauty was voluntary, the general intention was that those who joined would be thoroughly committed to Nazi ideals and would serve to reinforce the regime at the domestic level—after which they would settle into their intended role as wives and mothers.

The outbreak of war in September 1939 saw the BDM pressed into service to carry out several roles vacated by boys who went into the armed forces. While younger girls collected money for the Winter Relief fund, older girls went back to the country to assist with the harvest, while those remaining in the cities, especially later in the war, helped the victims of bombing. Some volunteered as nursing aides at military hospitals or at the front, while others helped wounded soldiers or refugees at train stations. Some assisted with the repatriation of wounded soldiers back to their hometowns, and yet others helped wounded soldiers still in the hospital. Secretarial assistance was also offered to local Nazi offices.

Later in the war, BDM girls helped Hitler Youth boys in the construction of antiaircraft barriers, while some were more aggressively active and joined paramilitary units serving in signals companies or as searchlight operators (*Flak Helferinnen*). Some, at the most desperate times, operated antiaircraft guns. At the very end of the war, some BDM girls joined the *Volkssturm*, established on October 18, 1944, as a Home Guard force. Although all males between the ages of 16 and 60 years not currently serving were conscripted, some BDM leaders received training in the use of handheld weapons, and others joined in this last-ditch defense of the Fatherland.

On October 10, 1945, after Germany's defeat and surrender, the *Bund Deutscher Mädel* was dissolved by *Kontrollratsgesetz Nr. 2* under Section 86 of the German Criminal Code administered by the Allied Control Council. Along with other arms of the Nazi Party, the League of German Girls and the Hitler Youth were designated unconstitutional organizations.

Further Reading

Heath, Tim. *Hitler's Girls: Doves among Eagles*. Barnsley, UK: Pen and Sword, 2017.
Reese, Dagmar. *Growing up Female in Nazi Germany*. Ann Arbor: University of Michigan Press, 2006.

LEBENSBORN

Lebensborn ("Fountain of Life") was the name given to the Nazi program of selective breeding for the purpose of creating a superior race.

Nazism embraced the notion of eugenics, a belief that humans could be bred to create a purer or more perfect race. The Nazi vision imagined an ideal Aryan who was Nordic, tall and physically beautiful, and had perfect features, including blond hair and blue eyes, and was fit and in perfect health. To achieve this refinement of German "blood," it was deemed necessary to exterminate the racially impure and to encourage the racially pure to multiply.

The *Lebensborn* program was established by the SS in Germany on December 12, 1935, in Munich, with an office created within the SS. On September 13, 1936, Heinrich Himmler wrote to members of the SS that the *Lebensborn* organization intended to serve the SS through the selection and adoption of qualified children; it was under Himmler's personal direction and was part of the Race and Settlement Central Bureau of the SS. Himmler stated that it was the duty of all leaders of the central bureau to become members of the organization and that they had to apply to join prior to September 23, 1936. In 1939, membership stood at 8,000, of which 3,500 were SS leaders.

Lebensborn was thus state-supported and an integral element of the Nazi racial system, with the aim of increasing the birth rate of Aryan children. This was to be achieved through the intensive breeding of German women—who met stringent physical standards of height, weight, blond hair, blue eyes, and athleticism—with SS officers, to whom they did not have to be married. The SS officers chosen for this purpose had already demonstrated their impeccable Aryan ancestry as a condition prior to joining the SS.

Lebensborn encouraged anonymous births by unmarried women, who would become impregnated in SS-run "stud farms." These were often luxury hotels and spas, where young women and men would meet prior to retiring discreetly to bedrooms, after which they would separate, never to meet again. *Lebensborn* provided welfare to its mostly unmarried mothers; upon conception, the women were sent to special maternity homes where they were cared for until the birth of their children. The *Lebensborn* program managers then arranged for the adoption of these children by likewise "racially pure" and healthy families thoroughly infused with Nazi ideals, particularly SS members and their families.

The Cross of Honor of the German Mother was awarded to women who bore the most Aryan children. Abortion was legalized by the Nazis for disabled children but strictly punished otherwise. The focus of the program was one of pure racial reproduction, in which Nazi concepts of racial hygiene would be in the foreground, to create pure-blooded Aryans for the Thousand-Year Reich.

Lebensborn established facilities in several occupied countries, and its activities were concentrated around Germany, Norway, and occupied northeastern Europe. The focus in occupied Norway was aiding children born to Norwegian women and fathered by German soldiers. About 8,000 children were born in *Lebensborn* homes in Germany, and between 8,000 and 12,000 children in were born in Norway.

Beginning in 1939, when Germany invaded Poland, the *Lebensborn* program also engaged in the **kidnapping** and transfer of children, mostly orphans, to families in Germany.

In other parts of Europe, the Nazis started to kidnap children from foreign countries—mainly from Yugoslavia and Poland, but also including Russia, Ukraine, Czechoslovakia, Romania, Estonia, Latvia, and Norway—for the *Lebensborn* program. They started to do this because they considered it their duty to remove the children from their environment. Himmler was alleged to have said that Nazism sought to "win over any good blood that we can use for ourselves and give it a place in our people." He encouraged his troops to kidnap an estimated 200,000 blond, blue-eyed Polish children from their homes or as they walked to school. They were moved to Nazi families and brought up as Germans, with little or no memory of their true ancestry. The SS tested the racial characteristics of individual children by measuring 62 parts of their body. If the child passed the test, he or she was sent away to be placed in German families for "Germanization." By 1942, the term *Lebensborn* had thus become a code word for the kidnapping of Polish and other children who met these idealized Nazi racial characteristics.

On May 1, 1945, a day after Hitler's death, American troops entered Steinhoering, the Munich base for the *Lebensborn* program. Here, they found 300 children, aged six months to six years. Most of the mothers and staff had fled. British and Soviet troops also found children at *Lebensborn* homes near Bremen and Leipzig. Most of these children were either put up for adoption or, if known, sent back to their birth families. Some of the children kidnapped in other countries who were living with families throughout Germany were repatriated to their native countries, but many had been "Germanized" to such a degree that they no longer fit in to their country of birth.

During World War II, it had been a matter of honor for a German woman to be carrying the child of an SS officer and, by doing so, creating a member of the new master race. After the war this abruptly turned into a matter of shame. The mothers were discouraged from revealing the facts of their wartime activities to their children or anyone else. Many of the children had been adopted, and their adoptive parents had no desire to divulge to them the truth about their backgrounds. After the war, a large number of the records relating to such births and kidnappings were lost; thus, no actual numbers can be accurately assessed.

Further Reading

Clay, Catherine, and Michael Leapman. *Master Race: The Lebensborn Experiment in Nazi Germany.* London: Hodder and Stoughton, 1995.

LESZCZYŃSKA, STANISŁAWA (1896–1974)

Stanisława Leszczyńska was born to a Polish Catholic family on May 8, 1896, in the city of Łódź, Poland. Her parents were Jan Zambrzycki, a carpenter, and his wife, Henryka. Before World War I, Jan was drafted into the Russian Army, and Henryka began working in a factory. This enabled Stanisława to attend a private school, but in 1908, when she was 12 years old, her parents decided to move to Rio de Janeiro in Brazil. Two years later they returned, and Stanisława completed her high school education in 1914.

On October 17, 1916, she married Bronisław Leszczyńska, a printer who came from Łódź. Four years later they moved to Warsaw, and Stanisława enrolled in the Midwifery School there, after which they returned to Łódź.

With the outbreak of war in September 1939, Stanisława and her family were forced to relocate when their district was formed into what became the Łódź ghetto. The family—by now including several children—decided to help Jews trapped in dreadful conditions in the ghetto. Among other activities, they smuggled in false documents and food—activities which, on February 18, 1943, led to their arrest by the Gestapo. Two sons were taken to Mauthausen-Gusen concentration camp, while Stanisława and her daughter Sylwia were sent to Auschwitz on April 17, 1943. Bronisław Leszczyńska and another son managed to escape, though Bronisław was killed during the Warsaw Uprising in 1944.

Believing she could be of assistance, at Auschwitz Stanisława approached a German doctor—most likely **Josef Mengele**—and told him she was a midwife. He assigned Stanisława and Sylwia (who was a medical student before the war) to the camp's "maternity ward," a place where it was expected that pregnant women would bide their time before their anticipated deaths.

In the usual run of events, most pregnant women at Auschwitz were sent to the gas chambers. A Jewish prisoner-doctor, **Gisella Perl**, performed abortions for pregnant women once it was learned that those discovered to be pregnant were usually summarily executed. Others would be sent to the "maternity ward." Two German midwives, "Sister Klara" (who acted as a kapo) and "Sister Pfani," oversaw the barracks. When babies were born, the role of the two German women was to declare them stillborn, before drowning them in a barrel or bucket. It was expected that Stanisława would do likewise.

A religiously devout woman who prayed in the morning, evening, before meals, and before work, Stanisława refused to murder the babies. When Mengele ordered her on pain of death to obey, she again refused. Instead, she delivered the babies alive—immediately after which she baptized the child with water and made a sign of the cross over the mother and baby.

Not every baby was immediately murdered. Beginning in 1943, a few hundred, with blue eyes and features conforming to the Nazi Aryan stereotype, were **kidnapped** and sent away to be given to German couples and Germanized as part of the Nazi **Lebensborn** program. Conscious of what was happening, Stanisława and her assistants did their best to tattoo these babies before they were taken, in the hope that they would later be identified and reunited with their mothers.

Of course, every time Stanisława delivered a baby, she risked her life, but despite knowing that most babies she delivered would be killed within a few hours, she worked to save as many of the mothers' lives as she could, working in impossible, unsanitary conditions. Assisted by her daughter and other prisoners, she later estimated that she had delivered 3,000 babies during her two years at Auschwitz. Of these babies born alive, medical historians Susan Benedict and Linda Shields have concluded that about half were drowned, another 1,000 died quickly of starvation or cold, 500 were sent to other families, and just 30 survived of the original number of 3,000 in the camp. It is believed that all the mothers survived childbirth.

Throughout this two-year period, Stanisława—whom the prisoners dubbed "mother" and "the angel of goodness"—kept bringing babies into the world, baptizing them, and caring as best as she could for the women in the barracks.

For their part, Sister Klara and Sister Pfani murdered by drowning over 1,500 babies. After the war, Klara was tried and imprisoned at Auschwitz for **infanticide**.

Stanisława remained the camp's midwife until it was liberated on January 26, 1945. Prior to this the Nazis had forced most of the remaining prisoners at Auschwitz to leave on death marches, but Stanisława refused to depart and stayed in the camp until its **liberation**.

After the war she resumed her career as a civilian midwife in Łódź and picked up the pieces of her family's shattered existence. Only after she retired, in 1957, did she begin to discuss her time at Auschwitz. On January 27, 1970, she attended a commemorative event in Warsaw, where several of those present were former prisoners from Auschwitz and their surviving children who had been born in the camp.

On March 11, 1974, Stanisława Leszczyńska died from cancer and has since been celebrated throughout Poland. Several hospitals are named in her honor, the main road leading to the Auschwitz museum is named after her, and in 1983 the School of Obstetricians in Kraków was named after her. In 1992 the Catholic Church announced that the process of her beatification, which could lead to sainthood, had begun.

Further Reading

Benedict, Susan, and Linda Shields (Eds.). *Nurses and Midwives in Nazi Germany: The "Euthanasia Programs."* New York: Routledge, 2014.

Gabryel, Kazimierz. *Stanisława Leszczyńska: 1896–1974.* Łódź: Diecezjalne Wydawn, 1989.

LIBERATION

On June 6, 1944—D-Day—American, British, and Canadian forces invaded Europe on the coast of Normandy in Operation OVERLORD, starting the military clawback that would lead to the liberation of Western Europe. In the East, the Red Army, after three years of bitter fighting, was pushing back German forces, and in late July 1944, the Majdanek death camp, in Lublin, was liberated. Here, in what was one of the best preserved of all the death camps, Soviet soldiers discovered the horrific machinery of the Final Solution—extermination sites outfitted with large gas chambers and crematoria. As 1944 unfolded the Red Army liberated or overran the sites of the other German death camps in Poland, at Sobibór, Bełżec, and Treblinka. In late January 1945 Auschwitz was liberated; the Soviet soldiers rescued the pitiful remnant that had been too sick or debilitated to be evacuated in the death marches.

In Western Europe Allied forces drove east, liberating Paris in August 1944 with the help of Free French units. The same month, the Allies invaded southern France in Operation DRAGOON. Throughout April and May 1945, American, British, Canadian, and Free French forces liberated camps through the western half of Germany. On April 11, the U.S. Third Army's 6th Armored Division rolled into Buchenwald, freeing 20,000 prisoners. Generals Dwight D. Eisenhower, Omar Bradley, and George S. Patton inspected many of the facilities in the surrounding towns, at the same time starting a trend repeated throughout the occupied areas of forcing local populations to visit the locations of the Nazis' deeds. Later, other American forces liberated camps such as Dachau and Flossenbürg. The British Army liberated Bergen-Belsen and other camps north of the American positions.

By mid-May the war was over in Europe. Once liberated, the survivors of the concentration camps faced a multitude of problems—disease, malnutrition, and the by-products of continued abuse. Thousands died after liberation, and tens of thousands of the living were now refugees, left with nothing and relying on the occupying Allied armies to help them reconstruct a new life. The relief and relocation process would take years to complete.

Very few Jewish children had survived, as systematic murder, abuse, disease, and **medical experimentation** took a huge toll. Of the estimated 216,000 Jewish children deported to Auschwitz, for example, fewer than 7,000 teenagers survived the selection process for forced labor; nearly all the others were murdered. When the camp was liberated on January 27, 1945, Soviet troops found just 451 Jewish children among the 9,000 surviving prisoners.

Undoubtedly the biggest challenge for children, once their safety had been secured, was becoming reconnected with members of their lost family. Most children who survived had done so either in hiding or by being placed with foster families. The joy of liberation was tempered by the major question of what to do next. For many, liberation was hardly enough. They were fed, they were free, but were unable to comprehend what their past and current experiences signified for them—and for their future—owing to their youth. In most cases, they were without parents or homes. Many were very sick or recovering.

As the children convalesced, their first thought was to start looking for their missing families. Bulletin boards throughout Europe posted messages every day from survivors looking for their loved ones. Children turned to the names and addresses of relatives overseas, the details of which they had learned before their families had been torn apart.

The difficulties were immense. Further, as the relatively few surviving parents went in search of their children, they were often confronted by different realities. Presuming the child could be located—in itself, a hazardous and sometime fruitless pursuit—then, after a period of years facing the most dreadful traumas, would the parents recognize their child? Would their child recognize them? If the child had been hidden with foster parents, would they be prepared to give the child up to strangers claiming to be their birth parents? Would the child accept them over those who had protected them during the war years? As it turned out, only a small percentage of parents were reunited with their children after 1945.

In the aftermath of the war, most survivors were relocated to one of the hundreds of displaced persons' (DP) camps that sprang up across Europe. Some were created in former concentration camps, whereas others were parts of towns that had been requisitioned by the Allies. Care of Jewish **child survivors** was a high priority and took various forms, with DP camp committees establishing special children's quarters where they could receive specialized care. Within the DP camps, survivors also searched for missing children, a task made easier, in some respects, by the fact that thousands of orphaned children were also to be found there. Reunions, however, were rare when compared to the vast number of people in this floating population of victims and orphans.

Approximately 185,000 Jews were in DP camps in Germany, 45,000 in Austria, and 20,000 in Italy. Referring to themselves as the *She'erit Ha-plaitah* ("The Saving Remnant"), they very quickly organized themselves due to an overwhelming concern for their own safety and future. The overwhelming majority of those who survived, whether in hiding or liberated from the camps, did not wish to remain in Europe, but preferred to emigrate—primarily to Palestine, which was under British control. The difficulty here was that the British denied Jewish admission so as not to offend the local Arab population, though for Zionists, entry to Palestine remained a primary objective.

Across the period 1945–1948, the illegal underground organized effort known as *Brichah* (escape) accounted for between 100,000 and 150,000 Jews being smuggled into Palestine. In 1946, through the Zionist movement known as Youth Aliyah established before the war by **Recha Freier**, thousands of Jewish children were given permission by the British government to migrate to Palestine and then to the state of Israel after its establishment in 1948.

Further Reading

Konigseder, Angelika, and Juliane Wetzel. *Waiting for Hope: Jewish Displaced Persons in Post–World War II Germany*. Evanston, IL: Northwestern University Press, 2001.

Niewyk, Donald L. (Ed.). *Fresh Wounds: Early Narratives of Holocaust Survival*. Chapel Hill: University of North Carolina Press, 1998.

LOINGER, GEORGES (1910–2018)

Georges Loinger was a Jewish resister and rescuer of children in Vichy France during the Holocaust. Though his efforts, hundreds of Jewish children survived the war through being transferred to Switzerland.

Born in Strasbourg in August 1910, at the age of 15, he entered the Zionist youth movement *Hatikvah* and became a group leader. In 1930 he attended a lecture from Dr. Joseph Weill, who advised him to devote himself to the education of Jewish youth and physically prepare himself for the trials that he believed were likely soon. A champion swimmer, in 1932 Georges moved to Paris, where he studied for a diploma in physical education and sports. After becoming an educator, he was instrumental in helping to create the city's first Jewish high school. In August 1934 he married his longtime girlfriend, Flore Rosenzweig, whom he had known since they were both youth leaders. He taught physical education at the school, and she became a secretary there.

While teaching, Loinger also became the chief instructor of physical education of the EIF. In 1937 a leading member of French Jewish society, Baron Edouard de Rothschild, brought 125 German Jewish children, aged between 8 and 14 years old, whose parents had been arrested and interned in camps in Germany, and placed them in the Château de la Guette. In this large property, owned by the Rothschilds near Paris, Flore Loinger was given responsibility for supervising the children's care.

Georges Loinger, in 2014, at the age of 104. Loinger was a leading rescuer of Jewish children in Vichy France during the Holocaust. Orchestrating the rescue activities of other resisters as well as through his own efforts, many hundreds of Jewish children survived the war by being passed across the border and into Switzerland. Born in Alsace in 1910, he lived until December 2018 and managed to impart his testimony on several occasions. (© Claude Truong-Ngoc/ Wikimedia Commons)

With the defeat of France in 1940, Loinger, serving in the French Army, was imprisoned with his unit and interned at Stalag 7A in Bavaria. Managing to escape with his cousin Marcel Vogel and returning to France by January 1941, after a period of rehabilitation, he saw the operation at the Château de la Guette dissolved in November 1941, with the children then placed in the care of the OSE.

Around the same time, he again met with Joseph Weill, who convinced him to become an OSE operative. By January 1943 he had been recruited to organize a means whereby secure **border crossings** to Switzerland could take place for several hundred Jewish children in and around the town of Annemasse, in Haute-Savoie. Throughout the period 1943–1944, Loinger, serving as a *passeur* (people mover), managed the successful passage of about 350 children. Some of the ways he was able to achieve these crossings were quite ingenious.

The best-known stories about Georges Loinger's life as a *passeur* include his heroism as he helped smuggle Jewish across the French-Swiss border by staging games of football, taking children on hikes, and then assisting them to cross during these activities. However, what is less known is the seriousness with which he undertook his missions. Loinger was to say later that "all the horror and injustice of the war are focused, for me, in that one moment, the departure of children, all these groups of children frightened and saddened by the separation from their families." As he saw it, the smuggling operations were the most important contribution to combatting Nazi genocide and the destruction of the Jewish people, for it was in the rescue of these children that the Jewish people could survive and recover after the Holocaust.

As a result he became an expert in crossing frontiers, and his efforts, together with the teams of *passeurs* he assembled (which included his cousin, **Marcel Marceau**) were overall successful in arranging the passage of convoys of children and youths to Switzerland. Two, however, were intercepted and had tragic outcomes: the stories of **Mila Racine** and of **Marianne Cohn**. Upon their capture, the former was sent first to Ravensbrück and then to Mauthausen, where she died; the latter was tortured and murdered brutally, but thanks to the intervention of the mayor of Annemasse, **Jean Deffaugt**, all of the children in her care were released and survived the war.

Describing his missions, Loinger explained later how he was eventually forced to modify his involvement with the process of smuggling Jewish children to safety. Between the summer of 1942 and late into 1943, he engaged in his smuggling activities, but after that he became a target for the Gestapo and had to stop. Instead, he engaged local *passeurs* to carry children across. Unlike Loinger and the members of the Jewish organizations, these smugglers worked for pay: Loinger was prepared to offer them gold coins (as he said, "because money was no longer valid"), so they made money from the distress of others—but the children were saved.

After the **liberation** Georges Loinger was given the task of creating a reception center in Annemasse for prisoners and deportees able to return to France. In 1946 he developed sporting activities in the OSE houses, at the same time establishing a school for sports instructors in Gournay-sur-Marne, near Paris. With the imminence of Israel's independence, in 1947 he began working for *Aliyah Bet* (the illegal immigration movement to Palestine), especially for the organization of the Exodus 1947 operation. By 1964 he was nominated as a *Chevalier de la Légion d'honneur* (Knight of the Legion of Honor) before retiring in 1978. In 1995 he became president of the association of Jewish resistance leaders in France, and in 1999 he was promoted to the rank of *Officier de la Légion d'honneur pour fait de Résistance*. In 2005 he was further elevated to the position of commander. In 2014 he was awarded honorary citizenship of the city of

Strasbourg, and in July 2016, he was made an officer in the Order of Merit of the Federal Republic of Germany. Georges Loinger died on December 28, 2018, aged 108.

Further Reading

Bartrop, Paul R., and Samantha J. Lakin. *Heroines of Vichy France: Rescuing French Jews during the Holocaust*. Santa Barbara, CA: Praeger, 2019.

Loinger, Georges. *L'odyssée d'un resistant: Témoignage d'un centenaire, enfrant d'Alsace*. Nice: Les Éditions Ovadia, 2016.

Loinger, Georges, and Katy Hazan. *Aux frontiers de l'espoir*. Paris: Le Manuscrit, 2006.

LORE

Lore is a short story set in immediate postwar Germany, written by British-born writer Rachel Seiffert. The story of Lore (Hannelore), a 12-year-old girl, is informed by the postwar experiences of Seiffert's mother, the daughter of Nazi parents who were arrested after the war. *Lore* is not a story about the war itself but rather about its aftermath in Germany and the impact the loss of the war had on the German people—a population that had been subjected to unrelenting Nazi propaganda concerning the greatness of Germany over the previous dozen years.

The story is set in the spring of 1945, just weeks after the defeat of Germany. Lore is the oldest of five children of a Nazi SS officer, Peter, and his wife, Asti, a Nazi functionary administering Hitler's racial policies. The children are Lore; her slightly younger sister, Liesl; two eight-year-old twin brothers, Jochen and Jurgen; and a baby, Peter. Lore is confronted with the shock of losing the war, as her father, returning from service on the front line, seeks to place his family on a farm in Bavaria, hoping to keep them safe there from the advancing Red Army.

Initially the farmer's family feeds them, but after leaving one day, the father fails to return; it is assumed he has been captured by the Russians. Lore's mother burns Nazi insignia and potentially incriminating photographs, which were all items of great pride and honor during the Third Reich. A short time after this, the occupying American forces come to the farm, and the farmer's son tells Lore that the Americans are going to put her mother into prison.

The mother orders Lore to go with the other children from Bavaria to her grandmother in Hamburg, giving instructions, including a map and an address, and hands her money and valuables, including her wedding ring, to buy train tickets and food for the journey. She tells Lore that she is going to a camp, not a prison, because a prison is for criminals. She then leaves her children, submits to the custody of the Americans, and is imprisoned. The children are on their own.

Lore has now become an embarrassment in the new Germany, the daughter of Nazis and therefore the wrong kind of German. Seiffert depicts a nation stunned and disbelieving, unable to vocalize its grief. The farmer and his wife come to Lore and say that the children cannot stay with them. They tell Lore that there are no trains and no postal service. The children pack their bags and set off on a 500-mile trek through the four zones of occupation to find their grandmother in Hamburg. On the road they meet local Bavarians who laugh at them as being Nazi children from the north.

On her journey through a conquered Germany, Lore sees dreadful images of concentration camps in photos shown to her by the Americans. She does not want to believe that her parents participated in this type of killing.

As the children pass through rural Germany, Lore meets a youth, Tomas, who bears a numbered tattoo on his arm and identity papers that classify him as a survivor of Buchenwald. As they proceed, Lore finds herself becoming emotionally dependent upon him but conflicted because he is Jewish and therefore, according to her upbringing, objectionable. The younger children begin to see him as a father figure. When one of Lore's twin brothers, Jochen, is killed trying to cross through the Soviet zone, she and her siblings find themselves depending on Tomas to take them to safety. After many awful experiences, including near rape, Lore, the rest of her siblings, and Tomas eventually manage to locate her grandmother in Hamburg, which has suffered from Allied bombings.

Lore and the other children do not feel able to explain Tomas, the Jew, to their grandmother, and while they keep him secret, they still visit him in the bombed-out building in which he is squatting. After Lore asks Tomas about the photographs of Nazi concentration camps she has seen, he runs away. Her younger brother then tells Lore that the identity papers Tomas had, and used to help Lore pass through checkpoints so she could find her grandmother and escape the Soviets, were stolen from a dead Jewish man.

The victims in this novel are not those who perished in the camps and ghettos but, controversially, German children struggling to understand what happened in their society. This is a dense account filled with ethical questions and ironies. In this story, the children of perpetrators appear to be victims as well.

Rachel Seiffert's novel from which the story of Lore is taken, *The Dark Room*, was published in 2001. Shortlisted for the Man Booker Prize, it was made into a feature film in 2012 entitled *Lore*, directed and co-written by Cate Shortland and starring Saskia Rosedahl in the title role. As with the book, the film shows the tensions and shame of German civilians after World War II, and we also see how Lore's ingrained dislike of Jews is so deeply embedded that hatred is in her culture and how, in her uncritical acceptance of that hatred, she, in her way, is also complicit.

Further Reading

Seiffert, Rachel. *The Dark Room*. London: Random House, 2001.

M

MAISON D'IZIEU

The Maison d'Izieu was a Jewish children's home in France originally established in April 1943 for their protection. As Jewish children were murdered without scruple by the Nazis, however, the story of the Maison d'Izieu is the story of one children's home that resulted in tragedy.

The peaceful village of Izieu looks out over the Rhone River, between the cities of Lyon and Chambéry in south-central France. During World War II, Izieu became the site of a Jewish children's home. It housed dozens of children and formed part of the network of homes created under the auspices of the OSE; it was run by Sabine Zlatin, a Jewish nurse and OSE activist.

Most of the children were not orphans but had been sent to Izieu for safekeeping by their families. Some of the children were French; others came from Algeria, Austria, Belgium, Germany, and Poland. The home was located in an area conducive to their welfare, as the Italian occupation forces were known to be less oppressive to Jews than other areas in the north that were under German control.

In September 1943, however, Italy surrendered to the Allies. Germany now occupied southern France, effectively snuffing out any semblance of Vichy independence; in next to no time, the Germans began to hunt down Jews with a view to deporting them to the euphemistically named "East." In October 1943 the Germans raided an OSE children's home near Marseille, sending the children to the transit camp at Drancy, on the outskirts of Paris. OSE decided from this point to shut down its children's homes, which included Izieu, and evacuate the children. It was hoped that the **Garel Network** would be able to take responsibility for most of the children from that point on.

Acting on a tipoff, on April 6, 1944, the local Gestapo, under orders from the "Butcher of Lyon," Klaus Barbie, entered the orphanage and arrested and forcibly removed the 44 children and their 7 supervisors, throwing the crying and terrified children onto their trucks. The children were imprisoned in Lyon and deported the next day to Drancy. After the raid Barbie sent a message to Gestapo headquarters in Paris, declaring that the children's home at Izieu had been removed and arrangements made for the deportation of its residents.

During the raid, Leon Reifman, a medical student who took care of the sick children, managed to escape and hide in a nearby farm. His sister, Dr. Sarah Lavan-Reifman, who was the resident doctor, together with their parents, Eva and

Moisz-Moshe, and their nephew, Claude Lavan-Reifman—all of whom lived in the home—were taken away; they were murdered at Auschwitz.

Using information obtained from the children detained in Lyon, the Germans tracked down some of their family members, who were also taken to Drancy. The children were put on the first available train toward the East, and 42 of the children and 5 of the adults were then gassed on arrival at Auschwitz. Two of the oldest children and the superintendent, Miron, who was Sabine Zlatin's husband and ran the home with her, were killed by a firing squad in Tallinn, Estonia.

Of the 44 children taken by the Nazis at Izieu, none survived. Of the supervisors there was one survivor, 27-year-old Léa Feldblum. She had false papers that would have enabled her to evade deportation to Auschwitz, but she chose to reveal her identity while in Drancy in order to remain with the children. On April 15, 1944, Léa and the children from Izieu arrived at Auschwitz, and she led the column of children to the selection point. When she informed the SS that these children were from a home, she was brutally separated from them. The children were gassed, and Feldman was processed into the general camp population. She survived Auschwitz and immigrated to Israel in 1946.

In the commune of Izieu, a young local assistant who worked at the home, Renée Paillares, succeeded in hiding a three-year-old Jewish girl in her home. The child, Diane Popowski, who had been born in in Luxembourg in 1940, survived the Holocaust.

Sabine Zlatin survived Klaus Barbie's raid on the home on April 6, 1944. On April 3 she had traveled to Montpellier to collect funds and look for possible hiding places for the Izieu children and was thus temporarily absent.

In 1987, Klaus Barbie was put on trial in France. Both Léa Feldblum and Sabine Zlatin testified and lived to see him convicted of crimes against humanity and sentenced to life imprisonment. Some 40 years after the events at Izieu, and toward the end of her life, Sabine Zlatin convinced the president of France, François Mitterrand, to turn the orphanage premises into a memorial. She died on September 21, 1996, aged 89.

Further Reading

Klarsfeld, Serge. *The Children of Izieu: A Human Tragedy.* New York: Harry N. Abrams, 1985.

MARCEAU, MARCEL (1923–2007)

Marcel Marceau was a French mime artist famous for his portrayal of "Bip the Clown." During World War II, while still young, he lived in hiding and worked with the French Resistance. As an activist, he managed to evacuate an entire orphanage of Jewish children just before they were to be deported to a concentration camp. Best known for this professional career as a mime, Marceau gave his first major performance to 3,000 troops after the liberation of Paris in August 1944. He then studied dramatic art and mime in Paris, referring to mime as the "art of silence"—an art he was to perform professionally for over 60 years.

Marcel Marceau was born as Marcel Mangel on March 22, 1923, in Strasbourg, France, to a Jewish couple, Charles and Anna Mangel. When he was only five years old, he saw his first Charlie Chaplin film, which inspired his later career.

In 1939, as Germany was poised to invade France, many of the Jews of Strasbourg were evacuated on short notice. At the age of 16, Marceau and his brother were sent to Perigord, in the south, and eventually they made their way to Limoges in west-central France. Eager to become a painter, Marceau enrolled in art school.

For two months after the German invasion in 1940, Marceau was hidden in the Paris suburbs at the home of a teacher, Yvonne Hagnauer. Living side by side in her institute were 90 Jewish and 100 non-Jewish children; if they had been denounced to the Gestapo or French gendarmes, they all would have been seriously endangered.

Marcel Marceau, photograph taken in the Netherlands on June 29, 1962, when he was already a major international star. While Marceau is perhaps best known as arguably the greatest ever exponent of the art of mime, less well-known were his activities during World War II, when he lived in hiding, worked as a French resister, and smuggled Jewish children from occupied France into Switzerland. (Dutch National Archives)

Marceau's cousin, **Georges Loinger**, a French resistance fighter, urged him to join the French Resistance, and within two years he and his younger brother, Alain, had joined the Resistance in Limoges. Because of his artistic talents, Marceau was used by the Resistance to forge identity papers for Jews and non-Jews, papers that showed the bearers to be younger than 18 years of age and therefore ineligible to be deported to Germany as forced labor. As well as bribing officials, he also forged papers for Alain and himself, changing their last name to Marceau, in honor of General Marceau from the French Revolution whom Marcel recalled reading about in Les Misérables.

Georges Loinger commanded a secret unit within the OSE, which smuggled Jewish children from occupied France to neutral countries. Toward the end of the war, Marceau also helped in the work of smuggling Jewish children. In one instance, he took charge of a group that had been hiding out in an orphanage; he dressed up as a Boy Scout leader, leading the Jewish children (also dressed as Scouts) through the woods to the Swiss border. Making this trip three times, Marceau successfully moved more than 70 children to safety into neutral Switzerland, calming them by using mime to keep them quiet during the dangerous trek through the forests to the border.

After the Allies landed on the shores of Normandy in June 1944, Marceau and Loinger joined the Free French Army and continued their push toward Berlin. What he later called the performance of his life as a soldier was when he, together with several others, captured an entire German unit. He acted as if he and his comrades were the advance guard of a much larger French force. In fact, the unit comprised Marceau and a few men, but the Germans surrendered rather than face a whole French division in battle.

Owing to Marceau's excellent command of English, French, and German, he worked as a liaison officer with U.S. General George Patton's Third Army. After the war, he returned to Strasbourg only to learn that his father had been captured in 1944 by the Gestapo and murdered at Auschwitz. His mother, Anna, had survived. He changed his name permanently to Marcel Marceau and soon thereafter rocketed to fame as the world's most prominent mime artist. He died in Paris on September 22, 2007, aged 84.

Further Reading

Martin, Ben. *Marcel Marceau: Master of Mime*. London: Paddington Press, 1978.

MEDICAL EXPERIMENTATION

German physicians played a decisive role in the racial programs of the Nazi state. Of all German occupational groups, they had the greatest proportion of members in the Nazi Party (almost 50 percent), and German medicine legitimized the Party's eugenic and racial programs. Such programs were implemented throughout the entire German health care system, with the Nuremberg Laws of 1935 extending state-enforced selection to include race, which was considered a medical issue. Racial inferiority certainly extended to the language of professional discourse that included concepts such as "life unworthy of life" (*lebensunwertes Lebens*).

As Nazi ideology viewed Jewish children as an existential threat, the Nazis sought to cut off the Jewish people for the next generation. As a result, children were foremost among Nazism's primary targets. Along the way, however, universities and research institutes saw opportunities for eugenic research in which Jewish children became human guinea pigs exploited for lethal medical experimentation. Having already been scientifically classified as "life unworthy of life," German medical science exploited the Nazi programs to acquire human specimens for institutes of anatomy, pathology, and neuropathology.

Nazi medical experiments were essentially pseudoscience in which the doctors blurred the distinction between science and sadism. The data was not recorded from scientific hypothesis and research; rather, it was inspired and administered through racial ideologies of mass murder and callous torture for its own sake.

Among the activities in which the Nazi doctors engaged, two types stood out. Medico-military experiments, in which the regime sponsored a series of inhumane experiments for alleged ideological, military, and medical purposes, included experiments in extreme hypothermia through freezing, high altitude, injections with seawater, sulfanilamide, tuberculosis, poison, and wounds. These were, however, for the most part restricted to victims who were adults, of military age, and usually (though not always) men. Racially motivated experiments, on the other hand, saw children targeted for "scientific" research by doctors focusing on achieving certain anthropological, genetic, and racial goals. These included experiments in sterilization; the study of twins and dwarves; and research on Jewish skeletons, skin, and skulls. Children in concentration camps were the most vulnerable. They, like countless adults, were subjected to high-pressure and freezing tests and experimented on with drugs.

In a celebrated case from early 1944, Kurt Heissmeyer, an SS physician, injected prisoners with various types of tuberculosis. He initially experimented on around 100 Jewish and Slavic adults, but these trials failed to deliver the hoped-for results. To complete his trials, he then appropriated Jewish children for his immunization against tuberculosis experiments. Twenty Jewish children, 10 boys and 10 girls, all between the ages of 5 and 12, were accordingly transferred from Auschwitz to the concentration camp at Neuengamme. As the already-weak children sickened, Heissmeyer removed their lymph glands and began injecting the tuberculosis bacteria into their lungs and bloodstreams. The children grew weaker and were confined to their barracks.

In March 1945, Heissmeyer sought advice as to what to do with the 20 sick and dying Jewish children, and it was decided by Rudolph Hoess, the commandant of Auschwitz, that the children should be murdered. He gave the task to *SS-Obersturmführer* Arnold Strippel. Lacking poison, Strippel was forced to improvise.

In 1943 the Hamburg SS had taken over **Bullenhuser Damm**, a bombed-out school, and converted it into a satellite camp of Neuengamme. Taken to this site on April 20, 1945, when the British were less than three miles away, the 20 children, along with their two French physicians and two Dutch caretakers, were murdered by being hanged on hooks in the basement at Bullenhuser Damm. Strippel and other officers supervised the murders.

Experiments took place in other ways as well. Under the program known by the euphemistic term of "euthanasia," patients medically defined as undesirable were selected for killing. Murder by gas chamber originated in the program, code-named Aktion T-4, with the task of turning on the gas assigned to a physician and designated as a medical act. Children with incurable diseases or psychological conditions were among the very first to be murdered according to this **child euthanasia** program, but some were reprieved temporarily so that they could be studied as objects of medical or scientific research prior to being sent to their deaths.

Probably the best known of all the medical experiments undertaken against children were those carried out by SS doctor **Josef Mengele**, known almost universally as the Angel of Death. He considered that **twins** held the mysteries behind how Aryan genetic features, such as blond hair and blue eyes, were passed on;

accordingly, he experimented on some 1,500 sets of twins, who, each day, had blood samples drawn from them. He attempted to change eye color by injecting chemicals or giving drops, injected lethal germs, carried out sex-change operations, and removed organs and limbs; he also attempted to create conjoined ("Siamese") twins by sewing their backs together and trying to connect blood vessels and organs. Among his other interests were conducting experiments on people with physical abnormalities.

Elsewhere, children were also subjected to experimental surgeries without anesthesia, as well as blood transfusions and isolation endurance. In the aftermath of these revelations, there arose to be considerable debate over the soundness of the Nazis' lethal experiments on unwilling subjects and whether data thereby gathered can be used in any way by the scientific community. Such "science" was, of course, completely fraudulent. Rarely did the responses of the victims represent the responses of those for whom the experiments were meant to benefit. Also, extreme doubts exist over the scientific integrity of the experiments when we consider the Nazi doctors' political aspirations and their enthusiasm for predetermined medical conclusions that proved Nazi racial theory. And the fact that the Nazi experiments were rarely, if ever, replicated raises further doubts about the data's scientific accuracy.

Further Reading

Lifton, Robert Jay. *The Nazi Doctors: Medical Killing and the Psychology of Genocide*. New York: Basic Books, 2000.

MEED, VLADKA (1921–2012)

Vladka Meed was a member of the Jewish underground in the Warsaw Ghetto from its inception. Born Feigele Peltel in Warsaw on December 29, 1921, to Shlomo and Hanna Peltel, she was educated in Yiddish but picked up Polish readily and became fluent while still young. At the age of 14 she became active in *Zukunft*, the **Jewish youth movement** connected to the Jewish Labor Bund. Attending a private school, she encountered antisemitism for the first time when, on the way to classes, she observed Jewish children being beaten by non-Jews in the street outside.

Feigele and her family were forced into the Warsaw Ghetto in 1940. Over time, her father died of pneumonia, and her mother, sister, and younger brother, Chaim, were sent to their deaths at Treblinka. With few other alternatives, Feigele decided to become part of the resistance movement in the ghetto, and she joined the *Żydowska Organizacja Bojowa* (Jewish Combat Organization, or ŻOB) soon after it was formed in 1942. She was inspired to join after hearing a Bund leader, Abrasha Blum, speak about the need for armed resistance. Blum was a member of the Jewish coordinating committee, a body that sought to unite the diverse political factions of the ghetto. It was at this time she assumed the resistance code name of Vladka, which she kept for the rest of her life.

Owing to her flowing red hair and typically Aryan appearance, and because she was fluent in Polish, she passed as a non-Jew outside the ghetto. Her major assignments involved working as a courier (*Kasharit*)—essentially of money, arms, and intelligence information. One of her most important missions was to smuggle a map of Treblinka out of the ghetto and into the hands of resisters outside, who would, it was hoped, forward it on to the Allies. This information was also vitally important in the ghetto itself as news spread more widely about where the deportations terminated. The upshot was a determination on the part of the ŻOB to resist further deportations by force, leading, in April 1943, to the Warsaw Ghetto Uprising.

Vladka also helped children escape the ghetto and arranged for them to be sheltered in Christian homes. She was impressed by the degree of resolve shown by many of the ghetto inhabitants; as she wrote later, "Some just refused to commit suicide, continued to educate their children in secret, [and] celebrated their holidays." Inspired by this determination to live, she decided to help keep the Jewish future alive and, on several occasions, managed to smuggle out children to be placed with sympathetic Christian families. She was, however, aware that such families were uncommon and that, as she saw it, most ethnic Poles were unsympathetic toward the Jewish fate.

During one such mission, Vladka met her future husband, Benjamin Meed, who was also working for the underground smuggling children into hiding places outside the ghetto. As the war continued, she used forged identification papers to work on both sides of the ghetto walls to obtain weapons and ammunition on the black market while at the same time finding hiding places for children and adults.

In addition, she acted as an information conduit for Jews searching for news about their relatives in labor and concentration camps or fighting with the partisans in the forest, and she assisted other Jews hiding on the Aryan side; and, for those who managed to survive the Warsaw Ghetto Uprising during April and May of 1943, she continued supplying money and papers to help them stay alive.

Vladka and Benjamin Meed were among the first survivors to reach the United States after the end of World War II, arriving in New York on May 24, 1946. Soon after her arrival, Vladka was approached by American Jewish organizations with a request that she provide lectures to the American public about her experiences; these would form the basis of a book published in Yiddish in 1948. An early firsthand account published about what later became known as the Holocaust, it would be published in English as *On Both Sides of the Wall* in 1972, with translations into other languages (including German and Polish) later. It was highly condemnatory of Warsaw's non-Jewish population, who, Vladka asserted, did little to help the Jews in the ghetto.

In 1962 the Meeds, with a group of several other survivors, established the Warsaw Ghetto Resistance Organization for the purpose of raising awareness about what they had experienced among the next generation. Vladka traveled and spoke widely about the Warsaw Ghetto Uprising and the Holocaust generally. Immediately after the World Gathering of Jewish Holocaust Survivors in Israel in June 1981, an American Gathering of Jewish Holocaust Survivors was established to prepare for a second gathering, to be held in Washington, D.C., in April 1983. On this occasion Benjamin Meed was in the forefront of the organizing process.

In recognition for her work in Holocaust education, Vladka received an award in 1973 from the Warsaw Ghetto Resistance Organization, and in 1989 she received the Morim Award from the Jewish Teachers' Association. These were followed by the 1993 Hadassah Henrietta Szold Award and the 1995 Elie Wiesel Remembrance Award. She also received honorary degrees from Hebrew Union College and Bar Ilan University.

Benjamin Meed died of pneumonia in Manhattan on October 24, 2006; Vladka Meed—Warsaw Ghetto resister and protector of Jewish children in the face of Nazi persecution—died a little over six years later, from Alzheimer's disease, at her daughter's home in Paradise Valley, Arizona, on November 21, 2012.

Further Reading

Meed, Vladka. *On Both Sides of the Wall*. New York: Holocaust Library, 1979.
Zuckerman, Yitzhak. *A Surplus of Memory: Chronicle of the Warsaw Ghetto Uprising*. Berkeley: University of California Press, 1993.

MENGELE, JOSEF (1911–1979)

Josef Mengele was an SS physician stationed at Auschwitz during World War II. A member of the team of doctors responsible for the selection of victims to be killed in the gas chambers and for performing deadly human experiments on prisoners, he was nicknamed "the Angel of Death."

Mengele was born in Günzburg, near Ulm, Bavaria, on March 16, 1911, the oldest of three sons of Walburga and Karl Mengele, a prosperous manufacturer of agricultural implements. As a boy he was cultured, bright, well-liked, and a good scholar. He graduated from Günzburg High School in 1930 and was accepted into Munich University. With no political interests until this time, at university he joined the Nazi Party to boost his career as a scientist. Mengele joined the *Stalhelm* (Steel Helmet) militia in 1931; in 1934 the SA incorporated the *Stalhelm* into its ranks, making Mengele, by default, a Brownshirt. Soon after this he developed a problem with his kidneys that required him to leave the *Stalhelm* but enabled him to concentrate on his studies. In 1935 he earned a PhD in physical anthropology, with a dissertation that dealt with racial differences in the structure of the lower jaw—allegedly enabling researchers to tell the difference between Jews and non-Jews.

In 1936 Mengele passed the state medical examination, after which he went to Leipzig to work at a clinic. In January 1937 he was invited to join the Institute for Hereditary Biology and Racial Hygiene in Frankfurt, where he became the assistant of Otmar von Verschuer, a leading scientific figure widely known for his research with **twins**.

In May 1938 he became a member of the SS. On July 28, 1939, he married Irene Schönbein, whom he had met while studying in Leipzig. Upon the outbreak of war in September 1939, Mengele was unable to enlist immediately because of his kidney problem, but in 1940 he was accepted into the Waffen-SS.

In 1941 the now-lieutenant Mengele was awarded the Iron Cross Second Class for his service in Ukraine. In January 1942 he was pronounced unfit for duty, promoted to the rank of captain, awarded the Iron Cross First Class, and posted to the Race and Resettlement Office in Berlin.

On May 24, 1943, Mengele's next assignment saw him appointed as medical officer of Auschwitz-Birkenau's *Zigeunerfamilienlager* ("Gypsy Family Camp"), where his work was funded by a grant from his mentor, Otmar von Verschuer. Here, he studied human genetics. In August 1944 the camp was liquidated. All its inmates were gassed, after which Mengele became chief medical officer of the main infirmary at Birkenau. (He was not, however, the chief medical officer of the Auschwitz complex overall; his superior was the SS Garrison Physician, Eduard Wirths.)

Selection was a process carried out by SS doctors on new arrivals to Auschwitz. The doctors "selected" (chose) those who were "fit" for work, with the others (children under 14, the elderly, sick, and women with children) sent to the line of those picked for immediate death. Some of the SS officers had to get drunk before a selection, but Mengele was reported to enjoy the process, and he even showed up at selections to which he was not assigned. He was the only doctor at Auschwitz to wear his medals; his uniform was always tailored, and he wore white gloves. He exploited his good looks to trick women into believing whatever he said. He had an unpredictable personality, and everyone, including other SS officers, feared him.

Mengele believed twins held the mysteries behind how Aryan genetic features, such as blond hair and blue eyes, were passed on. Accordingly, some 1,500 sets of twins were brought to him through the selection process. Once selected, they kept their own hair and clothes, were tattooed, measured in height and weight, and a brief history was taken. In the morning they reported for roll call and ate a small breakfast, and then Mengele would talk with some of them, give them candy, or even occasionally play a game.

Life for the twins was bearable until they were taken for experiments. Each day they had to give blood from fingers, limbs, and, for smaller children, from the neck. About 10 cubic centimeters of blood was drawn daily in a painful and frightening process. Sometimes so much blood was drawn that a twin would faint; huge blood transfusions were made from one twin to another. Mengele attempted to change eye color by injecting chemicals or giving drops that caused pain, infections, or temporary (and sometimes permanent) blindness. Other experiments included isolation endurance, spinal taps without anesthesia, castrations, amputations, the removal of sexual organs, and incestuous impregnations. Some samples of the bodies were sent to von Verschuer for further study. Of the 1,500 pairs of twins Mengele chose at Auschwitz, only 200 survived.

Mengele also had an interest in people with physical abnormalities, such as dwarves and hunchbacks, and on these, too, he carried out pseudoscientific experiments.

The SS abandoned Auschwitz on January 27, 1945, and Mengele was transferred to Gross-Rosen camp in Lower Silesia, working as the camp doctor. After Gross-Rosen was evacuated at the end of February 1945, Mengele worked in other camps for a short time, and on May 2, 1945, he joined a Wehrmacht medical unit led by Hans Otto Kahler, his former colleague at the Institute of Hereditary Biology and Racial Hygiene in Bohemia. The unit fled west to avoid capture by the Soviets, and members were taken as prisoners of war by the Americans. Unaware that Mengele's name already stood on a list of wanted war criminals, however, U.S. officials quickly released him.

From July 1945 until May 1949, Mengele, operating under false papers naming him as "Fritz Hollmann," worked as a farmhand in a small village near Rosenheim, Bavaria, staying in contact with his wife Irene and an old friend, Hans Sedlmeier. Sedlmeier arranged Mengele's escape to Argentina via Innsbruck.

In 1954, five years after Mengele escaped to Buenos Aires, his wife Irene divorced him. On July 25, 1958, in Nueva Helvecia, Uruguay, Mengele married Martha Mengele, widow of his deceased brother Karl. Given that his crimes were well documented at the International Military Tribunal and other postwar courts, West German authorities issued a warrant for his arrest in 1959. As "José Mengele," he received citizenship in Paraguay in 1959. In 1960 a request was issued for his extradition to West Germany. Alarmed by the capture of Adolf Eichmann in Buenos Aires, Mengele moved several times throughout South America, and in 1961 he apparently moved to Brazil, where he lived with Hungarian refugees Geza and Gitta Stammer, working as manager of their farm about 200 kilometers outside São Paulo. In the seclusion of his Brazilian hideaway, Mengele was safe.

In 1974, when his relationship with the Stammer family was coming to an end, other Nazis in hiding, including Hans Ulrich Rudel, discussed relocating Mengele to Bolivia, where he could spend time with Klaus Barbie. Mengele rejected this proposal, preferring to stay in São Paulo for the last years of his life. In 1977 his only son, Rolf, who had never known his father, visited him and found him to be an unrepentant Nazi who claimed that he "had never personally harmed anyone in his whole life." Mengele's health had been deteriorating for years, and he died on February 2, 1979, at a vacation resort in Bertioga, Brazil; he was swimming in the sea when he suffered a massive stroke and drowned. He was buried in *Embu das Artes*, under the name "Wolfgang Gerhard," whose identity he had used since 1976. The remains of "Wolfgang Gerhard" were exhumed on June 6, 1985, and a team of forensic experts determined that Mengele had taken Gerhard's identity, died in 1979 of a stroke while swimming, and was buried under Gerhard's name. Dental records later confirmed the forensic conclusion.

Mengele had evaded capture for 34 years. After the exhumation, the São Paulo Institute for Forensic Medicine stored his remains and attempted to repatriate them to the remaining Mengele family members, but the family rejected them and turned over his diaries to investigators. The bones have been stored at the São Paulo Institute for Forensic Medicine ever since.

Further Reading

Bartrop, Paul R., and Eve E. Grimm. *Perpetrating the Holocaust: Leaders, Enablers, and Collaborators.* Santa Barbara, CA: ABC-CLIO, 2019.

Kor, Eva Mozes, and Lisa Rojnay Buccieri. *Surviving the Angel of Death: The Story of a Mengele Twin in Auschwitz.* Terre Haute, IN: Tanglewood, 2009.

Kor, Eva Mozes, and Mary Wright. *Echoes from Auschwitz: Dr. Mengele's Twins. The Story of Eva and Miriam Mozes.* Terre Haute, IN: Candles, Inc., 1995.

Lifton, Robert Jay. *The Nazi Doctors: Medical Killing and the Psychology of Genocide.* New York: Basic Books, 2000.

Posner, Gerald L., and John Ware. *Mengele: The Complete Story.* New York: Cooper Square, 2000.

MISCHLING

Mischling is a German term, literally translated as "hybrid" but understood in the Nazi context to mean something like "mongrel," "half-breed," or "mixed breed." The plural form is *Mischlinge*. It denoted a person who was considered to have a background that was both Aryan and Jewish.

At the outset of the Third Reich in January 1933, it was not entirely clear what the Nazi racial agenda would be regarding Jews, other than finding ways to remove them from society and hope that they would seek to leave Germany. An initial step leading to their exclusion from Germany's daily life, however, was to define who would be considered a member of the Jewish "racial enemy."

The Nuremberg Laws of 1935 saw this process codified, in which a legal attempt was made to clarify who was a Jew, who was not, and who fell in between. Thus, those with four Jewish grandparents were "full Jews"; those with three Jewish grandparents were "three-quarter Jews"; those with two Jewish grandparents were considered *Mischlinge* of the first degree, provided they were not identified with the Jewish religion and not married to Jewish spouses; and persons with only one Jewish grandparent were *Mischlinge* of the second degree. In 1935, such persons in the latter two categories were said to number anywhere between 100,000 and 350,000.

Nazi antisemitism viewed Jews as a racial, biological category, not as a religious tradition. That said, few formal scientific tests were applied, other than the religious affiliation of a person's grandparents. There was nothing a child could do to demonstrate their ethnic "innocence" in the Third Reich; they had no say whatsoever over how the Nazi regime viewed them or what their fate would be. For the most part, however, *Mischlinge* of the first degree were classified as Jews, while those of the second degree were absorbed into German society, albeit with restrictions and discriminations.

The existence of *Mischling* categories enabled many Jews to survive the Holocaust due to Nazi reluctance to "kill off" the Aryan alongside of the Jew in each person. For a start, many intermarried Jews, especially women, were able to keep their heads above water (and those of their *Mischling* children) by virtue of their marriage to Aryan partners. Beyond this, some Aryan women were able to protect their children by claiming that they were the product of adultery or prostitution, rather than their legitimate children with their Jewish husbands. Illegitimate children were given preferential treatment in the courts when trying to prove that they were not Jewish. In many cases, of course, this was simply a ruse to help the children and, for the most part, had no bearing on the future of a married relationship.

For *Mischling* children, school was the first place that their status was put to the test. They were mostly those whose mothers were German, non-Jewish, but with Jewish fathers. Such children, it was recalled later, "had it from both sides." In state schools attended by both Aryan and *Mischling* children, the mothers of Aryan children could be members of the Nazi Party or were antisemites who did not want their children associating with Jews. On the other hand, some parents of *Mischlinge* were wary of the consequences of their children associating with Aryan children.

As the *Mischling* children grew, their tribulations did not diminish. They would be restricted in their choice of marriage partners, with first-degree *Mischlinge* requiring permission to marry—and this, in most cases, could only be to other *Mischlinge*. Permission to marry was suspended indefinitely from 1942, with the war given as the reason; in reality, this was the regime's opportunity to ensure that Jewish "blood" would no longer "pollute" future generations. *Mischlinge* had restricted access to higher education, and from 1942 they were generally forbidden from attending secondary schools or universities.

Further Reading

Burleigh, Michael, and Wolfgang Wipperman. *The Racial State: Germany 1933–1945*. Cambridge: Cambridge University Press, 1991.

Weiss, Sheila Faith. *The Nazi Symbiosis: Human Genetics and Politics in the Third Reich*. Chicago: University of Chicago Press, 2010.

N

NINAS RESA

A Swedish-Polish coproduction made in 2005, directed and written by Lena Einhorn. In English the film is entitled *Nina's Journey*, and it tells the story of the director's mother, Nina Rajmic, later Einhorn (Agnieszka Grochowska), as a Jewish teenager living under Nazi rule in Warsaw during the Holocaust.

The film's appearance was accompanied by a book in Swedish, also written by Lena Einhorn, entitled *Nina's Journey: A Survival Story*, which was awarded Sweden's August Prize for best nonfiction book of 2005. The movie premiered in November 2005 and won Sweden's Golden Ram award for Best Picture.

The film begins in the year 1937, and shows the life of Nina, then aged 12, and the happiness she enjoyed within a large, close-knit, loving Jewish family. We see how, as a young girl, she and her mother traveled to the United States to visit members of the family who had migrated there many years before; we also see how Nina's parents made the difficult decision to return to Poland just before the Nazis invaded in September 1939. Although they moved to Łódź, they were relocated as a result of the war to an apartment in the Warsaw Ghetto. It is here, in Warsaw, where most of the movie takes place.

As the story of her life unfolds, we see Nina doing what most teenagers do: coming of age, getting her first crush on a boy, going to parties, and graduating high school. In her case, however, all these things happen in wartime, under brutal occupation, and in the Warsaw Ghetto. The film shows Nina's efforts, with her mother (Maria Chwalibóg), to keep the family together; they are helped in no small measure by the audacity of Nina's brother Rudek (Paweł Iwanicki), who effectively acts in an unofficial resistance capacity to keep the family safe.

As Rudek is trying to find ways to avoid the Nazis who came into the ghetto, Nina and her mother are fortunate in obtaining vital war work in a clothing factory. This provides them with shelter, work for payment, and some small measure of protection from deportation to a death camp. Even that does not help them in the long term, however, as events during the spring of 1943 lead to the outbreak of the Warsaw Ghetto Uprising—further placing Nina in jeopardy. Only as a result of being smuggled out of the ghetto and into the safe hands of a friendly Polish family does she manage to survive. Her parents, on the other hand, are not successful in outlasting the Nazis, and they die in tragic circumstances.

We see Nina and Rudek survive, however, and are uplifted by their subsequent life path. Nina had always been keen to pursue an education, and we learn that after the war, she fled Poland and met a fellow student, Jerzy Einhorn (Andrzej

Niemczyk) in Copenhagen. They settled in Sweden where they completed their education, and Nina embarked on a career in medicine.

Ninas Resa is an engrossing coming-of-age tale about a courageous teenager who saw her life change as the Nazis invaded her country and her life. She lived under constant strain, continual threat, and saw most of her family die. Moreover, seemingly everyone else around her disappeared, too—not only her family, but also her friends, her schoolmates, and those familiar to her in her daily routine. To add to the movie's authenticity, it was shot in Warsaw, with Polish actors (many of whom were among the best-known in Poland when the film was made).

While the film could well have become a standard (though well-made) Holocaust drama of a young girl's struggle to survive the Warsaw Ghetto and her ultimate victory, *Ninas Resa* breaks with convention through the somewhat radical technique of adding documentary to the narrative through a running commentary from the director's mother, Nina Einhorn herself. Now an elderly lady being interviewed in Swedish, Nina is introduced at crucial times in order to develop her story in person. These interview segments are at once engaging and riveting—and they provide historical background and depth to Nina's story.

Nina was interviewed by her daughter prior to the production of the film but, sadly, did not live to see the finished treatment of her life at Lena's hands. She died in May 2002, before the film was released. What remains is a tribute by a daughter to her mother, certainly, but it is also a memorial to a generation that, in many cases, does not have someone to tell their story.

Further Reading

Einhorn, Lena. *Ninas Resa*. Stockholm: Prisma, 2005.

O

ŒUVRE DE SECOURS AUX ENFANTS

The *Œuvre de Secours aux Enfants* (Children's Aid Society, or OSE) is a Jewish organization created on October 28, 1912, by a group of doctors in St. Petersburg, Russia, as the *Obshchetsvo Zdravookhraneniya Yevreyiev* (Organization for the Health Protection of Jews, or OZE). It was, from the start, a specifically Jewish self-help body with an initial mission to protect, feed, and support Jewish children who were victims of poverty and persecution.

The Russian Revolution of 1917 and the ensuing civil war made its work increasingly necessary, while at the same time rendering its operations less and less tenable given the massive destruction and the onset of the communist state. In 1923 OSE relocated in Berlin; 10 years later, after the Nazis came to power in Germany in 1933, it was forced to relocate again, this time to France.

Prior to the outbreak of war in September 1939, OSE established and ran several homes for Jewish children who, for various reasons, were without parents or any other family to care for them. This was especially the case for refugee children, many of whom had been sent out of Nazi Germany by their parents or brought in by relatives—or, in some cases, had made their own way out of Germany and needed the assistance which only adults could provide. One of the organization's most important functions was therefore the running of the homes. In March 1939, several transports brought German Jewish children to France, while other children arrived either on their own or were brought by relatives. By May 1939, OSE children's homes held more than 200 refugees; in addition to providing a place to live, the homes served the children through the delivery of education and preparation for their future lives.

During the war years, the work of OSE increased exponentially as it rescued more and more children in danger. With the outbreak of war, children from Germany and Austria living in France now became enemy aliens in need of protection. Then, immediately after Germany's defeat of France in the summer of 1940, OSE found its field of operations expanded to include children displaced by the war. Because of the German-enforced division of the country, OSE operations were largely confined to southern France, in the so-called Vichy Zone. Jewish children needing OSE help came from a variety of backgrounds, particularly the Low Countries and northern France. They were installed in homes in the departments of Creuse and Haute-Vienne in a few villages where the local inhabitants were prepared to offer their support.

In the dark years of World War II from 1942 to 1944, OSE gradually turned into a resistance organization, particularly from the beginning of 1942 when it was forced to shift its focus from philanthropic work to that of active opposition to Nazi antisemitic measures. Its leaders, trainers, and educators became rescuers, hiding children under their responsibility behind false identities. OSE homes saw the provision of initial shelter for the children, after which they would be dispersed. Once the danger had passed, they would be reunited and provided with accommodation, food, clothing, education, and sports, just as before. One of the main figures in these activities was **Georges Loinger**, who became a key person **smuggling** Jewish children into Switzerland under OSE auspices from April 1943 onward. Loinger had already been long involved with the OSE homes, where he had organized sports competitions for the children to encourage their physical development in advance of whatever the future might hold.

Prior to this, in the middle of 1941, **Andrée Salomon**, the OSE delegate to the Gurs and Rivesaltes internment camps, had begun the process of organizing preparations for the emigration of interned Jewish children to the United States. She assembled 311 of these children and arranged for their transit to the United States with the assistance of other bodies such as the American Jewish Joint Distribution Committee. These children were required to leave their parents behind, however, and in many cases became orphaned as a result of the war.

In the summer of 1942, Vichy police began roundups and deportations of Jewish children, first to the transit camp at Drancy, outside Paris, from where they would be shipped to Nazi extermination camps. In response, OSE organized a smuggling operation to move the children to neutral countries, especially Switzerland and Spain. Families, convents, and boarding schools were prepared and made ready for the OSE children, who now operated from false papers. Despite this lifesaving work—which could only have been accomplished with the assistance of many individuals and parties, Jewish and non-Jewish—closing all the OSE homes took more than a year.

After September 1943, with the Italian capitulation and the German occupation of Vichy France, the task of cross-border rescue became more difficult, and the period between November 1943 and March 1944 saw the smuggling of children slow to a trickle. Beginning in March 1944, however—possibly due to the German invasion of Hungary that month, but certainly from June onward with the Allied landings in Normandy—rescues across the border resumed at an accelerated rate. These were carried out jointly by OSE in conjunction with the Jewish Scouts (EIF) and the activities of one of its groups, *La Sixiéme* (the "Sixth"), together with the militant *Mouvement de la jeunesse sioniste* (Zionist Youth Movement, or MJS).

In February 1944, time ran out for OSE. It had often operated in the full glare of Vichy and Nazi scrutiny but continued in its work of rescuing Jewish children despite the possible consequences. Early in 1944, Alain Mossé, the former chief of staff to the prefect of Savoy, was dismissed from service and immediately went over to serve OSE in Montpellier, Chambéry, and Aix-les-Bains. He provided the Resistance with Vichy police documents intended to remove foreign Jews, and, working alone during this critical time, he continued to distribute funds and find ways to conceal the children before they were conveyed across the Swiss border. On February 8, 1944, however, the entire staff of OSE at Chambéry was arrested. Mossé, tortured by SS officer Alois Brunner—the onetime assistant of Adolf Eichmann and commandant of the transit camp at Drancy—divulged nothing regarding OSE operations. Within 48 hours, all the remaining children's homes were evacuated, but Mossé and those working with him were sent to Drancy and then deported to their deaths at Auschwitz on March 7, 1944.

Following the **liberation** of France in August 1944, the work of OSE continued. Its immediate task was to repatriate the children still under its care and then to look after those who had been orphaned. It also helped in looking after others who had been freed from concentration camps. Children were sent to homes in France or to other countries, including pre-independence Israel and the United States.

Recognized for its rescue of more than 5,000 children during the war and the reception of child survivors of the camps, to this day OSE is renowned for its selfless actions in rescuing and valuing human life and upholding fundamental human values.

Further Reading

Bartrop, Paul R., and Samantha J. Lakin. *Heroines of Vichy France: Rescuing French Jews during the Holocaust.* Santa Barbara, CA: Praeger, 2019.

Loinger, Georges, and Katy Hazan. *Aux frontiers de l'espoir.* Paris: Le Manuscrit, 2006.

Zeitoun, Sabine. *L'Œuvre de secours aux enfants (O.S.E.) sous l'occupation en France: Du legalism à la résistance 1940–1944.* Paris: Éditions L'Harmattan, 2000.

OSLO JEWISH CHILDREN'S HOME

In Norway in 1939, the *Nansenhjelpen*, a humanitarian organization established by Odd Nansen, the son of Nobel Peace Prize laureate Fridtjof Nansen, applied on humanitarian grounds to admit 100 Czech Jewish children to Oslo's Jewish Children's Home. The Ministry of Justice, however—and with reluctance—decided to approve the entry of only 22 children. The first director of the home, Nina Hasvold (née Hackel), was recruited by Norwegian psychiatrist Nic (Carolina) Waal after they met in Berlin while attending the *Kinderseminar* (Seminar on Children) run by Wilhelm Reich. *Nansenhjelpen* board member Sigrid Helliesen Lund was also active in establishing the home. During the German occupation of Norway from 1940 to 1945, Waal was active in the underground resistance and, together with Hasvold and Lund, ensured the escape of Jewish children from Oslo, saving them from deportation.

The Children's Home in Oslo was established in 1938. Its first inhabitants were Jewish refugees from Vienna known as *Wienerbarna* ("the Vienna children"), who had arrived in June 1938 on the pretext of a summer vacation with the Norwegian Jewish community. With the German occupation of Oslo, however, the children had to be moved. After some time at the Jewish community's cabin at Skui in Bærum and in foster care, they moved into rented facilities in Industrigaten and finally into a building the Jewish community had acquired at Holbergsgate 21 in Oslo. Nina Hackel, who had fled St. Petersburg in 1918, became manager of the Jewish Children's Home.

Conditions worsened progressively for the Norwegian Jewish community after April 1940, and this affected the Jewish Children's Home. Though Sigrid Helliesen Lund had the foresight to burn the entire list of Czech Jewish refugees on April 9, 1940, the home eventually caught the attention of German and Quisling authorities. After the war broke out, parents in the former Czechoslovakia were contacted and asked if they wanted their children to continue to stay in Norway or return. The parents of seven children wanted a return; all of those subsequently perished in the Holocaust.

As manager of the home, Nina Hackel was much loved by the children, and this love was returned by children who arrived during the war in increasing number. In total, nine boys and five girls were living in the Jewish Children's Home when the situation began to tighten.

By autumn of 1942, Norway had been at war for two and a half years. The antisemitic measures had spread—all Jews had to register, and each had a J-stamp in their passport. Nina Hackel and Bertold Hasvold were introduced to each other, and a subsequent arranged marriage permitted Nina to remain in the country and obtain Norwegian residence.

The first group arrest of Jews occurred on June 18, 1941, four days before the German invasion of the Soviet Union. On October 25, 1942, Karl Alfred Marthinsen, the Norwegian commander of the SS and SD (*Sicherheitsdienst*, or security service), sent a telegram to all Norwegian police authorities announcing the arrests and detailing information on the confiscation of Jewish property. The law regarding Jewish property was signed the next day. Although Norwegian Jews were not confined in ghettos, on October 26, 1942, all Jewish males over 15 years with a J-stamp were arrested. The women had a daily duty to report to the police, and Nina Hasvold was required to register every day at the nearest police station.

On the morning of November 25, Sigrid Helliesen Lund responded to a ring on her doorbell. An unknown man delivered his brief message that there would be another visit that night—and the "small packages" (that is, the children) would be collected. She never discovered the identity of the messenger but had little doubt that the information came from sympathetic police working for the collaborationist authorities, who were concerned that she should leave and thereby save herself and the children. The message was a warning that this time women and children would be the victims. At the same time, Nic Waal received a similar message. Lund, who was involved with the Norwegian Resistance, realized she was in danger. The women working alongside her spent the day conveying warnings around Oslo and placing those threatened into safe homes.

Waal ignored the air raid sirens at 9:00 p.m. that night; as a doctor, she had been allowed to keep her small car, and often drove it on missions as a courier for the Resistance. She now she drove to the Jewish Children's Home. Together with Nina Hasvold, they woke up all 14 children and told them to dress in the finest clothes they had—and wear two of everything. The children were divided into two groups according to age. They held their shoes in their hands and slipped down the stairs from the third floor, being extra quiet because on the second floor, there lived a woman who had Nazi sympathies.

They put the younger children into the car and then traveled to the home of Gerda Tanberg, a friend who was willing to make her small apartment available. After that, Nic Waal went back and collected the older children. All were now crammed into Tanberg's two-room apartment. The situation was difficult; they needed food and drink, but there was precious little to go around due to rationing, and with other people living in the house, the children had to be as silent as possible.

Sigrid Helliesen Lund helped Gerda with supplies, obtaining ration cards so that the children could get food. Although the children were mostly with Gerda Tanberg, some were also farmed out to others not to arouse suspicion. As the time to flee to Sweden approached, all children returned to her apartment. It took a week to get the trip organized. A friendly taxi driver, Martin Solvang, was in the same resistance network as Nic Waal, and made repeated trips to the border area with his small charges, driving them from the Tanberg apartment to a small farm run by Ola Rauken near the frontier. Crossing the border, they met up with Ola Breisjøberget, who led them over the last part of the route to the Swedish border. Another member of the Norwegian Resistance, **Ingebjørg Sletten-Fosstvedt**, was also a vital member of the whole operation at the time.

When the children arrived in Sweden, they were led to a military outpost, but next to it was a school where they got cookies and cocoa. They were then transported to a hospital for delousing. As refugees, the orphans were all stateless. They were therefore sent to a holding location, separated from those who were Norwegian citizens, and they lived in Alingsås near Gothenburg until the war was over. Nic Waal and Tove Filseth (later Tau), who was secretary in the *Nansenhjelpen*, visited the children in Sweden.

When peace came in 1945, the children's home was visited by a Norwegian representative in Stockholm. He said that the children were stateless and should not hope to stay in Norway. Further, the orphanage had been sold during the war, with all its assets. The children, however, decided to go back regardless of whether Norway wanted them or not. All survived the Holocaust and subsequently found new homes in Norway, Sweden, Argentina, the United Kingdom, and the United States.

Of those who participated in the rescue effort, seven were recognized by Yad Vashem in Jerusalem as Righteous among the Nations in 2006. They were Caroline (Nic) Waal, Nina Hasvold, Gerda Tanberg, Martin Solvang, Ola Rauken, Ola Breisjøberget, and Sigrid Helliesen Lund. For her involvement in this and other activities, Ingebjørg Sletten-Fosstvedt had earlier been recognized, in 1967.

Further Reading

Abrahamsen, Samuel. *Norway's Response to the Holocaust: A Historical Perspective*. New York: Holocaust Library, 1991.

PASSING

The act of passing takes place when a person chooses to alter their identity by submerging themselves into a group with a different identity to their own. Passing most often results in separation—often, of necessity, a complete separation—from one's original identity, family, community, and lifestyle. During the Holocaust, some Jews managed to pass as Aryans—whether Germans, Poles, or any other non-Jewish group—as a means of self-preservation. To pass successfully, the Jew would have to be accepted into the non-Jewish community and not reveal their Jewish identity, which would have to remain concealed entirely.

Jews who decided to pass were forced to transform a wide range of what they had previously considered to be "normal"; this usually involved a name change but could also include their accent, their manner of dress, word choices, and other elements of their persona in order to blend in unnoticed with the non-Jewish majority around them.

There was nothing new in this. In order to escape antisemitism in earlier times, Jews had often converted to Christianity or presented themselves as Christians for the sake of survival. Passing, however, was not the same as assimilation, which is a more gradual and less urgently driven route to acceptance in the majority culture. Indeed, it was the assimilated Jew who was one of Adolf Hitler's major points of antagonism, as such people were often indistinguishable from others in German society. The Jew who passed, however, was always aware that his or her condition was only a temporary one that did not carry with it any personal commitment that would endure beyond the current crisis.

Thus, for some Jews, survival might be achieved by masking their identity and passing, in which case they could live an ostensibly free and legal existence through mixing with the local population. Very often, if the masquerade was incomplete or likely to be found out, this would be a preliminary step before going completely underground or living a life in hiding until liberation.

Trying to pass as a non-Jew was far from easy. The customs of the local population had to be understood instinctively, and, presuming the person in question could speak the local language, an equally instinctive appreciation of the shades and subtleties of regional jargon had to be obvious. Knowing something of popular history and politics could also help, as well as various forms of social interaction such as eating and drinking habits, cultural norms, and religious customs. There were often so many circumstances in which a Jew who was passing as a non-Jew could be given away through ignorance of local folkways that Jews passing were always looking over their shoulder in fear of being recognized.

Not everyone could adapt to this kind of hunted existence, and in urban areas, particularly in Eastern Europe, Jews could be given away by a sad or anxious look, a linguistic inflection, an obvious fear of authority, or any number of telltale signs showing that they did not quite fit in with those around them. The fear of exposure or denunciation was seemingly everywhere, particularly from Jewish informers keen to secure their own survival by working with the Gestapo—to say nothing of professional non-Jewish "rat catchers" who made a living out of locating Jews and handing them over to the authorities.

Where children were concerned, passing presented more problems than for adults. They needed to be able to explain, if questioned, why they were alone; such a moment was harrowing and confronting for many, able to give them away immediately. Moreover, how to respond, if challenged, was something for which children in wartime Europe in the 1940s were frequently not prepared, owing to the deference expected of those who were underage in an age-dominated society. A further element of that, of course, was the reality of not having parents from whom they could learn how to behave under the conditions in which they found themselves. And without parents, children, particularly orphans, could be devoid of appropriate or acceptable identity cards—another telltale sign of difference that would lead to immediate exposure.

Documents, moreover, had to be made out in a name that was not identifiably Jewish; therefore, questions arose for children as to whose name should be on the documents. In most cases, a new identity would have to be learned, often from scratch, and the child would have to memorize every aspect of it—and then know how to stick to the story so as not to be found out. Such a dramatic transformation was difficult enough for adults, but for children the issues were compounded owing to their youth.

Not only this, but if they were to pass in non-Jewish society, they had not only to possess money but also know how to use it—both elements of daily life for which they were often not prepared. Thus, help from friendly non-Jews for the procurement of identity and other documentation, as well as money, was indispensable, though children placing themselves in the hands of others was an obvious vulnerability that could see them undone.

Such everyday issues as clothing could also give away children who were passing in non-Jewish society. If they came in from outlying areas or had escaped from a ghetto into a non-Jewish area of a city, the clothing they wore, which might be especially shabby given the impoverishment of the ghetto, could signal that they were not local. And boys were especially vulnerable due to their **circumcision**, which was not a usual practice for non-Jews in Eastern Europe.

Passing might sometimes have been easier in Western Europe rather than further east, but in all societies, the problems were made more difficult for children. It was always going to be hard for children to forge new identities in another location where they were previously unknown, often rendering them defenseless.

Further Reading

Paldiel, Mordecai. *Sheltering the Jews: Stories of Holocaust Rescuers*. Minneapolis: Fortress Press, 1996.

PÈRE JACQUES (1900–1945)

Père Jacques de Jésus, OCD, was a French Carmelite friar and teacher responsible for accepting several Jewish children into his school, and for his efforts, he was arrested and imprisoned in various Nazi concentration camps. The combined effect of these experiences was to cost him his life.

Born Lucien-Louis Bunel in 1900, he was the third of seven children from a hardworking family in Normandy. Inspired by his father's deep piety, strong sense of social justice, and commitment to work, he decided to become a priest. In 1925 he was ordained in the diocese of Rouen and served in the St. Joseph seminary in Le Havre. He combined prayer and seclusion with social activism and was noted for his sermons and preaching. As a teacher of religion and English, he employed modern approaches to classroom management and was renowned for his intellect and sense of humor.

His longing for solitude and a life of contemplation, mixed with service to the poor, saw him consider joining a monastery. In 1930, upon deeper reflection, he entered the novitiate of the Carmelite Order and took his vows as Père Jacques three years later. In 1934, at the suggestion of his superiors, he opened a boarding school for boys, the *Petit Collège Sainte-Thérèse de l'Enfant-Jésus* in Avon, Seine-et-Marne.

Père Jacques remained at the school as principal until 1939, when he was called up for military service. When France surrendered to Germany in June 1940, however, he had little intention of resuming a quiet life. Returning to the school, he became an active member of the French Resistance.

He decided to resist in a novel way—not through physical confrontation but through the act of rescue. He made the school a refuge for Jews and opened its doors to young Frenchmen seeking to avoid conscription for forced labor in Germany. In January 1943 he enrolled three Jewish boys—Hans-Helmut Michel, Jacques-France Halpern, and Maurice Schlosser—as students. A fourth, Maurice Bas, was hidden in plain sight as a worker at the school, and Maurice Schlosser's father was protected by a local villager. When Lucien Weil, a distinguished botanist from the National Museum of Natural History in Paris, sought sanctuary, Père Jacques placed him on the faculty. In addition, he sought every opportunity to arrange for Jewish children to be placed with Catholic families.

On January 15, 1944, however, these initiatives came to an end. A former member of the school had been captured and tortured by the Gestapo to reveal what Père Jacques had been up to and learn of the hidden Jews' whereabouts. On February 3, 1944, the three students—Michel, Halpern, and Schlosser—together with Lucien Weil, his mother, and his sister, were taken to Auschwitz and gassed. Père Jacques was also arrested, and the school immediately shut down. One of the students in the school was Louis Malle, who grew up to become an Academy Award–winning film director. He later remembered that as Père Jacques was being led away, he turned to the watching students and said, "*Au revoir et à bientôt*" ("Good-bye and see you soon"). This farewell was to be the inspiration for Malle's celebrated autobiographical film from 1987, *Au Revoir les Enfants*.

At first Père Jacques was interned in the prison at Fontainebleau but was moved to a brutal German "reprisal camp" at Neue-Bremm, where he remained for three horrendous weeks during which 44 of the 51 prisoners who arrived with him perished. On April 22, 1944 he was transferred to Mauthausen, and immediately set about the task of trying to help others, sharing his rations, hearing confessions, and bringing whatever comfort he could. On May 18, however, he was sent to Gusen, a subcamp of Mauthausen. When the priests imprisoned there were transferred to the "priest block" at Dachau, Père Jacques hid his identity in order to remain at Gusen so he could continue ministering to the prisoners.

The 18 months of his captivity left him sick and exhausted. When American troops arrived to liberate the camp on May 5, 1945, Père Jacques, suffering from tuberculosis and weighing only 75 pounds, tried to restore order among the prisoners and helped organize the relief effort. On May 20 he was moved to a hospital near the Carmelite Friars in Linz but succumbed several days later and died on June 2, 1945, aged just 45. His body was returned to France and buried in the cemetery of Avon.

On January 17, 1985, Yad Vashem recognized Père Jacques as one of the Righteous among the Nations for his efforts in hiding Jewish students and saving their lives in his school during the Holocaust. Within the Catholic Church, he was honored further when the cause for his canonization was opened in 1990.

Further Reading

Yad Vashem. Lucien Bunel (Father Jacques), at https://www.yadvashem.org/righteous/stories/bunel.html.

PERL, GISELLA (1907–1988)

Gisella Perl was born on December 10, 1907, and grew up in Máramarossziget (Sighetu Marmației, sometimes called Sighet), then part of Hungary. After World War I, the town became part of Romania. In 1923, at the age of 16, she graduated first in her high school class. She was the only girl—and the only Jew—in that group. After graduation she asked her father to help her enroll in medical school, but his immediate response was to say that if she went, it would mean her breaking away from Judaism. Several months later she approached him again, this time swearing on a prayer book he had given her that she would always remain "a good, true Jew." Her father, Maurice Perl, relented, and she enrolled in medical school.

Gisella Perl became a successful and well-known gynecologist in Sighet. Married to another doctor named Krauss, she practiced medicine until early 1944, when the Jews of Hungary became the last major community targeted for extermination by the Nazis. First, she and her extended family were forced into a ghetto; soon thereafter, they were deported to Auschwitz. After they were separated by Dr.

Josef Mengele at a selection on the arrival ramp, she was never to see most of them again. Mengele assigned Gisella, with four other prisoner-doctors and four nurses, to operate a hospital ward in the camp. This had no beds, no bandages, no drugs, and no instruments. Within this environment, she tended to every disease and broken bone. She also performed surgery, without anesthesia, on women suffering from a variety of ailments, mostly camp-induced.

Mengele's most important role for the doctors, however, was for them to report to him every instance of pregnancy found in the camp. He instructed Gisella that she had a duty to do so, as he would arrange for them to be looked after and sent to a better camp. Gisella learned, however, that pregnant women were in fact subjected to **medical experimentation** at Mengele's hands; once she realized this, she decided that "never again would there be a pregnant woman in Auschwitz," and she would do all in her power to save their lives. To do so, she reasoned, she would have to prevent them from giving birth.

As both an inmate and head women's doctor at Auschwitz, she would save the lives of hundreds of women, performing abortions and terminating pregnancies—frequently at night—without any medical implements, anesthesia, bandages, or antibiotics. When she learned of a pregnant prisoner, she would explain to the expectant mother the situation she faced; if the SS knew she was pregnant, both her own life and that of her unborn child would be over. Sometimes the mother would ask her to bring a live baby into the world, only for the next step to take place immediately; Gisella would close her hand over the baby's mouth in order to save the mother's life.

The pressure generated by these actions was intense, and Gisella found herself thoroughly unprepared for the morally demanding work this involved. She was to say later, "No one will ever know what it meant to me to destroy those babies." She also knew, however, that if she had not done so, it would have meant the murder of both mother and child. Altogether, she saved hundreds of lives. Despite the grisly, lifesaving work in which she was engaged, women at Auschwitz called her affectionately "Gisi Doctor," a name that stuck after the war. The guilt and burden of the Holocaust weighed heavily on her, however, so much so that many years later, in 1947, she made an unsuccessful suicide attempt. Learning the fate of the rest of her family contributed to this, as she suffered from survivor guilt upon learning that practically no one else had survived.

In January 1945, as Russian forces approached, the Germans evacuated Auschwitz. Gisella was moved first to a camp near Hamburg; then, two months later, she was moved to Bergen-Belsen, where **liberation** came courtesy of British troops. She was to relate later that as the camp was being freed, she was delivering a baby—the first free child born at Belsen.

In the months that followed, Gisella remained in the camp, but in the fall of 1945, she left and began looking for her family. Within three weeks she learned that her husband had been beaten to death just before the liberation, and her teenage son, who had been taken from her when she was deported, had been gassed. Her parents and extended family had also been murdered. Soon after this Gisella made her suicide attempt. Surviving, she was taken to a convent in France to recuperate. Only later did she discover that her daughter, Gabriella, who had been one of thousands of **hidden children** during the war, had also survived the Holocaust.

In March 1947 Gisella journeyed to New York to address doctors and other professionals, sponsored by the Hungarian-Jewish Appeal and the United Jewish Appeal. She considered herself to be an ambassador of the 6,000,000 killed in the Holocaust. While there, she met former First Lady Eleanor Roosevelt, who encouraged her to resume practicing medicine. Until this time, Gisella had little interest in being a doctor anymore; she was, instead, driven to bear witness to what had happened at Auschwitz.

In 1951, sponsored by Representative Sol Bloom, Democrat of New York, she was granted citizenship. The process was not easy, as she was questioned by immigration authorities over the abortions she had carried out at Auschwitz and on suspicion of assisting the Nazi doctors of Auschwitz in carrying out human rights abuses. For a time, it seemed as though she would be denied citizenship. Sol Bloom, however, successfully petitioned the Justice Department to allow her to remain as a permanent resident of the United States.

Now an American, she opened a doctor's office on Park Avenue and joined the staff of Mount Sinai Hospital in obstetrics and gynecology, where over the rest of her career she delivered 3,000 babies and became an expert in treating infertility.

In June 1948 she wrote an account of her experiences during the war, entitled *I Was a Doctor in Auschwitz*. A movie, *Out of the Ashes* (dir. Joseph Sergeant, 2003), starring Christine Lahti as Gisella, was later made based upon the book.

In 1979, Gisella moved to Herzliya, Israel, to be with her daughter and grandson. She died in Israel on December 16, 1988, six days after her 81st birthday.

Further Reading

Perl, Gisella. *I Was a Doctor in Auschwitz*. New York: International Universities Press, 1948.

PIEPEL

The origin of the term *piepel* is not known. No one knows who coined it, or in what language it originated, but everyone in the world of the Nazi concentration camps, it seemed, knew what a piepel was: a preadolescent or young adolescent boy (mostly younger than 15 years old) who was forced to serve one of the kapos (prisoner functionaries). The boy was used to service all the kapo's needs, and this included sexual pleasure. Kapos were given authority by the Nazis to help control their fellow Jews in the concentration camps. For this, they were rewarded with better food and less cramped living conditions, among other things. Additional rewards, for those who wished to avail themselves, were the piepels. They, in return, would receive favored treatment, but given their situation, they were effectively sex slaves, subjected to rape for the gratification of the kapos and in return for extra food and patronage that could help to save their young lives.

The piepel assisted the kapo and served him physically. His special position was only guaranteed through being subservient to the older man, a collaborator who in turn served the Nazis. Exploiting their preferential position, some piepels were known to exhibit cruelty against other prisoners, whereas others sought to help their fellow Jews. Their understanding of the situation was often confused, however, particularly given their age and the morally uncertain world of the camps.

One piepel was the younger brother of a former concentration camp prisoner-turned-writer, Yehiel De-Nur, *né* Yehiel Feiner, who wrote under the name Ka-Tzetnik 135633. In his *House of Dolls* (1955), in which he described the "Joy Division" in which Nazis kept Jewish women as sex slaves in concentration camps, he already raised the issue of sexual violence committed by the Nazis against Jewish women. Another of De-Nur's books, *Piepel* (1961), dealt directly with Nazi sexual abuse of young boys through reference to the piepel himself.

Given that life was expendable in the concentration camp, it was always in the interests of a piepel to remain as attractive as possible for his kapo master. It was important to keep the kapo happy, and in such a pursuit, it was imperative that the piepel always appeared healthy. When a kapo tired of a piepel, or the piepel was no longer cooperative, it was relatively easy to find a new one. This was, after all, a slave environment, and piepels were slaves of a very specific kind, who could be raped—or killed—on a whim.

The topic of sexual violence against Jewish children during the Holocaust has barely been touched by academic writers, and it is only through documentaries such as ***Screaming Silence*** (dir. Ronnie Sarnat, 2015) that revelations are beginning to come slowly to light.

Further Reading

Wiesel, Elie. *Night*. New York: Hill and Wang, 1960.

PRITCHARD, MARION (1921–2016)

Marion Pritchard was a member of the Dutch resistance and a rescuer of Jewish children during the Holocaust.

Born Marion van Binsbergen in Amsterdam in 1921, she was the daughter of a Supreme Court judge and an English mother. In 1940, soon after the Nazi invasion and occupation of the Netherlands, Marion was a student at Amsterdam's School of Social Studies when she and a friend were arrested on suspicion of contact with members of the Dutch resistance. Although her friend had such contact, Marion did not, but she was classified as guilty by association and imprisoned for seven months.

In the spring of 1942, Marion saw children aged between two and eight loaded onto trucks and being taken away by Nazis. Shocked by what she had witnessed, she decided that from this point on, she would commit herself single-mindedly to rescue work.

At first, she provided essential items such as food and clothing to Jews in hiding. Assuming a more active role, a stranger handed her a baby girl for safe keeping; but on reaching her destination, she learned that her contacts had been arrested. Another couple, who were not originally part of the operation, took the baby off her hands, and Marion's new role as a smuggler of children had begun.

One Saturday in 1942, Marion was asked by the head of the social welfare organization where she was working if she would be prepared to find a safe place for a two-year-old Jewish boy named Jan Herben. Sheltering a Jew—even a child—was a criminal offense, but she immediately took the boy to her parents' apartment until she found a safer place. From this point, her rescue activities increased rapidly.

At the end of 1942 Marion moved to Huizen, North Holland, where she lived in a house

Erica Polak (1944), a Jewish baby that Marion Pritchard was hiding from the Nazis. Pritchard helped save approximately 150 Dutch Jews, most of them children, during World War II. She was imprisoned by the Nazis, worked in collaboration with the Dutch resistance, and killed a Dutch collaborator in order to save a Jewish child. (United States Holocaust Memorial Museum, courtesy of Marion Pritchard)

belonging to a friend of her parents. She was asked if she could shelter a Jewish family, Fred Polak and his three children, and she obliged. The house, which was secured by the Dutch resistance movement, was 150 miles outside of Amsterdam, and the Polaks stayed there until the end of the war. A friendly farmer brought them supplies of milk every day. Marion was successful in hiding them in a safe place they had dug under the floor; it was agreed that if the Nazis would launch a raid, the baby would be given a sedative in order to remain quiet.

Late one night in 1944, a suspicious Dutch Nazi entered the house, looking for Jews after a tipoff from a neighbor. Marion, aware that if the family was found, they would be sent to a concentration camp, reached for a revolver hidden close by and, without hesitation, shot and killed him. Her neighbor and friend, Karel Poons, a Jewish ballet dancer, came quickly to her aid. He walked to the village and arranged for the local baker to collect the body, while others, including a butcher and an undertaker, also got involved. The body was buried, the Polak family was safe, and there was no follow-up from the authorities.

Marion then placed 25 Jewish children with families in an area known as Het Gooi—a place near Hilversum characterized as the home of the rich and famous.

On another occasion she pretended to have a child of her own, born out of wedlock, and registered this Jewish baby at the city hall—a deception she repeated on several occasions in different towns and cities. Once, when staying as a house guest, Marion was given a little girl to place with a family. Having taken a nap, when she awoke, she found that the woman of the house was changing and feeding the baby, without asking questions or giving any sign of denunciation. This underscored Marion's sense that there was an underlying sense of right and wrong prevailing at the time, particularly with regard to innocent children.

Overall, during the Holocaust, Marion Pritchard safeguarded the lives of between 125 and 150 Jews, most of them children. She used whatever means were at hand; by 1945 she admitted that "I had lied, stolen, cheated, deceived, and even killed."

After the war Marion moved to Germany to work in displaced persons camps, hoping to learn the fate and possible location of Jewish friends who might have survived the war. It was here, in one of the refugee camps, that she met (and later married) Tony Pritchard, a former U.S. Army lieutenant. In 1947 they moved to the United States, where they settled in Vermont and raised a family. There Marion lectured extensively about her experiences during the war.

On March 31, 1981, Yad Vashem recognized Marion Pritchard van Binsbergen as one of the Righteous among the Nations, and in 1991 she was made an honorary citizen of Israel. In 1996 she was awarded the Wallenberg Medal from the University of Michigan, Raoul Wallenberg's American *alma mater*, placing her alongside other rescuers and upstanders such as Jan Karski, **Miep Gies**, Per Anger, Heinz Drossel, and **Nicholas Winton**.

Marion Pritchard died at age 96 on December 11, 2016.

Further Reading

Scrase, David, Wolfgang Mieder, and Katherine Quimby Johnson (Eds.). *Making a Difference, Rescue and Assistance during the Holocaust: Essays in Honor of Marion Pritchard*, Burlington: Center for Holocaust Studies, University of Vermont, 2004.

R

RACINE, MILA (1921–1945)

Mila Racine was a Jewish resister in France who saved the lives of Jewish children and others by smuggling them across the border from unoccupied France into Switzerland.

Born on September 14, 1921, in Moscow, she was the daughter of Georges (Hirsch) Racine and his wife Berthe (Bassia). One of three children, she had a brother, Emmanuel, and a sister, Sacha. Fleeing the Soviet Union and a climate of pogroms in the aftermath of the Russian Revolution, the family relocated to France and settled in Paris.

After Germany's invasion, partition, and occupation of France, the Racine family moved into the Vichy Zone. Mila joined the resistance on January 5, 1942. While her parents were in a safe house in Nice, Mila, Emmanuel ("Mola"), and Sacha worked for *Éducation Physique* (Physical Education), part of the MJS, as guides helping Jewish children reach safety.

Mila, operating under the alias of Marie Anne Richemond, came from a Zionist background and had been an active member of the Women's International Zionist Organization (WIZO). In the summer of 1943, she was given command of an MJS unit in Saint-Gervais-Le Fayet (Haute-Savoie) in the Italian zone, covering a region that included Toulouse, Gurs, Saint-Gervais, Nice, and Annemasse, under the overall command of Netanel ("Tony") Gryn.

Mila's activities, particularly around Annecy, saw her working in the "underground railroad," smuggling Jews to Switzerland. After Italy surrendered to the Allies on September 3, 1943, Jews in the alpine region took refuge in Nice. This provided Mila with the opportunity to drive convoys of children and adults to Annemasse, right on the border, from where they could reach Switzerland.

From then on, she helped hundreds of families and children who fled into her area. From her base in the French Alps, and often working close to German patrols, Mila and the other members of the MJS received children sent from French cities, often many miles distant. In order to protect them, they organized the children into small groups and then accompanied them to the border, where they were helped by Christian rescuers.

On October 21, 1943, she was conducting a convoy that included 30 children from the city of Nice, accompanied by a male member of the MJS, Roland Epstein. Logistically, this was a difficult group. It comprised children, an older couple, a young mother with a baby, and another couple with a small child. Without warning, they were intercepted by Germans with police dogs at Saint-Julien-en-Genevois. Gunshots rang out; one woman was killed and another wounded. Mila,

Roland Epstein, and the children were taken to Annemasse and incarcerated in the Pax Hotel, the prison located at Gestapo headquarters.

Suffering the torment of continual torture, Mila divulged nothing as the Nazis sought information regarding the smuggling operations. The mayor of Annemasse, **Jean Deffaugt**, managed to visit the prison and arranged with the Nazis to allow some of the children, including a baby of 14 months, to be freed and placed in a nearby children's home. Through the underground movement, he also managed to provide Mila with an escape plan. This was not something she could accept, however, as she had an instinctive feeling that the children (or perhaps Deffaugt) would be punished—or worse—if she was to escape.

Mila and Roland Epstein were transferred to the Montluc prison in Lyon. From there, Epstein was sent to the transit camp at Drancy and then deported to Buchenwald. He lived to see the end of the war and ultimate survival. Mila was deported, via the Royallieu transit camp at Compiègne, to Ravensbrück. From there, she was sent to Mauthausen, where she was put to hard labor repairing railways destroyed by Allied bombing. On March 22, 1945, on the eve of liberation, a British air raid targeted Mauthausen. Mila, on *aussenarbeit* (work outside the camp) at the time, was killed by shrapnel.

The work of Mila Racine did not end with her arrest, however. After her capture the MJS sent another resister, **Marianne Cohn**, to replace her in saving the lives of Jewish children. When she, in turn, was captured on the evening of May 31, 1944, she was replaced by yet another activist, Charlotte Sorkine. Such importance did the MJS place on the work of these young women that it determined nothing should stand in the way of their rescue activities on behalf of Jewish children, even at the risk of their very lives.

After the war, Mila Racine was posthumously awarded the *Medaille de la Resistance* and the *Croix de Guerre* by the French government. It is perhaps fitting that the recognition she received in Israel, many years later, was for a kindergarten and nursery in Tel Aviv to be named in her memory.

Further Reading

Lefenfeld, Nancy. *The Fate of Others: Rescuing Jewish Children on the French-Swiss Border*. Clarksville, MD: Timbrel Press, 2013.

RANJITSINHJI, DIGVIJAYSINHJI (1895–1966)

During World War II, hundreds of abandoned Polish children were taken into squalid orphanages deep in the interior of the Soviet Union. Orphaned Polish children—Jews and Catholics—faced uncertainty, but a kindhearted maharaja in Gujarat, India, agreed to accept them, rescuing them from a bleak future. His efforts saved the lives of hundreds of children.

Under the Molotov-Ribbentrop pact signed by Germany and the Soviet Union on August 23, 1939, both parties agreed to partition Poland. Germany attacked the western border on September 1, 1939, and 16 days later, Russia launched an eastern offensive. They carved up Poland, collaborating until Germany broke the pact in June 1941. Stalin's attack on Poland, however, had orphaned thousands of children, who were then moved to the interior of the Soviet Union and relocated to camps and temporary orphanages, where many died of illness or hunger.

In 1941 an amnesty permitting the evacuees to leave the Soviet Union was declared, and India was the first country to offer them shelter. The ruler of Nawanagar state, Maharaja Jam Saheb Digvijaysinhji Ranjitsinhji (born on September 18, 1895), then offered to house hundreds of children. The Hindu delegate to Britain's War Cabinet, the maharaja was already familiar with the situation, which prompted him to make his offer.

Hundreds of Polish children and women thus managed to escape the desperate circumstances of their exile. The Polish consulate in Bombay (Mumbai) had launched a drive to raise awareness in India about Jewish refugees and had been arranging for their travel to India during the war. Contradictory reports exist on how the children planned their escape, as they had already been turned away from every other country they approached for help.

Children leaving the USSR were brought to India by Anders's Army (the Polish Armed Forces in the East created from Polish soldiers in the Soviet Union), the Red Cross, the Polish consulate in Bombay, and British officials. When their ship docked in Bombay, the British governor immediately refused them entry. Maharaja Digvijaysinhji Ranjitsinhji Jadeja of Nawanagar tried to press the British government to let the refugees disembark, but facing this government intransigence and angry at the lack of compassion, the maharaja directed the ship to depart and then dock at Rosi Port in his state.

The maharaja greeted the women and children warmly as they disembarked, welcoming the orphans as his Nawnagari people and saying that just as he was the father of all the people of Nawanagar, so he was now also the father of the evacuees.

The children were set up in tents while the maharaja built the Balachadi camp, located near his summer palace 25 kilometers away from the capital city of Jamnagar. In response to persistent complaints by the British government regarding the entry of foreign refugees, the maharaja responded by claiming the evacuees as part of his family, even providing the government with adoption certificates for them.

Despite India itself suffering from a severe drought and famine at the time and civil strife over its demands for self-determination, the maharaja took many personal risks to ensure that more than 640 women and children found a safe refuge in Balachadi. He also ensured that they had special accommodation, schools, medical facilities, and opportunities for rest and recuperation at Balachadi, where he fed them well and built them a new school. The Indian people themselves showed no antagonism to the presence of the children, despite the local conditions.

When the war ended and the orphans had to return to Europe, both the children and the Maharaja were saddened. The Balachadi camp existed until early 1946; subsequently, the children were transferred to the Valivade camp in Kolhapur, where some remained until 1948. They emigrated with the help of the International Red Cross and the Polish Red Cross, which sought to successfully locate their relatives. Some children left for the United Kingdom or New Zealand, while others returned to Poland. The site of the camp today is part of 300-acre campus of the Sainik School, Balachadi.

After a reign of 33 years, Sir Digvijaysinhji Ranjitsinhji (who had been knighted in 1935 by King George V) died in Bombay on February 3, 1966, aged 70. He had never sought financial compensation for his action in taking in the children; his only wish was to have a street named after him in liberated Poland. After the war, however, the communist regime was unwilling to acknowledge the orphans' troubles, as it would have drawn attention to atrocities committed by the Red Army.

The maharajah's kindness was commemorated in postcommunist Poland, however, where he was posthumously awarded the Commander's Cross of the Order of Merit. He was also named the Honorary Patron of Warsaw's Bednarska High School. In 2013, the Polish government inaugurated the "Good Maharaja Square" in Warsaw in recognition for his help to refugees from Poland during the World War II, and the former evacuees themselves set up a "Survivors of Balachadi" group.

A documentary, *A Little Poland in India* (director/producer, Anu Radha), was made in 2016 with the collaboration of both the Indian and Polish governments to honor the efforts of Maharaja Jam Saheb Digvijaysinhji Ranjitsinhji.

Further Reading

Radha, Anu (director/producer). *A Little Poland in India.* Aakaar Films, 2016.

REYNDERS, HENRI (1903–1981)

Henri Reynders (Dom Bruno) was a Belgian priest credited with saving around 400 Jewish children during the Holocaust. Born in Brussels on October 24, 1903, he was the fifth child of eight in an upper-middle-class Catholic family. After completing his studies at a Catholic school, at the age of 17 he became a monk at the Benedictine Keizersberg Abbey in Leuven (Louvain). Between 1922 and 1925, he studied theology and philosophy at the Catholic University of Leuven and at Saint Anselm Athenaeum in Rome. After taking his vows in Rome in 1925, he led a monastic life at Mont-César Abbey. In 1928 he was ordained a priest, joined the Benedictine order in Belgium, and took the religious name of Dom Bruno. The University of Leuven awarded him a doctorate in theology in 1931.

Though devout, he dissented from some church doctrines, which led to his lecturing duties being curtailed; and as a result, he was assigned to mentor the son of the Duc de Guise, a claimant to the throne of France, living in Belgium. With the abbot's approval, however, he traveled widely, visiting church institutions to lecture. On one such visit, while lecturing to Catholic youths in Nazi Germany, he saw an elderly Jew being beaten, an incident he would later call the "shocking, revolting and nauseating" injustice and cruelty of Nazi antisemitism.

In response to the German invasion of Poland in September 1939, Belgium mobilized its army, and Dom Bruno was deployed to serve as a chaplain of its 41st Artillery Regiment. In May 1940 German troops invaded Belgium. In the course of the campaign, Dom Bruno sustained a leg injury and spent the next six months in prisoner-of-war camps at Wolfsburg and Doessel, Germany, where he gave religious and moral support to his fellow prisoners.

Upon King Leopold's meeting with Hitler, the Germans released many Belgian prisoners of war, including Dom Bruno. He returned to the abbey and resumed his teaching career. Motivated by his strong anti-Nazi beliefs and his hostility to the German invasion, he contacted elements of the growing Belgian resistance movement, helping to save downed Allied pilots and return them to Britain.

After his release, Jewish families began asking him to hide their children. With the help of the resistance, he enlisted families and Catholic institutions willing to care for Jewish children.

In 1942 the Nazi authorities began rounding up Jews for deportation to the newly completed death camps in Poland. With the permission of his abbot, Dom Bruno proceeded to the small village of Hodbomont to serve as chaplain at a home for the blind. Upon arrival he discovered that the manager of the home and many of the residents were, in fact, Jews in hiding. Both adults and children had found refuge there, with the assistance of Albert van den Berg, a noted lawyer working with Christian aid organizations opposed to Nazism. Dom Bruno and van den Berg quickly became close associates.

Later in 1942, the adults being shielded were rounded up and deported. It became unsafe to continue hiding Jewish children, so the home was closed, and van den Berg and Dom Bruno moved the children to other hiding places in rural areas. Using his influence with friends and acquaintances, he found refuges for the children in private homes, including his own mother's house and that of his brother, Jean Reynders. Dom Bruno was most successful in appealing to the protectors' Christian faith, resulting in Catholic boarding schools operating within the walls of convents or monasteries serving as places of refuge. He would personally escort the children and return to visit them, bringing news of their parents if they were also in hiding. He provided them with false identity papers with non-Jewish names and ration cards. Dom Bruno was only able to carry out his work with the willing cooperation of numerous officials, civil servants, and generous donors.

Dom Bruno returned to Mont-César Abbey and dedicated himself exclusively to finding further places of refuge for Jewish children. Initially he worked alone, though receiving financial support from Albert van den Berg and also assisted with funds by the Belgian banker and economist Jules Dubois-Pelerin. Over time, Dom Bruno expanded his contacts with other groups, but he found himself forced to move from place to place to avoid being caught by the Gestapo.

In saving as many Jews as possible from deportation, Dom Bruno found support among fellow monks at Mont-César, members of the Belgian church hierarchy, and family members, including his nephew Michel Reynders, who was later knighted in Belgium. Dom Bruno had to flee and go into hiding when the Gestapo raided the Mont-César Abbey, exchanging his monk's habit for civilian clothes and a beret to hide his shaved head. Another monk gave him a false identity card. Despite the serious risk, he continued to help Jews even while on the run. His courageous acts saved 400 Jewish lives, mostly children.

Dom Bruno built an underground network to successfully move and hide the children through the creation of contacts with active resistance groups as well as individuals engaged in rescue work. Several of these persons, including Albert van den Berg, paid with their lives for these humanitarian activities.

After Belgium's **liberation** in September 1944, Dom Bruno assisted with reuniting the hidden children with their parents or other surviving family members. Representatives of the Jewish community opposed the efforts of some Christian families to adopt Jewish orphans; sadly, many of the younger children who could not remember their Jewish origins wanted to stay with the families who had unofficially adopted them. Under the Nazi occupation, Dom Bruno did not allow the conversion of Jewish children to Catholicism, but he later changed this view, believing that the interests of each child should be the most important factor.

When the war ended, Dom Bruno briefly returned to the abbey but was reassigned by his order to other locations in Belgium, France, and Rome. His personal notebooks provided important information about his rescue work, and after the war, these notes, plus additional comments, were published in a book entitled *En Feuilletant mon cahier de Notes*. The book describes and names the hiding places of the Jews he helped, the names of others who assisted in this process, and details of his work forging identity documents, baptism certificates, money, and food coupons. These notebooks include 307 such entries, though Dom Bruno is known to have helped many more than this number.

On October 10, 1964, Yad Vashem recognized Henri Reynders, Dom Bruno, as one of the Righteous among the Nations. He retired to a nursing home, where he died on October 26, 1981, at the age of 78.

Further Reading

Paldiel, Mordecai. *The Path of the Righteous: Gentile Rescuers of Jews during the Holocaust*. Hoboken, NJ: KTAV, 1993.

Rabey, Steve. *Faith under Fire: Stories of Hope and Courage from World War II*. Nashville: Thomas Nelson, 2002.

"RHINELAND BASTARDS"

Those designated in the Third Reich during the 1930s as "Rhineland Bastards" (*Rheinlandbastarde*) were the children of mixed liaisons between German women and soldiers from French Africa who were stationed in the Rhineland as occupation forces between 1920 and 1930.

The term was thoroughly derogatory and related specifically to the children born of such unions rather than all Afro-Germans (many of whom were descendants from Germany's former African colonies). The "Rhineland Bastards," therefore, never numbered more than between 400 and 600 children in total, even though Germany's black population during the 1930s might have numbered up to 25,000. In view of the national humiliation Germany suffered at the hands of the French occupation, however—the more so given that it was a direct result of the

Treaty of Versailles—when the Nazis came to power, they decided to take action against those born as a result of the French African presence.

The origin of these children acted to their detriment, notwithstanding their skin color. With stories circulating of African soldiers raping German women and of what became known as the "'Black Horror on the Rhine," the children of Senegalese and other French colonial troops were maltreated from the start. The attitudes generated at the time and since had repercussions later, during World War II. On May 29, 1940, during the German assault against France, Germany's propaganda minister, Joseph Goebbels, stirred up German public opinion by drawing memories back to the "Black Horror on the Rhine"; as a result, in June 1940, German troops massacred thousands of Senegalese prisoners of war in a racial campaign of vengeance for the "crimes" of the Senegalese against German women in the 1920s.

The reality, however, was that children born in Germany, of German mothers, were German citizens. When the Nazis came to power in 1933, there was no legal basis upon which discriminatory measures could be brought against these children.

Earlier, in *Mein Kampf*, Adolf Hitler had little doubt that children resulting from relationships with African occupation soldiers contaminated the Aryan race, employing the opportunity provided by their presence to denounce Jews who, he wrote, had brought Africans into the Rhineland in the first place. However, the 1933 Sterilization Law and other racial legislation introduced by the Nazi regime were equivocal regarding what should be done about these children. Laws specific to the Afro-German children were not were enacted at first, as they were born from unions that preceded the Nuremberg Laws of September 1935. While these laws were not backdated, they did, however, forbid future sexual relations between races, and mixed marriages between so-called Aryans and non-Aryans were banned.

To bring some measure of order to this situation—it was said, on Hitler's direct order—in 1937 a new government body, designated as *Sonderkommission 3* ("Special Commission 3") was established for the purpose of preventing the "Rhineland Bastards" from procreating in the future. Headed by Dr. Eugen Fischer of the Kaiser Wilhelm Institute, local officials were ordered to identify all "Rhineland Bastards" in their areas and report their whereabouts to the commission. Anyone of mixed parentage was henceforth deprived of the right to marry, and boys and girls (some as young as 11) were arrested and compulsorily sterilized under the 1933 Law for the Prevention of Hereditarily Diseased Offspring. They often underwent this procedure without anesthetic. Whether or not they were informed about what was going to happen to them beforehand is unclear. Perhaps their parents were told, but in one sense, knowing or not knowing was of no consequence; they were going to be sterilized, regardless of what they or their families knew. To offset problems, anyone in this category could also request sterilization for themselves or a minor under their care, after which they were left alone. Altogether, hundreds were sterilized by the Gestapo in what was a secret state program.

The ordeals faced by these Afro-Germans did not end with their sterilization. Germans of African parentage—and these included those who were the progeny of Germany's own colonial past—experienced discrimination in a range of areas, such as employment, welfare, housing, and education. Mixed-race children were deprived of German citizenship. The regime was aware that if it did not adopt this measure, the children would, upon attaining their majority, have the right to vote, serve in the military, or be eligible to hold public office—notions that were anathema to the regime. The children of mixed German and African backgrounds were unwelcomed in the new Germany, and despite the Aryan half of their lineage, they were as denigrated within society as Jews were.

The fate of the "Rhineland Bastards" is complex. Their experiences were not uniform, and there was no coherent Nazi policy toward them throughout the 1930s and (once they had grown to maturity) the 1940s. During the Holocaust, some were subjected to **medical experimentation**. Others simply disappeared as "Night and Fog" prisoners, and still others were welcomed back into the Aryan fold and joined the **Hitler Youth**. A fundamental question needs to be asked regarding the Nazi perspective: Was there a plan that involved extermination for the "Rhineland Bastards?" This can be answered in the negative. Nazi racial ideology always had problems reconciling the killing of part-Aryans, as shown in the convoluted policies regarding **Mischlinge** (those of mixed Jewish and Aryan background). When it came to the Afro-Germans, it might be argued that similar confusion prevailed, which possibly saved them from becoming another group slated for annihilation.

Further Reading

Campt, Tina. *Other Germans: Black Germans and the Politics of Race, Gender, and Memory in the Third Reich.* Ann Arbor: University of Michigan Press, 2003.

RUBINOWICZ, DAWID (1927–1942)

Dawid Rubinowicz was a young boy who kept a diary for two years between 1940 and 1942, chronicling the destruction of his family at the hands of the Nazis through economic dispossession, indiscriminate brutality, degradation, and constant fear.

He was born on July 27, 1927, in Kielce, Poland, to a Jewish couple, Josek and Tauba Rubinowicz. He had a younger brother, Herszel, and a little sister, Mania (Malka). His parents moved to Krajno, a small agricultural settlement 170 kilometers south of Warsaw, near Bodsentyn in central Poland.

After the German invasion of Poland, beginning in October 1939, Jews had to register and were ordered to wear a six-pointed star when in public. Initially, not wearing the star was punishable by a fine or imprisonment, but from October 15, 1941 this was punishable by death.

As a result of the anti-Jewish laws, Dawid, in fourth grade and aged 12, was banned from attending school and from receiving an education. Shortly afterward he started keeping a diary, chronicling the daily experiences of his family and the Jewish community under Nazi occupation. His last entry ends mid-sentence on June 1, 1942.

The diary comprises his notes, sorted by date, contained in five school notebooks. Entries were written at irregular intervals, stretching from March 21, 1940, until June 1, 1942. For those two years, Dawid recorded the slow destruction of his family. On March 21, 1940, the diary records that Jews were no longer allowed to travel in vehicles—they had already been banned from using trains. On June 18, 1940, the family home was searched by soldiers who asked, "where all the things were," but nothing of value was there to be found. On August 5, 1940, it is recorded that all the Jews had to register with the Jewish Council (*Judenrat*). On August 12, 1940, the diary logged that Dawid was sad that he had to study on his own and could not go to school or go out anywhere. However, he wrote: "And when I think what wars are going on in the world, and how many people are killed every day by bullets, gas, bombs, epidemics and other enemies of man, I lose interest in everything."

The entry of July 10, 1941, reflected that the family used a month's reserve of food, but "now it is difficult to buy enough food for one day," and that everyone was struggling to find enough to eat.

Things deteriorated further, so that on December 12, 1941, the entry recorded that when he had gone the day before to Bodzentyn to get his tooth filled, he learned that the militia "had met a Jew who was driving out of town, and they immediately shot him for no reason, then they drove on and shot a Jewess, again for no reason. So two victims have perished for absolutely no reason." The entry for December 26, 1941, documented that "nowadays a person can be arrested for any trifle." In Dawid's entry on January 8, 1942, he noted that there were two more victims among the Jews in Bodzentyn; one was killed outright, and the other was wounded, arrested, and taken to the local police in Bieliny, where he would probably be beaten to death.

On January 11, 1942, the diary noted that the temperature was –20 degrees centigrade and that all Jews would have to be evacuated from the villages. On February 12, 1942, the diary recorded that a village policeman was putting up a notice. On the notice, a Jew was shown mincing meat and putting a rat into the mincer. Another Jew was pouring water from a bucket into the milk. In the third image, the Jew was shown stomping dough with his feet, and worms were crawling over him and the dough. The notice read "The Jew is a Cheat, Your only enemy." Dawid's entry recorded that the people were laughing as they read the poster and that he had "a headache from the shame the Jews suffer nowadays. God grant that this shame may soon end." On March 10, 1942, the diary recorded that the Rubinowicz family was forced to move from Krajno to the ghetto in Bodzentyn.

On April 10, 1942, the diary documented the murder of people for trivial or even no apparent reason. On May 6, 1942 Dawid noted that his father was picked up in a raid and sent to Skarzysko Kamienna, a forced labor camp 20 miles north of Bodzentyn and operated by a German explosives manufacturer. The diary ended in the middle of a sentence, in the entry describing Dawid's father's return, on June 1, 1942, because his arm had been injured at work. This is the last entry.

Between September 15 and 21, 1942, all Jews in the Bodzentyn ghetto (about 5,000 people) were ejected and forced to march to the Suchedniów train station, about 25 kilometers away. On September 21 sealed wagons left, arriving at their destination—the Treblinka extermination camp—the following day. It is likely that Dawid and his entire family were gassed a few hours after their arrival.

After the war the house where the Rubinowicz family had lived passed into the possession of Bodzentyn town authorities and was occupied by homeless Polish families. In August 1957 two residents, Artemiusz Wołczyk and his wife, Helena, found the diary in the attic. They understood the historical value of the text and gave the diary publicity. Beginning in October 1957, extracts were released on a local radio station, and in 1959 a journalist met the Wołczyks in Bodzentyn and collected the notebooks. In 1960 the first Polish edition of *The Diary of Dawid Rubinowicz* was published, and in succeeding years, it was translated and published in various languages.

Further Reading

Boas, Jacob (Ed.). *We Are Witnesses: Five Diaries of Teenagers Who Died in the Holocaust.* New York: Henry Holt, 1995.

RUDASHEVSKI, YITSKHOK (1927–1943)

Yitskhok Rudashevski was a teenager who kept a diary dating from the German invasion of Vilna (Vilnius) in June 1941 until April 6, 1943. As the Nazis forbade writing, let alone keeping diaries, making any sort of record was an act of resistance. The diary details life under occupation and the struggle of Jews crammed into the Vilna ghetto.

Yitskhok was born on December 10, 1927, the only child of Elihu and Rosa Rudashevski. He lived with his parents and maternal grandmother in Vilna, a city rich in Jewish cultural and intellectual life. His father was a typesetter for a Yiddish newspaper, and his mother was a seamstress.

In June 1940, under the Molotov-Ribbentrop Pact of August 23, 1939, Lithuania was placed under Soviet influence. The Jews of Vilna were reassured when they contrasted this with the Nazi oppression of Poland and its Jews. Yitskhok saw this period as one of joy and freedom. He became a Young Pioneer, leading a team of 10 students, and wore a red star on his jacket.

On June 22, 1941, Germany attacked the Soviet Union in Operation BARBAROSSA, breaking the Molotov-Ribbentrop agreement. Yitskhok hid all links with the Soviet Union; he saw the collaboration of Lithuanians with Germany against the Soviet government as a betrayal.

He was, however, confident in the ultimate victory of the Red Army. He diarized Lithuanian participation in the Nazi genocide, recording that by the end of June 1941, Lithuanian officers were knocking on people's doors to search and arrest Jews; providing soldiers who herded Jews into the Vilna ghetto in September 1941; recruiting the stormtroopers of Special Squad 11 who, in the ghetto, would arrest, rob, and herd thousands of people to the Ponary Forest for mass killings; searching for hideouts and accepting ransoms for a person's life; and serving as guards at the ghetto gates. Yitskhok's diary equated Lithuanians to Nazi collaborators—except in March 1943, when he recorded Lithuanian resistance against mobilization into the SS and the arrest of members of the local intelligentsia.

By September 6, 1941, the Rudashevski family and all Vilna's Jews had been forced into the ghetto, which Yitskhok described as being imprisoned in a box. Noting his fear and loneliness and the humiliation and mockery he experienced, he described that he and other children took over running their households, cooking, cleaning, and watching over younger siblings.

In spring 1942, Yitskhok enrolled at the reestablished Jewish gymnasium in the ghetto; this taught the prewar curriculum, though in atrocious circumstances. He wrote that the school gave his life meaning, providing an opportunity for self-expression and a sense of purpose. Involved in clubs for literature, poetry, and history, he thus documented ghetto life. He interviewed ghetto inhabitants, recorded their testimonies, and collected ghetto folklore—sayings, curses, blessings, songs, jokes, and stories. They were a treasure for the future.

His teachers were authority figures. Mira Bernshtein taught Yiddish and Hebrew and later became a legend of cultural resistance in the ghetto. Yakov Gershtein was a music teacher and head of the children's choir. Yitskhok identified with Gershtein's engaging personality and his instilling in children such values as national dignity, love for their mother tongue, music, and poetry. Gershtein died of hunger on October 27, 1942, and at a special evening to pay him tribute, Yitskhok stood on the stage of the Vilna Ghetto Theatre and read a eulogy to his dead teacher.

In addition, Yitskhok's diary detailed the history of cultural life in the ghetto and underlined the sense of civilization in the face of Nazi attempts to dehumanize and degrade them.

Yitskhok's last diary entry on April 6, 1943, recorded that Jews from Vilna were being taken to Ponary to be executed. When the liquidation of the ghetto began on September 23, 1943, Yitskhok, his family, and his uncle's family went into hiding. Approximately two weeks later, their hiding place was discovered by the Gestapo, and during the High Holidays of 1943, they were all taken to Ponary and murdered in mass graves. Yitskhok Rudashevski was murdered on October 1, 1943.

Only Sarah Voloshin, his 14-year-old cousin, escaped the ghetto and fled to the forests surrounding Vilna. She joined a Jewish partisan group, fought the Germans, and stayed with the partisans until the Soviet Army reoccupied Vilna on July 13, 1944. She returned to the family's hideout in Dysnos Street in the former ghetto, and in the attic, she found a small notebook written in Yiddish, its 200 pages filled with handwriting—some in pen, and some in pencil. It was Yitskhok Rudashevski's diary.

In July 1944 poets Avrom Sutzkever and Shmerke Kacherginski, both ghetto survivors, established a Jewish museum in Vilna. Yitskhok's notebook, handed over by Sarah Voloshin, was considered a valuable relic, which in 1946 was taken from Lithuania to Israel. In 1953 Sutzkever published the first edition of the diary in his journal of Yiddish literature *Di Goldene Keyt* (*The Golden Chain*). It was then published again in 1973 by the Ghetto Fighters' House in Israel. By 2017 excerpts from the diary were included in a school textbook of Lithuanian literature as a source for Holocaust education. A bilingual Yiddish-Lithuanian edition of Yitskhok Rudashevski's diary was published in Vilnius at the beginning of 2018.

Today, the original diary is kept at the YIVO Institute for Jewish Research in New York.

Further Reading

Boas, Jacob (Ed.). *We Are Witnesses: Five Diaries of Teenagers Who Died in the Holocaust.* New York: Henry Holt, 1995.

Rudashevski, Yitskhok. *The Diary of the Vilna Ghetto, June 1941–April 1943.* Kibbutz Lohamei HaGeta'ot, Israel: Ghetto Fighters' House, 1973.

Zapruder, Alexandra. *Salvaged Pages: Young Writers' Diaries of the Holocaust.* New Haven, CT: Yale University Press, 2015.

SALOMON, ANDRÉE (1908–1985)

Andrée Salomon (*née* Sulzer) was a Jewish resister in France who was head of the social service of the OSE in the Vichy Zone during World War II. Responsible for OSE social welfare programs, she organized various ways of saving children from Vichy internment camps. These children were usually placed in OSE homes and kept in hiding with false identities; when they were no longer able to evade deportation, arrangements were made for them to be smuggled out to more secure locations or across the border into Spain and Switzerland.

Andrée Sulzer was born in 1908 in Grussenheim, a small French town in Alsace right on the border with Germany. A legal secretary in Strasbourg and a Zionist by conviction, in 1931 she married a young scientist, Tobie Salomon. She began her rescue activities in a piecemeal fashion as early as 1937, but after Germany's *Kristallnacht* pogrom in November 1938, she started receiving children evacuated from the Third Reich. In 1939–1940 she began taking care of children in OSE homes, and in 1941 she was OSE delegate to the Gurs and Rivesaltes internment camps. Here, she prepared emigration papers for Jewish children leaving for the United States, simultaneously organizing assistance for interned families.

During this time, she was given responsibility for children's welfare in Clermont-Ferrand, where she was appointed Deputy Commissioner to the EIF by its leader, Robert Gamzon. The EIF was a prewar **Jewish youth movement** that evolved during the war into a rescue and resistance organization, with such activity especially pronounced through the activities of one of its groups, *La Sixième* (the "Sixth"). Though the EIF was neither religious nor Zionist by its nature, its idea of sending young Jews to the countryside was like the pioneering ideals of the Zionist movement who sought to prepare Jewish youth for life in Palestine.

Beginning in the summer of 1942, another Jewish resistance operative, Georges Garel (*né* Grigori Garfinkel), organized a secret network of escape routes to transport children to safe places when these were needed. The **Garel Network** came to cover four major regions in Vichy and was fully operational by the summer of 1943. Garel ("Gasquet") was born in Kiev and left Russia after the Revolution, settling first in Berlin before moving to Paris in 1926. In 1942 he began working with a Catholic priest, Father **Alexandre Glasberg**, and Charles Lederman (Garel's brother-in-law) to help Jews imprisoned in a camp at Vénissieux. From this base, he set up a child rescue network in Lyon, from where he coordinated everything and saw to it that sympathetic French families, as well as convents and boarding schools, were organized as places of refuge for the OSE children.

As Garel was organizing his network Andrée Salomon joined him, and in April 1943, following negotiations with Swiss authorities, the **smuggling** of unaccompanied OSE children into Switzerland began. After September 1943 the job became more difficult; organizing the smuggling parties to Switzerland was now entrusted to another rescuer, **Georges Loinger**. After a series of arrests between November 1943 and March 1944, the smuggling of children slowed down significantly as roundups were taking place all over Vichy France and the danger of capture for the *passeurs* intensified tremendously. In desperation, particularly after German forces defeated resistance fighters in March 1944 in a set-piece battle on the plateau of Glières in the *département* of Haute-Savoie, close to the Swiss border, activities resumed at an accelerated rate, carried out jointly by the OSE and other Jewish rescue organizations. Andrée Salomon, throughout this time, was a key player. In 1944 she also began organizing the clandestine movement of Jewish children into Spain.

In 1948 Andrée and Tobie Salomon welcomed their only child, a son named Jean. In 1952 Andrée became assistant general secretary of the French section of the Women's International Zionist Organization, or WIZO; maintaining her involvement in Jewish communal affairs, in 1957 she took up the position of general secretary of the French office of Israel Bonds. When she retired in 1970, she moved to Israel with her husband and son. Although nominated for various decorations, awards, and distinctions, she was consistent in her refusal to accept any that were offered.

Andrée Salomon's organization, the OSE, is remembered today as a key resistance organization. Her work, together with that of many others, hid children in non-Jewish institutions and was responsible for a secret network that saved the lives of more than 1,500 children and adults.

She died in Jerusalem on August 12, 1985.

Further Reading

Bartrop, Paul R., and Samantha J. Lakin. *Heroines of Vichy France: Rescuing French Jews during the Holocaust*. Santa Barbara, CA: Praeger, 2019.

Hazan, Katy, and Georges Weill. *Andrée Salomon, une femme du lumière*. Paris: Le Manuscrit, 2011.

SAUVAGE, PIERRE (b.1944)

Pierre Sauvage is a French-American documentary filmmaker and lecturer who was a child survivor of the Holocaust.

The son of French journalist and author Léo Sauvage (*né* Smotriez) and his Polish-born wife Barbara Sauvage, *née* Suchowolska, Sauvage was born on March 25, 1944 near **Le Chambon-sur-Lignon**, France. He and both parents survived the Holocaust, and in 1948 the family moved to New York, where his father became a correspondent for the French newspaper *Le Figaro*. In 1962 Sauvage returned to Paris to study at the Sorbonne but did not proceed with his studies; instead, he became enamored with cinema and began working for the film archivist Henri Langlois. When he returned to New York later, he became a story editor and writer, coauthoring a two-volume study, *American Directors* (1983), with Jean-Pierre Coursodon.

After several early projects in which he learned his craft as a producer and director, Sauvage devoted himself to producing a feature documentary that would tell the story of what happened at Le Chambon—which he described as "a conspiracy of goodness" that sought to save lives—and which saw the salvation of both him and his parents. When *Weapons of the Spirit* was released in 1989, he may not have realized that it would be the start of a lifelong commitment to seeing that the community of Le Chambon would be forever remembered.

Sauvage explored the goodwill of the people of Le Chambon using archival footage and interviews with surviving villagers, as the documentary was introduced by reference to his own experience. It was also the crowning achievement of one for whom this was also a voyage of personal exploration, as Sauvage did not know anything of his Jewish background before the age of 18, and journeying to Le Chambon helped him to locate his personal history while telling the story to a wider audience. *Weapons of the Spirit* won numerous awards and became a widely used teaching tool for Holocaust educators.

In 1982, well before *Weapons of the Spirit* appeared (though Sauvage had been giving it deep thought and preparation), Sauvage established Friends of Le Chambon, soon to be renamed the Chambon Foundation, the first nonprofit educational foundation dedicated to an exploration of the lessons of hope to be found amid the murderous dark that was the Holocaust. Since that time, the Chambon Foundation has been committed to ensuring that the memory of the righteous shall be everlasting. Then, in 2005, the Varian Fry Institute was created as a division of the Chambon Foundation, with a specific focus on the United States and the Holocaust and the goodness that was embodied in Varian Fry, who directed the most successful private American rescue effort of World War II.

In June 2004, as part of the 60th anniversary commemorations of D-Day, the Chambon Foundation, in partnership with the village of Le Chambon, organized a well-attended "Liberation Reunion," the first gathering of former refugees in the area of Le Chambon since 1986—an event that the Chambon Foundation had also played a key role in organizing. It included a conference featuring major participants from those times and leading historians of the war years in France. This, in turn, led to a visit to Le Chambon from French President Jacques Chirac, who had earlier been invited to provide a taped message to the Liberation Reunion. Instead, he addressed the community (and the world) in person on July 8, 2004. He used the opportunity to condemn racism and antisemitism, extolling the virtues of Le Chambon as the place where "the soul of the [French] nation manifested itself" and showed itself to be "the embodiment of our country's conscience."

One of Pierre Sauvage's additional ambitions was to create a historical museum in Le Chambon. The attention his film, lecturing, and other activities had generated assisted greatly in this process, galvanizing many in the community. Between 2010 and 2013, work was undertaken to create this memorial to the "conspiracy of goodness" until finally, in 2013, a museum and learning center, *Lieu de Mémoire au Chambon-sur-Lignon*, directed with enthusiasm by Le Chambon mayor Éliane Wauquiez-Motte, was inaugurated. Pierre Sauvage was invited to present the French version of *Weapons of the Spirit* as part of the inauguration.

The majority of Sauvage's documentary films have proceeded from the theme of good or righteous people during the Holocaust and how options could be found to save imperiled lives. Since the early 1980s, this child survivor and beneficiary of the goodness of a community that sought to protect Jewish children has been a pioneer in promoting the theme of rescuers of Jews. His is another dimension to the story of children of the Holocaust, showing that even after that horrible experience, survivors remember the goodness of those who rescued them and that their actions still have much that is of benefit to broader humanity.

Further Reading

Sauvage, Pierre (producer/director/writer). *Weapons of the Spirit*. Chambon Foundation, 1989.

SCHINK, BARTHEL (1927–1944)

Bartholomäus (Barthel) Schink was a member of the **Edelweiss Pirates** in Cologne during World War II. Born on November 27, 1927, he was active in the Ehrenfelder Navajo Group, and at the age of 16, he and 12 other members of that group were hanged in public by the Gestapo on November 10, 1944.

As a child, Barthel had witnessed the maltreatment of a Jewish barber at the hands of the SA and from this experience saw the injustice of Nazi persecution against Jews. During World War II, Barthel, together with his fellow Pirates Michael Jovy and Jean Jülich (who were also opposed to Nazi racial and antisemitic doctrines), admitted two Jewish youngsters—the Schwarz brothers—into their group. Shielding them thus, they permitted the brothers to escape deportation to Auschwitz. Later, they sheltered Friedel Krämer, a Jewish woman and her daughter Ruth, and a **Mischling** (mixed background), Paul Urbat, in a cellar.

Helping Jews became something of a specialty for Barthel and Jülich, and their opposition to the Nazi regime extended to obtaining and stockpiling ammunition and foodstuffs. Of course, they risked their lives by hiding Jews, but both their opposition to the regime and their commitment to the preservation of life motivated them to continue their activities.

Jovy had previously been arrested by the Gestapo in November 1939. In 1941 he was convicted by the *Volksgerichtshof* (People's Court) in Berlin on the charge of "preparation of high treason." He was sent to Siegburg, the large prison covering Cologne; it was there that he was put in contact with the Edelweiss Pirates through the 15-year-old son of a communist prisoner. The same year, all Jewish prisoners at Siegburg were deported to concentration camps, from which only a very few returned. In 1944 Jovy escaped and made his way to where the Cologne Pirates were based.

Jovy was met by another Pirate, Jean Jülich, aged 15. On October 10, 1944, Jülich was arrested by the Gestapo, who, on the orders of *Reichsführer-SS* Heinrich Himmler, was determined to break up the Edelweiss Pirates. Jülich was held in solitary confinement without trial, tortured for four months, and transferred to Rockenbach prison as the Allied troops closed in during February 1945. Here he survived beatings, starvation, and typhus until the camp was liberated by American troops in March 1945. He lived in Cologne for the rest of his life. Jovy, for his part, managed to escape by joining a reconnaissance work group and then crossing over to the Allied lines.

In the same roundup on October 10, 1944, Barthel Schink was also arrested. The only reason for his arrest was his membership with the Pirates. He was accused of planning to blow up the local Gestapo headquarters, which might have been true; it was said that he and Jülich had discussed just such an assault along with Hans Steinbruck, another member of the Cologne Edelweiss Pirates. Yet Barthel was at no time responsible for killing anyone, despite being slated for five murders. On the morning of November 10, 1944 Barthel Schink, aged 16, was executed as a criminal, without trial, on the public gallows at Ehrenfeld railway station, along with seven adults and five other Pirates. He was the youngest of those hanged; the executions took place on Himmler's direct orders.

On November 18, 1982, in recognition of their efforts in saving the lives of Jews, Yad Vashem recognized Michael Jovy, Jean Jülich, and Bartholomäus Schink as Righteous among the Nations.

SCHONFELD, SOLOMON (1912–1984)

Solomon Schonfeld was a British rabbi who rescued thousands of Jews (in particular, children) from Nazism before, during, and after the Holocaust.

Born on February 21, 1912, he was the son of Rabbi Dr. Victor Schonfeld. He studied at a yeshiva in Nitra, Czechoslovakia, where he was the student of Rabbi Chaim Michael Dov Weissmandl, who would later play his own part in the rescue of Jews in Slovakia. In 1940 Schonfeld married Judith Hertz, daughter of the Chief Rabbi of the United Kingdom, Dr. Joseph Hertz.

When Schonfeld was just 22 years of age, he became rabbi of the Adath Yisroel synagogue in North London, succeeding his father and at the same time becoming principal of the Jewish Secondary School, the first Jewish day school in Britain.

In the aftermath of the *Kristallnacht* pogrom of November 9–10, 1938, Julius Steinfeld, the head of Vienna's Agudath Israel community, contacted Schonfeld with the desperate plea that arrangements be made for a transport of children—a **Kindertransport**—for as many Orthodox Jewish children as possible from Austria and Germany to Britain. Schonfeld met with Yacob Rosenheim and Harry Goodman, respectively the founder and secretary of World Agudath Israel, to discuss what could be done. Traveling to Vienna, Schonfeld helped Steinfeld organize a transport for close to 300 children.

Prior to the transport's departure, Schonfeld arranged for 1,200 German rabbis and other Jewish religious leaders, together with their families, to be brought to the United Kingdom. In this endeavor, he had the advantage of his appointment as executive director of a new organization, the Chief Rabbi's Religious Emergency Council, which had been established by his father-in-law, Chief Rabbi Hertz, in 1938.

In the years that followed, Schonfeld developed excellent relationships with certain British officials who offered him their support despite the more negative mood prevailing in Whitehall at this time.

In the summer of 1942, Schonfeld negotiated with the Colonial Office for more than a thousand visas to be issued for Jews to enter the island of Mauritius. None arrived, but it was an indication of just how far he was prepared to go to secure some sort of protection to try to save Jews. As it turned out, many of those with such papers managed to enter Palestine instead, having already been granted access to a British territory.

Schonfeld was also highly creative. In December 1942 he organized broad support within Parliament for a motion asking the government to declare that Britain would be prepared to find a temporary refuge within the British Empire for Jews desperate to leave Nazi-occupied Europe. The declaration also extended to an invitation to other Allied governments to consider similar action. It received broad support and was endorsed by senior Christian clergy and leading members of the House of Lords. It ultimately gained the backing of 177 members of Parliament, and, although it failed in an overall vote, it was a strong indication of the kind of initiative Schonfeld was able to make and of how far the reach of his efforts extended.

All in all, Rabbi Schonfeld arranged for over 4,000 Jewish children to be brought to Britain. As an Orthodox rabbi, he sought to keep Orthodox children together in religious homes, and wherever possible he did so, at the same time providing them with a Jewish religious education. To help achieve this, he established an organization called the National Council for Religious Education, and then, in 1944, he founded a new school, the Hasmonean High School, to help further his religious day school aims. Among those he also sought to help were youths aged 16 to 18 who were ineligible for the *Kindertransports*. He brought them to Britain on the pretext that they were going to be studying in Jewish religious seminaries.

Schonfeld was a rabbi who lived his vocation and his faith. In 1940, after the refugees arrived in the United Kingdom and many were interned as "enemy aliens," he made a number of official visits to internment camps; he organized religious events for the Jewish festivals; and he worked to ensure that an uninterrupted supply of kosher food was available for those who were observant. Then, in 1943, he amassed a treasure-trove of tinned kosher food in preparation for postwar distribution to the expected influx of survivors from Nazi Europe—despite the fact that the Holocaust was still raging, and there was no certainty that there would actually be any survivors left to feed.

After the war, Schonfeld rescued hundreds more of those who had been **hidden children** during the conflict. By now, many of them were arriving from the communist-dominated countries of Eastern Europe. He also went into the displaced persons' camps, searching for survivors, and brought many out.

Rabbi Schonfeld was something of a maverick both as a rabbi and a rescuer. He worked independently of any political or religious group and preferred to operate as a one-man committee. His successes can be measured in their thousands—a most remarkable case of what could be done to rescue Jews during the Holocaust when political considerations did not cloud the will and necessity to save lives.

Rabbi Solomon Schonfeld died of a long-term brain tumor at the age of 72 on February 6, 1984. In 2013 he was recognized as a British Hero of the Holocaust.

Further Reading

Bartrop, Paul R. *Resisting the Holocaust: Upstanders, Partisans, and Survivors*. Santa Barbara, CA: ABC-CLIO, 2016.

SCREAMING SILENCE

Screaming Silence is a 2015 documentary produced by Israeli filmmaker Ronnie Sarnat. It deals with the topic of sexual violence against Jewish children during the Holocaust, considered to be one of the last taboo subjects not yet fully explored by scholars. It was broadcast on Israel's Channel 1 on the eve of Yom Hashoah (Holocaust Remembrance Day) in 2015.

Building on work undertaken by American scholars Rochelle G. Seidel and Sonja M. Hedgepeth and their colleagues at the Remember the Women Institute—which brought the story of sexual violence against Jewish women to a broad audience—Sarnat first encountered sexual violence against Jewish children while working on a documentary for Yom Hashoah, in which a man revealed that he had been raped by a German soldier when he was 13 years old. Once she knew of this story, Sarnat began a much broader search for others, but she encountered roadblocks along the way. No one, to this point, had been talking about child sexual abuse.

Searching for data in the form of people willing to speak on the record was the most difficult part of her search. First, it took her an inordinate amount of time in her six-year journey to locate survivors who had been victims of rape or sexual abuse as children or teenagers. After she broached the subject of her project to them, they then had to decide whether to reveal publicly what had happened to them. At first, she tried to study the topic through official or archival sources, but she found herself rebuffed constantly by institutional custodians who acted as gatekeepers of the research process. As Sarnat was to say later, "They argued that mentioning sex and Holocaust in the same sentence stains the memory of the Holocaust," which presented her with a dilemma: Should she seek to protect the sensitivities of the "politically correct" view, or expose the historic truth of what actually happened? Perhaps, she reasoned, taking the former position might even be a form of Holocaust denial. She decided to proceed, and the eventual result was *Screaming Silence*.

For the first time, survivors who had been raped or sexually abused as children or teenagers in ghettos and camps spoke publicly about what happened and how the experience had scarred them for the rest of their lives. In most cases, they had kept their ordeal a secret from even their closest family members. The film was essentially a collection of interviews; the film used no archival footage. Sarnat intruded little once the interviews got underway, preferring to allow the interviewees to relate their stories unprompted. Those interviewed—men and women—described having been sexually abused, raped, gang raped, or witnesses to forced prostitution, practices that Nazi ideology was supposed to have outlawed on the basis of *Rassenschande* ("race-shame," banned under the Nuremberg Laws on the ground that it was a form of racial mixing); and this, of course, is to say nothing of the illegality of the acts due to the ages of those involved. The testimonies in the documentary reveal an entirely different reality.

Of course, given the nature of the topic, it is impossible to ascertain how extensive the phenomenon of sexual violence against Jewish children was during the Holocaust. The young victims, for the most part, never spoke after the war about what had happened to them.

All of that aside, Sarnat's view (shared by others) is that research of this kind, cutting-edge though it is, must be done independently. Established Holocaust research institutions, she has argued, are reluctant to delve into the murky waters of sexual violence, whether against children or adults. Consequently—and determined to deal with this extremely difficult subject that others have refused to discuss—Sarnat found herself in largely unchartered territory. Noting, for example, that Israeli and German researchers assert that Jewish girls were not used as prostitutes and sex slaves, during her research she interviewed one who was a youth at the time who had firsthand encounters with such situations. She assembled testimonies affirming that Jewish girls worked in camp brothels, as did young boys (**piepels**), "often with a feminine look," who worked as sex slaves under the masquerade of "servants."

In this regard, Sarnat's work complemented—and, to a large degree, confirmed—that of a former prisoner-turned-writer, Yehiel De-Nur, known by his pen-name Ka-Tzetnik 135633, particularly his *House of Dolls* (1955), in which he described the "Joy Division" in which Nazis kept Jewish women as sex slaves in concentration camps. Another of De-Nur's books, *Piepel* (1961), dealt directly with Nazi sexual abuse of young boys. Some Israelis opposed the teaching of De-Nur's books in schools, on occasion describing them as kitsch bordering on pornography, something Sarnat would have understood as further reinforcement of the preference not to know about these horrible things that took place during the Holocaust.

Sarnat's documentary is difficult to watch. Listening to the survivors' descriptions, some viewers undoubtedly find the revelations hard to deal with. Yet Sarnat's conclusion is that if the details of the rapes were left out of the story, it would have done injustice to those being interviewed. Further, it is important to realize that as with many other cases of child sexual violence, the victims had lives that were most often permanently damaged as a result of the assaults committed against them. As Sarnat was to conclude later, one finishes watching the documentary with one abiding question: "How come this topic hasn't been addressed before?"

Further Reading

Ghert-Zand, Renee. "Holocaust film reveals long-hushed child sex abuse." *Times of Israel*, April 15, 2015; at https://www.timesofisrael.com/documentary-reveals-secrets-of-sexual-abuse-of-children-in-the-holocaust/.

Hedgepeth, Sonja M., and Rochelle G. Saidel (Eds.). *Sexual Violence against Jewish Women during the Holocaust*. Lebanon, NH: Brandeis University Press/University Press of New England, 2010.

SECOND GENERATION

As the mortality of the Holocaust generation approaches, the children of survivors, known collectively as the Second Generation, play an increasingly crucial role in keeping alive the memory of the Holocaust experience. With many feeling as though they were obligated to preserve their parents' memories, the responsibility is often quite crushing—perhaps more so because of what has come to be known in psychoanalytic literature as "transmitted trauma," anguish that is transferred from the survivors to their children (and, now, adult grandchildren) as a result of complex post-traumatic stress disorder (PTSD) processes. Most members of the Second Generation have been affected by their parents' experiences in one way or another, and to varying degrees.

Many of the Second Generation view the Holocaust differently from their parents, often possessing a far more complex understanding of it, owing to a broader range of influences and approaches that have contributed to their knowledge of what happened during the war years. They are forced to assess the Holocaust in this different way while at the same time accepting that they must remain respectful of what they have been told while growing up, and not question the veracity of their parents' accounts of what happened.

There can be no doubt that many in the Second Generation carry conveyed emotional scars, frequently the result of their parents' untreated PTSD. Many Holocaust survivors suffered from lifelong emotional and mental afflictions. As children, some in the Second Generation were embarrassed at their parents' passivity or victimization during the Holocaust; some also felt unease as their parents displayed socially dysfunctional behavior out of alignment with the norms of wider society. For still others, the question was not why their parents' experiences led them to be classed as socially aberrant but rather, in view of all they had lived through, why they were so "normal." These issues significantly affected some in the Second Generation, but they also affected their relationships with their parents. Further, some in the Second Generation are prone to emotional disturbances of their own bordering on a form of Holocaust-related PTSD, even though they did not experience the Holocaust themselves.

In recent times, consideration has been given also to the grandchildren of Holocaust survivors, the last generation of Jews who will have had any sort of direct link to the period of the Third Reich.

While their experiences are, for the most part, less traumatic and more nuanced than those of their parents in the Second Generation, they are frequently just as committed to preserving Holocaust memory and communicating it to their own children and to the wider community with whom they interact. Often seeing themselves as the custodians of an important legacy, they are taking the first-person experiences of the Holocaust generation into the future, so that after their grandparents have gone, there will still be those who can say—deep into the 21st century—that they had personal experience with those who lived through the Holocaust.

As a way to bring some sense of order and support to the often bewildering stresses and strains experienced by those who can now be termed the "Generations of the Shoah," an organization was formed in October 2002 in the United States as a result of the merger of a number of localized second- and third-generation groups. Generations of the Shoah International (GSI) now acts as a worldwide network of children and grandchildren of Holocaust survivors, linked together with the common goals of preserving and honoring their legacy, sharing resources and programming ideas, providing emotional support to members, and tackling issues of mutual interest.

Further Reading

Hass, Aaron. *In the Shadow of the Holocaust: The Second Generation.* Cambridge: Cambridge University Press, 1996.

SENDLER, IRENA (1910–2008)

Irena Sendler was a Polish social worker who, as head of children's section of the underground resistance movement **Żegota**, was instrumental in saving thousands of Jewish children from the Nazis.

Born Irena Krzyżanowska on February 15, 1910, in Otwock, a short distance from Warsaw, her father was Dr. Stanisław Krzyżanowski, a physician and one of the earliest members of the Polish Socialist Party (*Polska Partia Socjalistyczna*, or PPS). He had a profound influence on the formation of many of Irena's ideas regarding social justice. When her father died in 1917, Jewish community leaders, out of gratitude for his efforts to reduce medical costs among poor Jews, offered to help pay for her education. She attended the University of Warsaw, studying Polish literature, and married Mieczysław Sendler. Although their marriage ended in divorce in 1947, she kept her married name for the rest of her life.

When Germany invaded Poland in September 1939, the 29-year-old Irena Sendler was a senior administrator in Warsaw's Social Welfare Department, providing meals, financial aid, and other services for orphans, the elderly, the poor, and the destitute throughout the city. With the onset of war, given the introduction of Nazi antisemitic measures, she also began aiding Jews. Through her office she arranged for the provision of clothing, medicine, and financial aid. Jews receiving assistance were registered under fictitious Christian names, with more than 3,000 false documents being forged to help Jewish families in need. Once the ghetto into which the Jews had been forced was sealed in November 1940, however, the options for continuing this kind of aid were rendered effectively impossible.

Despite this, Irena was determined to continue providing aid to the Jews of the now-isolated ghetto. Therefore, when Żegota, the Council to Aid Jews, was established in October 1942, she was among its most enthusiastic supporters. Żegota existed under the auspices of the Polish government-in-exile and operated through the Polish resistance, with the express purpose of aiding the country's Jews and finding places of safety for them within occupied Poland.

Irena saw her specific role as one of rescuing Jewish children. To do so, she needed to be able to enter the heavily guarded ghetto on some sort of official business, and in pursuit of this, she secured a pass from Warsaw's Epidemic Control Department. With this in hand, she was able to visit the ghetto daily, enabling her to reestablish earlier contacts and thereby arrange the rescues that were so urgently needed. Żegota played a vital role in this enterprise. Two dozen other Żegota members helped get Jewish children out as well as assisting Jews remaining in the ghetto—in hiding, seeking hiding places, and paying for their upkeep and medical care.

In August 1943, Irena—known by her *nom de guerre*, "Jolanta"—was appointed to head Żegota's Department for the Care of Jewish Children. This enabled her to formalize her rescue activities, and with the help of each of the 10 centers of the Social Welfare Department, from where she recruited people to assist her, she issued hundreds of false documents with forged signatures—at least 400 on her own responsibility.

Irena cooperated with others in Warsaw's Municipal Social Services Department and the RGO (Central Welfare Council), a Polish relief organization tolerated under German supervision. Her team then organized a smuggling operation, sneaking out babies and small children in ambulances and trams. Sometimes they were taken out in sacks or disguised as packages; others were hidden deep inside freight consignments. All and any means were taken to try to get the children out of the ghetto and to safety.

Children were then hidden with kindly Polish families, but finding homes willing to provide refuge was never easy. It was no small thing to ask parents to risk the lives of their own children if the Nazis were to find out what they were doing. Often, Irena relied on the good graces of the church to assist. Various Catholic convents were successfully prevailed upon to open their doors, and the Sisters of the Family of Mary orphanage enabled Jewish children to pass through with changed identities. Irena retained the real names of the children through adopting a private code. She kept the only record of their identities in a set of jars buried, ironically, not far from a German military barracks. These jars, which were located later, contained the names of 2,500 children. The exact number of children saved is unknown.

Not all were rescued by Irena alone, but her group, comprising about 30 volunteers, managed collectively to achieve these remarkable rescues. So far as it was humanly possible, Żegota did its best to ensure that the children would be returned to their Jewish families when the war was over, but unfortunately, all too often, there were no family members left alive by 1945.

On October 20, 1943, Irena Sendler's run ended abruptly when she was arrested. The Gestapo sought full disclosure of all Żegota operations regarding the **hidden children**, particularly their secret identities and their locations. Interrogation and imprisonment led to torture. She had her legs broken and her feet crushed but refused to divulge anything that would give away the children or her coconspirators. Sent to the notorious Pawiak prison, she was sentenced to death. Only at the last minute was her life spared, when Żegota activists managed to bribe one of the Gestapo officers. She escaped from prison, spent the rest of the war in hiding, and continued her work for Jewish children while continuing to head the children's section of Żegota. At the end of the war, she and her surviving helpers gathered as many of their records as could be located and passed them on to the General Secretary of Żegota, Adolf Berman, at the Central Committee of Polish Jews.

On October 19, 1965, Israel's Yad Vashem recognized Irena Sendler as one of the Righteous among the Nations for her efforts on behalf of Jewish children, and in 1991 she was made an honorary citizen of Israel. She was awarded Poland's Order of the White Eagle on November 10, 2003, and in 2008 she appeared on a Polish commemorative silver coin. In 2003 she was also declared the recipient of the Jan Karski Award for Valor and Courage, and in 2007 she was nominated for the Nobel Peace Prize. She died in Warsaw on May 12, 2008, aged 98.

Further Reading

Paldiel, Mordecai. *The Path of the Righteous: Gentile Rescuers of Jews during the Holocaust.* Hoboken, NJ: KTAV, 1993.

Tomaszewski, Irene, and Tecia Werbowski. *Code Name: Żegota: Rescuing Jews in Occupied Poland, 1942–1945: The Most Dangerous Conspiracy in Wartime Europe.* Santa Barbara, CA: Praeger, 2010.

Zimmerman, Joshua D. *The Polish Underground and the Jews, 1939–1945.* Cambridge: Cambridge University Press, 2015.

SIERAKOWIAK, DAWID (1924–1943)

Dawid Sierakowiak was born in Łódź, Poland, in July 1924, to Majlech and Sura Sierakowiak. He and his younger sister, Nadzia, lived a happy family life with their parents. A bright boy, Dawid earned a scholarship to study at a private Jewish high school in Łódź.

On June 28, 1939, just before his 15th birthday, he began keeping a diary. In this he displayed excellent skills of observation, noting not only the events around him but also recording his own feelings, moods, and opinions. From the time the gates closed on the ghetto in Łódź on April 39, 1940, Dawid wrote about his hopes and doubts; he also described, with the keen eye of an intellectual, perceptive, and idealistic young man, the many tragedies swirling around him in the ghetto.

Although only a teenager, Dawid was drawn to Marxism, like many other young Jews of the same generation with a left-wing outlook who had been drawn to **Jewish youth movements**. His views led him to oppose the many class divisions existing within the ghetto hierarchy, divisions that affected all those living in the direst circumstances—especially through the onset of murderous hunger that destroyed people's will to go on, tore relationships apart, and eventually killed in large numbers. Dawid also chronicled the importance of work for one's survival, noting on one occasion his concern for children and those unable to work at a time when the Germans had begun deporting those deemed unfit to be of any use.

Although sometimes compared to the *Diary of a Young Girl*, written by another teenager, **Anne Frank**, Dawid's diary is of a different nature. Anne, hidden in her Amsterdam attic, was remote from the horrors of the Holocaust and the brutality of daily life suffered by Jews facing the Nazis directly. Dawid's diary, on the other hand, describes the day-to-day barbarism of the Łódź ghetto, from which one can only recoil in disgust when reflecting that this took place in the heart of Europe during the 20th century.

The diary is preserved in five notebooks. It is presumed that two other notebooks existed but have been lost—possibly by people who took over the apartment where he and his family had been living and the notebooks were burned and used for heating. There are also gaps in the existing notebooks, where pages have been torn out. Still, what remains, covering a period of nearly four years, makes the diary one of the longest and most sustained individual accounts of daily life in a ghetto during the Holocaust. The diary may truly be considered a day-to-day record of life in the ghetto.

Dawid began his diary at the age of 14, in June 1939. His final entry ended abruptly on April 15, 1943. In this final entry he mentions the prospect of getting a job in the ghetto bakery, where he would be warm and able to eat. After this entry, however, there is nothing. Although he had another four months to live, we know nothing of how he spent that time—though it can be speculated that he was worn down by hunger, despair, and sickness. The diary is a testament not only to Dawid's life but also to the story of the Łódź Jewish community under the Nazis.

The slow destruction of Dawid's family took place along similar lines to thousands of others within the awful conditions of the ghetto. His mother was deported and murdered in September 1942; his father died of illness in March 1943. Although the fate of his sister Nadzia is unrecorded, it is believed she was deported to Auschwitz and murdered there. Dawid himself succumbed in August 1943, four months after he wrote his last entry. He perished in the Łódź ghetto on August 9, 1943, probably from tuberculosis complicated by starvation and exhaustion.

After the war, the diary was discovered by Wacław Szkudlarek, a non-Jewish Pole who had lived before 1939 on the site of what became the ghetto. Returning to his home after the **liberation** of Łódź by Soviet troops in 1945, he found the notebooks lying among some trash and duly informed officials of his find.

Holocaust scholar Lucjan Dobroszycki, himself a survivor of the Łódź ghetto, edited the first two notebooks and published them in Poland in 1960. In 1967 a leading Łódź journalist, Konrad Turowski, purchased the three surviving notebooks and was preparing them for publication, but Poland's communist regime held up further progress. Several years passed before a full version of all five surviving notebooks was finally published and made available to the public. In 1996 Alan Adelson, an American director and writer, arranged for a comprehensive version of the full work to be published in English.

Further Reading

Adelson, Alan (Ed.). *The Diary of Dawid Sierakowiak: Five Notebooks from the Łódź Ghetto.* New York: Oxford University Press, 1996.

SLETTEN-FOSSTVEDT, INGEBJØRG (1908–1991)

Ingebjørg (Inge) Sletten was a Norwegian journalist born in 1908. During the Spanish Civil War, she went to Spain as a reporter and received accreditation from the Republican government. An antifascist, she was in Madrid during the last days of the Civil War before returning to Sweden.

On April 9, 1940, Norway was attacked by Germany. The Germans hoped to establish naval bases there to counter the British in the North Sea and to secure important raw materials for the war effort. Although the Norwegian military put up a spirited defense, the Germans secured the country by late May. On June 7, King Haakon VII, along with much of the Norwegian government, fled and established a government-in-exile in London. The Germans then recruited Vidkun Quisling, a self-proclaimed fascist, to act as head of state.

The first anti-Jewish measure was introduced just a month after the beginning of the Nazi occupation, in May 1940, when radios belonging to Jews were confiscated. After this, between June 1940 and June 1941, there were relatively few restrictions placed on Norway's Jews. However, with Operation BARBAROSSA (the invasion of the Soviet Union), the Germans arrested Jews in northern Norway during the summer of 1941. In January 1942 a decree was issued requiring all Jews to have a red "J" stamped in their identification papers, and in October 1942, mass arrests of Jewish males over the age of 15 began, followed by arrests of women and all children under 15. At the same time, Jewish property was confiscated. On November 26, 1942, 530 Jews were deported by sea on the *Donau*, heading toward Poland. Another mass deportation of Jews followed in February 1943. These Jews were transported to Auschwitz, where women, the elderly, and children were sent directly to the gas chambers.

Many Norwegians objected to the arrests and deportations, either hiding Jews or tipping them off about planned arrests. Some 900 Norwegian Jews fled to neutral Sweden, where they took refuge until the end of the war.

During the German occupation, Inge Sletten, a member of the Norwegian underground, worked hard to save Jews by assisting them to cross the border into Sweden. She helped the family of the Norwegian rabbi Julius Samuel, himself deported and killed in Auschwitz, to flee to Sweden. In a highly celebrated case, she took charge of refugee children from Vienna who were placed in the **Oslo Jewish Children's Home**. Hearing one day that they might be deported to Eastern Europe, she worked with Nina Hasvold, Nic Waal, and others in smuggling 14 of the children out of the home after an anonymous call warning of imminent mass arrests of Jewish women and children. The children were subsequently hidden in several apartments in Oslo. After a week they were sent in small groups to a farm near the Swedish border; from there, the children walked toward the border accompanied by Norwegian border guides Ola Rauken and Ola Breisjøberget.

They covered about 20 kilometers before they reached sanctuary on the other side of the frontier.

In 1943, Inge learned that she was being watched by the Gestapo. Realizing that her life was in danger, she used her own escape routes in order to leave Norway for Sweden, where she remained for the duration of the war. At war's end, she married another former member of the Norwegian underground, and they both became teachers in a high school in Oslo.

Overall, only 25 of the 795 deported Jews survived incarceration in Nazi concentration and death camps during the Holocaust. The German occupation of Norway lasted until the war ended in Europe on May 8, 1945.

On April 4, 1967, Yad Vashem recognized Ingebjørg Sletten-Fosstvedt as one of the Righteous among the Nations. She died in 1991.

Further Reading

Abrahamsen, Samuel. *Norway's Response to the Holocaust: A Historical Perspective.* New York: Holocaust Library, 1991.

Nissen, Henrik S. (Ed.). *Scandinavia during the Second World War.* Minneapolis: University of Minnesota Press, 1983.

SMUGGLING

The term *smuggling* relates to the illegal transportation of any of a variety of items (whether articles, animals, or people) from one place to another in violation of the authority or authorities that dominate a specific domain.

During the Holocaust, smuggling took place in several ways, especially through the movement of Jewish refugees from German-occupied Europe to places of safety beyond the Nazi grasp. It also involved the illegal transfer of food, weapons, and other commodities to Jewish communities, particularly in the ghettos. There was some large-scale smuggling, especially of arms; but most smuggling on a day-to-day basis was small.

The oppressive environment in which Jews found themselves saw a desperate need for rescue, and in this regard, both Jews and non-Jews risked their lives. Those who could afford it bribed police not to notice. Throughout Europe they constituted but a fraction of the population that might have helped—even by the most generous estimates, less than half of 1 percent of the total population under Nazi occupation—but their importance transcended their numbers. As Jews were progressively stripped of their rights, segregated, and isolated from the rest of the community, people smugglers sustained them materially and emotionally. They conspired to hide Jews and move them out of harm's way, and as it became clear that Jews were marked for extermination, they helped them maintain an underground existence, often sheltering them within their own homes for at least part of the time.

Within the ghettos, where the German administration deliberately limited food supplies to an absolute minimum, starvation was present from the very beginning. Smuggling food from the "Aryan side," mainly by children, was often the only option of providing the ghetto with supplies. The severe shortage of food in the Warsaw Ghetto, for example, exacerbated the situation. At its peak, in April 1941, a population of well over 400,000 people were crammed into a tiny walled-in fraction of the city. Of these, 85,000 were children aged 14 and under.

Smuggling by children never ceased and took place anywhere an opportunity presented itself: through gaps in the ghetto walls, through the blind spots in and near the gates, via underground tunnels, through sewers, and through houses and other buildings bordering on the walls. Children scaled walls to smuggle food into the ghettos, despite the Germans doing all in their power to seal off the ghetto hermetically, fixing barbed wire and broken glass to the top of the wall and ordering the Jewish Councils (*Judenräte*) to build the wall higher to stop smuggling and escapes. The walls were rarely guarded by the Germans themselves; for the most part, Jewish ghetto police and Polish police, each on their own side, ensured that security was maintained.

Despite this, smuggling still took place, most often by children. Their small size and dexterity enabled them to pass through breaches in the ghetto walls, often able to avoid detection that would be inevitable for adults. Others acted as lookouts at the wall and at the openings. Those designated to do the smuggling were sometimes very young children aged as young as 5 and 6 years old, though the majority were probably between 10 and 14. Crawling through narrow openings in the walls, these young traffickers in contraband were a vital resource for the general population as well as their own families, as the ghetto inhabitants relied increasingly on smuggled food to stay alive. They had to find a way through the wall and obtain the goods they were seeking through various means, ranging from purchase (much less likely), to begging, to outright theft. It was hazardous getting out, once through to the other side, and then getting back into the ghetto again the way they had left.

Of course, they risked their lives in this endeavor; if they were caught smuggling anything—no matter how paltry—the penalty was death. Ludwig Fischer, the chief administrator (and then, from 1941, governor) of the Warsaw District issued a proclamation imposing a mandatory death penalty on Jews who left the ghetto, which sealed the fate of all smugglers, children and adults alike. Pursuant to this, German soldiers shot child smugglers in great numbers. And even if they were, for some reason, not killed, they were at the very least severely punished; if lucky, they might escape with a beating from a ghetto policeman.

Although they faced such grave danger every day, they did not stop. Various groups might devise a system of smuggling bags of turnips and potatoes through a hole in the ghetto wall; others engaged in forced labor outside might grab potatoes, vegetables, or bread to bring back in; they might hide these few items in their sleeves or under their shirts. Frequently, such small-scale smuggling activities would be discovered, and the goods had to be surrendered upon arriving back in the ghetto, after which the children would await their fate.

Henryka Łazowertówna was a Jewish poet generally considered to be one of the most eminent to come out of Poland. Born in Warsaw in 1909, in 1941 she wrote her best-known poem, "Mały szmugler," translated into English as "The Little Smuggler." It tells the story of a small child who supports his starving family by bringing over food supplies from the Aryan side into the ghetto. The text of the poem, in Polish, Hebrew, and English, is today inscribed on the Monument to the Memory of Child Victims of the Holocaust located on Okopowa Street in Warsaw. The poem was first published in 1947.

Over the walls, through holes, through the guard posts,
Through the wire, through the rubble, through the fence,
Hungry, cheeky, stubborn,
I slip through, I nip through like a cat.

At midday, in the night, at dawn,
In snowstorms, foul weather, and heat,
A hundred times I risk my life,
I stick out my childish neck.

A rough sack under my arm,

Wearing torn rags on my back,
With nimble young legs
And in my heart constant fear.

But you have to bear it all,
And you have to put up with it all,
So that tomorrow you
Will have your fill of bread.

Over the walls, though holes, through bricks,
At night, at dawn, and in day,
Cheeky, hungry, crafty,
I move as quietly as a shadow.

And if the hand of fate unexpectedly
Catches up with me one day in this game,

It is an ordinary trap of life.
Mother, don't wait for me anymore.
I will not be coming back to you again,
The voice will not be heard from afar;
The dust of the streets will bury
The fate of the lost child.

And I have only one request,
And the grimace is set on the lips:
Who, Mother, will bring you
Your bread tomorrow?

Henryka Łazowertówna was murdered at Treblinka in August 1942. Before her deportation, friends offered to find a safe house in which she and her mother could live. She refused to accept this, however, arguing that she was needed by the orphaned and homeless children for whom she was caring at the time.

Further Reading

Miron, Guy (Ed.). *The Yad Vashem Encyclopedia of the Ghettos during the Holocaust.* New York: New York University Press, 2009.

Plotkin, Diane. "Smuggling in the Ghettos: Survivor Accounts from the Warsaw, Łódź, and Kraków Ghettos." In Eric J. Sterling (Ed.), *Life in the Ghettos during the Holocaust.* Syracuse, NY: Syracuse University Press, 2005, pp. 84–119.

SÜSKIND, WALTER (1906–1945)

Walter Süskind was a German-born Jewish businessman of Dutch background. Born on October 29, 1906, in Ludenscheid, Germany, he became a manager in 1919 for the German company Bolak. In 1935 he married Johanna (known as Hanna) Natt, and in March 1938, they, together with Johanna's mother Fran Natt and Walter's mother Frieda Süskind, moved to Amsterdam. With other family members already in the United States, the intention was to find a way to migrate there later.

After the German invasion of the Netherlands in May 1940, however, the family became trapped. In July 1942 the Nazi-imposed Amsterdam Jewish Council (*Joodse Raad*) appointed Süskind to manage the *Hollandsche Schouwburg* (Dutch Theater), which was renamed the *Jüdische Schouwburg* and utilized for the purpose of holding Dutch Jews who were apprehended prior to being sent to the transit camp at Westerbork. From there—though it was not widely known—they were deported regularly to their deaths at Sobibór and Auschwitz.

Right opposite the Dutch Theater was a children's nursery, where the Nazis preferred to place young Jewish children. Süskind, together with another member of the Theater administration, Felix Halverstad; and the director of the nursery, Henriette Henriques Pimentel, established a means whereby the children could be rescued. Children were brought secretly to the *Hervormde Kweekschool* (Reformed Teacher Training College), two houses from the theater, and, with the assistance of the college director, **Johan van Hulst**, passed through the garden and into the theater.

Süskind and Halverstad then manipulated the Dutch Theater records, to show that these children were not registered; in this way, their names did not appear in any official capacity. They would sneak the children out from under the Nazis' gaze using a variety of ruses, whisking them off to safer locations out of the city. During the 18 months that Süskind oversaw the Dutch Theater he was able to save the lives of some 600 Jewish children. In this he was helped by several different Dutch resistance groups.

Such rescue came at a price, however. In order to remain at his post, he had to show himself to be an effective administrator of Nazi dictates, which meant organizing the deportation of thousands of Jews to the euphemistically named "East." Moreover, to achieve such effectiveness, he was obliged to develop a relationship with the Nazi in charge of the deportations, Ferdinand aus der Fünten, at that time a senior official in Amsterdam's Central Office for Jewish Emigration. Süskind was therefore seen by many Jews to be a collaborator, especially as he used his position to secure the safety of his wife, Hanna, and their daughter, Yvonne.

During the entire operation in which children were rescued, Süskind and those around him were never betrayed or discovered by the Nazis, even as he worked seemingly hand-in-hand with aus der Fünten. Only a few people, moreover—those directly involved with the escapes—ever knew the details of Süskind's activities.

Süskind experienced considerable turmoil over his role, particularly over the dilemma of saving his family or saving others. Leaders of every Jewish Council throughout Europe were confronted with this fundamental question: Should the Nazis be met with opposition, or should one work with them if by doing so it would be possible to save at least some lives? Does one become a traitor or a hero? After his realization of what the Nazis were doing by sending transports to the East, he sought to thwart their deportation plans as far as the children were concerned.

On September 2, 1944, time and luck ran out for the Süskind family. They were arrested and sent to the transit camp at Westerbork, but even there, Süskind attempted to find a way to help people escape. In this endeavor, however, he failed. From Westerbork, in October 1944, the family was deported to **Theresienstadt**. As this happened, a forged letter, purportedly from a high-ranking Nazi, was in Süskind's possession. It described how Süskind had been valuable to the Nazi administration in Amsterdam, and he hoped it could serve as some sort of guarantee for him and his family. He attempted to present it to the commandant of Theresienstadt, Karl Rahm, but a kapo got in the way and instead pushed him into a railcar headed for Auschwitz.

Johanna and Yvonne Süskind were murdered immediately upon arrival. The fate of Walter Süskind himself has been disputed. Most accounts argue that he died on February 28, 1945, on a death march somewhere in Central Europe, but another version is that he was murdered by Dutch prisoners in Auschwitz who believed he was a collaborator.

In 2012, a Dutch film, the eponymously titled *Süskind* (directed by Rudolf van den Berg) was made about the exploits of Walter Süskind, starring Jeroen Spitzenberger in the title role. The dilemmas Süskind faced in real life were clearly delineated. In one scene, for instance, the film shows the character of aus der Funten forcing Süskind to decide between putting 13 orphaned children onto the next transport or sending the 13-member Jewish orchestra instead. The film compares well, in several areas, to what is possibly the best-known of all Holocaust movies, *Schindler's List* (directed by Steven Spielberg, 1993).

In fact, several parallels can be drawn between the two movies. One vitally important difference can be observed, however, apart from the obvious fact that Oskar Schindler was not Jewish, while Walter Süskind certainly was. Unlike *Schindler's List*, there is nothing remotely resembling a happy ending in *Süskind*. The heartbreaking end of the movie mirrors the tragic reality that was Walter Süskind's own story.

Further Reading

Paldiel, Mordecai. *Saving the Jews: Amazing Stories of Men and Women Who Defied the "Final Solution."* Rockville, MD: Schreiber Publishing, 2000.

SWING KIDS

Swing Kids (directed by Thomas Carter, 1993) is an American motion picture film relating to a relationship between two best friends during the Third Reich. High school students Peter Müller (Robert Sean Leonard) and Thomas Berger (Christian Bale) go through their daily routine via a close adherence to the subculture of American swing music, an expression of rebellion against the closed and disciplined society of Nazi Germany.

The boys' act of defiance takes the form of an attempt to be "swing kids" by night and **Hitler Youth** by day, a decision that eventually proves to be impossible for Thomas, who is increasingly seduced by positive feelings for the sense of exclusivity that Nazism has imparted on German youth. Whereas Peter becomes progressively depressed through his involvement with the Hitler Youth—indeed, he retreats into sullenness and stubborn defiance owing to his enforced membership—Thomas becomes more and more of an ardent young Nazi, never thinking there is anything wrong with being part of the movement.

Things come to a head in a situation involving a third member of the swing kids, Arvid (Frank Whaley). A young man with a physical disability, Arvid is severely beaten by a group of Hitler Youth, including Emil Lutz (Noah Wyle), another swing kid–turned-ardent-Nazi. Shocked by this treatment of one of their own by one of their own, Thomas then accuses Emil of selling out. Emil replies, "I am not a traitor. I just wised up. You will too." From this moment on, Thomas begins to see his Nazi future, seduced by power and the advantages that can come from it, and begins to internalize Nazi ideology more fully. His attitude is summed up with the realization that "Nazis go anywhere they want, do anything they want, everyone gets out of our way."

When the inevitable confrontation takes place between Peter and Thomas, Peter is emphatic, saying, "If you side with the Nazis, Thomas, then we're at war." Referring to the Nazi attitude toward those with physical disabilities, Thomas tells Arvid, who is still recovering from his beating, that "we're coming for you next." Peter, furious, shouts, "You're turning into a Nazi!" Thomas responds, "Oh, so what if I am?"

A number of storylines then unfold: Arvid, realizing there is no future for him in Germany and no hope of escape, commits suicide; Peter is asked to spy on his boss, whom the Nazis suspect is working against the Reich; and Thomas denounces his father for making anti-Hitler statements at home. Ultimately there is a form of reconciliation between Peter and Thomas, but only before the film's climax that sees a still-defiant Peter taken to a concentration camp.

While there are few overt expressions of antisemitism in *Swing Kids*, the film offers a great deal of insight regarding the conditioning of German youth into accepting Nazi racial propaganda. Thomas and Emil (and those like them) show us how it was possible for the Nazis to seduce compliance from those who did not identify its evil, even as its members were sucked more and more deeply into the Nazi quagmire.

Further, the film considers the many ways adolescent Germans in the 1930s were confronted with choices that young people should never have to face: whether to choose their own lifestyle over one imposed by the state; whether to betray their friends for principles in which they themselves did not believe; whether to turn against the helpless because they were told to; and whether to follow the crowd or chart their own course despite the many pressures to the contrary. Peter went one way and paid the price. Thomas went the other, achieved status and power, and never really understood what doing so represented.

The Nazis, for their part, sought both political compliance and the transformation of society such that those growing up would know no other way but that of the Nazis. While the intention regarding opponents was that they would be scared into submission or suffer the consequences, the position with respect to those of the younger generation was that they would be socialized into behaving only according to the objectives the Nazis demanded. This, of course, was to lead whole classes of young Germans into a moral universe over which they had no control. *Swing Kids*, in short, portrays the conflicts of some members of German youth at a time simultaneously confusing and demanding conformity.

The reality the film portrays relates to so-called Swing Youth (*Swingjugend*), young devotees of jazz and swing music during the 1930s. Comprising mainly boys and girls in the 14 to 21 age bracket, they defined themselves through their music; as such, they ran up against opposition from the Nazi state and found themselves confronting those of similar ages in the Hitler Youth and the **League of German Girls**. Dancing at home in private as well as in clubs and rented halls, the swing kids effectively formed a subculture (even a counterculture) in Nazi Germany, and when their music became illegal, their expression of it became a political statement. Initially apolitical, swing culture developed into a nonviolent refusal to be cowed into submission by the Nazi regime.

Jewish swing kids were for the most part welcomed by others, though for these devotees, their adherence became even more dangerous than if they were not Jews. On August 18, 1941, over 300 swing kids—mostly non-Jews but including some who were Jewish—were arrested. Those known to the authorities from earlier confrontations were sent to concentration camps, the boys to Moringen youth camp and the girls to Ravensbrück. Others, like other recalcitrants such as the **Edelweiss Pirates**, had their heads shaved or were subjected to beatings before being sent home.

Further Reading

Kater, Michael. *Different Drummers: Jazz in the Culture of Nazi Germany*. New York: Oxford University Press, 1992.

Peukert, Detlev J. K. *Inside Nazi Germany: Conformity, Opposition and Racism in Everyday Life*. London: B. T. Batsford, 1987.

SZTEHLÓ, GABOR (1909–1974)

Gabor Sztehló was a Christian minister in Budapest who rescued hundreds of Jewish children during the Holocaust.

The son of a lawyer, Marta Maria Józefa, he was born in Budapest on September 29, 1909. He attended the Sopron Lutheran grammar school, and in 1931, he obtained a degree in Lutheran theology. The following year he was ordained a pastor. From 1933 to 1935, he served a congregation in Hatvan, northern Hungary, before moving to Nagytarcsa in central Hungary, where he was stationed between 1935 and 1942.

On October 20, 1942, under the direction of Pastor Gyula Muraközy and the sponsorship of the Universal Convent of the Reformed Church of Hungary, the Good Shepherd Committee was established. This became Hungary's major association of Jews converted to Protestantism. Its leadership was entrusted to Pastor József Éliás, himself of Jewish background. The Hungarian Evangelical Church became affiliated with the Committee in May 1944, when Bishop Sándor Raffay appointed Sztehló as its representative in charge of converts from Judaism and dependents of those called up for forced labor, providing food, clothing, and succor. Before Hungary was occupied by Nazi Germany in March 1944, the Committee had already supported Jewish and non-Jewish refugees through aiding those interned in various camps.

After Germany invaded Hungary, Sztehló and the Good Shepherd Committee began rescuing abandoned Jewish children. This intensified considerably in October 1944 after the antisemitic, fascist Arrow Cross party took power and unleashed a full anti-Jewish campaign of terror.

Éliás and Sztehló had prepared for this, seeing to it that the children in their care would be fed, housed, and looked after with the cooperation of the International Red Cross, which established a special department (Section B) especially for this purpose. Responsibility for the protection of the children fell almost exclusively on Sztehló's shoulders as Éliás was targeted by the Arrow Cross, having antagonized them one too many times before they came to office.

Most of those helped were children of converts and Christian orphans, but Sztehló soon extended his rescue activities to all Jewish children, regardless of status. By Christmas 1944, 32 homes had been designated as havens in which the children could be sheltered. One of these was the castle of Ney Ákos, former director of railways in Hungary and a hero of World War I. Sztehló provided documents for approximately 1,500 children, stating that they were not Jewish, saving them from likely deportation and execution. Although some of the homes were raided by Arrow Cross and police, no harm came to any of the children housed in them.

On December 26, 1944, Soviet units began the encirclement of Budapest, signaling the start of a siege that would claim the lives of some 38,000 civilians. During the battle, many of Sztehló's homes were damaged, rendering them useless for continued use as shelters for the children. With the escalation in fighting, Sztehló moved 33 children to the basement of his own home, and he and his family protected them for nearly three weeks. The city surrendered to the Russians unconditionally on February 13, 1945, and Sztehló then managed to move the children to something more permanent until they were either claimed by their families—unfortunately, all too infrequently—or until Jewish organizations accepted them.

When liberation came, and the war finally ended, Sztehló continued to care for children once it became known that their families had succumbed to the Holocaust. He established a school in which the children not only received an education but also learned technical skills that would permit them to re-enter society. In 1951 the homes were taken over by Hungary's communist regime.

Sztehló's family moved to Switzerland in 1956. Anxious to continue his work, he remained in Hungary and persisted in the development of charity homes as part of the work of the Lutheran Church. In 1961, however, during a visit to Switzerland, he suffered a stroke, which necessitated him remaining there on medical advice. Upon recovery, he resumed his pastoral activities in his new home. When his passport expired, it was not renewed by the Hungarian government; he was not even permitted to return to Hungary as a visitor. It took over 10 years before he finally received permission to return, but he died on May 28, 1974, just two months prior to his scheduled visit. He was cremated, and his ashes were returned for their final interment to Budapest's Farkasréti cemetery.

In 1972 Pastor Gabor Sztehló was recognized as one of the Righteous among the Nations by Yad Vashem for his work in saving the lives of Jewish children. He became the first Hungarian to be so acknowledged. Then, in 1973, he was also nominated by the Swiss government for the Nobel Peace Prize. Overall, the acts of resistance undertaken by Gabor Sztehló saw some 1,600 Jewish children and 400 Jewish adults saved from the Holocaust.

Further Reading

Paldiel, Mordecai. *The Path of the Righteous: Gentile Rescuers of Jews during the Holocaust.* Hoboken, NJ: KTAV, 1993.

Silver, Eric. *The Book of the Just: The Unsung Heroes Who Rescued Jews from Hitler.* New York: Grove Press, 1992.

T

THERESIENSTADT

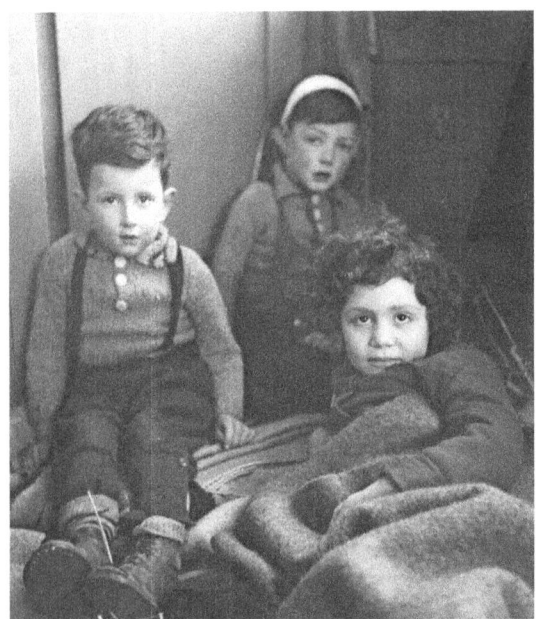

In this image, taken in February 1945, in a children's camp in St. Gallen, Switzerland, we see three Jewish children who managed to be rescued from Theresienstadt. Located in the town of Terezín, some 35 miles from Prague in northwestern Czechoslovakia, Theresienstadt was established by the Nazis as a ghetto for Jews as well as a concentration and transit camp. As a way station for Jews on the road to Auschwitz, children were hit especially hard; of approximately 15,000 (12,000 of whom were under the age of 15) who passed through the camp, it is estimated that only about 100 survived until the end of the war. (United States Holocaust Memorial Museum, courtesy of Stadtarchiv [Vadiana] St. Gallen)

Located in the town of Terezín, some 35 miles from Prague in northwestern Czechoslovakia, Theresienstadt was established by the Nazis as a ghetto for Jews as well as a concentration and transit camp. It was originally built as a military fortress and garrison town by the Habsburg emperor Joseph II, who named it in honor of his mother, Empress Maria Theresa. Construction of the Theresienstadt fortress began in October 1780; it was then built over the next decade.

On November 24, 1941, the site became operational as a Nazi ghetto camp and was designed to fulfill two primary functions. First, it served as a transit point for Czech Jews being deported to the euphemistically named "East"; second, it was a labor camp where elderly, disabled, or prominent Jews were housed. Theresienstadt became more than that, however, as the Nazis employed the location in order to perpetrate an elaborate hoax on neutral countries and watchdog organizations such as the International Committee of the Red Cross by implying that those located at Theresienstadt were being well treated in a town where there was a measure of Jewish self-government and where social services were a central concern.

Indeed, based on this ruse, Theresienstadt developed a reputation for being a "privileged" or "humane" camp. The Jews of Czechoslovakia, as well as elderly Jewish men and women, Jews married to Aryans, and well-known Jewish personalities from Germany and Western Europe, were treated very differently from those sent to other camps. The location became known as a "model" or "ideal."

In 1942, however, its character changed when the head of the Reich Security main office, Reinhard Heydrich, ordered that the camp henceforth be utilized as a transit camp for Jews being sent to the extermination camps farther east. Over 140,000 prisoners from across Europe would ultimately pass through Theresienstadt, and of these, 90,000 were transferred to their deaths. Tens of thousands of others died at the camp before they even left.

Despite this appalling death rate, the Germans continued to refer to the camp in glowing terms in an effort to disguise their activities and keep the outside world from learning about the true scale of the Holocaust. In June 1944 the Germans permitted representatives of the International Committee of the Red Cross (ICRC) to visit the camp after receiving negative press about the deportation of Dutch Jews there. The ICRC officials were impressed, reporting back favorably on what they had seen. Gardens had been cultivated, barracks were clean and renovated, and buildings were freshly painted. The streets were clean, there were well-stocked provisions in shop-front establishments, and smartly dressed inmates appeared to be gainfully employed. Fake stores, cafes, kindergartens, and a bank were opened, and little flower gardens were planted throughout the ghetto. After the visit, a propaganda movie was made about the life of the Jews under the auspices of the Third Reich. By the time the positive ICRC report was issued, however, the Jews on whom it was based had already been sent to their deaths at Auschwitz. When the ICRC personnel left, deportations from Theresienstadt resumed, and they continued through to October 1944.

Children were hit especially hard; of approximately 15,000 (12,000 of whom were under the age of 15) who passed through the camp, it is estimated that only about 100 survived until the end of the war. The continued arrival of Jews from Western Europe, Czechoslovakia, and Germany created terrible overcrowding, and in a bid to alleviate this situation, men were separated from women and placed in different barracks, thus splitting family groups. In order to make conditions better for the children, the Jewish Council initiated the movement of some into special homes, known as *kinderheim*. Here, the children were educated, were able to receive better food rations than the adults, and, for many hours of the day, were under the direct supervision of Jewish youth leaders such as **Fredy Hirsch**.

A group of dedicated adults, such as Rabbi **Regina Jonas**, devoted themselves to caring for the children—and not just by taking care of their physical needs. As the children were separated in different barracks from their parents, morale was vitally necessary, and adult helpers went out of their way to shield the children as much as possible from the depressing reality of life in which they found themselves.

Unlike most other concentration camps, and possibly on account of the Nazi **deceptions**, Theresienstadt was a place in which cultural activities played an important part in people's daily activities. Among others, the camp housed artists, writers, teachers, actors, and musicians; accordingly, concerts, plays, lectures, art exhibits, and other cultural happenings were frequent occurrences. The children could, for example, enjoy stage performances, notably the staging of **Brundibár**, a children's opera by Czech Jewish composer Hans Krása with a libretto by Adolf Hoffmeister. Another aspect of this activity saw children given the opportunity to paint and draw and even take classes from renowned artists. These classes had a privileged position within the children's care program and became an important aspect of clandestine activity. And in addition to the paintings and drawings, children also engaged in creative writing, particularly poetry. All these documents to the horrors of daily life constitute some of the most poignant expressions of children's lives during the Holocaust.

In 1964, Hana Volavková, a Holocaust survivor and curator at the Central Jewish Museum in Prague, edited a collection of these paintings, drawings, and poems, entitled *I Never Saw Another Butterfly*. The artworks she reproduced chronicled the children's daily misery, at the same time displaying some of their hopes for a brighter future. Certainly, they showed that the children had an understanding of what was happening around them, and their surviving artworks demonstrated how art could be employed as therapy under the most trying of conditions.

On May 2, 1945, with Adolf Hitler dead and Soviet forces pressing in from the east, camp personnel turned over control of Theresienstadt to the ICRC. Soviet troops officially liberated the camp on May 8. It was one of the last Nazi camps to be liberated.

Further Reading

Adler, H. G. *Theresienstadt 1941–1945: The Face of a Coerced Community*. Cambridge: Cambridge University Press, 1955.

Redlich, Egon. *The Terezin Diary of Gonda Redlich*. Lexington: University Press of Kentucky, 1992.

Volavkova, Hana. *I Never Saw Another Butterfly*. New York: Schocken Books, 1994.

TIEFENBRUNNER ORPHANAGE

Yona Tiefenbrunner was a young Orthodox Belgian rabbi who saved hundreds of Jewish orphans from Nazism during World War II. Born in Germany, he married Ruth Feldheim, and the two had started building a family in Brussels before the war broke out, and then the Jews of Belgium came under an increasing set of restrictions over successive months and years.

In 1942, a Jewish orphanage was created by Belgium's occupation government near Antwerp, with Tiefenbrunner—not yet 30 years old—agreeing to serve as its director. Seemingly overnight, he became a father figure to hundreds of traumatized war orphans—boys, girls, toddlers, and teenagers. At least 100 children were given refuge in the orphanage, in which Rabbi Tiefenbrunner, in the face of Gestapo scrutiny, created and led a religiously observant community of young Jews who maintained the full range of Jewish rituals: bar mitzvah, Shabbat observance, fulfillment of the various requirements of the Festivals, and the like. He created what was effectively an island of refuge amid the horrors of Nazism.

Children in the orphanage referred to him simply as "Monsieur," the name by which he is remembered today among those who survived and their descendants. The fact that the orphanage was in Antwerp made Tiefenbrunner's achievement even more remarkable.

On the eve of the German invasion in May 1940, Antwerp had a Jewish population of about 50,000, the majority of whom were either recent immigrants from Eastern Europe or refugees from Nazi Germany and Austria. The city was home to several local pro-Nazi and antisemitic parties and groups that collaborated with the Nazis in their anti-Jewish measures. On April 14, 1941, these attitudes boiled over into what became a wartime pogrom against Antwerp's Jewish quarter. In scenes reminiscent of the *Kristallnacht* in Germany just two and a half years earlier, some 200 rioters, armed with iron bars, sticks, and other weapons, and spurred on by the German occupation authorities, set fire to the Van den Nestlei and the Oostenstraat synagogues, burned a number of Torah scrolls, smashed the windows of Jewish-owned shops, and harassed the Jewish population. They then turned their attention toward the home of Rabbi Marcus Rottenburg, chief rabbi of Flanders.

The Jews of Antwerp proactively tried to save themselves and others, and local Zionist youth groups became active in helping to smuggle Jews to secure hiding places. It has been estimated that perhaps as many as 3,000 Jews managed to hide in the Antwerp area during the war, including some 800 who remained in the city.

Of these, Rabbi Tiefenbrunner's orphanage was a refuge of the first order for the city's children. Despite the ever-present danger of deportation, Tiefenbrunner not only went about his daily activities but also stood up to the Gestapo whenever the welfare of the children was imperiled. Risking his life on more than one occasion, Tiefenbrunner would enter Gestapo headquarters if the life of a Jewish child was at risk, demanding the child's release into his care. Following halachic (i.e., Jewish religious) law that the preservation of life comes before almost all other religious strictures, Rabbi Tiefenbrunner would break Shabbat laws in order to travel to see the Gestapo if it was necessary to demand the release of a child, always aware of the fact that he could be shot on the spot or deported without trace for making such a demand.

He seemed, however, to enjoy a charmed life, as did the children he was protecting. He took all comers: from those left by their parents for safekeeping, to those handed across by non-Jews who could no longer look after them, to children who simply arrived out of the blue, needing somewhere to stay. The children whose lives were saved—and it should not be forgotten that this included Rabbi Tiefenbrunner's own three daughters—numbered in the hundreds over the course of the war.

At war's end, Rabbi Yona and Ruth Tiefenbrunner, despite having their own young family, continued to nurture those who remained in the orphanage and had nowhere else to go. In the two decades that followed, the rabbi remained in his position as director until the last child had grown and married. The orphanage closed in 1960, and Tiefenbrunner, his life's work completed, died in August 1962, aged just 48. In August 2002, on Rabbi Yona Tiefenbrunner's 40th *yahrzeit* (the anniversary of his death), surviving orphans from Antwerp met in Jerusalem to remember "Monsieur" and pay tribute to the work he did on their behalf during the war. One of those present, Moniek Kerber, noted, "He gave us the will to continue with our lives. He restored the human spirit within each of us after the desolation of the Holocaust. We are all a living monument to his blessed memory."

Further Reading

Weinstock, Malky. *Angel of Orphans: The Story of R' Yona Tiefenbrunner and the Hundreds He Saved.* New York: Menucha Publishers, 2009.

TROCMÉ, ANDRÉ (1901–1971)

André Trocmé was a French Huguenot pastor who, with his wife, Magda, directed a remarkable rescue effort of Jewish children and other refugees in the village of **Le Chambon-sur-Lignon** and its surrounding areas, a rural mountainous region in south-central France known as the Plateau Vivarais-Lignon.

Born in Saint-Quentin-en-Tourmont in northern France on April 7, 1901, Pastor Trocmé was the son of a French father and German mother and the product of a strict bourgeois Huguenot upbringing. As an eyewitness to the horrors of World War I, he was shattered by its tremendous violence and the decimation of an entire generation, and he advocated for the resolution of conflict through nonviolent means. In 1926 he married the equally dedicated Magda Grilli di Cortona, whom he had met while conducting graduate work at the Union Theological Seminary in New York. They would have four children: Nelly, Jean-Pierre, Jacques, and Daniel.

Pastor Trocmé became an outspoken proponent of nonviolence, making him a controversial figure in the French Protestant church. In an effort to limit his influence, he was sent to the remote parish of Le Chambon; once there, he did not hesitate to impart his pacifist convictions into his work. In 1938, he and Pastor Edouard Theis, who came to the village to assist him, opened the *École Nouvelle Cévenole*, a coeducational secondary school based on the principles of tolerance, pacifism, and internationalism.

Pastor Trocmé's preaching was also politically shaded. He spoke out against Nazism in neighboring Germany, pointing out its discriminatory policies toward Jews. With the coming of World War II, both his opposition of the Nazis and his pacifism would be tested in a manner he did not anticipate.

In 1940 France capitulated to Germany within a few short weeks. On June 23, 1940, the day after the armistice was signed, Pastors Trocmé and Theis emphasized their views in a celebrated sermon directed squarely at their Protestant Huguenot congregation: "The duty of Christians is to resist the violence brought to bear on their consciences with the weapons of the spirit—we will resist whenever our adversaries try to force us to act against the commands of the Gospel. We will do so without fear, but also without pride and without hatred." When deportations of Jews began in France in 1942, Pastor Trocmé urged his congregation to give shelter to "the people of the Bible," especially as the village and its outlying areas were quickly filled with hundreds of fleeing Jews. Pastor Trocmé showed the way by enjoining his congregation to take in refugees, particularly children in need of sanctuary. From this point on, the people of Le Chambon would prove repeatedly that they were willing to open their doors courageously to Jews and other persecuted refugees seeking shelter.

Magda Trocmé also assisted refugees in their search for safe havens, connecting them with those prepared to take them in. While not part of any formal resistance network, the efforts of the Trocmés to assist Jews overlapped with the work of many others who were supporting rescue efforts in the area.

As a result, large numbers of people found permanent shelter in and around Le Chambon, and others were sheltered temporarily until a way could be found to smuggle them across the border into Switzerland. They were housed with local townspeople and farmers, in public institutions, and in children's homes. There were many ways people provided help. It was not only a matter of families being prepared to accommodate the Jewish refugees; when the children (nicknamed "Testaments" by the villagers) arrived at the local train station, designated members of the community would meet them before spiriting them away to their new homes. Schools found ways to accommodate increased enrollments, and fabrications of school registers were made so it appeared as though the children—with changed names—had always been there. With very few dissenters, the entire community of Le Chambon, it seemed, banded together as one in order to rescue Jewish children.

While the people of Le Chambon were effectively hiding the children "in plain sight," Vichy French authorities learned of Pastor Trocmé's clandestine work. Accordingly, in January 1943, he and Pastor Theis, together with the local headmaster, Roger Darcissac, were arrested and imprisoned for several weeks in the St. Paul d'Eyjeaux internment camp for political prisoners, near Limoges. When he was arrested and first told to desist from his rescue activities, Pastor Trocmé made a statement that became famous: "These people came here for help and for shelter. I am their shepherd. A shepherd does not forsake his flock. . . . I do not know what a Jew is. I know only human beings."

After a period of imprisonment, they were released through the intervention of several individuals—including Pastor Trocmé's cousin Daniel Trocmé, who was also involved in refugee work in Le Chambon and who was himself later arrested. Deported to Majdanek, he died in 1944.

Following his release, Pastor Trocmé continued his efforts on behalf of Jewish children in Le Chambon, but he was forced to go into hiding for several months. His absence did not deter the residents of Le Chambon or close the rescue operation he had begun. They continued welcoming persecuted Jews into their homes, providing a sanctuary for them and enabling many to see out the war in relative safety.

No one knows precisely how many Jewish refugee children were hidden or saved at Le Chambon during World War II. Some estimates consider a figure of about 3,500; others range as high as 5,000, considering those Jews who at least passed through Le Chambon and vicinity as well as those who remained for any length of time.

After the war, André and Magda Trocmé continued the cause of nonviolent resolution of problems, with André serving as European secretary for the International Fellowship of Reconciliation, a nongovernmental pacifist organization founded during World War I in response to the horrors of war in Europe. He spent his final years as pastor of a Reformed church in Geneva.

On January 5, 1971, Yad Vashem recognized Pastor André Trocmé as one of the Righteous among the Nations, with Magda receiving the same recognition on May 14, 1984. In an unprecedented move, in 1998 Yad Vashem presented this honor to the entire village of Le Chambon-sur-Lignon.

Pastor André Trocmé died on June 5, 1971, in Geneva, followed by his wife Magda on October 10, 1996, in Paris. Both are buried in the family grave in Le Chambon.

Further Reading

Grose, Peter. *A Good Place to Hide: How One French Community Saved Thousands of People during World War II.* New York: Pegasus Books, 2015.

Hallie, Philip. *Lest Innocent Blood Be Shed: The Story of the Village of Le Chambon, and How Goodness Happened There.* New York: Harper Perennial, 1994.

Moorehead, Caroline. *Village of Secrets: Defying the Nazis in Vichy France.* New York: HarperCollins, 2014.

TWINS

Twins are two offspring produced by the same pregnancy. In view of the Nazi determination to breed both a superior "race" and at the same time one of greatly enlarged size, medical experiments on twins were undertaken during the period of the Third Reich to see whether their breeding could be scientifically engineered. Foremost among those engaged in this activity was an SS medical doctor, **Josef Mengele**. During 1943 and 1944, he performed experiments on nearly 1,500 twins at Auschwitz.

The general idea was that if heredity could be planned and controlled, the future would be guaranteed for the Aryan people. Twins, it was felt, held the secret to creating a blond-haired, blue-eyed population. Where Mengele was concerned, Auschwitz had an abundance of twins available for experimentation and was therefore the perfect place to undertake his research.

On entering Auschwitz, women and children were separated from men in a process known as selection. New arrivals were sorted into those who were considered able or not able to work; those unfit for work would be gassed immediately, and the others were put to slave labor. Where twins were identified, they were separated from their mothers; and after a period of processing, they were sent to Mengele's office. He would then inspect them, looking for common and unusual characteristics, before commencing a program of **medical experimentation**.

To begin with, the twins were arranged by age and sex. Their day began with roll call at 6:00 a.m., following which they would return to their barracks. Sometimes they would be given the chance to play games. Typically, each day, every twin had blood drawn, following which measurements of various parts of their bodies would be taken. Prisoner doctors working in Mengele's laboratory undertook routine work of this kind, following which Mengele would begin his experiments. If, however, any of the twins went missing, Mengele would react angrily; his scientific project could be jeopardized if word got out as to what he was doing.

He was obsessed, for example, with blue eyes. In an attempt to create blue eyes artificially, Mengele would administer extremely painful eyedrops or injections composed of various chemical solutions in the eyes of one twin, while the other would be used as a control. Not only would the drops or injections cause intense pain, but infections and sometimes even blindness would result.

The twins were also injected with various infections such as tuberculosis, typhus, and other diseases—sometimes to one twin and not the other. When the injected twin died of the disease, the other would likely be killed so the effects on their bodies could be compared.

Among Mengele's experiments on twins could be counted lumbar puncture, in which a needle is inserted into the spinal canal to help diagnose diseases of the central nervous system, including the brain and spine. This extremely painful (and, if administered incorrectly, crippling) procedure was routinely administered without anesthesia. Other surgeries, also carried out without anesthesia, involved amputation, removal of organs, and even castration. Sometimes, bizarrely, Mengele would vary his experiments by attempting to create conjoined ("Siamese") twins by sewing their backs together and trying to connect blood vessels and organs; after a few days, however, gangrene would set in, and the twins inevitably died.

In another experiment, more than 100 twins were singled out for a special experiment in which they were given injections of bacteria that cause Noma disease, a rapidly progressive and often gangrenous infection in which mucous membranes of the mouth develop ulcers and rapid, painful tissue degeneration ensues.

After most experiments of whatever kind, both twins would be euthanized with injections of phenol to the heart or through overdoses of chloroform. Sometimes they were killed intentionally simply in order to study them during autopsy, when Mengele would examine them one last time.

With an interest in the genetic propensity of parents having twins, Mengele had a seemingly unlimited supply of twins to study. A Jewish prisoner doctor forced to work for Mengele later calculated that there were upward of 732 pairs of twins, bringing the total close to 1,500 altogether. Of these, perhaps no more than 200 survived the war and the experiments.

When the Soviet Army liberated Auschwitz in January 1945, some surviving twins remained. Units then set to work filming the children and taking down their statements so that the world would know what they had experienced and what Mengele's experiments entailed. At that time, the Soviets learned of Mengele's other pseudoscientific experiments, particularly on dwarves, giants, and Roma.

As they grew, the surviving children coped with their appalling ordeals in different ways. Perhaps the best-known survivor of Mengele's experiments on Jewish twins was **Eva Mozes Kor**, a Romanian survivor, along with her twin sister, Miriam.

She went on to establish the organization CANDLES ("Children of Auschwitz Nazi Deadly Lab Experiments Survivors") in 1984. Through this program she managed to locate 122 other survivors. Building on this foundation, in 1984 she founded the CANDLES Holocaust Museum and Education Center in her American hometown of Terre Haute, Indiana. This is a center dedicated to the mission of educating the public about eugenics, the Holocaust, and the power of forgiveness.

On January 27, 1995, during the 50th anniversary of the liberation of Auschwitz, another SS doctor, Hans Münch, returned to Auschwitz at the behest of Eva Mozes Kor, in which he took the opportunity to sign a document verifying that the gas chambers had existed and that cruel experiments had taken place against twins. Eva Mozes Kor, in a highly publicized statement, then publicly forgave him and the Nazis for what had been done to her, having come to the realization that for her to heal, she must forgive those who had tormented her as a child.

Further Reading

Kor, Eva Mozes, and Lisa Rojnay Buccieri. *Surviving the Angel of Death: The Story of a Mengele Twin in Auschwitz*. Terre Haute, IN: Tanglewood, 2009.

Kor, Eva Mozes, and Mary Wright. *Echoes from Auschwitz: Dr. Mengele's Twins. The Story of Eva and Miriam Mozes*. Terre Haute, IN: Candles, Inc., 1995.

Lagnado, Lucette Matalon, and Sheila Cohn Dekel. *Children of the Flames: Dr. Josef Mengele and the Untold Story of the Twins of Auschwitz*. New York: William Morrow, 1991.

Lifton, Robert Jay. *The Nazi Doctors: Medical Killing and the Psychology of Genocide*. New York: Basic Books, 2000.

Posner, Gerald L., and John Ware. *Mengele: The Complete Story*. New York: Cooper Square, 2000.

W

WEINER, PAVEL (1931–2010)

Born in Prague on November 13, 1931, into the middle-class Jewish family of Ludvik and Valy Weiner, and with an older brother, Handa, Pavel Weiner enjoyed a comfortable and cultured upbringing. Prior to the Nazi takeover of Czechoslovakia and then the onset of war, his family led an active social life. They enjoyed going to museums and concerts, traveling, and playing sports. The family was not especially religious, though most of the family friends were members of Prague's Jewish community.

In May 1942 Pavel and his family were deported to the **Theresienstadt** (Terezín) concentration camp/ghetto. The family was separated and assigned to different barracks, and Pavel was sent to Room 7 in building L417, which was the designated *kinderheim* (children's home) for Czech boys. At Terezín most of the children lived in *kinderheims*, separated for boys and girls, as the Jewish Council tried to shield the children from the camp's realities by providing better food and living conditions than experienced by many of the adults. Pavel would spend three years of his childhood at Terezín, between the ages of 10 and 13. While there, he kept a diary covering a year of his life in the camp, dated from April 1944 until the camp's **liberation** in April 1945. Many years later this was edited by Holocaust scholar Debórah Dwork and published as *A Boy in Terezín: The Private Diary of Pavel Weiner, April 1944–April 1945*. The diary shows the development of this 12-year-old boy as he lived through the horrors of Theresienstadt during its most taxing period.

Many young people kept **diaries and journals** while in Terezín, and Pavel Weiner's fits in well with those few remaining. What makes his valuable, however, is the depth of detail in which he wrote over a concentrated and uninterrupted period of one year.

In the *kinderheim*, Pavel shared his room with nearly 40 other boys. It was expected that they would perform labor for the Nazis, but together with other children under 14 years of age, they would attend secretly run classes in the morning, always on the lookout for guards who could close them down. Pavel was keen to maintain his studies, and whenever possible, he studied Hebrew, Czech, English, and French. Other subjects included mathematics, history, and geography.

Another activity in which the boys engaged was writing—in particular, the creation of magazines that would keep them alert and try to overcome their daily trauma. In as many as 10 secret periodicals, they produced poems, drawings, and paintings in which they produced a rich record of life as they experienced it. They also poured out their hopes for a better world that might one day come to pass. One of Pavel's pet projects was a magazine named *Neshar* ("Eagle"), of which he was the editor. The boys he lived with called themselves *Nesharim* ("the eagles"), and the magazine would be eagerly devoured and discussed, secretly, each Friday night. Pavel's articles reflect his character and attitude, in particular his hope, patriotism, maturity, and belief in the victory of truth.

Much of the diary focused on daily life in the *kinderheim*, dealing with Pavel's relationships with those around him as well as his ongoing struggles on a personal level, such as the search for food, education, concerns about his family, the making and breaking of friendships, and the like. His relationships, in fact, were not always happy ones, as he often found himself alienated from those around him due to his introspection and sensitive nature.

In August 1944 Pavel reflected on the two years of life the Nazis had stolen from him, and he undertook to write about his feelings in his diary so that he might learn from them. He also affirmed his desire to study hard and start a new life for himself, even within the ghetto walls.

Then, in late September 1944, Pavel learned that his father and brother, Handa, were to be deported. He had done his best to stay in touch with his parents and Handa from his position in the *kinderheim* and worried about them constantly, everyone in his family, other than his mother, succumbed to the Holocaust. The same was true for most of the original 40 boys in Pavel's room. Of these, only 10 survived until liberation.

In his diary entries, Pavel wrote about the things that mattered for him at ground level, with larger events—for example, relating to politics—reduced in importance. He wrote about loss, of longing for companionship, and about the debilitating condition of imprisonment, in which he lost motivation to continue striving for excellence. Yet despite these disheartened feelings, he did manage to continue with his studies and maintained a commitment to his diary. Throughout, he expressed his thoughts about hope for a better future and an optimistic belief in humanity.

The diary ended in May 1945. It was a precious record of daily life in Theresienstadt and took its place alongside other important chronicles of this most challenging of times.

After the war, Pavel Weiner and his mother returned to Prague, but in 1948, after the communist takeover of Czechoslovakia, they migrated to Canada. After completing high school in Montreal, Pavel moved to the United States to study chemistry and became a chemical engineer in New York. He died in January 2010, aged 78.

Further Reading

Weiner, Pavel. *A Boy in Terezin: The Private Diary of Pavel Weiner, April 1944–April 1945.* Evanston, IL: Northwestern University Press, 2012.

WESTERWEEL, JOHAN (1899–1944)

Johan Gerard (Joop) Westerweel was a Dutch resister and rescuer of Jews during World War II. He was born in the small city of Zutphen on January 25, 1899, and as a young man developed a belief in nonviolent resistance. He became a teacher in the Dutch East Indies, but as a conscientious objector, he was expelled from the colony for refusing to be drafted into the army. His pacifism became the basis of his moral compass as he grew older, with a strict Christian upbringing having implanted in him a sense of universal justice and a belief in the basic goodness of humanity.

In 1940 Joop and his wife, Wilhelmina (Wil, or Willy), moved to Rotterdam, where he had been offered a position as principal of a Montessori school. In earlier appointments he had already encountered Jewish refugee children, most of whom had begun arriving from Germany during the 1930s. In Rotterdam he began his resistance activities against the Nazis, who had occupied the Netherlands in May 1940.

He could not reconcile his humanistic worldview with what he was seeing around him, as Jews were being segregated from non-Jews and Dutch society was becoming fragmented by the Nazi occupation. He gathered a group of people from among his family and friends with a view to developing a network that would try to save Jewish lives and mitigate the worst effects of Nazi antisemitism. They would come to be known as the Westerweel group.

He organized for German and Polish Jewish refugees to be received into safe houses and found the means to enable their children's education to continue. As time went on, Dutch Jews also began to help, particularly teenagers and those in their early 20s who were often members of **Jewish youth movements** such as *Hechalutz*. Many of the *Halutzim*, as they were called, comprising young Jews aged between 15 and 19, originated from Central and Eastern Europe, and had come to the Netherlands before the war to undertake agricultural training prior to migrating to Palestine.

Members of the Westerweel group included Willy Westerweel; Joachim Simon ("Schuschu"); Letty Rudelsheim; Giel Salome; Frans Gerritsen and his wife, Henny Gerritsen-Kouffeld; Jan Smit; Paula Welt Kaufman; Menachem Pinkhof; and Miriam Pinkhof.

By 1942 Joop Westerweel had organized a rescue network that was so effective that anywhere between 300 and 400 people had been helped, many of whom had been hidden or managed to escape to Palestine. Throughout this time, Joop and Wil continued to live in the open, with Joop continuing to teach and the four Westerweel children going about their daily routines in school.

In December 1943 Wil Westerweel was arrested by the Germans during an attempt to free one of the *Hehalutz* youth members, Lettie Rudelsheim, from the Scheveningen prison. Wil was taken to the Vught concentration camp, where she remained incarcerated for nearly a year. She was later transferred to Ravensbrück, where she was put to work at hard labor. Although severely weakened by her experience, she survived the war, was repatriated to Sweden as part of a prisoner exchange, and returned to Holland after the war.

Immediately after Wil's arrest, Joop arranged for their children to go into hiding. He then quit his position at the school and went underground.

One of those with whom he worked in the Westerweel group was Bouke Koning, a young man who had begun rescue work on his own initiative before joining Westerweel in the summer of 1942. Among his tasks was accompanying refugees across the Belgian border, from where they headed southward. On March 11, 1944, while escorting two young Jewish women to the frontier, Koning and Westerweel were arrested. Joop Westerweel was returning to the Netherlands, having just visited several young Jews hidden in the Pyrenees. Upon his arrest he was taken to Rotterdam, where he was imprisoned at the police station at Haagseveer. He was severely tortured for information regarding his network and resistance activities prior to being transferred to the concentration camp at Vught, where he was again tortured.

It soon became clear to him that his life was forfeit and that one day he would be executed for his continued refusal to provide the Gestapo with any information. In July 1944 he wrote a poem entitled "*Avond in de Cel*" ("Evening in the Cell"), which helpers managed to send out of the camp. It was to be his last communication with the outside world.

> *It is the hour of sentences*
> *Now, now that evening is falling,*
> *When the light comes from within*
> *Our being is beaming.*
> *A cell, four white walls*
> *The door is closed firmly;*
> *In these late hours*
> *Shines a moderate light.*
> *I fold my hot hands*
> *I close my eyes;*
> *I feel the pain burning so much*
> *I seek eternal light.*
> *My soul seeks the reason*
> *From her abandonment;*
> *I long for peace*
> *In this loneliness.*
> *The sunlight is now going to fall;*
> *It is the last hour:*
> *I see the weak rays*
> *Against the blind wall.*
> *The wall, that's the order*
> *Around our lonely place*
> *And from the law of the horde*
> *The very last word.*
> *It is the hour of sentences*
> *Now the evening has fallen*
> *And now the light from within*
> *My being shines.*

Very soon after this, on August 11, 1944, Joop Westerweel, with four others, was executed at Vught. Wil Westerweel, at that time still at Vught, was forced to witness her husband's execution.

After the war Joop Westerweel was remembered fondly by the Dutch government. Several streets and a school were named in his honor, as were as other public areas. In March 1947 the Joop Westerweel Park was built, and on June 16, 1964, Joop and Wil were recognized by Yad Vashem as Righteous among the Nations.

Further Reading

Paldiel, Mordecai. *The Path of the Righteous: Gentile Rescuers of Jews during the Holocaust.* Hoboken, NJ: KTAV, 1993.

WIESEL, ELIE (1928–2016)

Elie Wiesel was a Romanian-born American writer, thinker, and teacher, world renowned for his work in raising awareness of the Holocaust and its relevance for contemporary society. For many, he was the conscience and expression of all Holocaust survivors. A youth during the Holocaust, he later became a prolific author whose written work dealt essentially with the moral responsibility of all people to fight hatred, racism, and genocide.

Wiesel was born in Sighet on September 30, 1928. As a child his world essentially revolved around family, religious study, community, and God. Sighet was occupied by Hungary in August 1940, and with the Nazi invasion in March 1944, this all changed. Wiesel's entire village was first incarcerated in two ghettos, and then deported to Auschwitz. While not yet 16, Wiesel was crammed into a freight car along with his parents and three sisters and sent to Auschwitz, where he was tattooed with the number A-7713. He and his father were separated from his mother and sisters and sent to work as slave labor at the Bunawerke, a subcamp of Auschwitz. They remained together for a year, surviving a death march to Buchenwald in the winter of 1944–1945, until his father died just a short time before **liberation** by the Americans in April 1945. Both of Wiesel's parents and one of his sisters perished during the Holocaust.

After the liberation, Wiesel was taken to Paris, where he lived in an orphanage. Between 1947 and 1950, he studied Talmud, philosophy, and literature at the Sorbonne, attending lectures by Jean-Paul Sartre and Martin Buber. Working as a teacher of Hebrew and a choirmaster to supplement his income, he then became a journalist. He steadfastly refused, however, to write about or discuss his Holocaust experiences. A meeting with the 1952 Nobel Laureate for Literature, François Mauriac, however, convinced him of the need to begin writing about his experiences, and this was to lead him on an altogether unexpected path as the recognized voice of Holocaust survivors everywhere.

His best-known work is his Holocaust memoir, *Night*. This was first written in Yiddish, Wiesel's first language. In its initial incarnation, it ran to more than 800 pages. A version of this, published in 1956 in Argentina, *Un di Velt Hot Geshvign* (*And the World Remained Silent*), was substantially shorter at 245 pages. Wiesel then halved the manuscript in French, publishing it in 1958 as *La Nuit*. The book was then further translated into English as *Night* and published in 1960.

The success of this version has been nothing less than phenomenal. It has been translated into 30 languages, and millions of copies have been sold in the United States alone.

Night is a work of considerable linguistic power, proceeding from a style that is at once stripped of all extravagance and consisting of a multitude of memorable phrases. Nearly every line, it seems, is quotable. Wiesel, the religiously pious teenager from a country village, appears as an anguished soul tortured by having survived an experience that took his parents, sister, and so many others. The book witnesses the death of his innocence and belief in God. Recurring themes throughout *Night*, in fact, are his increasing disgust with mankind and his loss of faith. A single question gnaws at him and does not allow him to rest: How can a loving God, the same God in whom he had once placed his very being, have allowed the events of the Holocaust to occur? The book is filled with descriptions and reflections that are inspirational and worthy of citation, and its very readability, coupled with the story it relates, has led to it being adopted in school curricula the world over. It is arguably as well-known to generations of schoolchildren as *The Diary of a Young Girl* by **Anne Frank**.

Night is a work about Wiesel's experience with his father at Auschwitz and Buchenwald during 1944–1945. Beyond simple autobiography, it explores the inversion of the parent-child relationship, in which his father deteriorates into a state of helplessness and Wiesel becomes the one to teach his father how to survive. It also shows how, when his father was unable to cope and became weaker and weaker, Wiesel's childhood was lost.

It was from this moment, perhaps, that for Wiesel any future life would be dedicated to ethical issues and the will to bear witness to the Nazi horror. *Night*, in recording Wiesel's experience, came to be a symbolic recording of the experience of all Jews, and as a result, he dedicated his life to ensuring that no one can forget what happened. For Wiesel, "Never Again!" was more than a phrase; it became his life's mission, to ensure that no one could be allowed to say they hadn't been told about the reality he tried to convey.

In 1955 Wiesel moved to the United States and made his home in New York, and he became a U.S. citizen in 1963. From 1972 to 1976, he was the Distinguished Professor of Judaic Studies at the City University of New York, and in 1976 he was appointed Andrew W. Mellon Professor in the Humanities at Boston University. Wiesel's work received recognition from the U.S. government in 1978, when he was appointed chair of the Presidential Commission on the Holocaust established by President Jimmy Carter. In 1980 the Commission was renamed the U.S. Holocaust Memorial Council, and Wiesel remained chair until 1986. In further acknowledgment of his contribution to the betterment of society, he was awarded the Congressional Gold Medal of Freedom in 1985, the Nobel Peace Prize in 1986, and an honorary knighthood from Britain's Queen Elizabeth II in recognition of his advocacy of Holocaust education in the United Kingdom. He was elected to the American Academy of Arts and Letters in 1996.

Having survived the Holocaust, Elie Wiesel did all in his power to foster the kind of understanding that will enable people to see the necessity of developing an appropriate degree of compassion to defeat indifference and thereby prevent more atrocities and other genocides. He died on the morning of July 2, 2016, at his home in Manhattan, aged 87.

Further Reading

Berenbaum, Michael. *The Vision of the Void: Theological Reflections on the Works of Elie Wiesel.* Middletown, CT: Wesleyan University Press, 1979.
Fine, Ellen S. *Legacy of Night: The Literary Universe of Elie Wiesel.* Albany: State University of New York Press, 1982.
Wiesel, Elie. *Night.* New York: Hill and Wang, 1960.

WINTON, NICHOLAS (1909–2015)

Sir Nicholas Winton was a British stockbroker who organized a rescue operation that brought 669 children, almost all of them Jewish, from Czechoslovakia to safety in Britain before the outbreak of World War II.

He was born Nicholas Wertheim on May 19, 1909, in West Hampstead, England. His parents were Rudolf and Barbara Wertheim, German Jews who came to London in 1907. To acculturate, they changed their name to Winton, converted to Christianity, and ensured that their son was baptized into the Church of England. Rudolf Wertheim-Winton, a successful banker, saw that his family wanted for nothing, and Nicholas was raised to a life of some comfort. After attending the Stowe School in Buckingham (where he began but left without graduating), Winton followed in his father's footsteps as a banker, learning his profession working in banks in Hamburg, London, Berlin, and Paris. In 1931, after working for the *Banque Nationale de Crédit* in Paris, he returned to England and began his career at the London Stock Exchange.

As a young man, Winton held progressive views on several issues, aligning himself with many matters close to the agenda of the Labour Party. He was opposed to the Conservative government's policy of appeasement and expressed apprehension over German Nazism.

In December 1938 Winton was about to leave for a Christmas skiing holiday in Switzerland when he received a phone call from his friend Martin Blake—a teacher at London's Westminster School and an associate of the British Committee for Refugees from Czechoslovakia—asking him to forgo his vacation and instead come immediately to Prague. The British Committee had been established in October 1938 to assist refugees after Germany's annexation of the Sudeten regions following the Munich Agreement the previous month. Winton was happy to do so, and upon his arrival in Prague, Blake introduced him to his colleague, Doreen Wariner, arranging for him to visit refugee camps filled with Jews and political prisoners.

Winton was appalled by what he saw, and Blake and Wariner invited him to assist Jews in danger of their lives. He decided to act and began to establish an organization to aid Jewish children.

The timing could not have been more opportune. On the night of November 9–10, 1938, the Nazis launched the pogrom that became known as *Kristallnacht*,

WINTON, NICHOLAS (1909–2015)

Nicholas Winton in October 2007, at the age of 98. Winton was a British stockbroker. Learning that the *Kindertransport* rescue initiative applied only to Germany and Austria, in 1939 he set about putting together a small team to help organize a rescue operation for Jewish children in the lands that had comprised Czechoslovakia. In an unofficial capacity, his rescue operation brought 669 children, almost all of them Jewish, to safety in Britain before the outbreak of World War II. In 2002 he was knighted by Queen Elizabeth II. (Courtesy of Li-sung)

and Winton learned that in the aftermath, the British government had approved a measure to allow the entry of Jewish refugees younger than 17 on the proviso that they had a place to stay and landing money of £50 to enable them eventually to return home. He then also learned of how some Jewish relief organizations in Britain were planning to rescue German and Austrian Jewish children on what became known as the **Kindertransport** program. This was an initiative that eventually brought some 10,000 unaccompanied children to safety in Britain.

Winton was told, however, that whereas the *Kindertransport* initiative applied to Germany and Austria, there was no organization in Prague to deal with Jewish refugee children.

Accordingly, he put together a small team to help organize a rescue operation for children in the Czech lands. Without authorization, he established a Children's Section of the British Committee for Refugees from Czechoslovakia and began taking applications from parents in Prague. Racing against the clock to find foster homes in Britain, raise funds, and obtain exit papers, Winton opened an office on Vorsilska Street in which his appointees, Trevor Chadwick and Bill Barazetti, worked continually to assist the thousands of parents who soon began lining up, trying to find a haven for their children. After Winton returned to Britain, leaving Chadwick in charge in Prague, he contacted foreign governments to ask if they would be prepared to accept the children. Only Sweden and Britain agreed to do so.

In trying to save as many children as possible, Winton worked to arrange facilities for their reception in Britain. He faced many obstacles. The Dutch government had closed its borders to Jewish refugees after *Kristallnacht*, and Winton knew he would have to negotiate an agreement in order to enable the children to transit through Holland for embarkation to Britain. He also had to find foster homes, so that he could assure the Dutch authorities that the children had somewhere to go and would not remain in the Netherlands. To secure places in

British homes and hostels, he placed newspaper advertisements seeking families prepared to accept the children, and then arranged for their transportation. He also had to raise money to fund this and the British government's £50 guarantee required for each child.

At every turn he was successful, and on March 14, 1939—one day prior to the German occupation of the Czech lands—the first of Winton's transports left Prague by plane for London. He then arranged another seven transports, leaving Prague by train across Germany to the Netherlands, and then by ferry to Britain. In London, the children were met by their British foster parents. The last trainload of children to arrive in Britain from Prague left on August 2, 1939.

One final group of 250, the biggest thus far, was scheduled to leave Prague on September 1, 1939. They did not make it. On that day Germany invaded Poland, and all German borders were closed. Two days later, Britain and Germany were at war, and all further rescue activities ceased. The train carrying the 250 children was shunted out of sight, and the children were never seen again.

Overall, Nicholas Winton found homes in Britain for 669 children, many of whose parents would later perish at Auschwitz. After the war, Winton's rescue efforts remained practically unknown and unremembered. In 1988, his wife Grete—whom he had married in 1948, and who knew nothing of this earlier episode in his life—found a scrapbook from 1939 chronicling the full story. His attitude was that he did not think anyone would have been interested.

Winton's achievements were recognized around the world, particularly in Britain and the Czech Republic. In 1993 Queen Elizabeth II awarded him an MBE (Member of the British Empire), and on October 28, 1998, the president of the Czech Republic, Václav Havel, recognized his achievement with the award of the Order of T. G. Masaryk. Queen Elizabeth then went further than her earlier award and knighted him on December 31, 2002, for his services to humanity. In 2008 the Czech government nominated Winton for the 2008 Nobel Peace Prize, and in 2010 he was named a Hero of the Holocaust by the British government. On October 28, 2014 he was awarded the highest honor of the Czech Republic, the Order of the White Lion, by Czech President Miloš Zeman; and finally, on February 23, 2015, he was awarded the Freedom of the City of London. Winton's Jewish ancestry disqualified him from being declared Righteous among the Nations by Yad Vashem.

Sir Nicholas Winton died peacefully in his sleep on the morning of July 1, 2015 at Wexham Park Hospital in Slough. He was 106 years old.

Further Reading

Emanuel, Muriel, and Vera Gissing. *Nicholas Winton and the Rescued Generation: Save One Life, Save the World.* Edgeware, UK: Vallentine, Mitchell, 2001.

Smith, Lyn. *Heroes of the Holocaust: Ordinary Britons who Risked Their Lives to Make a Difference.* London: Edbury Press, 2012.

Winton, Barbara. *If It's Not Impossible . . . : The Life of Sir Nicholas Winton.* Leicester: Troubador Publishing, 2014.

WORLD FEDERATION OF JEWISH CHILD SURVIVORS OF THE HOLOCAUST AND DESCENDANTS

The World Federation of Jewish Child Survivors of the Holocaust and Descendants is an international organization of child Holocaust survivors and their children in the **Second Generation** and beyond. Its mission is to bring together survivors and descendants to share their families' unique histories and to keep alive the memory of the Jewish victims of the Holocaust, including 1.5 million children. The key objectives of the organization are to represent the interests of the child survivor community and to support each other, and to pass on their legacy to future generations. It pursues these objectives by relating accounts of their survival, by community interaction, education, and by holding conferences and fighting antisemitism.

The organization was established in 1985 at an American Gathering of Holocaust Survivors meeting in Philadelphia, Pennsylvania, when Dr. Judith Kestenberg, a child psychiatrist who had founded the International Study of Organized Persecution of Children, convened a session during the gathering. During the 1970s Kestenberg had earlier treated several patients in her psychoanalytic practice who were child Holocaust survivors, and the more she studied their issues, the more she recognized that while they were often too young to fully remember their experiences, they were, nonetheless, traumatized by them. This led to her studying the conditions facing Jewish children during the Holocaust in order to help them recover their memories and combat their traumas.

Child survivors from all over the United States and Canada attended that Philadelphia meeting. Addressing the gathering, Kestenberg noted that those who had survived as children were often overlooked by the older generation of survivors, and for many who were there, it validated their own feelings and experiences.

A group of child survivors had met a few years earlier in Los Angeles at the instigation of a California therapist, Dr. Sarah Moskovitz, author of *Love Despite Hate: Child Survivors of the Holocaust*. During her travels, she convened groups who had survived as children, and informal groups arose.

It was agreed in Philadelphia that, building on this start, further gatherings should be organized. Small groups were established in a number of communities worldwide, essentially for the purpose of offering mutual support in a safe and understanding environment. Soon, the World Federation of Jewish Child Survivors of the Holocaust and Descendants was formed. The founders wanted to give their organization a name that would include all who had survived as children, regardless of the circumstances of their survival—whether in camps, the **Kindertransports**, in hiding, or by escaping to places outside the Nazi grasp.

Following this, annual conferences began to be held in cities across the United States and Canada as well as in Amsterdam, Prague, Jerusalem, Warsaw, and Berlin. The intention of the conferences was to build connections between the survivors and create a caring community where they could share personal histories, support each another, and celebrate life. It did not take long before the organization also began also to include the generations of the descendants, recognizing that they, too, bear traumatic scars from the Holocaust.

Members of the World Federation have since established a speakers' bureau, volunteering to address schools, the general public, and community events. Among other topics discussed, they relate their personal histories of survival and loss, of resilience, of the heroism of Jews who helped other Jews (this is a key feature of the Federation's activities), and of rescuers designated as Righteous among the Nations. The descendants honor the memory of the survivor families by telling their histories and contributing to continued programs of Holocaust remembrance around the world. Further, the World Federation of Jewish Child Survivors of the Holocaust and Descendants is in the forefront of the fight against antisemitism and all forms of bigotry, striving to impart the lessons of the Holocaust—the lessons of tolerance, democratic values, and empathy for humanity as a whole.

Further Reading

World Federation of Jewish Child Survivors of the Holocaust and Descendants, at https://www.holocaustchild.org/.

Y

YAD VASHEM CHILDREN'S MEMORIAL

Yad Vashem, Israel's Holocaust Martyrs' and Heroes' Remembrance Authority, was established in 1953 by an act of Israel's Knesset to commemorate the six million Jewish men, women, and children murdered by the Nazis and their collaborators during the Holocaust. Located on the western slope of Mount Herzl on the Mount of Remembrance in Jerusalem, the site was chosen specifically because the area was not, at that point, crowded out with competing draws of historical significance.

The site consists of a large complex containing the Holocaust History Museum, memorial sites such as the Children's Memorial and the Hall of Remembrance, the Museum of Holocaust Art, sculptures, outdoor commemorative sites such as the Valley of the Communities, a synagogue, a research institute with archives, a library, a publishing house, and an educational center named the International School for Holocaust Studies.

A view of the entrance to the Children's Memorial at Yad Vashem. Yad Vashem, Israel's Holocaust Martyrs' and Heroes' Remembrance Authority, is located on the western slope of Mount Herzl on the Mount of Remembrance in Jerusalem. The Children's Memorial at Yad Vashem commemorates the approximately 1.5 million Jewish children who were murdered by the Nazis and their collaborators during the Holocaust. Here, the names, ages, and birthplaces of those known to have died, taken from Pages of Testimony in Yad Vashem's Hall of Names, are continually recited. (Courtesy of Bahnfrend)

The Children's Memorial is a tribute to the approximately 1.5 million Jewish children who were murdered by the Nazis and their collaborators. Here, the names, ages, and birthplaces of those known to have died are continually recited. The names are taken from Pages of Testimony in Yad Vashem's Hall of Names.

The Children's Memorial is unique and dominated by symbolism. Standing in front are a cluster of stark-looking, unfinished cement pillars of different heights, reminding visitors that children of all ages and stages of life were murdered in the Holocaust. This leads to a descending entrance ramp cut from the rock, which takes visitors down a hall that decreases in size as they proceed, implying a sense of growing confinement. Indeed, to traverse this, visitors are required to walk in single file. This, in turn, heads toward an underground cavern, also hollowed out from the living rock. Inside, an octagonal room is lit by a memorial candle, reflected in a series of semireflective glass panels and mirrors which line the walls, floors, and ceiling, scattering sparks of light like stars in the universe. In the background a voice intones the names and ages of the children, their countries of origin, and the camps in which they died. To the left, just beyond the entrance, the walkway opens onto an area devoted to displaying large images of diverse black-and-white pictures of these children's faces. Visitors walk through the reflecting lights, exiting to a terrace overlooking the Judean Hills.

In 1976, the Holocaust Martyrs' and Heroes' Remembrance Authority appointed architect Moshe Safdie to design a museum devoted to the children who perished in the Holocaust. To the idea of a museum, Safdie presented a counterproposal: a children's memorial that he would design that would be in keeping with his understanding of Yad Vashem's mandate, which is to commemorate the Jews murdered by the Nazis, recognize the destroyed communities, and establish appropriate projects of memorialization. The challenge he then faced was to create the setting for a horrific narrative that would, at the same time, culminate in an uplifting celebration of renewal. The Children's Memorial, opened in 1987, is the result. It was funded through a donation from Abe and Edita Spiegel, Holocaust survivors and philanthropists, whose son Uziel was murdered in Auschwitz at the age of two and a half.

The Yad Vashem Children's Memorial is a place of memory and contemplation. Its revolutionary design is intended to promote a true comprehension of the nature of the Holocaust while raising questions of the nature of war, yet each person's comprehension of the experience will differ—as though the objectives of the design team would be for individual reflection rather than some sort of directed appreciation which could, in the long run, be meaningless. Although no one can visualize 1.5 million dead children, the intimacy of the Memorial gives a glimpse of the experience that can serve as an aid to understanding.

Further Reading

Gutterman, Bella, and Avner Shalev (Eds.). *To Bear Witness: Holocaust Remembrance at Yad Vashem*. Jerusalem: Yad Vashem, 2005.

Ockman, Joan, Moshe Safdie, Avner Shalev, and Elie Wiesel. *Yad Vashem: Moshe Safdie—The Architecture of Memory*. Jerusalem: Yad Vashem, 2006.

Z

ŻEGOTA

The term *Żegota* was a shorthand name for the Konrad Żegota Committee, part of the Polish underground movement's Council to Aid Jews (*Rada Pomocy Żydom*). The Council operated from late fall 1942 until the liberation of Poland in 1945. Unlike many such organizations during World War II, it did not go by an acronym.

The Council originated as the Provisional Committee for Aid to Jews (*Tymczasowy Komitet Pomocy Żydom*), founded on September 27, 1942, by writer Zofia Kossak-Szczucka and a member of Poland's social elite, Wanda Krahelska-Filipowicz ("Alinka"). This was a largely Catholic group and was transformed into Żegota on December 4, 1942. Żegota became a broad-based joint organization of Jews and non-Jews from different political orientations. It was the brainchild of Henryk Woliński, a member of the Home Army; its general secretary was a member of Poland's Socialist Party, and its treasurer was a member of the Polish Democratic Party. Its fundamental aim was the common cause of saving Jews in danger from the Nazis, and in this regard, Poland was the only country in Nazi-occupied Europe where such an organization, run jointly by Jews and non-Jews from a wide range of political movements, existed.

After a circuitous route, by the late spring of 1944, much of the funding it received was arriving from the Polish government-in-exile in London. The financial resources needed to save even one Jewish life ranged from 6,000 to 15,000 złotys. Depending on the situation, Żegota's monthly budget ranged from 500,000 to 2 million złotys, which, though seemingly large, did not meet the needs of saving many Jewish lives. As a result, and wherever possible, Żegota operatives sought to prop up their resources in alternate ways.

The means it employed to help save Jews were many, but it was found to be much easier to assist Jews if they were outside ghettos and on the Aryan side. Medical attention was provided for Jews in hiding, along with food and false identity documents. Żegota attempted (and often succeeded) in providing help for Jews in forced labor camps, while financial aid was provided when possible. Sometimes it was able to assist in escapes, though these could often not be planned; it was more likely that advantages had to be made of local circumstances as and when they presented themselves. One of Żegota's major tasks related to the forging of documents, such that on average, Żegota was said to have been producing up to 100 sets of forged papers per day.

Żegota also played an important role in saving Jewish children by placing them with foster families or relocating them to orphanages and convents. In Warsaw the head of Żegota's children's section, a Polish social worker named **Irena Sendler**, assumed near-legendary status by personally taking care of over 2,500 Jewish children. Sendler, who was one of many members of Żegota recognized by Israel's Yad Vashem as Righteous among the Nations, was nominated for a Nobel Prize before her death in 2008.

By the time the Council was established, most of Poland's Jews had been killed, but the organization's activists, at enormous personal risk, managed to help several thousand Jews. Indeed, it has been estimated that about half the Jews who survived the Holocaust in Poland—a figure representing over 50,000 people—were helped by Żegota in one way or another.

To as great an extent as possible, Żegota operated as a professional organization. Although extensive in its spread, its work was based on smaller cells, with up to 100 of these in Warsaw alone. Elsewhere, it operated in Kraków, Vilna (Vilnius), and Lvov (L'viv), with specific departments dealing with issued such as legal, housing, clothing, children's welfare, medical care, and finances, among others.

Poland, the only Nazi-occupied country where helping Jews was punishable by death, was also the only country that saw the establishment of an organization such as Żegota. It has been estimated that during the war, perhaps up to 20,000 members of Żegota were captured and executed by the Germans, with thousands of others imprisoned and sent to concentration camps. It was remarkable that the location of Żegota's head office in Warsaw, at 24 Zurawia Street, was well known to Poles but was never raided by the Germans. Żegota was a truly unique phenomenon within the horror of the Holocaust, which bought the lives of tens of thousands of Jews at the cost of tens of thousands of Poles. In an environment in which the history of Polish relations with Jews has frequently been soured by expressions of antisemitism, this stands as a shining example of what could have been done throughout the rest of Europe if more people of goodwill had decided that it was necessary to make a stand.

Further Reading

Tomaszewski, Irene, and Tecia Werbowski. *Code Name: Żegota: Rescuing Jews in Occupied Poland, 1942–1945: The Most Dangerous Conspiracy in Wartime Europe.* Santa Barbara, CA: Praeger, 2010.

Primary Source Documents

The documents that follow, selected from a vast number of possibilities, represent a snapshot of some of the ways children were affected by the Holocaust. The Third Reich affected children in myriad ways between 1933 and 1945, as the many reference entries shown throughout in this book demonstrate. Often, however, records are hard to locate, particularly where there were no survivors of a specific situation or when, owing to the clandestine nature of rescue activities, records were not kept for fear of exposure or denunciation. An attempt has therefore been made here to provide a varied range of sources that will give readers an idea of the types of documents that can be accessed to illustrate the experience of children during the Holocaust.

1. *The Jewish Question in Education* (1937)

Der Stürmer, a weekly Nazi newspaper edited by notorious antisemite Julius Streicher, printed a pamphlet for teachers in 1937 outlining how to teach German children about Jews and the so-called Jewish Question. The pamphlet was entitled The Jewish Question in Education (Die Judenfrage im Unterricht) *and was written by Nazi supporter Fritz Fink. Introduced by Streicher, the pamphlet's tone is clear from the start, when it refers to "the monstrous character and dangerousness of the Jew." It urged teachers to incorporate antisemitic tropes into every part of the curriculum. Students were exposed in the classroom to* The Jewish Question in Education, *with passages assigned pointing out the different physiognomy of Jews that made them a danger to Aryan society. Seeing that children were the future in the Nazi campaign against the Jews, Fink criticized teachers who did not give themselves wholeheartedly over to antisemitic propaganda. Streicher, for his part, ensured that the pamphlet was given considerable publicity in* Der Stürmer, *and he republished it and gave it wider coverage almost as soon as it was released.*

The National Socialist state brought fundamental changes into all spheres of life of the German People.

It has also presented the German teacher with some new tasks. The national socialist state demands that its teachers instruct German children in social questions. As far as the German people is concerned the racial question is a Jewish question. Those who want to teach the child all about the Jew must themselves have a thorough knowledge of the subject. School Inspector Fritz Fink, with his publication "The Jewish Question and school instruction," will help the teacher in acquiring some knowledge of the subject. He can and is entitled to do this, for he himself has been called upon by circumstances to take part in a struggle which enabled him to gain experience and knowledge concerning Jewish blood and its influence on the

German People. Those who take to heart all that has been written with such feeling by Fritz Fink who for many years has been greatly concerned about the German People, will be grateful to the creator of this outwardly insignificant publication. . . .

Racial and Jewish questions are the fundamental problems of the national socialist ideology. The solution of these problems will secure the existence of National Socialism and with this the existence of our nation for all time. The enormous significance of the racial question is recognized almost without exception today by all the German people. In order to attain this recognition, our people had to travel through a long road of suffering. In order that the coming generation be spared this suffering, let us, the German educators of our youth, instill in their hearts, from their early childhood, all there is to know about the Jews. No one should be allowed to grow up in the midst of our people without this knowledge of the monstrous character and dangerousness of the Jew. . . .

Knowledge of racial and Jewish questions must grow organically out of our general system of school education. The racial doctrine and the Jewish question must be like a red thread marking the education of all age groups in our school education. There is no subject from which cannot be drawn an unsuspected full measure of valuable knowledge of the Jewish question.

The attached pamphlet, "The Jewish question and School Instruction," was brought out in an urgent desire to show up some of these possibilities. . . .

The Jewish Question and School Instruction

From the ranks of the teachers comes now the question: "How should we represent the Jew to our pupils?" Only one answer can be given to this question: "In all his monstrosity, horror and dangerousness." Such as he is. . . .

A teacher who has come to a thorough understanding of the Jewish question will make use in his work of the "Stürmer." He reads to the class extracts from an Article which describes how a Jew deceived a peasant etc.

Thus we glide from the purely outward appearance of the Jew to his inner nature. Our fight against the Jew is not for the reason that he is different in body to ourselves. The bodily difference is not the dangerous part of the Jew. We must make it clear to a child that in the strange appearance of a Jew, which is immediately conspicuous to us, lies a soul, which is fundamentally different in all its emotions and manifestations, from our souls. We must point out that the Jew thinks, feels, and behaves in a different manner from ourselves. That his way of thinking, of feeling and of behaviour is diametrically opposed to our morals and our laws.

Jewry is Criminality

But the fact, that in deceit, usury, murder, etc. Jews see no crime but consider them as acts pleasing to their God when they are directed against non-Jews—will appear most monstrous to our children. At first it will frighten the children and they will shake their heads incredulously. In the same way as millions of people in Germany scornfully shook their heads when the national socialists and foremost of all the "Stürmer" exposed the criminal methods and criminal laws of the Jews. "But deceit, usury, falsehood are sins." A boy in the class will cry out, "We are forbidden to commit them!" The teacher will ask: "Who forbade you to commit them?" "Our conscience. The laws of the State, God."

But if deceit, usury, falsehood, etc. are not crimes, not sin in the eyes of the Jews, then a Jew must have a different conscience, different laws, and a different God than we have, and thus the teacher and his pupils will suddenly find themselves thoroughly involved in the Jewish question and in its most serious aspect.

The manner in which he (the teacher) pursues the question with the children should make clear to them the fundamental reason for all Jewish acts.

One who has reached this stage of understanding, will inevitably remain an enemy of the Jews all his life and will instill this hatred into his own children.

Source: *Nazi Conspiracy and Aggression*, Office of the United States Chief of Counsel for the Prosecution of Axis Criminality (Washington, D.C.: U.S. Government Printing Office, 1946), Red Series, vol. VIII, pp. 30–32, Doc. M-46.

Commentary

Soon after assuming office, the Nazis reformed Germany's education system in order to indoctrinate the country's youth. In fact, no sector of the Nazi new order took higher priority than Germany's young. After ensuring that all Jews had been removed from the public education system, the Nazis focused on changing what students learned, altering the core curriculum to place an emphasis on sport, history, and racial science. Textbooks had to be approved by the Ministry of Education, and teachers had to become members of the Nazi Party or be dismissed. By 1937, 97 percent of all teachers belonged to the National Socialist Teachers' Union, and every member of the union had to submit a table of ancestry demonstrating that they were true Aryans.

The Jewish problem as addressed within the Nazi curriculum was definitively dealt with in a pamphlet written by Nazi supporter Fritz Fink and published in the pages of Julius Streicher's *Der Stürmer* in 1937. It was entitled *Die Judenfrage im Unterricht* (*The Jewish Question in Education*), parts of which are reproduced in this document.

The author, Fritz Fink, wrote a piece containing guidelines in which he spelled out how to identify Jews, and his pamphlet urged teachers to incorporate antisemitism into all parts of the national curriculum. He asserted that knowledge of "the racial and Jewish Question must grow organically from the whole curriculum of our schools."

In the introduction written by Julius Streicher, the editor of *Der Stürmer* stated, "The National Socialist state requires its teachers to teach German children racial theory. For the German people, racial theory means the Jewish problem." As a result, the manual asserts that German children are already innately opposed to Jews, though perhaps they do not quite know why. It is therefore up to the teachers to draw out this opposition and facilitate the children's hatred.

The document reproduced here contains parts of the introduction by Julius Streicher as well as some of Fink's text. In some respects, the message is the same in both; indeed, the two pieces could practically have been written by the same pen. These, however, only touch on the core content of the pamphlet, in which Fink addresses a variety of important areas intended to condition students to the importance of race-thinking. Thus, intermarriage between Germans and Jews is portrayed as unnatural because in the Nazi conception, racial intermixing is contrary to nature. The Jews are an eternal enemy of the German people: the teacher will convey the message that "if deceit, usury, falsehood, etc. are not crimes, not sin in the eyes of the Jews, then a Jew must have a different conscience, different laws, and a different God than we have." The notion of the Jew as a deadly enemy of everything German must be made clear in the classroom, and the teacher's guide suggests that visual depictions of stereotypical Jews should be posted on the blackboard adjacent to those of perfect Aryans. This will not only serve a pedagogic role, teaching students how to spot a Jew; it will also reinforce the racial superiority of those in the ideal German classroom.

The Jewish Question in Education concludes by looking at the record of history, showing how Jews had always been in the forefront of the destruction of major civilizations such as Egypt, Persia, and Rome; the lesson was a salutary one. Germans (and this meant German children in school) should always be on their guard to ensure that Jews, who posed a danger to the very existence of German society, are identified and rooted out wherever they could be found.

The pamphlet shows that with solid racial teaching, an opportunity is presented for the child to go from being a passive recipient of information on the destruction caused by Jews to an active participant in the war against them. Nazi propaganda is therefore viewed here from within an adult frame of reference. Teachers reading this manual will see that children can be provided with an immediacy that can show them that the racial struggle is in their own interests, as well as in that of the nation overall. Although they might have instinctive negative feelings toward Jews, how to channel these feelings is something that must be carefully taught. Doing so will help the children understand why their prejudice is necessary and desirable in the Nazi state.

2. *The Poisonous Mushroom* (1938)

Published in 1938, The Poisonous Mushroom (Der Giftpilz) *was a Nazi propaganda book for children containing 17 short stories, each with its own brightly colored illustration. It was written by Ernst Hiemer, illustrated by Philipp Rupprecht (Fips), and published by Julius Streicher, the infamous publisher of the Nazi newspaper* Der Stürmer. *The book's title is explained in its first story. While searching in the forest for mushrooms, a mother tells her young son that bad mushrooms are poisonous and look very much like good ones that are edible, making it hard to tell one from the other. The distinction between mushrooms becomes the model for the distinction between Germans and Jews: Germans are good people, and Jews are bad people who can disguise themselves, making their evil hard to recognize. The mother tells her son about the different kinds of "poisonous Jews," each of which is depicted in its own chapter of the book: the Jewish peddler, the Jewish cattle dealer, the kosher butcher, the Jewish doctor, and so on. Each story depicts the very worst of antisemitic stereotypes, and each one ends with a short "jingle," such as that in the first of three excerpts included in this document.*

THE POISONOUS MUSHROOM [Der Giftpilz]

A Stürmer book for young and old Fables by Ernst Hiemer
Pictures by Fips

"It is almost noon," he said, "now we want to summarize what we have learned in this lesson. What did we discuss?"

All children raise their hands. The teacher calls on Karl Scholz, a little boy on the first bench. "We talked about how to recognize a Jew."

"Good! Now tell us about it!"

Little Karl takes the pointer, goes to the black board and points to the sketches.

"One usually recognizes a Jew by his nose. The Jewish nose is crooked at the end. It looks like the figure 6. Therefore, it is called the 'Jewish Six.' Many non-Jews have crooked noses, too. But their noses are bent, not at the end but further up. Such a nose is called a hook nose or eagle's beak. It has nothing to do with a Jewish nose."

"Right!" says the teacher. "But the Jew is recognized not only by his nose . . ." The boy continues. The Jew is also recognized by his lips. His lips are usually thick. Often the lower lip hangs down. That is called "sloppy." And the Jew is also recognized by his eyes. His eyelids are usually thicker and more fleshy than ours. The look of the Jew is lurking and sharp. . . .

Then the teacher goes to the desk and turns over the black board, on its back is a verse. The children recite it in chorus:

> From a Jew's countenance—the evil devil talks to us,
> The devil, who in every land—is known as evil plague.
> If we shall be free of the Jew—and again will be happy and glad,
> Then the youth must struggle with us—to subdue the Jew devil. ...

Inge sits in the reception room of the Jew doctor. She has to wait a long time. She looks through the journals which are on the table. But she is most too nervous to read even a few sentences. Again and again she remembers the talk with her mother. And again and again her mind reflects on the warnings of her leader of the BDM [League of German Girls]: "A German must not consult a Jew doctor! And particularly not a German girl! Many a girl that went to a Jew doctor to be cured, found disease and disgrace!"

When Inge had entered the waiting room, she experienced an extraordinary incident. From the doctor's consulting room she could hear the sound of crying. She heard the voice of a young girl: "Doctor, doctor leave me alone!"

Then she heard the scornful laughing of a man. And then all of a sudden it became absolutely silent. Inge had listened breathlessly.

"What may be the meaning of all this?" she asked herself and her heart was pounding. And again she thought of the warning of her leader in the BDM.

Inge was already waiting for an hour. Again she takes the journals in an endeavor to read. Then the door opens. Inge looks up. The Jew appears. She screams. In terror she drops the paper. Frightened she jumps up. Her eyes stare into the face of the Jewish doctor. And this face is the face of the devil. In the middle of this devil's face is a huge crooked nose. Behind the spectacles two criminal eyes. And the thick lips are grinning. A grinning that expresses: "Now I got you at last, you little German girl!"

And then the Jew approaches her. His fleshy fingers stretch out after her. But now Inge has her wits. Before the Jew can grab hold of her, she hits the fat face of the Jew doctor with her hand. Then one jump to the door. Breathlessly Inge runs down the stairs. Breathlessly she escapes the Jew house.

The *pimpf* [Hitler Youth boy between 10 and 14] so far has not said anything. Suddenly he stops. Then he grasps his two friends by the arm and pulls them away. They stop in front of a bill-board. They read a large poster. It says Julius Streicher makes an address in the People's Hall about "The Jews are our misfortune."

"That is where we go!" shouts Konrad, "I wanted to hear him speak for a long time." "I have heard him once before at a meeting two years ago," says Erich. "Do tell us all about it!" the two *pimpfs* beg.

The Hitler youth recounts:

"The meeting was overcrowded. Many thousands of people attended. To begin with, Streicher talked of his experiences in the years of struggle, and of the tremendous achievements of the Hitler Reich. Then he began to talk about the Jewish question. All he said was so clear and simple that even we boys could follow it. Again and again he told about examples taken from life. At one time he talked most amusingly and cracked jokes, making all of us laugh. Then again he became most serious, and it was so quiet in the hall that one could hear a needle drop. He talked of the Jews and their horrible crimes. He talked of the serious danger which Judaism is for the whole world.

"'Without a solution of the Jewish question there will be no salvation of mankind.'

"That is what he shouted to us. All of us could understand him. And when, at the end, he shouted the 'Sieg-Heil' for the Führer, we all acclaimed him with tremendous enthusiasm. For two hours Streicher spoke at that occasion. To us it appeared to have been but a few minutes."

Source: *Nazi Conspiracy and Aggression*, Office of the United States Chief of Counsel for the Prosecution of Axis Criminality (Washington, D.C.: U.S. Government Printing Office, 1946), Red Series, vol. IV, pp. 358–360, Doc. 1778-PS.

Commentary

Der Giftpilz was the title of a children's book published by Julius Streicher in 1938. Intended as antisemitic propaganda, it was a collection of 17 short stories written by Ernst Hiemer and illustrated by Philipp Rupprecht (known professionally as *Fips*).

The core purpose of the book, aimed at children and sometimes used in schools, was to show how Jews were the most detestable enemy of the German (Aryan) people and that children should always be on their guard against them. As such, the aim of the stories contained in the book was to indoctrinate German children to despise Jews at every turn. Further, as suggested in the book's title, Jews often camouflaged themselves as Germans, making it difficult to tell them apart from regular society—just as poisonous mushrooms are frequently difficult to discern from those that are edible. The first of the stories recounts a German mother explaining to her son how, just as there are good and bad people, there are edible and poisonous mushrooms: "Just as it is often hard to tell a toadstool from an edible mushroom, so too it is often very hard to recognize the Jew as a swindler and criminal." The Jews, she says, are a "poison" inside Germany, and, "Just as a single poisonous mushroom can kill a whole family, so a solitary Jew can destroy a whole village, a whole city, even an entire folk."

Preying on the anxieties of German children, the book warns them about the dangers posed by all Jews. However, the book's seductive approach does not stop there. The stories do not simply portray the Jews as evil and dangerous; the appeal is made to the children that they can themselves be heroic in identifying Jews and thereby support their parents and save Germany. As children learn "the truth" about the Jews, they demonstrate that they are trustworthy boys and girls who will grow up to become good German citizens.

The depictions of Jews in all the stories are intended both to frighten children and to alert them to the dangers Jews pose. Communism is portrayed as being led by Jews who wish to sacrifice Germany to Russia. Jews are depicted as being abusive toward their German servants; Jewish dietary laws cause extreme suffering to innocent animals. The book warns of Jews concentrated in various occupations, such as business, the law, or certain trades, where Jews make it a practice of cheating honest Germans. Throughout the book, Jews are revealed as people who enjoy it when good Germans suffer; the Jews, on the other hand, are evil and treacherous and revel in their own filth.

Jewish men are presented as pedophiles and sexual predators. As shown in the extract here, Jewish doctors are child molesters, particularly of German girls. The chapter from which this extract came also accused Jews of kidnapping Christian children to use their blood in Passover matzah, in a restatement of the age-old blood libel accusation. One of the book's final chapters blames the Jews for the death of Jesus, who, it is affirmed, the Jews consider to be their greatest enemy.

Focusing on any disquiet children might have as to where the Jews derive their malevolence, the book addresses the foundations of Jewish belief in the Talmud. A chapter relates numerous false claims, such as that the Talmud forbids Jews to do manual labor, that Jews are only permitted to engage in trade, that non-Jews ("Goys") are meant to be slaves, and that Jews are permitted to cheat non-Jews.

The book was viewed by the Nazi hierarchy as a boon for teachers, who were encouraged to utilize *Der Giftpilz* in the classroom when indoctrinating their students about racial hierarchy. In one story, shown in this extract, after appropriate instruction from the teacher, a boy in the class describes Jewish features: "One usually recognizes a Jew by his nose. The Jewish nose is crooked at the end. It looks like the figure 6. Therefore, it is called the 'Jewish Six.' Many non-Jews have crooked noses, too. But their noses are bent, not at the end but further up. Such a nose is called a hook nose or eagle's beak. It has nothing to do with a Jewish nose." In the text accompanying this picture, the young German boy is portrayed as crying out to his brother in horror: "Those sinister Jewish noses! Those lousy beards! Those dirty, standing out ears! Those bent legs! Those flat feet! Those stained, fatty clothes! Look how they move their hands about! How they haggle! And those are supposed to be men!"

Illustrated carefully for maximum effect, the accompanying captions leave their young readers in no illusions as to the conclusions to be drawn. Overall, the stories in *The Poisoned Mushroom* present the broad notion that Jews are inescapably evil and that all good German children should hate them.

3. Heinrich Himmler on the Responsibility to Beget Children (October 28, 1939 and January 30, 1940)

Initiated in 1935, the Nazi program of selective breeding of its population to produce a superior or "master" race, named Lebensborn, *or the "fountain of life," was established with the aim of increasing the birth rate of Aryan children. This was to be achieved by promoting the birth of German children conceived by couples with "racially pure" blood—in particular through the close breeding of German women who met stringent physical standards with SS men who met the same standards of height, weight, blond hair, blue eyes, and athleticism. It was not necessary for the couple to be married; all that mattered was that there should be an increase in the Aryan population. Reichsführer-SS Heinrich Himmler, who started the program, directed that it was the responsibility of SS men to expand the German population, and that "German women and girls of good blood" should become mothers "even out of wedlock," with incentives and rewards offered by the government for each child born. In this document, Himmler outlines the responsibilities of the SS men, explains the help that will be provided to pregnant women, and, in a subsequent statement, clarifies that the program was not to extend to SS men approaching the wives of soldiers in the field.*

Berlin, October 28, 1939
SS ORDER FOR THE ENTIRE SS AND POLICE

Every war causes the best blood to be shed. Many a victory of arms meant for a people at the same time a disastrous loss of living strength and blood. But unfortunately inevitable death of its best men, deplorable as that may be, is not the worst. Of much more disastrous consequences is the lack of those who were not begotten by the living during, and by the dead after the war.

The old saying that only those who have children can die in peace must again become an acknowledged truth in this war, especially for the SS. Only those who know that their kind, that all for which they and their ancestors have striven, is continued in their children, can die in peace. The possession most prized by the widow of a fallen soldier is always the child of the man whom she loved.

Though it may perhaps be considered an infraction of necessary social standards and convention in other times, German women and girls of good blood can fulfill a high obligation even out of wedlock by becoming mothers of children of soldiers going to the front, whose eventual return or death for Germany lies entirely in the hands of fate—not because of promiscuity, but because of the deepest sense of ethics. It is the sacred duty also of these men and women whose place has been determined by the state to be on the home front, to become parents of children again, especially now.

Let us never forget that the victory of the sword and of the spilled blood of our soldiers remains fruitless if it is not succeeded by the victory of the child and the colonizing of conquered soil.

In past wars, many a soldier has decided, out of a deep sense of responsibility, to beget no more children during the time of war, so as not to leave his wife and an additional child in want and distress in case of his death. You SS men need not have such worries; the following regulations eliminate them.

1. Special commissioners, personally appointed by me, shall be entrusted in the name of the Reich Leader with the guardianship of all legitimate and illegitimate children of good blood whose fathers were killed in action. We shall support these mothers and humanely assume the responsibility for the education and upbringing of these children so that no mother and widow need to have any material worries.
2. During the war the SS will care for all legitimate and illegitimate children begotten during the war and for pregnant mothers in cases of need and distress. After the war, the SS will generously grant additional material aid should these fathers who return request so. SS men and you mothers of these children, the hope of Germany show that in your belief in the Fuehrer and your willingness to do your share in the perpetuation of our blood and people, you are just as willing to continue the life of Germany as you have had the courage to fight and die for it.

Berlin 30 January 1940
TO ALL MEMBERS OF THE SS AND THE POLICE

You are all familiar with my order of October 28, 1939, in which I reminded you of your duty to become fathers of children if possible during the war.

This proclamation, which has been made in all decency and which considers, if correctly interpreted, problems to be faced in the future, has been greatly misunderstood by some people. I therefore deem it necessary for each and every one of you to know fully what doubts and misunderstandings have come up and what has to be said about them.

1. People are always shocked by the clearly expressed fact that there exist illegitimate children and that a number of unmarried women and girls have become mothers of such children, outside of matrimony. There is nothing to be discussed about that.

2. The greatest misunderstanding, however, resulted from the following statement: "Though it may perhaps appear an infraction of necessary social standards and convention in other times, German women and girls of good blood can fulfill a high obligation even out of wedlock, by becoming mothers of children of soldiers going to the front, whose eventual return or death for Germany lies entirely in the hands of fate-not because of promiscuity, but because of the deepest sense of ethics."

Many have misconstrued this statement and think it is an encouragement for SS men to approach wives of soldiers who are in the field. Impossible as it is for this thought to be understood, it must nevertheless be cleared up.

a. That no one approach the wife of a soldier who is in the field is as much matter of fact to us SS men as it is to every other German. This is a simple and natural law of ethics and comradeship.
b. I further assert that out of the app. 250,000 SS men before the war, 175,000 are under arms today, mostly with the Wehrmacht in the front lines, others with the SS units and regiments of Verfuegungstruppen, SS Death Head Units, military police, and with the SS Death Head Units on the Eastern front. That should be more than ample proof that the majority of SS are themselves at the front and not at home.
c. It is also feared that this order would tend to destroy family and honor, and that this order would cause men to be unwilling to marry. This can be refuted clearly by the following data: The percentage of married SS men on January 1, 1939, was 39 percent, while a year later it was 44 percent. These data speak for themselves and have not been surpassed by anyone so far as we know.
d. Another point comes up in connection, with this question: What do these people who spread or repeat such opinions, think of the German women? Even should some one man out of a population of 82 millions have the baseness or the human weakness to approach a married woman, then there are still two prerequisites necessary for seduction: the one who does the seducing and the other who lets herself be seduced.

We do not only believe that it is unethical to approach the wife of a comrade but also that the German woman herself is probably the best guardian of her marriage. Any other opinion should be regarded by all men as an insult to German women.

e. The question why, according to the order of October 28 1939, the women of the SS and the policemen are accorded special care which is not being granted to other women, is also being raised.

The answer is very simple: because the comradeship and the will to sacrifice has induced SS leaders and men to make voluntary contributions which incidentally have been paid for years to the organization "Lebensborn"—thus raising the necessary means.

This should have cleared up all misunderstandings. It is up to you SS men, however, to make all German men and women understand the full implication of this so vital and sacred a question so much above any frivolity and ridicule, as must always be done in epochs where people are representatives of ideologies.

Source: *Nazi Conspiracy and Aggression*, Office of the United States Chief of Counsel for the Prosecution of Axis Criminality (Washington, D.C.: U.S. Government Printing Office, 1946), Red Series, vol. V, pp. 466–469, Doc. 2825-PS.

Commentary

The Nazi conception of racial hygiene (*Rassenhygiene*) was first introduced and developed in 1894 by German physician Alfred Ploetz and picked up by many others in the early part of the 20th century. It was a concept that had at its base the notion of eugenics, the branch of knowledge dealing with the production of genetically superior human beings through improvements in their inherited qualities. For some, this translated into proposals calling for the compulsory sterilization of physically and psychologically "inferior" humans; for others, added to this could be measures designed to control the breeding of those with criminal tendencies, with incurable diseases (or even those that were curable, such as venereal disease), or with social abnormalities such as chronic alcoholism.

The fear of a degeneration in the German "race" should such things go unchecked became a crucial element of Nazi ideology, and it was attractive to the racial thinking that dominated the National Socialist world view—to such a degree that sterilization and, later, compulsory euthanasia became state policy for the purpose of ensuring the health and virility of the German people in the future.

An important element of this position could be found in Nazi population policy, in which breeding programs could be controlled and enhanced. After the passage of the Nuremberg Laws in 1935, it became compulsory for both marriage partners to be tested for hereditary diseases in order to preserve the perceived racial purity of the Aryan race. Members of the SS were cautioned to carefully interview prospective marriage partners to make sure they had no family history of hereditary disease or insanity.

Pursuant to this, also in 1935, the Nazi program of selective breeding known as *Lebensborn* (Spring of Life) was established. A series of clinics dispersed throughout Germany were created. This saw the introduction of a selective breeding scheme for the purpose of producing a superior race, the aim being to increase the birth rate of Aryan children. The focus of the program was one of pure racial reproduction, in which Nazi concepts of racial hygiene would come to the fore.

In the *Lebensborn* homes, the pregnant women—most of whom were single—went to deliver their babies in secret, where both mother and child were cared for in strictly controlled conditions by SS doctors and nurses. In most cases the mothers gave their children up for adoption to carefully screened SS families, and as abortion was illegal in Germany (other than for disabled children), the enhancement of the population was viewed as a patriotic duty.

To be accepted into the *Lebensborn* program, women had to have the right "racial" characteristics (such as blond hair and blue eyes) and prove that they had no genetic disorders. Without benefit of marriage, the program encouraged anonymous births by unmarried women who would become impregnated in SS-run "stud farms." These were often luxury hotels and spas where young women and men would meet prior to retiring discreetly to bedrooms, after which they would separate, never to meet again. Many of these SS officers already had their own legitimate families, but Heinrich Himmler, as shown in this document, encouraged his men to create children outside of marriage as a way of building a German master race.

An initiative of the SS, the program was state supported and an integral element of the Nazi racial system. Upon conception, the women were sent to special maternity homes where they were cared for until the birth of their children, following which the children would be adopted by parents who would be equally "racially pure" and thoroughly imbued with Nazi ideals. Although figures are difficult to ascertain, perhaps anywhere between 6,000 and 8,000 children were born to the program in Germany between 1936 and 1945. After the war, many of the actual records of such births were lost; thus, no actual numbers can be accurately assessed.

The document reproduced here, created two months into World War II, is a statement issued by *Reichsführer-SS* Heinrich Himmler to officers and men of the SS, outlining to them the urgent need to procreate. Racial purity dominated Himmler's mind-set, and with the war certain to take a toll of German life, he ordered the men of the SS to impregnate "German women and girls of good blood"—even "out of wedlock" if necessary—before going into battle. He told the SS that women, single or married, should, out of patriotic duty, allow themselves to be impregnated by soldiers who were about to go to war. Widowed women and orphaned children, Himmler promised, would be nurtured by the Nazi state. Himmler's procreation order was both a war measure to cover anticipated losses and a eugenic precaution to ensure the continuation of Aryan bloodlines.

4. Testimony of John Freund

A young Jewish boy living in Czechoslovakia, John Freund, and his family were citizens of the territory overrun by Nazi Germany in March 1939. The changes wrought by this development were immediate, but to a nine-year-old boy, their impact was somewhat muted. As shown in this account, the resilience of children provided John and his friends with the opportunity to recalibrate their lives in such a way as to maximize their childhood pleasures while they were able to do so, in an environment of increasing gloom. It is a memoir of light in an ever-darkening world in which the innocence of children offered hope to those around them—and provided each with the support they needed to prevail over the system that would have destroyed them.

I was nine years old in 1939 when the German army rolled across the Austrian border into our town. It was a grim day. The scenery was full of armoured trucks, tanks, soldiers in dark green uniforms and the occasional low-flying airplane. With them, the Germans brought their dreadful Nazi ideology. They were led by their leader, Adolf Hitler, perhaps the greatest criminal political leader of all time.

When the Germans came, most people stayed indoors, but there were some who welcomed them. These were people who hated the Jews. These people were envious of those with more than they and now it was their turn to show their true colours. Nobody knew what would happen. The war had not yet started; the Czech army was ordered not to resist the invaders. The Germans took over quickly and people were arrested on the first day of the invasion. Soon, orders began appearing on bulletin boards and in newspapers.

We Jews were hit the hardest. Signs that read "Jews not permitted" appeared in cinemas, coffee houses, streetcars, public buildings, public parks and elsewhere. Schools were ordered not to allow us in and public swimming areas became prohibited to us. Once, as I walked near my home alone, I noticed my Grade 3 teacher across the street. He crossed toward me and, as we passed, he shook my hand and quickly said, "Be brave." He took a great risk, as even talking to a Jew was regarded as a crime.

Discussion among the adults at home was often in German – perhaps so that we children could not understand. At night, we would listen to the news from England on our shortwave radio, as Czech radio was now in the hands of the Germans. At this time, there were pessimists and there were optimists. The pessimists thought that in one to two years all would be back to normal, while the optimists thought weeks. In the end, the war lasted six years and, for us, things never got back to normal.

I could no longer play with my non-Jewish friends. My friendship with Zdeněk and other non-Jewish boys came to an end. There were about three hundred Jewish families in town, and I did not know many of them. Some were professionals like us—doctors and lawyers. Others were small storekeepers and several were wealthy manufacturers. I became good friends with a group of four boys who were all my age. In our group, there were two Rudis, one Henry, one Paul and me. Before the war, Henry and one of the Rudis were rich. The other Rudi and Paul were poor. After the Germans took everything from us, we were all poor. We were required to wear a yellow Star of David on our outer garments, over our lapels. Our parents warned us to stay away from certain parts of town where it was known that there were hooligans and Nazis. I do not think that we were subjected to too much abuse at that time. Did all this drive us to despair? No way. Life went on. We wore our Stars of David, but not in shame.

In our town there were about two hundred Jewish youngsters and about one hundred of us were between the ages of 10 and 18. Excluded from the general community, we formed our own. My schooling moved from the schoolhouse to our living room. Groups of children met and were instructed by young Jewish teachers. Schooling was improvised; the older boys and girls taught the early grades. I was 10 years old when I had my first Latin lessons. I still remember "amo, amas, amat" and my introduction to algebra. We read about animals and distant lands. We sang songs in Hebrew which, for me, was a strange language that until that point had been used only in prayer. We dreamed about the faraway land of Palestine where Jews were making a fresh start. Occasionally, a father of a friend would be arrested and would disappear. We had to give away our car. Father was forced to close down his medical office and we had to live off his savings.

Another Jewish family lived in our building. They were simple, poor people who lived next to the butcher's store. Their place was warm and smelled of cooked meat. I don't remember their names, but their daughter Anna and I became friends. I often visited their warm apartment, where we sat around, talked and played cards. In time, we were ordered to give up half of our apartment. We lost two of our four rooms to some insurance office. Our maid, Maria, had to leave us, but she would often come to visit.

Some friends succeeded in leaving the country. They went to Palestine, England, Canada and the United States. It became more and more difficult to get permission to leave. My father was among the optimists and thought that all would soon return to normal. He and his friends liked to joke about Hitler and the Nazis. Unfortunately, the whole thing was far from a joke.

Among the more pleasant memories from this time—1940 to 1941—were the summer days spent along the River Vltava. Although we were banned from public swimming, we were allowed to swim along a narrow strip of land by the road. This strip was a half-hour walk from town, or a ten-minute ride by bicycle, and was near a railway bridge. It was called U Vorisku, named after the Voriseks family who owned and leased us the patch between the fields and the river. We bicycled, jogged, walked or ran to U Vorisku. It soon became a hub of activity. Swimming past the shoreline was treacherous, especially for younger children. The older boys had a tiny boat that was used to rescue the daredevils who tried. The water in the river was filthy, with pieces of raw sewage floating on the surface; one never put one's face into the water. Yet it was a place where we could cool off and have fun.

We were permitted to set up benches and changing rooms along the river. We had space for four ping-pong tables and when everything was cleared we even had room for a small soccer field. Someone brought a soccer ball and volleyball net. We played soccer along the narrow field and when the ball ended up in the river—as it often did—it took several minutes to retrieve it. I was 10 and would always play soccer with the older boys. I played the defence position. I was small, tough and daring, and stopped every attack on my team's goalie. My real success, however, was in ping-pong. We had two tables situated underneath a shelter behind the changing cabin. I played as often as I could. There was a tournament toward the end of the summer of 1941. We were divided into three age groups: under ten, ten-to-fourteen, and fifteen and older. I had early success, eliminating most of my opponents quickly. In the semifinals and the finals, I won every game. At an evening ceremony, I was awarded a brand-new white cork racquet and a plaque with my name engraved on it. There was dancing and singing. That evening, I felt that everyone liked me. These youngsters were my friends. There were the Harrys, Jirkas, Pavels, Karels, Rudlas, Lilkas, Ritas, Ankas, Suzans, Lidias and Cecilias. There were Poppers, Kopperls, Kohns, Herzes, Holzers, Frishes, Stadlers and Levys. There were even more, but I have forgotten most of the names. We were young, enthusiastic and mischievous, but we were always good to one another. Great warmth was established among us young people and we developed a deep love and respect for each other. The two summers of 1940 and 1941 were among my happiest.

Some days we worked on the Voriseks' farm, helping with the harvesting. I held a large canvas bag under a chute and filled it with oats or wheat. For our work, we received a large slice of fresh white bread, thickly covered with goose liver and fat.

We all had daytime duties. The older boys and girls were learning trades. Under orders from the Nazis, the Jewish community had to submit information about our properties and compile lists of our addresses, so the younger children, like myself, delivered this information in sealed envelopes. The moment we finished our duties, we would rush to our favourite spot along the river. We played team sports and our friendships intensified. Every moment in the sun was cherished and when it rained we would huddle under trees. In addition to athletics and games, we would sing. Sometimes there were fights, usually ending with someone coming home with a black eye.

When the days began to shorten and the cool air returned, we knew our beautiful summer was coming to an end. Several of the older boys decided that we must not hibernate but continue with our friendships. They started a handmade magazine named *Klepy* (Gossip). It was typed and illustrated and only one copy of each issue was printed. One issue had a picture of me kicking a ball on the front cover. The first issue merely gossiped about our summer activities at the river. However, subsequent issues had stories and jokes. Contributions by the readers were sought and published. All readers were given a chance to read the single printed copy and were asked to comment on the issue. There were 20 issues of *Klepy*. Here is an excerpt from an early issue:

> *What is the goal and purpose of our* Klepy? *First of all, to prove that a healthy spirit and sense of humour is within us and that we are not diminished by the difficulties of our days. We are capable, in moments of rest from our labour, to occupy our minds with worthwhile thoughts and humour.*

During this time, two boys were afflicted with epilepsy. The worst case was Fricek K. He was new to Budějovice, having come from the Sudetenland a few years earlier. Fricek was always with his cousin Erich. They were both 10 years old. Fricek had frequent epileptic fits, sometimes as often as every half hour. He would fall to the ground, lie on his back, and emit terrifying shrieks. When this would happen, his cousin Erich would open Fricek's mouth, which was full of froth, and pull out his tongue, caressing his forehead. The sick boy would shake wildly for three to four minutes and then appear to be in a deep sleep for a few minutes. After that, he would get up, looking weak and dizzy. This frightening event occurred many times each day.

Another person who had the same affliction was an older man we called Mr. Papa. He was a confectionery vendor. He had a wagon with candies, apples and chocolate bars. He could always be found in the shade under the large railway bridge. I used to buy a chocolate rum ball from him whenever I could afford it. His epilepsy was quite different. His attacks came only once every two weeks. When they occurred, he would fall on his back, breathing heavily, and lie in this state for almost a full hour. There was nobody qualified to do anything for him, other than give him a glass of water when he finally came to. After an attack, he would not show up to work for a few days. But when he did come back, it was always with a fresh supply of apples, chocolate bars and candy.

The summer of 1940 passed and we had only our memories to keep us warm. We looked forward to next summer—until it came. During the summer of 1941, our lives were in imminent danger. These threats were not from our fellow citizens, but from the mad dictator in Berlin. As the days became shorter and cooler, we cherished each day and prayed that the summer of 1941 would never end. For many, this would be their last summer.

Around this time, we, the Jews of Budějovice, started to take some interest in religion again. Our beautiful, tall synagogue had two steeples and many beautiful entrances and was located in a fine part of the city. It was built in the late 1800s. The Germans could not stand competition from another God, so they blew up the synagogue—completely wiping out any trace of the original building. Without the synagogue, services were held in a large, decorated warehouse. Our rabbi, Rudolf Ferda, inspired the participation of the children, and soon Friday night services were full of girls and boys. A chorus of ten-to twelve-year-old girls and boys was organized and their beautiful voices made many at the services tremble with joy. The boys learned to pray and, both in fun and seriousness, imitated our cantor by holding services at home. Rabbi Ferda was a good man. His long sermons always included the theme that Jewish history winds itself like a red thread through the ages. He spoke in Czech with a German accent, and sometimes we could not keep from bursting into laughter. However, when he ordered us out of the sermons, we were really sorry.

A special relationship developed among the young Jews who were shunned by the general community and vilified in newspapers and on radio. We found new strength and helped each other through the hard times. When a very poor family came to town with many children, room was quickly found to help them. Our family took in a little girl who lived with us for a while.

My father was no longer permitted to practise medicine and spent the summer days working in a friend's garden. He loved it. We worried about what would happen when our savings were gone. We got used to eating less and eating cheaper food: bread without butter, potatoes and, only rarely, meat.

The summer of 1941 came to an end. We still went to U Vorisku in the fall and sometimes in the winter, where we would walk around and look forward to the next summer. But this was not to be. In April 1942, the whole Jewish community (just under a thousand people) were taken from their homes and resettled in the ghetto Terezín (Theresienstadt, in German).

Source: John Freund. *Spring's End*. Toronto: Azrieli Foundation, 4th Edition, 2014, pp. 15–21. Used by permission.

Commentary

On March 15, 1939, Adolf Hitler completely abrogated his earlier pledges regarding the sovereign state of Czechoslovakia, and German forces swept into the country. The Czech lands of the renamed Bohemia and Moravia were now made into a German "protectorate."

The Munich Agreement of the previous September saw Czechoslovakia lose its Sudetenland regions, handed across by Britain and France to Hitler on the ground that they were peopled by German-speakers who could be "returned" to the Reich (notwithstanding that the Sudetenland had never belonged to Germany). At this time the Czechs also lost the backbone of their northern defenses, a carefully constructed state-of-the-art series of mountain fortifications and bunkers.

In the same grab for territory, Czechoslovakia's other neighbors—the jackal states of Poland and Hungary—chipped in for their share, helping themselves to parts of the Czech state, which they thought should also be theirs.

The relative ease with which Adolf Hitler managed to negotiate Czechoslovakia into this position—in which its territorial integrity was impossibly compromised—emboldened him to consider further adventures. While the Munich Agreement removed the immediate threat of war and gave Britain and France a breathing space to hasten their preparation for potential conflict, Hitler's confidence grew that he could get what he wanted without war. He had never discussed a complete occupation of Czechoslovakia, though he (and other Nazi leaders like Hermann Göring) expressed continual racial contempt for the Czechs and Slovaks.

However, with the occupation of the Sudetenland, Hitler considered that the rest of what was termed "rump Czechoslovakia" should also be occupied. Over the winter of 1938–1939, he became convinced that, considering their capitulation at Munich, Britain and France would not use force to resist any further German expansion.

The severely wounded Czechoslovak government now began to be undermined from within, through calls for the secession of Slovakia. Slovak People's Party leader and Catholic priest Jozef Tiso received aid and encouragement directly from Germany for this purpose. And then, on March 14, 1939, after a period of agitation further undermining central resolve, Slovak parliamentarians voted in favor of a complete break with Czechoslovakia, with Tiso making a public appeal to Hitler to step in and guarantee the defense of what was now essentially a German puppet state.

Under these circumstances, Czech President Emil Hácha had little idea how to deal with the situation. He requested an audience with Hitler, who summoned him to Berlin and then used the opportunity to intimidate Hácha, threatening a *Luftwaffe* attack on Prague if he did not order the surrender of the Czechoslovak Army. During the meeting Hácha suffered a heart attack and had to be resuscitated by medical staff. Weakly, he eventually gave in to Hitler's terms of total capitulation.

The Czech lands were henceforth to be formed into a new German Protectorate of Bohemia-Moravia, with German troops entering what remained of Czechoslovakia early in the morning on March 15, 1939. That same evening, Hitler made a triumphal entry into Prague and took up temporary residence at the Hradčany Castle, from which he could now look forward to becoming master of Europe. He installed Konstantin von Neurath, the former German foreign minister, as Reich Protector of Bohemia-Moravia. Slovakia became an independent state under the leadership of Jozef Tiso, who established an ethnic nationalist, fascist, authoritarian, one-party dictatorship allied to Nazi Germany.

In Prague, German citizens turned out and waved swastika flags as German troops and military equipment marched in. For the powerless Czechs, however, the German takeover was as great a tragedy as could be imagined. Many gathered in Wenceslas Square, where they repeatedly sang the national anthem until this was suppressed. A portrait of the founder of the Czech state, Tomáš Masaryk, was placed on the Tomb of the Unknown Soldier; this was later destroyed on the orders of the occupiers.

For children such as John Freund, these events did not pass unnoticed, though it was the little things that they really mattered. Most notably, as John shows in this document, relationships were tested by the new order. Here, however, we see the adaptability of youth under strain, as John and his friends find newer and more interesting ways of enjoying each other's company as though there were no Nazis or international crises.

The Western Allies surrender at Munich was supposed to end Hitler's territorial ambitions in Europe and guarantee the future peace. The occupation of Czechoslovakia, however, showed that Hitler's guarantees in fact guaranteed nothing. The invasion made it clear that Hitler could not be trusted to keep his promises, and from this point onward, Britain and France, with enormous reluctance, started preparing for war. They now declared that if Hitler set his sights on Poland, they would have little option but to defend it. Convinced—finally—that there were no limits to Hitler's territorial ambitions, they saw no alternative; they would have to prevent German domination of Europe. And if this had to be through force, then so be it. Appeasement was over, and the road to war lay open.

Established as a new state in 1918, Czechoslovakia managed only two decades of national existence before disappearing from the map in tears and sorrow. And in the six years that followed, of up to 320,000 Czech civilians who died during World War II, at least 275,000 were Jewish victims of the Holocaust.

5. Testimony of Ann Szedlecki

Ann Szedlecki, a 14-year-old Jewish girl from the city of Łódź, describes here the chaotic, frightening first few months of the German occupation, and how it was played out daily. With the keen eye of an observer, she not only shows how life changed but also offers several specific details characterizing the new arrangements: shortages, curfew, arbitrary punishments, and executions. Eventually, we see how Ann made up her mind to take her life into her own hands by leaving the stifling ghetto with her older brother, Shoel. While this was a huge step for one so young, Ann was also excited at the prospect—while at the same time not quite realizing that "my happy and carefree childhood was over."

Our lives changed abruptly in the fourth week of August 1939 when a loud knock at the door work us up at five o'clock in the morning. It was one of my father's employees letting us know that he wouldn't be coming to work—the government had announced a mobilization and he had been called up; he was being sent to the border. After he left, I opened the balcony door and stepped outside. I saw a lot of movement, mostly men in uniform on horseback and in horse-drawn carriages setting out to fight the enemy. Even at my age I could see that they were going to be sitting ducks. The newsreels and the newspapers told us how well the Germans were prepared. They had already occupied Czechoslovakia and claimed Austria as their own without firing a single shot. The Germans knew that they couldn't fail because the rest of the world had turned a blind eye to what was going on.

When my brother-in-law, Janek, was called up, we faced a serious problem. He had decided to sell his hardware store in Lodz that summer and relocate to the nearby smaller town of Koluszki, about 20 kilometres east, but he had received his draft orders before he could close the deal. My sister went to the authorities to explain that he was in Koluszki, but they assumed it was an excuse and that he was planning to desert, so they gave him 24 hours' notice to show up or face court martial. Luckily, Manya was able to get in touch with him. He came to say good-bye, wearing a uniform, and that was the last time we saw him. We later heard rumours that he had been taken as a prisoner of war on the outskirts of Warsaw and shipped to a camp in Romania. But there was no way to know for sure.

September 1, 1939 arrived and the Nazis started sealing the fate of European Jewry. Murder and unimaginable horrors were in store for us. The city was actually very quiet—the calm before the storm—except for newsboys shouting, "Extra!" and proclaiming that Poland was preparing Hitler's coffin to bury him. Everyone said that with England and France on our side, it was going to be a short war. We read in the newspapers that the Germans were shooting with ersatz ammunition, and that it was up to Poland to finish the beast. Nevertheless, we started buying up food and other supplies.

Then, in the days immediately before the Germans entered Lodz, the looting of stores began, particularly Jewish and liquor stores. My sister's store was no exception, even though there wasn't much to steal since most of the merchandise had already been moved to Koluszki. We decided to close up our apartment and move in with Manya. We didn't know what the next day was going to bring, but we had a premonition of things to come. We grew closer to each other, as if there was safety in numbers.

Lodz wasn't bombed at all, but for days, every time we looked up at the sky there were hundreds of German planes flying on their way to bomb Warsaw into surrender. The weather was perfect for flying and bombing accurately and the invaders took advantage of it. Soon the capital city was under siege.

Panic broke out as news of the Germans approaching Lodz reached us. People started leaving the city by the thousands by whatever means possible. We wanted to go but our father, intent on keeping the family together, wouldn't let us. He may have been right to make us stay. All those poor people ended up trapped outside the city and were bombed mercilessly by low-flying planes; dead bodies littered the highways. There was nowhere to run.

A week of uncertainty ended when German troops marched into Lodz on Friday, September 8, 1939. It was a warm, sunny day and I walked to the Plac Wolności to watch the arrival of the occupiers. They came on foot and in trucks, looking immaculate in their uniforms, boots shining. Many of them carried flowers from the German population of the city. City Hall and other buildings were decked out with huge flags with swastikas. In other words, the city rolled out the red carpet to welcome the invaders, whom some regarded as liberators. The large German population of the city opened their arms for their brethren, even though the community had lived in Poland for generations. There weren't many sad faces in the throngs, and there were fewer Jews.

Signs of things to come appeared almost immediately. I witnessed a soldier pulling an elderly Jewish man's beard and kicking him to the ground because he wasn't working fast enough to fill the trenches that had been dug only a few days before to stop the German tanks. I remember how enthusiastic and patriotic we had felt when we dug those trenches.

At the end of September, after weeks of siege and relentless bombing, Warsaw capitulated and the triumphant German army occupied the city on October 1, 1939. In the conquered capital city, burned out, demolished buildings bore witness to the results of modern warfare. A beautiful, cultural city was reduced to rubble. Most of Warsaw's defenders were dead, and while the valiant survivors could resist no longer they were full of spirit.

My sister's store faced the Zielong Rynek, the Green Market. On one Sunday soon after the Germans arrived, the stalls in the market were closed and some boys were playing soccer there when a truck with German soldiers went by. They stopped and joined the boys in the game, which frightened everybody. Another time, when I took my niece for a stroll in the park—this was before the harsh laws banning us from parks were passed—an older soldier next to me started playing with Miriam. With tears in his eyes, he told me that he had left a baby the same age back in Germany. I don't remember any other demonstrations of kindness. Maybe the same soldier would think nothing of bashing a Jewish baby's head against a wall to kill it. These examples are just too minor when you consider what was about to happen to us.

The Germans dynamited the monument to the Polish hero Tadeusz Kościusko at the centre of Plac Wolności as soon as they entered Lodz. I remember walking by one day and seeing it lying on the ground. Its head was separated from the torso and a victorious German soldier was having his picture taken with his arm around his girlfriend and his foot on Kościusko's head.

Before long, all kinds of decrees and restrictions started appearing, each one more dehumanizing than the last. There were so many of them that it's hard to remember them all, although a few stand out in my memory. No Jews were allowed to attend school or institutes of higher learning, regardless of age, which brought my formal education to and end at 14. We were banned from using public transportation and from entering any park, theatre or cinema. A curfew was imposed from seven at night until seven in the morning. We had to get off the sidewalk when a German soldier approached. Most shameful of all, we had to wear an armband as a sign of our Jewish identity on our sleeves. Disobeying this rule was punishable by death.

It wasn't safe for a male Jew of any age to be in the street. They were constantly being caught and put to work in forced labour, whether the Germans needed them or not. One of them was my father. We didn't see him once for a whole day and were very relieved when he came home with a loaf of bread after working in a bakery.

One evening, just before the curfew, I was walking home past the Deutsche Shul after visiting a girlfriend and saw a big crowd gathered. I stopped and watched in horror as soldiers rolled in barrels full of tar and set the building on fire.

"It's a great day," gloated one Pole.

"Don't be so happy," warned his friend. "They will start with the Jews, and finish with the Poles."

I couldn't stay too long to eavesdrop because it was so close to curfew. When I went past the synagogue the next day, there was nothing left except the lingering smell of fire. Another sign of things to come.

There was a public hanging of a Jewish man named Radner and two Polish men in the poor Jewish section of Lodz. Although the bodies were on display for some time, I wasn't allowed to go see them. I don't know what their crimes were. In Radner's case, it may have been that he wasn't wearing his armband, or some other "heinous" crime.

The bread lines were now longer and whenever a Jew got to the front of the line, he or she was pointed out and sent back to the end. Many times people went home without any bread. Some Jews thought they didn't look Jewish and didn't wear the armbands, putting themselves in terrible danger. Even if the Germans couldn't identify them, the Poles had no trouble spotting them and pointing them out. Sometimes I was able to get in line by four o'clock in the morning and, with any luck, came home with bread.

Any kind of social life stopped for us altogether. Our radios had been confiscated immediately after the Germans occupied Lodz. Ours had been a beautiful Philips short-wave radio with a "magic eye," a cathode tube for adjusting the station. I missed being able to listen to the music from France, the international news from Moscow, or short-wave broadcasts from the United States—even though I didn't understand what they were saying. All of the newspapers except German ones published in Polish had been shut down. My favourite had been *Express*. The curfew kept us from venturing out from early evening until morning, so we were left with each other for company. Our only joy was watching little Miriam, who at six months old was a delight. We hadn't heard any news from Malka's husband.

Poland's independence, which had lasted between the two world wars, was now ended. Germany occupied most of the western part of Poland and, because of the pact between the Soviet Union and Germany signed by Soviet minister Vyacheslav Mikhailovich Molotov and German foreign minister Joachim von Ribbentrop earlier in 1939, the Soviets now occupied the eastern part. For a brief period in 1939, the Germans allowed people to cross into the eastern parts of pre-war Poland now under Soviet administration. A steady exodus started, and my brother, Shoel, along with a few friends, decided to join the mass of people fleeing. Just a few days after leaving, however, Shoel returned home minus the gold watch and money that had been taken as payment by a guide who promptly disappeared. When Shoel returned home, we were relieved to be a family again and face our future together.

But the situation in Lodz was getting worse every day, so my brother decided to give it another try. His intent this time was to go to Soviet-occupied Bialystok, some 330 kilometres to the northeast, find a place to stay and then come back for the rest of the family. As things turned out his plan was impossible. My parents wouldn't leave Manya alone with baby Miriam and she had decided to stay in Lodz until she heard from her husband. As November 1939 drew to a close, my brother decided he would go alone. I, however, had a plan of my own—I wanted to go with him. For some reason, my parents didn't object. Did they have a premonition?

Shoel and I were ready to leave at the end of November, taking quite a bit of luggage with us. A horse-drawn carriage was called to take us to the railroad station and we said tearful goodbyes, not realizing that it would be the last time we'd ever see each other. We kissed for the last time and went out into the cold, dark night to face the unknown. As I entered the carriage, I heard my mother calling me. She rushed out of the house, took the pink wool shawl off her shoulders and wrapped it around me. She kissed me again and said the words that I would always remember: "Be decent."

I stuck to these principles in spite of terrible difficulties. I would have made her proud had she known. I was good and decent, but at what price? I was rewarded with years of hunger, loneliness and homelessness. And yet, I always felt her protective arms around me. Even though her woolen pink shawl was later stolen, it kept me warm—if only in the abstract. She kept watch over me.

There would be no more listening to family stories, no more bananas or mandarins when I was sick. No more being blessed every night before bedtime. No more goodnight kiss.

From now on, life for me was going to be serious business, just trying to survive. As we were pulled away from our home, I turned for the last time to see my mother. She was wiping her eyes and waving. I waved back until we disappeared from each other's view. The truth is that I didn't feel apprehension about leaving. I was excited and ready for the first adventure of my life. But as it turned out, my happy and carefree childhood was over. I just didn't know it yet.

Source: Ann Szedlecki. *Album of My Life*. Toronto: Azrieli Foundation, 2nd Edition, 2009, pp. 53–61. Used by permission.

Commentary

On September 8, 1939, the Germans occupied the Polish city of Łódź, annexing it to the Reich and renaming it Litzmannstadt. The persecution of Jews began immediately. Within 10 days, all Jewish-owned enterprises had been taken over by Germans; Jews could no longer use public transportation or leave the city without special permission; they were not allowed to own cars, radios, and various other items. Synagogue services were banned, and Jews were required to keep their shops open on Jewish holidays.

Despite these restrictions, however, the Łódź ghetto became the longest-surviving and most profitable of all of Poland's ghettos. Up to 34 percent of the city's prewar population were Jews, a statistic compounded when the Nazis drove large numbers of other Jews to the ghetto from Germany, Austria, Luxembourg, and other Polish cities. Łódź was the first ghetto to be sealed, in May 1940, and the last to be liquidated, in August 1944. Starved, diseased, and deported, only 5 percent of ghetto residents survived.

The German occupation instituted drastic changes to the daily lives of the residents. From the very first days, Jews were seized in the city streets for arduous forced labor. Those trying to hold body and soul together were subjected to draconian lifestyles in which they were required to stand in line for hours on end to receive food rations. Bread and other foodstuffs were only distributed once every few days; if families missed out on receiving their rations because they had been picked up to perform labor, they were forced to make do until the next distribution. Most of the population starved, with the nature and quality of the rations—often the soup was so thin that potato peelings became precious commodities—leading to most people starving after three months. Overall, some 43,500 people, about 21 percent of the ghetto population, died of starvation, cold, or disease. In this community, however, the population was constantly replenished.

Anti-Jewish regulations dominated everything. Home radios had to be handed over; Jews were forbidden to travel by train. Non-Jews were forbidden to purchase or lease Jewish-owned businesses without a special permit; bank accounts belonging to Jews were blocked. And of course, Jews were forbidden to leave the closely guarded ghetto under penalty of death.

The Nazis intended that the ghetto, while making money for them, would pay for its own upkeep and not cost the occupying authority anything of its own. As a result, the Jews were required to pay for their own food, security, sewage removal, and all other expenses. To meet these costs, the ghetto was run on behalf of the occupying Germans by the Nazi-appointed Jewish Council (*Judenrat*), led by the controversial Chaim Rumkowski. His view was that work meant salvation and that productive Jews equated with value in the eyes of the Nazis. If the ghetto could earn a huge profit for the Nazis, lives could be saved.

Yet the productive life of the ghetto came at a cost for its factory workers, among whom were large numbers of child laborers.

Ann Szedlecki was one of these children. Born Chana Frajlich in Łódź in 1925, when the war broke out, she was just 14 years old. Part of her memoir, recounted in this document, shows the extent to which her life, and that of those around her, changed as a result of the German invasion and the subsequent ghettoization of the Jews. Along the way, she also provides an insight into how others—Poles—viewed these developments. By November 1939, Ann and her brother Shoel had had enough. Anticipating worse things to come, they decided to escape the ghetto and make for a safer location.

As it turned out (though we do not see it in this excerpt), they fled across the demarcation line between the German and Soviet-occupied sections, hoping to ride out the crisis and then return for the rest of the family later. Instead, Ann ended up spending most of the next six and a half years alone in the Soviet Union, enduring the harsh conditions of northern Siberia under Stalin's Communist regime. After the war, she returned to Łódź to find that every member of her family had perished during the Holocaust. In 1950, she married and immigrated to Israel and then, in 1953, to Toronto. Ann Szedlecki died in Canada in 2005.

6. Mordecai Chaim Rumkowski, Łódź Ghetto (September 4, 1942)

In the Łódź ghetto, as elsewhere, the Nazis required that a Judenrat (Jewish Council) be established to administer the ghetto and to implement Nazi orders. Mordecai Chaim Rumkowski was appointed as chair. Rumkowski was convinced that the ghetto would remain intact—or, at least, that its destruction would be delayed—if the Nazis saw it as providing a benefit to the war effort. He thus made every effort to have as many Jews as possible working in various factories throughout the ghetto. Rumkowski's domineering personality led to him assure the Germans that the number of Jews to be deported on a given date would be at the designated gathering place, at the appointed hour. Yet he faced an almost impossible position in that he sought to keep the ghetto viable while at the same time showing deference to Nazi demands for more and more people to be deported to their deaths. In this document—one of the most infamous speeches made by a Jewish leader—Rumkowski had to explain why it was necessary to deliver up for deportation all children under the age of 11 along with the elderly. He explained that he had no choice and that the Germans were asking for the "best we possess." He said, "I must stretch out my hands and beg: Brothers and sisters! Hand them over to me! Fathers and mothers: Give me your children!"

The ghetto has been struck a hard blow. They demand what is most dear to it—children and old people. I was not privileged to have a child of my own and therefore devoted my best years to children. I lived and breathed together with children. I never imagined that my own hands would be forced to make this sacrifice on the altar. In my old age I am forced to stretch out my hands and to beg: "Brothers and sisters, give them to me!—Fathers and mothers, give me your children. . . ." (Bitter weeping shakes the assembled public) Yesterday, in the course of the day, I was given the order to send away more than 20,000 Jews from the ghetto, and if I did not—"we will do it ourselves." The question arose: "Should we have accepted this and carried it out ourselves, or left it to others?" But as we were guided not by the thought: "how many will be lost?" but "how many can be saved?" we arrived at the conclusion—those closest to me at work, that is, and myself—that however difficult it was going to be, we must take upon ourselves the carrying out of this decree. I must carry out this difficult and bloody operation, I must cut off limbs in order to save the body! I must take away children, and if I do not, others too will be taken, God forbid . . . (terrible wailing).

I cannot give you comfort today. Nor did I come to calm you today, but to reveal all your pain and all your sorrow. I have come like a robber, to take from you what is dearest to your heart. I tried everything I knew to get the bitter sentence cancelled.

When it could not be cancelled, I tried to lessen the sentence. Only yesterday I ordered the registration of nine-year-old children. I wanted to save at least one year—children from nine to ten. But they would not yield. I succeeded in one thing—to save the children over ten. Let that be our consolation in our great sorrow.

There are many people in this ghetto who suffer from tuberculosis, whose days or perhaps weeks are numbered. I do not know, perhaps this is a satanic plan, and perhaps not, but I cannot stop myself from proposing it: "Give me these sick people, and perhaps it will be possible to save the healthy in their place." I know how precious each one of the sick is in his home, and particularly among Jews. But at a time of such decrees one must weigh up and measure who should be saved, who can be saved and who may be saved.

Common sense requires us to know that those must be saved who can be saved and who have a chance of being saved and not those whom there is no chance to save in any case.

Source: Yitzhak Arad, Yisrael Gutman, and Abraham Margaliot (Eds.). *Documents on the Holocaust, Selected Sources on the Destruction of the Jews of Germany and Austria, Poland, and the Soviet Union.* Jerusalem: Yad Vashem, 1981, pp. 283–284. Reproduced by permission of Yad Vashem Publications.

Commentary

The Łódź ghetto, located in Poland, was established in February 1940 and was the longest lasting of the Polish ghettos. It operated, overall, for more than four years.

The city of Łódź, Poland's second city, is located about 75 miles southwest of Warsaw. During the Holocaust its Jewish population was second only to that of Warsaw, with some 230,000 Jews. It was occupied one week after Germany's invasion that began on September 1, 1939. Renamed Litzmannstadt, it was incorporated into Germany as part of the Warthegau, run by Gauleiter Arthur Greiser.

The initial months of the German occupation of Łódź were difficult for the Jewish community, characterized by a combination of hard labor, arrests, random beatings, terror and humiliation, and widespread plunder. The application of the Nuremberg Laws restricted and marginalized the Jews, and in mid-November 1939, the city's four major synagogues were burned to the ground.

The ghetto was established in February 1940 in the northern section of the city. The number of Jews forced into its very small area of only 1.5 square miles ranged from 160,000 to 164,000. It was sealed on May 1, 1940, surrounded by a wooden fence, barbed wire, and armed guards.

Conditions for the Jews saw overcrowding, disease, atrocious sanitation, and the absence of electricity and running water. Hunger, leading to death by starvation, was perhaps the ghetto's greatest burden. Unlike in some other ghettos, there was virtually no successful smuggling of food into Łódź.

As elsewhere, the Nazis required that a *Judenrat* (Jewish Council) be established to administer the ghetto and ensure that Nazi orders were carried out. Mordecai Chaim Rumkowski was appointed as chair. In that capacity practically every important decision was made by him.

Rumkowski organized administrative services within the ghetto that were essential for the survival of the Jews, such as departments for health, education, supplies, housing, registration, and a Jewish police force. Schools were established for the ghetto's thousands of children. Orphanages, prayer services, and cultural activities helped to make the ghetto as livable as possible in such a terrible situation. Without running water or sewerage systems, the need for a sanitation department—which he established—was critical, yet despite these efforts the terrible conditions of life were the direct cause of the death of one out of every five people.

With food the most needed of all essentials, Rumkowski's primary concern was to convince the Germans to provide additional sustenance. His solution dovetailed perfectly with his broader plan for the survival of the ghetto and its inhabitants. He was convinced that only by making the Jews indispensable to the German military machine could he forestall their murder. Accordingly, he sought to make Łódź an industrious center of German manufacture. He established factories and workshops making textiles, German uniforms, munitions, and whatever else the Nazis looked upon as necessary. His goal was to have a job for everyone who wanted one; his hope was that this would protect as many Jews as possible from being killed or deported.

The Nazis accepted the industrialization of the ghetto and agreed to a proposal by Rumkowski to pay those working in the more than 100 ghetto factories in the form of food. His plan was simple: work was a form of protection and a means of getting critically needed food into the ghetto.

Despite what would seem to be a well-deserved place in Holocaust history as a hero among the *Judenrat* leaders, Rumkowski was—and remains today—perhaps the most controversial. His governance style was dictatorial, his attitude imperious. He rode through the ghetto in an opulent carriage pulled by white horses. He and his inner circle of family and officials seemed to be well fed, and they were always among those not on the deportation lists.

Apart from his domineering personality, his responsibility to assure the Nazis that the number of Jews to be deported on a given date would be at the designated gathering place and at the appointed hour invariably left him vulnerable to criticism by desperate Jews who saw him as assisting the Nazis in their task of extermination. Others, however, saw him as a tireless leader trying to administer Nazi orders in a way that would cause the least pain and keep alive as many Jews as possible.

His position can best be seen in the heartbreaking speech he made on September 4, 1942, known generally as the "Give me your children" speech. In it he had to explain why it was necessary to deliver up for deportation all children aged under 11, together with the elderly. He explained that he had no choice and that the Germans were asking for the "best we possess." He said, "I must stretch out my hands and beg: Brothers and sisters! Hand them over to me! Fathers and mothers: Give me your children!"

Deportations were halted from September 1942 through May 1944 due to the German Army's need for the munitions from the ghetto factories. In February 1944, however, Himmler ordered the ghetto's liquidation. By August 1944 the 75,000 Jews still alive were deported to Auschwitz-Birkenau. By the time the Soviets entered the ghetto on January 19, 1945, fewer than 10,000 of the 230,000 Jews of Łódź had survived.

7. Heinrich Himmler: "The Difficult Decision" (October 4 and 6, 1943)

On October 4, 1943, Reichsführer-SS Heinrich Himmler spoke for three hours to a secret meeting of SS officers in the town hall of Posen (Poznań), in occupied Poland. This was followed by a second speech two days later. The significance of the two speeches lay in the fact that, for the first time, a senior Nazi spoke openly about the reality of Germany's extermination of the Jews. The speech of October 4 justified the crimes already perpetrated, commending the audience of SS officers for their commitment to the task and noting that those under their command had, through it all, remained "decent fellows." In the second speech, dated October 6, Himmler revealed what he considered a "difficult decision," namely, the "eradication" of Jewish women and children—a decision that had to be made in order to ensure that no one would be able to wreak revenge on "our sons and grandsons." The document reproduced here contains excerpts from both speeches.

Speech of October 4, 1943

I mean the evacuation of the Jews, the extermination of the Jewish race. It's one of those things it is easy to talk about, "the Jewish race is being exterminated," says one party member, "that's quite clear, it's in our program—elimination of the Jews, and we're doing it, exterminating them." And then they come, 80 million worthy Germans, and each one has his decent Jew. Of course the others are vermin, but this one is an A-1 Jew. Not one of those who talk this way has watched it, not one of them has gone through it. Most of *you* know what it means when 100 corpses are lying side by side, or 500, or 1,000. To have stuck it out and at the same time—apart from exceptions caused by human weakness—to have remained decent fellows, that is what has made us hard. This is a page of glory in our history which has never been written and is never to be written.

Speech of October 6, 1943

I ask of you that what I say in this circle you really only hear and never speak of. We come to the question: how is it with the women and the children? I have resolved even here on a completely clear solution. That is to say I do not consider myself justified in eradicating the men—so to speak killing or ordering them killed—and allowing the avengers in the shape of the children to grow up for our sons and grandsons. The difficult decision had to be taken, to cause this Volk [people] to disappear from the earth.

Source: Speech by *Reichsführer-SS* Heinrich Himmler before senior SS officers in Poznan, October 4 and 6, 1943. United States Evidence Files, Record Group 238, National Archives Collection of World War II War Crimes Records, 1933–1949. U.S. National Archives.

Commentary

Heinrich Himmler was one of the most notorious members of Adolf Hitler's inner circle in Germany's Nazi Party. As head of the SS, he oversaw the mass murder of Jews and others during the Holocaust of World War II.

When World War II broke out in 1939, the SS seized responsibility for the liquidation of "enemies" of the German Reich in the occupied territories. The *Einsatzgruppen*, special killing squads, began the systematic mass murder of Jews,

Roma, partisans, communists, Slavs, and others considered to be "subhuman" all over Eastern Europe and the Soviet Union. Those Jews who were not summarily shot were herded into ghettos and then later into extermination camps, where they were gassed to death and burned in crematoria. Himmler was intimately involved in these actions, often personally visiting execution sites and the camps, and it was he who was most active in translating Hitler's murderous hatred of Jews into an actual program of extermination.

With the Final Solution operating at its peak during 1943, in the first speech Himmler addressed a secret meeting that included nearly 100 senior SS officers in the town hall of Posen (Poznań), in occupied Poland, on October 4, 1943. He spoke again in a second speech, this time to senior party and government representatives, on October 6. Excerpts of these two speeches are reproduced in this document.

The speech on October 4 was—in the overall context of the Holocaust—extremely important and is unquestionably Himmler's most quoted speech. Here, for the first time, was a recorded acknowledgement of the crime then taking place, accompanied by a recognition that the events then taking place would have to be guarded under a blanket of permanent secrecy. Referring explicitly to the genocide of the Jews then being carried out, Himmler stated that "I mean the evacuation of the Jews, the extermination of the Jewish race," conflating the two words "evacuation" and "extermination" to mean the same thing. Considering that doing this fed right into the fundamental ideals of the Nazi Party, this was, nonetheless, at the same time "a page of glory in our history which has never been written and is never to be written."

In the speech on October 6, Himmler also specifically dealt with another issue that had, until that time, not been discussed openly. While the extermination of the Jews was now an open secret for a broader spread of the SS hierarchy, an issue that caused disquiet among those carrying it out—the murder of Jewish children—had also to be addressed. Those charged with the task of implementing the Final Solution at ground level, such as members of the *Einsatzgruppen*, found difficulty in shooting children into open pits or at other killing sites. Himmler, however, asserted that Jewish children had to be killed so that a group of "avengers" did not grow up who would come after "our sons and grandchildren." Thus, he argued, "[t]he difficult decision" had to be made to have the Jews "disappear from the earth."

In this context, Himmler enabled those doing the killing to think that they were protecting the lives of their own children by murdering the children of their racial enemy. Saying that this was "the most difficult decision of my life," Himmler was letting slip, perhaps, a deeply-held reflection regarding the humanity of the children being killed—an anathema to all true-believing Nazis. The response from those present was enthusiastic, however, as for them it underscored Himmler's own sensitivity while at the same time recognizing his commitment to the task at hand.

As a follow-up, on June 21, 1944, Himmler spoke once more, this time to a gathering of generals in Sonthofen, deep in the Bavarian Alps. Here again, he mentioned "the most terrible task" he had to carry out, issuing the most "terrible order which could have been given to an organization." It is clear, however, that

Himmler said such things for effect: in the same speech, he also said, "It is good that we had the severity to exterminate the Jews in our domain."

8. Affidavit of Szloma Gol on the Killings at Ponary (1944)

The Ponary (Paneriai) Forest was a wooded area about six miles south of Vilna (Vilnius), Lithuania, on the road to Grodno. Before war came to the area in the summer of 1941, it was a place known to the residents of Vilna for holidays and recreation, and they would often go there on weekends to gather berries and mushrooms, as well as for their summer vacations. Between July 1941 and July 1944, Ponary was used as the principal site for the mass murder of up to 100,000 people, mostly Jews, as well as Polish intelligentsia and Russian POWs. The murders took place near the Ponary train station and were carried out by German SD, SS Einsatzgruppen, and Lithuanian collaborators. During the killing spree, at least 70,000 Jews were murdered in Ponary, together with estimated 20,000 Poles and 8,000 Russians. Between September 1943 and April 1944, prisoners in what became nicknamed the Burning Brigade were tasked with destroying the evidence of the killings, and each day members of the unit had to exhume the contents of the mass graves in the forest. Szloma Gol was one of these prisoners, and in this affidavit to the Nuremberg Tribunal after the war, he described how three Jewish boys, aged 12 and 13, were required to wash gold fillings extracted from the bodies of Jews murdered by the Nazis.

I, SZLOMA GOL declare as follows:

As the corpses were taken from the mass graves, and before they were placed on the pyre, two persons were charged with extracting the gold from the teeth of the bodies with prongs, and two or three other persons simultaneously washed the gold in benzine. <u>The washing of the gold thus extracted was done by three Jewish boys aged 12 to 13</u> who were among the 80 persons in the pit. The gold was packed in boxes each weighing 8 kilograms. During the period of my stay in the pit 7 or 8 such boxes were filled with dental gold. LEGEL ordered the boxes to be neatly packed because they were to be sent to Berlin. MURER personally took the boxes with him [emphasis added].

I declare the above to be correct.
[signed] SZLOMA GOL
August 10, 1946.

Source: *Nazi Conspiracy and Aggression*, Office of the United States Chief of Counsel for the Prosecution of Axis Criminality (Washington, D.C: U.S. Government Printing Office, 1946), Red Series, Supplement A, 1176–1177.

Commentary

When the Nazis attacked the Soviet-occupied part of eastern Poland in the summer of 1941, all Jewish civilians, including infants, became targeted for destruction. Moved from hometown villages to larger ghettos, most eventually arrived at the much larger ghetto in the Lithuanian city of Vilna—known colloquially as "the Jerusalem of Lithuania"—where almost all were murdered in the enormous bloodletting that took place in the Ponary Forest, an area that had traditionally been a recreational area used for vacations and weekends away for Vilna's residents.

Ponary, indeed, became the primary murder site of the Jews of Vilna and the region surrounding it. The forest was situated just a few miles south of Vilna, on the road to Grodno. The pre–World War II Jewish population of Vilna was nearly 100,000, making up around 45 percent of the city's total. By July 1944, the population had been reduced to slightly over 20,000.

Vilna had been part of the reconstituted state of Poland after the Great War, but following the start of World War II and the Soviet invasion of eastern Poland in September 1939, the city was transferred by the Soviets to Lithuania; the whole country was then annexed to the Soviet Union in June 1940. In the summer of 1941, Lithuania was invaded by Germany during Operation BARBAROSSA, and the killing of Jews began almost immediately. *Einsatzkommando* 9, part of the notorious *Einsatzgruppe A*, descended on Vilna, rounded up 5,000 Jewish men from the city, took them to Ponary, and shot them there.

The first executions took place on July 8, 1941. One hundred Jews at a time were brought from the city to Ponary, where they were ordered to undress and hand over whatever money or valuables they had in their possession. They were then marched naked, in single file, in groups of 10 or 20 at a time, holding hands to the edge of pits that had been dug by the Soviet Army to store fuel. They were then shot into the pit by rifle fire. A thin layer of sand was placed over them, and the next group was led to the edge of the pit, where they, too, were shot. The killing went on for hours, as in a production line. The killings then continued throughout the summer and fall of 1941. By the end of the year, more than 20,000 Jews had been murdered, but this was only the beginning.

With the creation of the Vilna ghetto in September 1941, the Nazis had a ready pool of slave labor at their disposal, so the pace of the killing slowed during the early part of 1942, but with the changing fortunes of war, the murders intensified toward the end of the year.

During 1943 information about the massacres at Ponary began to spread beyond the local area, and with the advance of the Soviets westward, *Reichsführer-SS* Heinrich Himmler ordered the establishment of a special unit, *Kommando 1005,* whose task it was to burn the bodies of mass murder victims and hide any traces of the killings. In Vilna this translated to a unit made up of Jewish prisoners tasked to perform this grisly task. In August 1943 the Germans returned to Ponary and began to exhume and burn the corpses. The Burning Brigade, numbering 80 Jewish prisoners, was sent to Ponary at the end of September 1943. After disinterring the bodies and burning their remains for seven months, on the night of April 15, 1944, they managed to escape after having dug a tunnel under Ponary, but almost all were captured, and they, too, were murdered. Fifteen of them succeeded in escaping and managed to reach the partisans in the Rudniki forests. The work of burning the bodies continued, however, and by the end of 1944, upward of 60,000 corpses had been burned at Ponary.

So far as can be ascertained, the total number of victims by the end of 1944, Jewish and non-Jewish, was anywhere between 70,000 and 100,000, with the latter figure taken as the most likely possibility. With the end of the war, only 24,000 of Lithuania's total Jewish population survived. Ninety percent of the prewar total had been murdered.

9. Sir Herbert Emerson: Memorandum on Refugee Children in France, Belgium, and Switzerland (December 11, 1944)

In mid-1938 Britain's India Office was requested to provide the name of a senior ex-civil servant from India who could be nominated to serve as the next League of Nations High Commissioner for Refugees. Sir Herbert William Emerson, formerly the British governor of the Punjab, thereby became the new Commissioner. He took office on January 1, 1939, in an office that combined both the existing High Commission and the Nansen Office. It was generally assumed that he would be dealing primarily with Jewish refugees from Nazism, though of course no one at that time could foresee the extent to which his brief would take him. By the late stages of World War II, Emerson, together with renowned Swiss jurist Dr. Gustav Kullmann (who had acted as Deputy High Commissioner before and during the war), undertook a study of the situation pertaining to children in France, Belgium, and Switzerland as the Nazis were in retreat throughout Western Europe. This document is their report, noting—with some sense of satisfaction—that the organizations that, to that point, had stepped forward to assist the children had led to a situation in which "the children are safe."

1. During the occupation of France and Belgium, very fine work was done by a number of agencies inside those countries, and in Switzerland, towards the rescue of children whose parents were deported by the Nazis, or had to flee from Nazi persecution. It is feared that many of the parents have been killed. The persecution was not confined to Jews, but was almost universal in their case, and was of a particularly brutal character. During our recent visit to France, Belgium and Switzerland, Dr. Kullmann and I investigated, so far as we could, the problem of the Jewish children, with special reference to the assistance by the Intergovernmental Committee and the means by which such assistance might best be given. While, owing to a lack of communications and other causes, completely accurate facts and figures are not yet available, the position is sufficiently clear to give a general picture of the size and nature of the problem.

2. The children now in question are those who were separated during the occupation from both their parents. The majority of them were concealed under false names and papers in their own countries, and were maintained in private facilities or religious institutions. The Churches gave great assistance. There were secret organisations operating in the countries, and also from Switzerland. The movement was financed partly by private contributions, but largely by the Joint Distribution Committee of America. In the later stages, the Intergovernmental Committee was able to give some financial assistance through the Joint Distribution Committee, which acted as its agent. In Belgium, the Belgian authorities gave a good deal of secret financial help. Some children were removed to Switzerland, which at the time of

liberation, was giving asylum to about 1,000. The number there is now slightly less, since some children have been able to return to France.
3. The great majority of the Jewish children fall into three classes:
   (i) The children of Belgian or French nationals.
   (ii) The children or other nationals, mainly Poles, who have been long established in France or Belgium.
   (iii) The children of refugees from Nazi persecution, mainly of German and Austrian origin, who had been given temporary asylum in either France or Belgium.

In addition to the children of refugee parents, the mandate clearly includes these children who had to be removed to Switzerland when, as was frequently the case, the situation of the children was a direct consequence of the deportation or flight of their parents from their country of residence, it would seem ungenerous to hold that the children should be excluded from the benefits of the mandate merely on the ground that in order to save their lives, they did not in fact leave their countries of residence. I would hope therefore, that when the time comes to consider what practical help the Intergovernmental Committee can give towards a solution of this problem, the Executive Committee will approve a broad interpretation of the mandate.

4. The figures so far ascertained are approximately as follows:
   (i) <u>France</u>: 8,000 children. Figures are not available about the distribution of these among the three classes mentioned in paragraph 3 above but it is probable that the majority of them are children of Polish parents long established in France. There may be as many as 500 children of German and Austrian refugees.
   (ii) <u>Belgium</u>: about 1,500 children who were concealed who had neither parent with them. Of these a considerable proportion are of German and Austrian refugees, the rest being children of Polish parents long established in Belgium.
   (iii) <u>Switzerland</u>: <u>About 1,000 divided among the three</u> classes.

5. The Jewish community, as a whole, which is giving very serious thought to the future of these children. There are certain organisations which took a very active part in their rescue and preservation. Such as the Comite de Defense in Belgium and the OSE, operating mainly from Switzerland. The Joint Distribution Committee is very closely interested because of the financial help it has already given, and the still greater help it may be called upon to give. The Jewish Agency for Palestine is prepared to make a considerable number of certificates available for immigration into Palestine. The French Government has in contemplation a general scheme relating to the welfare of war orphans, among whom most of the children now in question would be included. Under this scheme the French Government would be the legal guardian of the children and would apparently provide for their maintenance, welfare and education. The Belgian Government may consider a similar scheme, although we have no definite information of

this point. The Swiss Government contemplates the return of the children now in Switzerland to the countries from which they were received, but it has no wish to make this an immediate issue, and is prepared to continue the care and maintenance of them for the time being. Among the children are (some) who have reached an age where they are capable of making up their own minds as to what they wish their future to be. We were told, for instance, of 500 in Switzerland who have long made their plans to go to Palestine. About them there is no difference of opinion between the various Jewish interest. It is agreed that these youths should decide for themselves. About the others, the present attitude of the organisations which have been directly concerned with their rescue and preservation, is that no final decision about the future of a child should ordinarily be made until every reasonable effort has been made to trace one or both of his parents. Very good progress has been made in this direction. In France, for instance, 2.500 children have been united since liberation with one or both of their parents, and 500 more are in the process of being united. There is also at present a strong feeling among the organisations mentioned that provision should be made in France or Belgium, as the case may be, for the care, education, maintenance and training of many of the children. In France several homes previously in existence have been re-opened for the purpose, and others are in contemplation. Until the details of the scheme of the French Government are known, the Jewish community is not in the position to form an opinion as to how far it will assist their problem. Thus there are several matters outstanding which can be only decided by the Jewish community itself.

Meanwhile, the children are safe, and are being well cared for. Many are still in the homes of their foster parents, some of whom are loathe to give them up, a matter which will require tact and patience for its solution.

<u>Additional Comment</u>: In a later report dated 8 January 1945, Sir Herbert Emerson states that the French Government has indicated its interest in establishing "a system of State guardianship and State care for all children who have lost their parents, including those within the mandate of the Intergovernmental Committee. Pending the introduction of that system, the children are being maintained from voluntary sources. Fourteen homes have already been opened, and others are in contemplation. The rest of the children are still with foster parents. A few of the children who were given asylum on Switzerland have returned, and a considerable number are likely to return in the near future.

Source: War Refugee Board, Ira Hirschmann Papers, Box 3. New York Public Library.

Commentary

As Allied forces began to liberate the countries of Western Europe during 1944, questions arose as to what was to be done with Jewish children whose lives had been saved during the war. Various stratagems had been employed to do so: hiding them with accepting Christian families; placing them in orphanages; concealing them in plain sight in various communities such as at Le Chambon; conveying them across natural borders, for example, Switzerland and Spain; and hiding them in religious institutions like monasteries and boarding schools. Now, with the liberation, the children could come out of their places of refuge and return home.

This caused problems for refugee agencies such as those described in this document by Sir Herbert Emerson. The end of the war would see millions of displaced people across the continent seeking out their former homes—or new ones—among the urban and rural remains of cities, towns, and villages. The return was far from straightforward. In some places, a resurgence of antisemitism resulted in Jews being not welcomed; in others, the same phenomenon saw Jews resisting repatriation. Some tried to return home so they could search for missing relatives or retrieve lost property, only to find strangers living in their houses.

Governments and relief organizations such as those mentioned by Emerson worked hard to facilitate where they could go. And among those who were uprooted and newly liberated were vast numbers of children. What to do about Jewish children after the Holocaust was one of the most intractable problems at the end of the fighting. The standard solutions for displaced children were family reunification, when immediate relatives could be traced, or at least repatriation. But a vast number of those who survived the war had lost their entire families. Soon they would be sent to newly established displaced persons camps, but while the war was still raging—even though heading toward its endgame—agencies such as those highlighted by Emerson relied on individual governments to assist in finding a solution.

Most of these children were unaccompanied; their care during the war might have been underwritten by charitable homes or institutions, but when reality was faced, they might still be alone or, perhaps, be accompanied by a brother, sister, or cousin. In what followed, these children would often become the objects of custody battles when their parents reappeared, or when foster parents or religious institutions claimed a right to guardianship. Various claimants might make declarations regarding where the children should rightfully land; having been protected during the war, assertions were now often made that their rightful place should be with those who had saved their young lives, often provided them with a new identity, and even, sometimes, with a new religious faith. For many years, these children had lived far from the family home and often had no identity other than that of those who had shielded them.

While Emerson's report (and the additional report annexed to the document, dated January 8, 1945) focused on many of the positive aspects of the situation as it pertained to children facing their new future in France, Belgium, and Switzerland, the situation in the first two countries was, of course, different from that in the third. In December 1944, when the report was compiled, Paris had been liberated since August, but there were still parts of France that had yet to come under Allied control. The liberation of Belgium from German occupation had begun when Allied forces entered on September 2, 1944, and was completed only on February 4, 1945. Thus, when Emerson and Kullmann were compiling their report, there was still a long way to go before firm conclusions could be reached regarding the ultimate safety of those about whom they were writing.

Where Switzerland was concerned, there were additional concerns. Up to the spring of 1944, a large proportion of all refugees who made it to Switzerland and were refused entry were Jewish. It is impossible to tell how many of these were children, but the balance of probabilities would suggest that the figure numbered several thousand. Rescuing Jewish children across the border during the war, moreover, had been an illegal act in both Vichy France and in Switzerland. Now, with the war coming to an end, it was in many cases just as difficult to get the children back across the border into France, and this, too, was going to be a problem for the refugee agencies until the war was finally over and normal diplomatic relations could be resumed.

In short, the issues highlighted by Emerson's memorandum pointed to the need for a wholesale consideration to be made of the entire repatriation issue in the future, something that was finally resolved when the United Nations Relief and Rehabilitation Administration (UNRRA) became fully operational during the fall of 1945.

10. Testimony of Fanny Lesser

Fanny Lesser, one of eight children in her family, was born in Czechoslovakia. In 1944 the whole family was sent from the Chust (Khust) ghetto, then under Hungarian rule, to Auschwitz. They were among the 5,000 or so ghetto inhabitants who were deported in four transports in late May and early June of that year. Most were sent directly to the gas chambers of Auschwitz, but a few, such as Fanny, managed to stay alive as a result of being sent on farther. In this memoir, Fanny describes these and other developments through to her selection by Dr. Josef Mengele for slave labor and deportation with 300 other women to Weisswasser, a Nazi labor camp, later in 1944.

The freight cars we traveled in were closed cars with no toilets. The toilet was a hole in the floor to use to go to the bathroom but only when the train was moving. We were on this train for quite a few days. We had only the food we had brought. We had no water. I have no idea how people managed. Every time the train stopped, people would scream: "Water! Water!" The SS would then spray the train with water, tantalizing us.

Whenever the train stopped between Chust and Auschwitz-Birkenau, the SS used to come and holler, "If you have any gold or money, surrender it now. They will kill you, when you get there, if you still have money or gold." At every stop people gave the SS their jewelry and money.

Grandfather Noah and Grandmother Ethel, my mother's parents, were with us. Grandfather had sold a cow for 300 pengars. My father said to him, "Noah, give us the money. We have to tear it up and throw it out." Grandfather would reply, "We have to have money. What will we do when we arrive at this place? We need to buy food for the little ones." My father became very stern with him, saying, "Noah, you have to give us the money. You see what is happening." He finally gave the money to my father. We chewed it up into little pieces and threw it down the toilet hole.

The last stop! What it was, was Auschwitz! . . .

When we arrived at Auschwitz, the doors opened and I saw many SS officers with their dogs. I also saw boys in striped uniforms; I didn't know then that they were our own people. The SS told us to get out of the freight car. I had my little sister, Ruhala, on my arm. One boy in a striped uniform came over to me and said, "Whose baby is that?" I answered, "My mother's." He told me, "Give the baby to your mother." I thought, "Why is he saying this?" I gave Ruhala to my mother. I stayed with my cousin, Blanka, who was on our transport.

We got out of the freight car and they took us to the right. We were not allowed to turn around. I never saw my mother or Ruhala again. A friend told me that she had seen my father and older brothers alive after the selection. I prayed to G-d that they would survive.

Sarah—I never saw her again. She didn't come with Blanka and me. Solomon was in line with my father and two older brothers, but he saw Mommy and insisted on going with her. Lea was young, so she went with my mother, as did Yosef and Ruhala. My sisters—Saran and Lea—and my brothers, Yosef and Solomon, all were murdered, as well as my mother's parents.

My uncles and aunts were in other ghettos, such as the Munkacs ghetto. My father had four sisters; three sisters from Munkacs died with all their families. In Korosmezo, another of my father's sisters and a brother survived. This sister, Suri (Sarah), lost two children but after the war found her husband and had two more children that she named after the two that had been murdered—Zipporah and Moishe—now in Israel. My cousin Blanka survived with her three sisters: Ruska, Suri, and Helen, but her mother and father and four younger children died in Auschwitz. My father also had brothers with so many children that did not survive. My mother's brother, Alex, who had married in 1940, survived in Budapest, Hungary, but his wife died in Auschwitz. He is still alive and living in Florida.

With the deportations from Hungary, the role of Auschwitz-Birkenau as an instrument in the German plan to murder the Jews of Europe achieved its highest effectiveness. Between late April and early July 1944, approximately 440,000 Hungarian Jews were deported, around 426,000 of them to Auschwitz. The SS sent approximately 320,000 of them directly to the gas chambers in Auschwitz-Birkenau and deployed approximately 110,000 at forced labor in the Auschwitz concentration camp complex. The SS authorities transferred many of these Hungarian Jewish forced laborers within weeks of their arrival in Auschwitz to other concentration camps in Germany and Austria.

After our selection at Auschwitz-Birkenau, the SS led us to a big hall. They shaved us everywhere. They made us stand nude for a long time until we had received the clothes they gave out. We were unrecognizable. I was not tattooed, although my brothers were. I got a number but I don't remember what it was. Then we walked to Birkenau that was only a few kilometers away. There we went to Block (Street) C to Barrack 16. There were 32 barracks in Camp C, two of which were washrooms.

In Block C everyday selections occurred but in different barracks. Every day people were selected to go to work or to go to death. When I came into the barracks, I did not know about the gas chambers but there were girls who had been in Auschwitz since 1942 and 1943. They told us right away: "Don't think about if you have a mother or a father. All are dead!" I was 14 years old. I cried. I still did not believe what they were saying.

They gave us very little food, watery coffee and soup, and a small piece of bread. We were always hungry. Every night we talked about cooking and baking. We were going to bake huge loaves of bread and never peel potatoes so we wouldn't waste even the peels.

In Block C, my cousin Blanka met this *Kapo*, Peter, a Polish prisoner, who cooked for the SS. He told Blanka that he would give her some food. I used to go to Peter, and he would give me a tin container of soup or stew. By the time I reached my barrack with this container, I had given away nearly all of the food; Blanka and I had hardly anything.

One day I said to Peter, "Oy! The cherries are in season. I love cherries." Soon after, Peter went to Krakow and brought back cherries for us. Oh, my G-d! I remember how they tasted.

Even raw potatoes—if we could find one—tasted like the best dessert.

Before this the International Red Cross had come in and the SS had showed them how well they were treating the prisoners. "Why there is even a Czech family camp!" the SS told the Red Cross. The Red Cross never got off the lorries (trucks). The Nazi propaganda seemed to fool the Red Cross. However, they had killed them all, just as they had done to those in the Gypsy camp.

Dr. Mengele selected us. Mengele came every day and did the selections. Mothers and daughters were not supposed to be together. It was a law to separate families. People hid their relationships. My cousin, Blanka, and I were always together; this was dangerous.

Another danger was pregnancy. I remember a girl, Miriam, from the same city as my cousin Blanka. The *aelteste* (barrack leader) kept asking us, "Is Miriam pregnant? If she is, we will all be in trouble." Blanka answered her, "No! She does not even understand what pregnant is." But Miriam was pregnant, although she didn't know it—she was so innocent. Soldiers had raped her and she had a baby in the barracks. My cousin had learned to be a nurse and had worked in a hospital. She delivered the baby boy. Miriam was surprised when she saw the baby. He was a big boy but stillborn. I put him in a pail and went to the toilet and buried him. I had to do this to protect Miriam and the rest of the women in the barracks. Miriam survived and later lived in Israel.

Another case of a pregnant woman occurred in another barrack. One group consisting of four sisters and a cousin were together. The oldest sister was married and pregnant. Her sisters and cousin knew the SS would get rid of any pregnant woman. I risked my life helping her to hide out during selections. We knew which barrack would go through the selection process that particular day. When I heard there would be a selection in her barrack, I used to take her into my barrack, and I went to her barrack and answered for her during roll call—*Zahlappel*. The baby was born in the *Revier* (medical clinic). Her sisters took the baby out the *Revier's* little window, took the baby to the gate, and gave the baby to Germans who said they would give the baby to German people. The sisters didn't know for sure that the baby would survive. But, for sure, they tried to save the baby. They did save the mother, and all the sisters survived.

The SS officers would have roll call and count every single morning and night. We would line up—five to a row. If the count were off, no matter what, they would count again and again. Do you know where they found the missing? They found them dead. It was not possible to escape. During the day we stayed in the yard. Sometimes we were not allowed to stand up so we had to kneel for a long time. I heard in some barracks that they had to hold bricks up in the air when they were kneeling.

After roll call, we would go to the washroom where there was running water once a day. In back of the barracks there were holes where we could have gone to the bathroom. Our stupid *aelteste*, the head of the barracks, would not let us go to the bathroom behind the barrack because then she would have to clean up the area by hosing it down. She would hit us if she caught us.

We feared even more Irma Griese, the beautiful camp leader. She would beat us for the smallest thing; when I cut off my hem and used this material for a headscarf, she saw this and beat me. During the Nuremberg Trials after the war, Griese was sentenced and hanged.

In August of 1944, Mengele selected from C Block three hundred women. He selected young ones, examining our eyes and hands. We didn't know why. We were crying because we were afraid that he was sending us to the front to the soldiers. After we were selected, we waited four weeks in B Camp, across the wires, for a transport.

This waiting for the transport was especially bad because of the conditions. We were waiting on the other side of the barbed wires for the transport. We waited four weeks to go to Mährisch-Weisswasser, one of the 97 sub-camps of the Gross-Rosen, a Nazi slave labor camp in Poland. While waiting for the transport, we had no running water. Trucks brought water that we had to catch in our hands. Early in the morning, we would go into a little stream and wash ourselves because there were no washrooms.

One morning I saw outside many nude women. They had been on a transport that was turned back because the trains had been bombed. The SS brought the women back and then took all their clothes. Nobody could go anyplace. What they did was for spite—for no reason. I gave them something to wear. Among these women I saw my cousin, also named Fanny, and Aunt Rozia. Both survived and went to Israel.

Finally one day our transport arrived. We left for Mährisch-Weisswasser, a slave labor camp, in Germany.

Source: Fanny Lesser. *Lives Entwined: Fanny and Max Lesser, Holocaust Survivors*. Margate, NJ: ComteQ Publishing, 2007, pp. 32–38. Used by permission of ComteQ Publishing.

Commentary

Khust (Hungarian, Huszt) was a Czechoslovak city located in the Carpatho-Rus region. A city of around 20,000 inhabitants, it contained approximately 8,000

Jews. The day after the collapse of Czechoslovakia on March 14, 1939, the Khust city government proclaimed independence as Carpathian Ukraine on March 15, 1939. The next day, on March 16, 1939, Hungarian troops invaded Khust and claimed it as part of Hungary.

With the city under Hungarian rule, its Jews began to suffer antisemitic repression. During the war years, Jewish men of military age were forced into labor battalions, with some sent to support Hungarian units on the eastern front. Many died, and hundreds of Jews without Hungarian citizenship were deported to Ukraine and murdered there.

When Germany invaded Hungary in March 1944, there were 5,351 Jews in Khust. As the Final Solution was brought to bear against Hungary's Jews, a ghetto and a *Judenrat* were established, a situation not helped when another 5,000 Jews from the surrounding area were brought in.

The mass deportation of Hungarian Jews began in May 1944. In Khust, all the town's Jews were expelled from the ghetto and from late May to early June all the inhabitants were deported in four transports. Driven toward the train station, they were placed on railcars and, after a journey of three days, deported to Auschwitz. Most were gassed there or worked to death at forced labor. Later in June 1944 the town was declared by the Nazis to be *Judenrein*—that is, "cleansed of Jews."

The family of Fanny Lesser was among those deported. Originally from the small town of Majdan, then in Czechoslovakia but now in southeastern Poland close to the border with Slovakia, they were included in the transports that were collected and sent to Khust prior to the deportation. As Fanny explains in this document, an excerpt from her memoir, at Auschwitz she and her family underwent "selection," the process carried out by SS doctors on new arrivals to Auschwitz. The doctors then identified those whom they considered fit for work, with the others (children under 14, the elderly, sick, and women with children) sent to the line of those slated for immediate death.

Fanny's heart-wrenching description of the selection of her family upon their arrival at Auschwitz is matched by her account of what happened to those who managed to survive this initial attack. Upon being sent to the barracks, Fanny was confronted with the awful truth that those of her family from whom she had been separated were already dead. At the age of 14, she had to find ways to stay alive, despite the trauma and the poor food—in which "even raw potatoes . . . tasted like the best dessert."

The turn in Fanny's fortunes came when she was forced to undergo another selection, this time, in August 1944, at the hands of the infamous Dr. Josef Mengele, the so-called Angel of Death at Auschwitz. Moreover, Mengele was particularly interested in children as subjects for bogus medical experiments, which he conducted as a scientist searching for some hidden mystery.

Fanny, fortunately, did not catch his eye in this respect, though she was among some 300 women he selected, somewhat unusually, for a transport out of Auschwitz. As Fanny describes, this was to Mährisch-Weisswasser women's labor camp (*Frauenarbeitslager*), a subcamp of the main camp at Gross-Rosen (located in the German village of Gross-Rosen, now the modern-day Rogoźnica in Lower Silesia, Poland). Working as slave labor at Weiswasser, Fanny was later rescued by the Swedish Red Cross, survived the war, and eventually moved to the United States where she lived out the rest of her life in New Jersey.

Chronology

1919	January 5: German Workers' Party (DAP) founded by Anton Drexler and Karl Harrer
	September 12: Adolf Hitler joins the DAP
1920	February 24: Nazi Party established when the DAP is renamed; it becomes the National Socialist German Workers' Party (NSDAP); Hitler presents a 25-point Program, the Nazi Party Platform
1923	November 9: Hitler leads an attempt to overthrow the government of Bavaria; he fails
1924	February 24: Trial of Adolf Hitler for treason begins; he is found guilty and sentenced to five years in prison
	December 19: Hitler released from Landsberg having served just eight months of his five-year sentence
1925	February 27: Hitler declares the Nazi Party to be reestablished, with himself as leader (Führer)
1933	January 30: Adolf Hitler appointed chancellor of Germany by President Paul von Hindenburg
	February 27–28: Reichstag fire; arrests of political opponents of the Nazis begin almost immediately
	March 5: Reichstag elections: Nazis gain 44 percent of vote in manipulated elections
	March 20: Dachau concentration camp established
	March 27: Enabling Act passed
	April 1: Jewish businesses boycotted across Germany
	April 26: Hermann Göring establishes the Gestapo
	May 10: Books written by Jews and "undesirables" are publicly burned
	July 14: Law for the Prevention of Offspring with Hereditary Defects passed, forcing many Germans with "undesirable genes" to be sterilized
1934	June 30: *Sturmabteilung* (SA) leadership purged during what becomes known as the "Night of the Long Knives"

	August 2: German president Paul von Hindenburg dies; Hitler declares the office of president abolished and names himself Führer of Germany
1935	September 15: Nuremberg Laws announced at the annual Party Rally
1936	July 1: Hitler Youth membership becomes compulsory for all Aryan boys
	August 1: Summer Olympic Games begin in Berlin
1937	March 21: Papal encyclical *Mit Brennender Sorge* issued by Pope Pius XI
	July 19: Buchenwald concentration camp established
1938	March 12: *Anschluss* (union) of Austria with Germany; all German antisemitic decrees are applied immediately to Austria
	July 6–14: International conference on refugees held at Evian, France
	August 1: Central Office of Jewish Emigration established to speed up the pace of Jewish emigration from Germany
	August 8: Mauthausen concentration camp established in Austria
	August 17: Nazis require Jewish women to add "Sarah" and men to add "Israel" to their names on all legal documents
	August 19: Swiss government refuses entry to Austrian Jews seeking sanctuary
	September 27: German Jews banned from practicing law
	September 29–30: Munich Conference: Britain and France surrender the Sudetenland regions of Czechoslovakia to Germany by negotiation
	October 5: Passports belonging to German Jews are marked with the letter "J" to indicate their Jewish identity
	November 7: Ernst vom Rath, Third Secretary in the German Embassy in Paris, is shot and mortally wounded by Herschel Grynszpan; vom Rath dies on November 9, precipitating Kristallnacht
	November 9–10: Kristallnacht pogrom occurs in Germany and Austria. Nazi figures give 91 Jews killed, and up to 10,000 arrested; 267 synagogues are destroyed; figures are likely much higher
1939	March 15: Germany invades, occupies, and dismembers Czechoslovakia
	May 15: The first prisoners arrive at Ravensbrück

June 17: The SS *St. Louis*, a ship carrying 936 Jewish passengers, returns to Europe after being denied entry into the United States and Cuba

August 23: Nazi-Soviet Non-Aggression Pact signed

September 1: Germany invades Poland; curfew imposed on German Jews

September 3: France and Britain declare war against Germany

September 17: Soviet Union invades Poland

September 21: Reinhard Heydrich orders *Einsatzgruppen* commanders to establish ghettos in German-occupied Poland

September 27: Warsaw surrenders; Jewish Councils (Judenräte) established in Poland

November 23: Yellow stars required to be worn by Polish Jews over the age of 10

1940 February 8: Łódź ghetto is established

April 1: Thousands of refugees permitted into Shanghai, China

April 9: Denmark and southern Norway are invaded and occupied by Germany; Heinrich Himmler issues a directive to establish a concentration camp at Auschwitz

April 30: The Łódź ghetto is sealed off from the outside world

May 7: Nearly 165,000 inhabitants are sealed in the Łódź ghetto.

May 10: France, the Netherlands, Belgium, and Luxembourg are invaded by Germany

May 20: Auschwitz concentration camp established for Polish political prisoners

June 4: Neuengamme concentration camp opens

June 22: France surrenders to Germany; Marshal Philippe Pétain leads the pro-Nazi government established in Vichy

July 17: First anti-Jewish measures taken in Vichy France

September 7: German forces begin aerial bombings of Britain

October 3: Vichy France passes its own version of the Nuremberg Laws

October 16: Germans officially establish the Warsaw Ghetto

November 4: Jewish civil servants in the Netherlands dismissed

November 16: Warsaw Ghetto, containing nearly 500,000 Jews, is sealed

1941 January 21–26: Romanian Iron Guard annihilates hundreds of Jews

February 9: Dutch Nazis riot against Amsterdam Jews

March 1: Construction of Birkenau begins

April 21: Natzweiler-Struthof concentration camp opens in France

May 14: Over 4,000 Jews are rounded up in Paris at the Vel' d'Hiv

June 22: Germany violates its nonaggression pact with the Soviet Union and invades (Operation BARBAROSSA)

June 27: Białystok occupied by Nazis; Białystok ghetto established

July 2: Ukrainian nationalists murder thousands in Lvov (Lv'iv)

July 17: *Einsatzgruppen* ordered to execute captured communists and Jews during Soviet campaign

July 20: Minsk ghetto established

July 31: Adolf Eichmann appointed to prepare the "Final Solution"

September 1: German euthanasia program formally ended, following the deaths of some 100,000 people

September 6: Vilna Ghetto established

September 19: Jews in Germany ordered to wear armbands bearing the yellow Star of David

September 29: *Einsatzgruppen* murder some 34,000 Jews at Babi Yar ravine, outside Kiev

October 7: Birkenau is established as the primary mass murder site of Auschwitz

October 22–24: Romanian and German forces massacre an estimated 50,000 Jews in Odessa

October 28: Approximately 9,000 Jews are killed outside of Kovno (Kaunas)

November 8: Plans are made for the creation of a ghetto in Lvov (Lv'iv)

November 24: Theresienstadt (Terezín) ghetto/concentration camp established

December 7: Japan attacks Pearl Harbor, drawing the United States into World War II

December 8: Chełmno extermination camp becomes fully operational; some 320,000 Jews will be murdered here

December 11: Germany and Italy declare war on the United States

1942

January 10: *Armée Juive* (Jewish Army) created in France

January 16: Deportations from Łódź begin

January 20: Wannsee Conference takes place

February 23: Some 768 Jewish passengers, after being refused entry into Palestine, drown when the *S.S. Struma* sinks off of the Turkish coast.

March 1: Extermination by gas begins at Sobibór

March 17: Killings begin at Bełżec extermination camp

June: First anti-Nazi resistance pamphlet published by the White Rose group of Hans and Sophie Scholl

June 1: Jews in France, Holland, Belgium, Croatia, Slovakia, and Romania ordered to wear yellow stars

June 1: Treblinka extermination camp begins operation

July 13: 1,800 Jews are massacred in Jozefów, Poland, by German Reserve Police Battalion 101

July 14: Mass deportation of Dutch and Belgian Jews to Auschwitz begins

July 16: Over 4,000 children taken from Paris and sent to Auschwitz; overall, some 12,887 Jews in Paris are sent through Drancy

July 22: Mass deportation of Jews from the Warsaw Ghetto to Treblinka begins

July 23: Adam Czerniaków commits suicide in Warsaw

July 28: The Jewish Combat Organization is formed in the Warsaw Ghetto

August 7: Dr. Janusz Korczak and 200 orphans under his care are gassed in Treblinka

August 17: Kurt Gerstein visits Bełżec death camp and witnesses the gassing of up to 3,000 Jews

August 29: The Reigner Telegram is sent

September 2–3: Revolt of the Łachwa ghetto, arguably the first ghetto revolt of the Holocaust

October 15: The SS slaughters 25,000 Jews near Brest-Litovsk

October 25: The deportation of Norwegian Jews begins

October 28: First transport of Jews sent from Theresienstadt (Terezín) to Auschwitz

December 24: Armed operations by the Jewish Combat Organization against German troops in Kraków

1943

January 18–21: Renewed deportations of Jews from the Warsaw Ghetto begin following a visit from Himmler; Jewish resistance begins in the ghetto

February 22: Christoph Probst, Hans Scholl, and Sophie Scholl are executed after admitting to distributing White Rose pamphlets

February 26: The first Roma arrive at Auschwitz

March 13–14: Liquidation of the Kraków ghetto

March 23: Nazi deportation of Greek Jews begins

April 5: Approximately 4,000 Jews are massacred in the Ponary Forest, outside Vilna

April 19: New deportations from the Warsaw Ghetto; first day of Warsaw Ghetto Uprising; Britain and the United States begin the Bermuda Conference

May 1: Bermuda Conference ends

May 8: Nazi forces capture the Jewish Combat Organization's command bunker at Miła 18; Mordecai Anielewicz is among the dead found there

May 16: SS General Jürgen Stroop reports that the "Jewish quarter of Warsaw is no more"

May 19: Nazis declare Berlin to be Judenfrei ("cleansed of Jews")

June 2: 3,000 Jews killed following resistance in Lvov; another 7,000 are sent to the concentration camp at Janowska

June 11: Himmler orders liquidation of all ghettos in occupied Poland

August 2: Treblinka uprising

August 15–16: Uprising of the Białystok ghetto

October 1–2: German police begin deportations of Danish Jews; Danes respond with a rescue effort that saves the lives of 90 percent of the Jewish population

October 14: Sobibór uprising

October 16: Major Nazi raid and *razzia* (round-up) against the Jews of Rome, who are sent to Auschwitz

October 21: Minsk ghetto liquidated

1944

January 22: U.S. President Franklin D. Roosevelt creates the War Refugee Board

March 19: Germany begins its occupation of Hungary; Adolf Eichmann sent from Berlin to oversee the deportation of the Hungarian Jews

May 15: Beginning of the deportation of Jews from Hungary to Auschwitz; Jews from Ruthenia and Transylvania are deported

May 16: Germans offer to free 1,000,000 Jews in exchange for 10,000 trucks

July 9: Raoul Wallenberg arrives in Hungary, where he distributes Swedish passports and sets up safe houses for Jews

July 11: Deportations from Hungary are halted by order of Regent Miklós Horthy

July 24: Majdanek extermination camp is liberated by the Russians

August 1–October 4: Warsaw Revolt

August 2: Germany destroys the so-called Gypsy camp at Auschwitz, gassing some 3,000 in the process

August 6: Łódź, the last Jewish ghetto in Poland, is liquidated with 60,000 Jews sent to Auschwitz

October 7: *Sonderkommando* revolt at Auschwitz; one of the gas chambers is destroyed, and 15 SS guards and 400 members of the *Sonderkommando* are killed

November 8: Deportations resume in Budapest

November 19: The Vatican and four other neutral powers in Budapest issue a collective protest to the Hungarian government calling for the suspension of Jewish deportations

November 28: Himmler orders the gas chambers at Auschwitz destroyed

December 24–29: Hungarian Arrow Cross fascists attack Jews in Budapest

1945

January 5: Roza Robota, Estusia Wajcblum, Ala Gertner, and Regina Safirsztajn, accused of supplying gunpowder to the Auschwitz *Sonderkommando*, are executed

January 18: The evacuation of Auschwitz begins

January 19: The Soviet Army liberates Łódź

January 28: Soviet forces liberate Auschwitz

April 9: Evacuation of Mauthausen begins

April 11: American forces liberate Buchenwald

April 15: British forces liberate Bergen-Belsen

April 27: Soviet forces liberate Sachsenhausen

April 29: American forces liberate Dachau; Soviet forces liberate Ravensbrück

April 30: Hitler commits suicide

May 1: Joseph Goebbels kills his wife and children before shooting himself as Berlin is surrounded by the Soviet Army

May 2: Soviet forces capture Berlin

May 3: Theresienstadt is surrendered to the International Committee of the Red Cross

May 5: American forces liberate Mauthausen

May 7: Germany surrenders to the Allies in Reims

May 9: Wilhelm Keitel signs surrender documents in Berlin

May 23: Heinrich Himmler commits suicide

September 1: Japan surrenders to the Allies after the United States detonates atomic bombs at Hiroshima and Nagasaki, ending World War II

October 18: International Military Tribunal of major war criminals begins at Nuremberg

1946 July 4: Forty-two Jews are killed in a pogrom in Kielce, Poland

October 1: International Military Tribunal ends

October 15: Hermann Göring commits suicide in his cell at Nuremberg

October 16: Death sentences carried out at Nuremberg as those condemned are hanged

Glossary

Aktion: A Nazi operation involving operations by Nazis against Jews from villages or ghettos who were then assembled, deported to labor or death camps, and, in many cases, murdered.

Allies: The collective term for the countries fighting Nazi Germany, Italy, and Japan during World War II; these comprised primarily the United States, Britain and the Commonwealth, and the Soviet Union, with many other countries aligning with the aims of these major combatants.

Anschluss: German for "political union," used to describe the annexation of Austria by Germany on March 13, 1938.

Antisemitism: An umbrella term for a variety of negative beliefs or actions held or taken against Jews for the sole reason that they are Jewish. Not to be spelled as "anti-Semitism," as there is no such thing as "Semitism" against which hostility can be directed.

Aryan: A term applied in Nazi ideology to people of Northern European racial background, in stark contradiction to other peoples (particularly Slavs, Latins, and especially Jews).

Concentration camp: Camps established from 1933 onward for the nonjudicial imprisonment and forced labor of those identified by the Nazis as enemies of the Third Reich; these would ultimately include political opponents, Jehovah's Witnesses, Roma, homosexuals, asocials, and Jews.

Crimes against humanity: A legal category within international law that identifies punishable offences for gross violations of human rights, atrocities, and mass murder of noncombatant civilians. Acts that can be considered as crimes against humanity include, but are not confined to, murder, extermination, enslavement, deportation, imprisonment, torture, rape, and persecutions on political, racial, and religious grounds.

Death march: Forced transfer and deportation of concentration camp inmates toward the end of World War II, undertaken to prevent their liberation by the Allies; these resulted in a vast number of deaths.

Displaced persons: Survivors of the Holocaust or other World War II–related population dislocation at war's end and who had no home to which they could immediately return.

DP camps: Special camps set up by the Allies to house, medically assist, and then enable displaced persons to find new homes, often outside of Europe.

***Einsatzgruppen*:** SS mobile killing squads that followed the German military operations, largely in Poland and the Soviet Union after June 1941; supported by units of German police and local volunteers, they executed over a million Jews and others, mainly through shooting and the use of gas vans.

Euthanasia: In the Third Reich, the adoption of eugenic measures to improve the quality of the German "race" through the murder of those with incurable psychological problems, the permanently disabled, or those with physical and emotional disorders.

Extermination camp: A site to which Jews and others were deported for the purpose of their annihilation. The Nazis located six of these in occupied Poland: Auschwitz-Birkenau, Bełżec, Chełmno, Majdanek, Sobibór, and Treblinka.

Final Solution: The euphemistic cover name for the Nazi plan to exterminate the Jewish population of Europe (*Endlösung der Judenfrage*). Beginning in the late fall of 1941, Jews were rounded up in occupied German territories and sent to death camps to be murdered. To ensure compliance, they were told beforehand that they were going to be "resettled" in the east.

Gas chamber: A sealed room or other enclosed space in which a number of victims could be killed simultaneously by inhaling poison gas (such as carbon monoxide or by hydrocyanic acid (HCN), known by its commercial name of Zyklon-B).

Gestapo: Germany's secret state police force (*Geheime Staatspolizei*) and a branch of the SS, employed as a detective policing agency charged with creating a climate of fear and hunting down enemies of the State throughout occupied Europe.

Ghetto: A designated area where all Jews from a city and its surrounding areas were forced to reside. The ghetto would be surrounded by barbed wire or walls, and it became a very clearly defined district, guarded from the outside. Established mostly in Eastern Europe, ghettos were usually sealed so that those imprisoned inside were prevented from leaving (or others from entering).

Holocaust: One of the terms (along with Shoah and Churban) used to describe the destruction of approximately six million Jews by the Nazis and their collaborators in Europe and North Africa between the years 1933 and 1945. Among all those murdered by the Nazi regime during this period, only the Jews were marked for complete and utter annihilation.

***Judenrat*:** Jewish Council (plural, *Judenräte*), established by the Nazis in ghettos, especially in Eastern Europe. The role of the Council was to carry out German administrative directives, usually resulting in the deportation of the Jews prior to the ghetto's liquidation.

Judenrein: A term used to describe an area which has been cleansed or purified of all Jews by deportation and/or murder. Areas designated as having been "cleansed of Jews" were those where all Jews had been either murdered or deported.

Kapo: Concentration camp prisoners chosen to direct and discipline their fellow prisoners into complying with camp rules and regulations, allowing the camps to operate with fewer SS staff.

Kristallnacht: "Crystal Night" or "Night of Broken Glass," was a pogrom directed on November 9–10, 1938, throughout Germany and Austria by Nazis against Jews and conducted by SA forces and civilians. Synagogues were burned; Jewish homes, schools, and businesses were vandalized; 91 Jews were murdered. About 35,000 Jewish men were sent to labor or concentration camps.

Labor camp: Camp where Jews and other prisoners were forced to engage in hard labor in conditions of slavery.

Massacre: The intentional, random, and often brutal killing of a significant number of relatively defenseless people by a more powerful group or state force.

Master race: A concept in racial ideology in which a "superior" race is deemed the highest in racial hierarchy. Adolf Hitler sought to eliminate all "inferior" and undesirable peoples, especially Jews, whom he considered the "source of all evils."

Nazi: Member of the National Socialist German Workers' Party (*Nationalsozialistische Deutsche Arbeiterpartei*), which was founded after World War I and which Adolf Hitler led from 1921.

Nuremberg Laws: A series of antisemitic and racial laws in Nazi Germany. The first two of these laws were enacted by the Reichstag on September 15, 1935, at a special meeting convened during the annual Nuremberg Party Rally. These were the Law for the Protection of German Blood and German Honor, and the Reich Citizenship Law. These laws deprived German Jews of citizenship; removed Jews from German political, social, and economic life; and created definitions of Jewishness based on biological descent.

Nuremberg trials: The prosecution by the Allies in 1945–1946 of the key Nazi leaders for crimes committed during World War II. Most were sentenced to imprisonment or death by hanging.

Persecution: The systematic abuse of a person or group by others, usually based on difference in religion, race, or politics. The persecutor causes physical torment, harassment, isolation, imprisonment, fear, or pain, with the intention of causing severe suffering.

Pogrom: A term usually associated with mob attacks against Jewish communities, it has also come to be applied more generally when violence takes place against any persecuted group. During much of the 20th century, the term implied any attack on Jews regardless of the degree of official input and irrespective of whether the attack was spontaneous or planned. The destruction wrought by pogroms varied from situation to situation and could involve murder, rape, pillage, physical assault, and wanton or random destruction. Pogroms could also lead to genocidal massacres.

Propaganda: Biased information used to manipulate recipients and promote an agenda by generating an emotional rather than a rational response. Propaganda can be produced by governments, activist groups, companies, religious organizations, and the media through paintings, cartoons, posters, pamphlets, films, radio shows, television shows, and websites. The Nazis achieved the acceptance, among both opponents and admirers, of the most blatant falsehoods.

Racism: The prejudicial belief that biological characteristics such as skin pigmentation, facial features, bone structures, and hair quality are the primary determinant of human abilities, and that the human species is unequally divided along superior and inferior lines based on such attributes. Racism can lead to active forms of discrimination in the areas of politics, society, culture, economics, religion, and the military, and can be expressed through laws, socioeconomic exclusion, discrimination, violence, and genocide.

Refugee: A person who has been forced to leave their nation, state, or place of living as a result of war or general unrest; cannot return home safely; and carries a well-founded fear of persecution should they attempt to do so.

Reichstag: The German parliament, which enacted Nazi laws from 1933 to 1945.

Righteous among the Nations: Non-Jews who, at the risk of their own lives, saved Jews from their Nazi persecutors, as recognized by Yad Vashem in Jerusalem.

SA (*Sturmabteilung*): The Nazi Party's original paramilitary or stormtroopers, called "Brownshirts" from the color of their uniforms. Organized in 1921, and led by Ernest Röhm, it supported Hitler's rise to power in the 1920s and 1930s by providing protection for Nazi rallies and assemblies, disrupting the meetings of opposing parties, fighting against the paramilitary units of the opposing parties and boycotting Jewish businesses.

Sonderkommando: The term given to work units in Nazi death camps, usually prisoners who were forced to work in the gas chambers, undressing rooms, and crematoria.

SS (*Schutzstaffel*): Also called "Blackshirts" from the color of their uniforms. From a small personal bodyguard unit created for Hitler in 1925, the SS became a major paramilitary organization which was, from 1929 until the Nazi collapse in 1945, the primary agency of security, surveillance, and terror within Germany and German-occupied Europe. After Nazi Germany's defeat, the SS was judged by the International Military Tribunal at Nuremberg to be a criminal organization.

Third Reich: When Adolf Hitler became chancellor on January 30, 1933, the Nazi state was declared to be Germany's Third Reich (Empire), intended to last for a thousand years. The First Reich was the medieval Holy Roman Empire (800–1806). The Second Reich (1871–1918) was united Germany under the Hohenzollerns (1871–1918).

War: A state of organized, armed conflict between different states, or different groups within a state, that is usually open and declared. War is characterized by aggression and violence, is often prolonged, and is usually waged by military forces fighting against each other. Conflict taking place during war is typified by high mortality, economic and social disruption, and physical devastation in the areas where fighting takes place.

War crimes: Acts committed during armed conflict that violate the international laws, treaties, customs, and practices governing military conflict between belligerent states or parties. War crimes are a legal category within international law, identifying punishable offenses for serious violations (so-called grave breaches) of the accepted international rules of war. War crimes recognize individual criminal responsibility where such violations occur, enshrining the idea that individuals can be held accountable for their own actions during wartime, provided a moral choice was able to be made at the time of the offense.

Yellow star: In Germany in 1937, Jewish prisoners in concentration camps were to wear a yellow triangle. By 1941 the yellow star was the standard emblem for all Jews over the age of six years throughout the Greater Reich. The yellow color was associated with cowardice. If caught outside the ghettos without it, Jews were subject to beatings, imprisonment, and sometimes worse. Inside the death camps, such visible badges of separation and identification were also in use. Though variations existed depending on the country under Nazi hegemony, sometimes the star alone, sometimes with the word Jude, Jood, or Juif, it was the wearing itself that had the most obviously devastating effect.

Bibliography

The bibliography that follows is intended as a starting point for researchers and students of the Holocaust, with a specific focus on children. In some cases these works are intended to serve as further reading on a specific topic, or a broader context in which it can be placed. The bibliography does not claim to be a complete listing of all works relating to children of the Holocaust but, rather, an aid for deeper investigation.

New works are appearing literally every day, but there are some general works that should be consulted at a bare minimum as the core of any research project on children during the Holocaust period. See the following, especially: Debórah Dwork. *Children with a Star: Jewish Youth in Nazi Europe*. New Haven, CT: Yale University Press, 1991; Lynn H. Nicholas. *Cruel World: The Children of Europe in the Nazi Web*. New York: Knopf, 2005; Nicholas Stargardt. *Witnesses of War: Children's Lives under the Nazis*. London: Jonathan Cape, 2005; and Patricia Heberer. *Children during the Holocaust*. Lanham, MD: Alta Mira Press, 2011.

Abrahamsen, Samuel. *Norway's Response to the Holocaust: A Historical Perspective*. New York: Holocaust Library, 1991.
Adelsberger, Lucie. *Auschwitz: A Doctor's Story*. Boston: Northeastern University Press, 1995.
Adelson, Alan (Ed.). *The Diary of Dawid Sierakowiak: Five Notebooks from the Łódź Ghetto*. New York: Oxford University Press, 1996.
Adler, H. G. *Theresienstadt 1941–1945: The Face of a Coerced Community*. Cambridge: Cambridge University Press, 1955.
Aly, Götz, Peter Chroust, and Christian Pross. *Cleansing the Fatherland: Nazi Medicine and Racial Hygiene*. Baltimore: Johns Hopkins University Press, 1994.
Amkraut, Brian. *Between Home and Homeland: Youth Aliyah from Nazi Germany*. Tuscaloosa: University of Alabama Press. 2006.
Barnouw, David, and Gerrold Van Der Stroom (Eds.). *The Diary of Anne Frank: The Critical Edition*. New York: Doubleday, 1989.
Bartoszewski, Władysław, and Zofia Lewin. *The Samaritans: Heroes of the Holocaust*. New York: Twayne Publishers, 1970.
Bartrop, Paul R. "Barkman, Frances (1885–1946)." *Australian Dictionary of Biography*, vol. 13. Melbourne: Melbourne University Press, 1993, p. 114.
Bartrop, Paul R. *Resisting the Holocaust: Upstanders, Partisans, and Survivors*. Santa Barbara, CA: ABC-CLIO, 2016.
Bartrop, Paul R., with Gabrielle Eisen (Eds.). *The Dunera Affair: A Documentary Resource Book*. Melbourne: Schwartz and Wilkinson, 1990.

Bartrop, Paul R., and Eve E. Grimm. *Perpetrating the Holocaust: Leaders, Enablers, and Collaborators*. Santa Barbara, CA: ABC-CLIO, 2019.

Bartrop, Paul R., and Samantha J. Lakin. *Heroines of Vichy France: Rescuing French Jews during the Holocaust*. Santa Barbara, CA: Praeger, 2019.

Bauer, Yehuda. *Jews for Sale? Nazi-Jewish Negotiations, 1933–1945*. New Haven, CT: Yale University Press, 1994.

Bauman, Janina. *Winter in the Morning: A Young Girl's Life in the Warsaw Ghetto and Beyond, 1939–1945*. New York: Free Press, 1986.

Ben-Ami, Fanny. *Le Journal de Fanny: L'histoire vraie d'une jeune fille au destin hors du commun*. Paris: Éditions de Seuil, 2011.

Bender, Sara. *The Jews of Białystok during World War II and the Holocaust*. Boston: Brandeis University Press, 2008.

Benedict, Susan, and Linda Shields (Eds.). *Nurses and Midwives in Nazi Germany: The "Euthanasia Programs."* New York: Routledge, 2014.

Berenbaum, Michael. *The Vision of the Void. Theological Reflections on the Works of Elie Wiesel*. Middletown, CT: Wesleyan University Press, 1979.

Berg, Mary. *The Diary of Mary Berg: Growing up in the Warsaw Ghetto*. London: Oneworld Publications, 2006.

Birenbaum, Halina. *Hope Is the Last to Die: A Personal Documentation of Nazi Terror*. New York: Twayne, 1971.

Bitton Jackson, Livia E. *Elli: Coming of Age in the Holocaust*. New York: Times Books, 1980.

Blackburn, Gilmer W. *Education in the Third Reich: Race and History in Nazi Textbooks*. Albany: State University of New York Press, 1984.

Blatt, Thomas (Toivi). *From the Ashes of Sobibor*. Evanston, IL: Northwestern University Press, 1997.

Boas, Jacob (Ed.). *We Are Witnesses: Five Diaries of Teenagers Who Died in the Holocaust*. New York: Henry Holt, 1995.

Brown, Gordon. *Wartime Courage: Stories of Extraordinary Courage by Exceptional Men and Women in World War Two*. London: Bloomsbury, 2008.

Burleigh, Michael, and Wolfgang Wipperman. *The Racial State: Germany 1933–1945*. Cambridge: Cambridge University Press, 1991.

Byers, Ann. *Saving Children from the Holocaust: The Kindertransport*. Buchanan, NY: Enslow Publishers, 2011.

Campt, Tina. *Other Germans: Black Germans and the Politics of Race, Gender, and Memory in the Third Reich*. Ann Arbor: University of Michigan Press, 2003.

Chalmers, Beverley. *Birth, Sex and Abuse: Women's Voices under Nazi Rule*. Surbiton, UK: Grosvenor House, 2015.

Clay, Catherine, and Michael Leapman. *Master Race: The Lebensborn Experiment in Nazi Germany*. London: Hodder and Stoughton, 1995.

Cohen, Adir. *The Gate of Light: Janusz Korczak, the Educator and Writer Who Overcame the Holocaust*. Madison, NJ: Fairleigh Dickinson University Press, 1994.

Cohen, Asher, and Yehoyakim Cochavi (Eds.). *Zionist Youth Movements during the Shoah*. New York: Peter Lang, 1995.

Cohen, Beth B. *Child Survivors of the Holocaust: The Youngest Remnant and the American Experience*. New Brunswick, NJ: Rutgers University Press, 2018.

Coleman, Fred. *The Marcel Network: How One French Couple Saved 527 Children from the Holocaust*. Washington, D.C.: Potomac Books, 2013.

David, Janina. *A Square of Sky: A Jewish Childhood in Wartime Poland*. London: Hutchinson, 1964.

David, Janina. *A Touch of Earth: A Wartime Childhood*. London: Hutchinson, 1966.
Einhorn, Lena. *Ninas Resa*. Stockholm: Prisma, 2005.
Emanuel, Muriel, and Vera Gissing. *Nicholas Winton and the Rescued Generation: Save One Life, Save the World*. Edgeware, UK: Vallentine, Mitchell, 2001.
Enzer, Hyman A., and Sandra Solotaroff-Enzer (Eds.). *Anne Frank: Reflections on Her Life and Legacy*. Urbana: University of Illinois Press, 2000.
Fine, Ellen S. *Legacy of Night: The Literary Universe of Elie Wiesel*. Albany: State University of New York Press, 1982.
Flinker, Moshe. *Young Moshe's Diary: The Spiritual Torment of a Jewish Boy in Nazi Europe*. Jerusalem: Yad Vashem, 1965.
Frank, Anne. *The Diary of a Young Girl*. New York: Doubleday, 2003.
Friedlander, Henry. *The Origins of Nazi Genocide: From Euthanasia to the Final Solution*. Chapel Hill: University of North Carolina Press, 1995.
Gabryel, Kazimierz. *Stanisława Leszczyńska: 1896–1974*. Łódź: Diecezjalne Wydawn, 1989.
Garel, Georges with Katy Hazan. *Le sauvetage des enfants juifs par l'OSE*. Paris: Le Manuscrit, 2012.
Georges, Olivier. *Pierre-Marie Gerlier, le Cardinal Militant*. Paris, Desclée de Brouwer, 2014.
Geve, Thomas. *Youth in Chains*. Jerusalem: Rubin Mass, 1958.
Ghert-Zand, Renee. "Holocaust Film Reveals Long-hushed Child Sex Abuse." *Times of Israel*, April 15, 2015, at https://www.timesofisrael.com/documentary-reveals-secrets-of-sexual-abuse-of-children-in-the-holocaust/.
Gies, Miep. *Anne Frank Remembered*. New York: Simon and Schuster, 1987.
Glas-Wiener, Sheva. *Children of the Ghetto*. Fitzroy, Victoria: Globe Press, 1983.
Gossels, Lisa, and Dean Wetherell (producers). *The Children of Chabannes*. Good Egg Productions, 1999, at https://childrenofchabannes.org/.
Grose, Peter. *A Good Place to Hide: How One French Community Saved Thousands of People during World War II*, New York: Pegasus Books, 2015.
Gross, Alan G., and Ray D. Dearin. *Chaim Perelman*. Albany: State University of New York Press, 2003.
Gutterman, Bella, and Avner Shalev (Eds.). *To Bear Witness: Holocaust Remembrance at Yad Vashem*. Jerusalem: Yad Vashem, 2005.
Hallie, Philip. *Lest Innocent Blood Be Shed: The Story of the Village of Le Chambon, and How Goodness Happened There*. New York: HarperPerennial, 1994.
Hart, Kitty. *I Am Alive*. London: Transworld Publishers, 1962.
Hart, Kitty. *Return to Auschwitz: The Remarkable Story of the Girl Who Survived the Holocaust*. London: Atheneum, 1983.
Hazan, Katy and Georges Weill. *Andrée Salomon, une femme du lumière*. Paris: Le Manuscrit, 2011.
Heath, Tim. *Hitler's Girls: Doves among Eagles*. Barnsley, UK: Pen and Sword, 2017.
Hedgepeth, Sonja M., and Rochelle G. Saidel (Eds.). *Sexual Violence against Jewish Women during the Holocaust*. Lebanon, NH: Brandeis University Press/University Press of New England, 2010.
Heyman, Éva. *The Diary of Éva Heyman*. New York: Shapolsky, 1988.
Holliday, Laurel. *Children in the Holocaust and World War II: Their Secret Diaries*. New York: Pocket Books, 1995.
Im Hof-Piguet, Anne-Marie. *La Filiere in France Occupée, 1942–1944*. Yverdon-les-Bains: Éditions de la Thièle, 1985.
Israeli, Raphael. *The Death Camps of Croatia: Visions and Revisions, 1941–1945*. New Brunswick, NJ: Transaction Publishers, 2013.

Iturbe, Antonio. *The Librarian of Auschwitz*. New York: Henry Holt, 2012.
Joffo, Joseph. *A Bag of Marbles*. Chicago: University of Chicago Press, 2000.
Kamenetsky, Christa. *Children's Literature in Hitler's Germany: The Cultural Policy of National Socialism*. Athens: Ohio University Press, 1984.
Karas, Joža. *Music in Terezín, 1941–1945*. New York: Beaufort Books, 1985.
Kater, Michael. *Different Drummers: Jazz in the Culture of Nazi Germany*. New York: Oxford University Press, 1992.
Keren, Nili. "The Family Camp." In Michael Berenbaum and Yisrael Gutman (Eds.), *Anatomy of the Auschwitz Death Camp*. Bloomington: Indiana University Press, 1998, pp. 428–440.
Klaphek, Elisa. *Fraulein Rabbiner Jonas: The Story of the First Woman Rabbi*. San Fransisco: Jossey-Bass, 2004.
Klarsfeld, Serge. *The Children of Izieu: A Human Tragedy*. New York: Harry N. Abrams, 1985.
Koch, H. W. *The Hitler Youth: Origins and Development 1922–45*. London: Macdonald and Jane's, 1975.
Koehl, Robert L. *RKFDV: German Resettlement and Population Policy 1939–1945*. Cambridge, MA: Harvard University Press, 1957.
Konigseder, Angelika, and Juliane Wetzel. *Waiting for Hope: Jewish Displaced Persons in Post–World War II Germany*. Evanston, IL: Northwestern University Press, 2001.
Kor, Eva Mozes, and Lisa Rojnay Buccieri. *Surviving the Angel of Death: The Story of a Mengele Twin in Auschwitz*. Terre Haute, IN: Tanglewood, 2009.
Kor, Eva Mozes, and Mary Wright. *Echoes from Auschwitz: Dr. Mengele's Twins. The Story of Eva and Miriam Mozes*. Terre Haute, IN: Candles, Inc., 1995.
Krell, Robert. *Child Holocaust Survivors—Memories and Reflections*. Victoria, BC: Trafford Publishing, 2007.
Küchler-Silberman, Lena. *One Hundred Children*. New York: Doubleday, 1961.
Kulski, Julian Eugeniusz. *Dying, We Live*. New York: Holt, Rinehart and Winston, 1979.
Lagnado, Lucette Matalon, and Sheila Cohn Dekel. *Children of the Flames: Dr. Josef Mengele and the Untold Story of the Twins of Auschwitz*. New York: William Morrow, 1991.
Lathey, Gillian. *The Impossible Legacy: Identity and Purpose in Autobiographical Children's Literature Set in the Third Reich and the Second World War*. Bern: Peter Lang, 1998.
Lazare, Lucien. *The Mission of Abbé Glasberg in the French Resistance during WWII*. Oegstgeest, Netherlands: Amsterdam Publishers, 2016.
Lee, Carol Ann. *The Hidden Life of Otto Frank*. New York: HarperCollins, 2003.
Lefenfeld, Nancy. *The Fate of Others: Rescuing Jewish Children on the French-Swiss Border*. Clarksville, MD: Timbrel Press, 2013.
Levine, Karen. *Hana's Suitcase* (Anniversary Edition). Sydney: Allen and Unwin, 2014.
Lifton, Betty Jean. *The King of Children: The Life and Death of Janusz Korczak*. New York: Collins, 1988.
Lifton, Robert Jay. *The Nazi Doctors: Medical Killing and the Psychology of Genocide*. New York: Basic Books, 2000.
Loinger, Georges. *L'odyssée d'un resistant: Témoignage d'un centenaire, enfrant d'Alsace*. Nice: Les Éditions Ovadia, 2016.
Loinger, Georges, and Katy Hazan. *Aux frontiers de l'espoir*. Paris: Le Manuscrit, 2006.
Lomović, Boško. *Heroine from Innsbruck: Diana Obexer Budisavljević*. Belgrade: Svet Knjige, 2014.
Lukas, Richard C. *Did the Children Cry? Hitler's War against Jewish and Polish Children, 1939–1945*. New York: Hippocrene Books, 2001.

Martin, Ben. *Marcel Marceau: Master of Mime*. London: Paddington Press, 1978.
Meed, Vladka. *On Both Sides of the Wall*. New York: Holocaust Library, 1979.
Megargee, Geoffrey P., and Joseph R. White (Eds.). *The United States Holocaust Memorial Museum Encyclopedia of Camps and Ghettos, 1933–1945*, vol. III, *Camps and Ghettos under European Regimes Aligned with Nazi Germany*. Bloomington: Indiana University Press, 2018.
Melson, Robert. *False Papers: Deception and Survival in the Holocaust*. Champaign: University of Illinois Press, 2000.
Miller, Mary. *Jane Haining: A Life of Love and Courage*. Edinburgh: Birlinn, 2019.
Miron, Guy (Ed.). *The Yad Vashem Encyclopedia of the Ghettos during the Holocaust*. New York: New York University Press, 2009.
Moorehead, Caroline. *Village of Secrets: Defying the Nazis in Vichy France*. New York: HarperCollins, 2014.
Moskovitz, Sarah. *Love Despite Hate: Child Survivors of the Holocaust and their Adult Lives*. New York: Schocken Books, 1983.
Muller, Melissa. *Anne Frank: The Biography*. New York: Metropolitan Books, 1998.
Nelson, David Conley. *Moroni and the Swastika: Mormons in Nazi Germany*. Norman: University of Oklahoma Press, 2015.
Niewyk, Donald L. (Ed.). *Fresh Wounds: Early Narratives of Holocaust Survival*. Chapel Hill: University of North Carolina Press, 1998.
Nissen, Henrik S. (Ed.). *Scandinavia during the Second World War*. Minneapolis: University of Minnesota Press, 1983.
Ockman, Joan, and Moshe Safdie, Avner Shalev, and Elie Wiesel. *Yad Vashem: Moshe Safdie—The Architecture of Memory*. Jerusalem: Yad Vashem, 2006.
Paldiel, Mordecai. *The Path of the Righteous: Gentile Rescuers of Jews during the Holocaust*. Hoboken, NJ: KTAV, 1993.
Paldiel, Mordecai. *The Righteous Among the Nations: Rescuers of Jews during the Holocaust*. New York: Harper, 2007.
Paldiel, Mordecai. *Saving One's Own: Jewish Rescuers during the Holocaust*. Philadelphia: Jewish Publication Society, 2017.
Paldiel, Mordecai. *Saving the Jews: Amazing Stories of Men and Women who defied the "Final Solution."* Rockville, MD: Schreiber Publishing, 2000.
Paldiel, Mordecai. *Sheltering the Jews: Stories of Holocaust Rescuers*. Minneapolis: Fortress Press, 1996.
Palmer, Glen. *Reluctant Refuge: Unaccompanied Refugee and Evacuee Children in Australia, 1933–1945*. Sydney: Kangaroo Press, 1997.
Pearl, Cyril. *The Dunera Scandal: Deported by Mistake*. Sydney: Angus and Robertson, 1983.
Perl, Gisella. *I Was a Doctor in Auschwitz*. New York: International Universities Press, 1948.
Peukert, Detlev J. K. *Inside Nazi Germany: Conformity, Opposition and Racism in Everyday Life*. London: B. T. Batsford, 1987.
Pike, Robert. *Defying Vichy: Blood, Fear and French Resistance*. Stroud, UK: The History Press, 2018.
Plotkin, Diane. "Smuggling in the Ghettos: Survivor Accounts from the Warsaw, Łódź, and Kraków Ghettos." In Eric J. Sterling (Ed.), *Life in the Ghettos during the Holocaust*. Syracuse, NY: Syracuse University Press, 2005, pp. 84–119.
Polak, Joseph A. "The Lost Transport." *Commentary*, September 1995, at https://www.commentarymagazine.com/articles/the-lost-transport/.
Porat, Dan. *The Boy: A Holocaust Story*. New York: Hill and Wang, 2010.

Posner, Gerald L., and John Ware. *Mengele: The Complete Story*. New York: Cooper Square, 2000.

Pressman, Steven. *50 Children: One Ordinary American Couple's Extraordinary Rescue Mission into the Heart of Nazi Germany*. New York: HarperCollins, 2014.

Prorokova, Tatiana. "The Holocaust in Film: Witnessing the Extermination through the Eyes of Children." *Holocaust Studies* 23, no. 3 (2018), pp. 377–394.

Rabey, Steve. *Faith under Fire: Stories of Hope and Courage from World War II*. Nashville: Thomas Nelson, 2002.

Radha, Anu (director/producer). *A Little Poland in India*. Aakaar Films, 2016.

Rashke, Richard. *Escape from Sobibor*. Boston: Houghton Mifflin, 1982.

Redlich, Egon. *The Terezin Diary of Gonda Redlich*. Lexington: University Press of Kentucky, 1992.

Reed, Walter W. *The Children of La Hille: Eluding Nazi Capture during World War II*. Syracuse, NY: Syracuse University Press, 2015.

Reese, Dagmar. *Growing up Female in Nazi Germany*. Ann Arbor: University of Michigan Press, 2006.

Rempel, Gerhard. *Hitler's Children: The Hitler Youth and the SS*. Chapel Hill: University of North Carolina Press, 1989.

Rittner, Carol (Ed.). *Anne Frank in the World: Essays and Reflections*. Armonk, NY: M. E. Sharpe, 1997.

Rudashevski, Yitskhok. *The Diary of the Vilna Ghetto, June 1941–April 1943*. Kibbutz Lohamei HaGeta'ot, Israel: Ghetto Fighters' House, 1973.

Samuels, Diane. *Kindertransport*. London: Nick Hern Books, 2010.

Sauvage, Pierre (producer/director/writer). *Weapons of the Spirit*. Chambon Foundation, 1989.

Schwarberg, Günther. *The Murders at Bullenhuser Damm: The SS Doctor and the Children*. Bloomington: Indiana University Press, 1984.

Scrase, David, Wolfgang Mieder, and Katherine Quimby Johnson (Eds.). *Making a Difference, Rescue and Assistance during the Holocaust: Essays in Honor of Marion Pritchard*, Burlington: Center for Holocaust Studies, University of Vermont, 2004.

Selzer, Anita. *I am Sasha*. Melbourne: Penguin Books Random House, 2018.

Sieffert, Rachel. *The Dark Room*. London: Random House, 2001.

Silver, Eric. *The Book of the Just: The Unsung Heroes Who Rescued Jews from Hitler*. New York: Grove Press, 1992.

Silverman, Emily Leah. *Edith Stein and Regina Jonas: Religious Visionaries in the Time of the Death Camp*. London: Routledge, 2014.

Siret, Mal. "Child Holocaust witness reveals lucky escape aboard The Lost Train." BBC News, August 6, 2019, at https://www.bbc.com/news/world-europe-49233817.

Sliwowska, Wiktoria (Ed.). *The Last Eyewitnesses: Children of the Holocaust Speak*. Evanston, IL: Northwestern University Press, 1998.

Smith, Lyn. *Heroes of the Holocaust: Ordinary Britons Who Risked their Lives to Make a Difference*. London: Edbury Press, 2012.

Stephens, Elaine C., Jean E. Brown, and Janet E. Rubin. *Learning about the Holocaust: Literature and Other Resources for Young People*. Hamden, CT: Library Professional Publications, 1995.

Tomaszewski, Irene, and Tecia Werbowski. *Code Name: Żegota: Rescuing Jews in Occupied Poland, 1942–1945: The Most Dangerous Conspiracy in Wartime Europe*. Santa Barbara, CA: Praeger, 2010.

Valent, Paul. *Child Survivors of the Holocaust*. Melbourne: William Heinemann, 1993.

Vasvári, Louise O., and Steven Tötösy de Zepetnek (Eds.). *Imre Kertész and Holocaust Literature*. West Lafayette, IN: Purdue University Press, 2005.

Volavkova, Hana. *I Never Saw another Butterfly*. New York: Schocken Books, 1994.

Vromen, Suzanne. *Hidden Children of the Holocaust: Belgian Nuns and their Daring Rescue of Young Jews from the Nazis*. Oxford: Oxford University Press, 2008.

Waxman, Zoë. *Women in the Holocaust: A Feminist History*. Oxford: Oxford University Press, 2017.

Weiner, Pavel. *A Boy in Terezín: The Private Diary of Pavel Weiner, April 1944–April 1945*. Evanston, IL: Northwestern University Press, 2012.

Weinstock, Malky. *Angel of Orphans: The Story of R' Yona Tiefenbrunner and the Hundreds He Saved*. New York: Menucha Publishers, 2009.

Weiss, Helga. *Helga's Diary: A Young Girl's Account of Life in a Concentration Camp*. New York: Norton, 2013.

Weiss, Sheila Faith. *The Nazi Symbiosis: Human Genetics and Politics in the Third Reich*. Chicago: University of Chicago Press, 2010.

Wiesel, Elie. *Night*. New York: Hill and Wang, 1960.

Williams, Frances. *The Forgotten Kindertransportees: The Scottish Experience*. London: Bloomsbury, 2013.

Winton, Barbara. *If It's Not Impossible . . . : The Life of Sir Nicholas Winton*. Leicester: Troubador Publishing, 2014.

World Federation of Jewish Child Survivors of the Holocaust and Descendants, at https://www.holocaustchild.org/.

Yad Vashem. "Geulen's List: Andrée Geulen-Hersovici," at https://www.yadvashem.org/righteous/stories/geulen-herscovici.html.

Yad Vashem. Jeanne Daman-Scaglione (Belgium), at https://www.yadvashem.org/yv/en/exhibitions/righteous-women/daman.asp.

Yad Vashem. Kanabus Family, at http://db.yadvashem.org/righteous/family.html?language=en&itemId=4043969.

Yad Vashem. Lucien Bunel (Father Jacques), at https://www.yadvashem.org/righteous/stories/bunel.html.

Yad Vashem. Women of Valor: Stories of Women Who Rescued Jews during the Holocaust, at http://www.yadvashem.org/yv/en/exhibitions/righteous-women/gunden.asp.

Zapruder, Alexandra. *Salvaged Pages: Young Writers' Diaries of the Holocaust*. New Haven, CT: Yale University Press, 2015.

Zeitoun, Sabine. *L'Œuvre de secours aux enfants (O.S.E.) sous l'occupation en France: Du legalism à la résistance 1940–1944*. Paris: Éditions L'Harmattan, 2000.

Ziemian, Joseph. *The Cigarette Sellers of Three Crosses Square*. London: Vallentine Mitchell, 1970.

Zimmerman, Joshua D. *The Polish Underground and the Jews, 1939–1945*. Cambridge: Cambridge University Press, 2015.

Zuckerman, Yitzhak. *A Surplus of Memory: Chronicle of the Warsaw Ghetto Uprising*. Berkeley: University of California Press, 1993.

Index

Note: Page numbers in **bold** indicate the location of main entries. Page numbers in *italics* indicate photos.

Abadi, Moussa, **1–3**
  death of, 2
  on depersonalization, 2
  early years and education, 1
  and Marcel Network, 1–2
  marriage, 2
  pseudonym (Marcel Samade), 1
  rescue activities, 1–2
Adelsberger, Lucie, **3–5**
  and death march, 4
  death of, 4
  duties at Auschwitz, 3–4
  early years and education, 3
  as *Judenbehändler* (attendant of Jews), 3
  and liberation, 4
  medical practice and publications, 3
Aliyah Bet, 102, 172
Amitié Chrétienne, 92–93, 101
André, Joseph, **5–6**
  and *Comité de Défense des Juifs,* 6
  death of, 6
  early years and education, 5
  Jewish children's rescue network founded by, 5–6
  postwar activities, 6
  rescue activities, 5–6
  Righteous among the Nations recognition, 6
Anne Frank House, **7–8**
  and Anne Frank Foundation, 7–8
  established as museum, 8
  front of, 7
  and Gies, Miep, 8
  history of, 7–8
  location, 7
  purpose of, 84–85
  refurbishment and rededication, 8
  Secret Annex, 7
Anschluss, 304
Antifascism
  and Abadi, Moussa, 1
  and Sletten-Fosstvedt, Ingebjørg, 227
  and Spanish Civil War, 134–135, 227
Association of Children of the Holocaust, **8–10**
  commitments and activities, 9
  funding, 10
  meetings and General Assemblies, 10
  membership, 9, 10
  origins and history of, 9
  purpose, 8–9, 10
  and Righteous among the Nations, 9–10
Auschwitz-Birkenau extermination camp (Poland), 27, 32–33, 34, 79, 81–82, 134, 196, 288
  Białystok deportations to, 16, 17
  Birkenau established as primary mass murder site, 306
  children and mothers at, 3, 4, 126, 127, 228
  children's block (Block 31), 118–119, 149–150
  construction of Birkenau begins, 306
  crematoria at, 56
  and death marches, 4, 97
  deportations of Parisian Jewish children to, 307
  deportations to Neuengamme from, 30
  destruction of gas chambers, 309
  establishment of Auschwitz, 305
  evacuation of, 309
  Family Camp BIIb, 149
  first arrival of Roma at, 307

Auschwitz-Birkenau extermination camp (Poland) (*Continued*)
  first deportations of Hungarian Jews to, 308
  first deportations to, 55, 137, 158, 307
  first transport of Jews from Theresienstadt to, 307
  food shortages and starvation, 3, 150
  "Gypsy camp" destroyed at, 309
  and Haining, Jane, "Scottish Angel of Auschwitz," 105–106
  Hoess, Rudolph, commandant of Auschwitz, 30, 179
  Lesser, Fanny, testimony of, 297–302
  and Leszczyńska, Stanisława, 167–168
  liberation of, 18, 84, 169, 245, 309
  library and librarians at, 149–150
  in literature and memoirs, 4, 47–48, 77, 97, 107–109, 113–114, 139–140, 199, 252–253
  Łódź deportations to, 309
  Maison d'Izieu deportations to, 176
  medical experimentation at, 112, 144–146, 149, 167, 182–184, 197–198, 244–246
  and Mengele, Josef, 112, 144–146, 149, 167, 182–184, 197–198, 244
  Perl, Gisella, testimony of, 199
  resistance movement, 117–119
  selection process at, 112, 139, 169
  Sonderkommando revolt, 309
  survivors, 2, 18, 77, 82, 84, 97, 99, 100, 102, 109–111, 112–113, 139–140, 149–150, 176, 251–252
  Wiesel, Elie, at, 251–252

Barbie, Klaus, 175–176, 184
Barkman, Frances, **11–12**
  and Australian Jewish Welfare Society, 11–12
  death of, 12
  early years and education, 11
  and Frances Barkman Houses, 12
  Jewish welfare activities, 11–12
  postwar activities, 12
Bauman, Janina, **12–14**
  death of, 14
  A Dream of Belonging, 14, 46
  illness of, 13
  and Jewish youth movements, 13
  marriage, 14
  postwar activities, 14
  and Warsaw Ghetto, 12–14
Bełżec extermination camp (Poland), 19, 111, 152, 169, 307
Ben-Ami, Fanny. *See Le Voyage de Fanny*
Berg, Mary, **14–15**
  and *A Bouquet of Alpine Violets* (adapted play), 15
  diary of, 14–15, 67
  The Diary of Mary Berg: Growing Up in the Warsaw Ghetto, 15
  and invasion of Poland, 14
  and Korczak, Janusz, 15
  marriage, 15
  postwar activities, 15
  and Warsaw Ghetto, 14–15
Bergen-Belsen concentration camp (Germany), 2, 111, 150
  Frank, Anne, at, 82, 83, 84, 99
  liberation of, 158, 169, 198, 309
Bermuda Conference, 308
Białystok children, **16–17**
  and Białystok ghetto uprising, 16
  deportations to Auschwitz, 17
  deportations to Theresienstadt, 16, 17, 118
  location of Białystok, 16
  murders of, 17
  rescue operations, 16–17
Białystok ghetto, 16–17, 306, 308
Birenbaum, Halina, **18–19**
  at Auschwitz, 18
  honors and awards, 19
  Hope Is the Last to Die: A Personal Documentation of Nazi Terror, 19
  and invasion of Poland, 18
  marriage, 19
  postwar activities, 18–19
  and selection process, 18
  in Warsaw Ghetto, 18
Blatt, Thomas "Toivi," **19–21**
  death of, 21
  From the Ashes of Sobibor, 21
  interview with Karl Frenzel, Sobibór SS guard, 20
  postwar activities, 20–21

at Sobibór, 19–20
Sobibor, the Forgotten Revolt: A Survivor's Report, 21
Border crossings, **21–23**
   dangers and difficulties of, 21–23
   and *passeurs* (people movers), 21–22, 53, 64, 89, 157, 161, 162, 172, 216
   See also Cohn, Marianne; Marceau, Marcel; Racine, Mila
Bouty, Pierre and Marguerite, 62
The Boy: A Holocaust Story, **23–24**
   background and inspiration, 23
   photographs, 24
   Porat, Dan, author, 23–24
   and Warsaw Ghetto Uprising, 24
Brady, Hana. *See Hana's Suitcase*
Brundibár, **25–27**
   Krása, Hans, composer, 25–27, 240
   Krása, Hans, murder of, 27
   meaning of the term, 25
   poster, 25
   postwar performances, 27
   staged at Theresienstadt, 25–26, 118, 240
   victory chorus, 26
Buchenwald concentration camp (Germany), 135, 140, 174, 204
   death march to, 97, 251
   establishment of, 304
   liberation of, 97, 139, 169, 309
   and Strippel, Arnold, war crimes trial and conviction, 30
   Wiesel, Elie, at, 251, 252
Budisavljević, Diana, **27–29**
   death of, 29
   diary and records of, 28, 43
   honors and awards, 29
   and kidnapping, 28
   marriage, 27
   postwar activities, 29
   rescue activities, 27–29, 42
   visit to women's camp at Stara Gradiška, 28
Bullenhuser Damm, **29–31**
   conversion to satellite camp of Neuengamme, 30, 179
   and Heissmeyer, Kurt, 29–31
   massacre at, 30
   and postwar trials, 30–31
   and Strippel, Arnold, 30–31, 179

Camps. *See* Concentration and extermination camps
Carter, Jimmy, 252
Central Office of Jewish Emigration, 304
Château de la Hille, **32–34**
   French police raid of, 32–33
   and *Kindertransport,* 32
   location, 32
   and Näf, Rösli, 32–33
   and Ott, Emma, 33
   rescue activities at, 32–34
Chełmno extermination camp (Poland), 100, 306
Chevrier, Félix, **34–36**
   death of, 35
   and Œuvre de Secours aux Enfants, 34–35
   postwar activities, 35
   rescue activities, 34–35
   and Resistance, 35
   Righteous among the Nations recognition, 35
Child euthanasia, **36–38**
   and Aktion T-4, 36, 179
   and Brandt, Karl, 36–37
   and infanticide, 126
   original intention of program, 36
   program expansion, 36–37
   and Reich Committee for the Scientific Registration of Serious Hereditary and Congenially Based Diseases, 36
   See also Infanticide
Child survivors, **38–39**
   definition of, 38
   and Holocaust memorialization, 39
   loss suffered by, 38
   postwar lives, 38–39
   and Second Generation, 39
   See also World Federation of Jewish Child Survivors of the Holocaust and Descendants
Children and film, **39–42**
   broadness of Holocaust theme, 39–40
   notable examples, 41
   sense of place and period, 41
   and sentimentality trap, 40
   See also La Colline aux Mille Enfants; Le Voyage de Fanny

Children's concentration camps, Croatia, **42–45**
  and Budisavljevic, Diana, 42
  death rates in, 42–43, 44
  history of, 42
  Jasenovac Memorial Museum, 44
  re-education of children, 44
  survivors, 43
  See also Jastrebarsko children's concentration camp (Croatia); Sisak children's concentration camp (Croatia); Stara Gradiška concentration camp (Croatia)
Children's literature of the Holocaust, **45–49**
  and allegory, 48
  diaries and journals of children who did not survive, 45
  fictional works, 46–47
  readership ages, 48
  reminiscences, 45–46
  themes in, 46–47
  See also Bauman, Janina; David, Janina; Diaries and journals; Frank, Anne; Glas-Wiener, Sheva; Heyman, Éva; Küchler-Silberman, Lena; Rubinowicz, Dawid; Wiesel, Elie
Children's Memorial. *See* Yad Vashem Children's Memorial
Chirac, Jacques, 132, 217
The Cigarette Sellers of Three Crosses Square, **49–50**
  characters and story of, 49–50
  publication of, 50
  writing of, 50
  Ziemian, Joseph, pseudonymous author, 49–50
Circumcision, **51–52**
  and covenant of *brit milah,* 51
  definition of, 51
  in Jewish tradition, 51
  and passing, 51, 195
  and persecution, 51
  "uncircumcization" procedures, 51–52
  and Żegota, 51
Cohn, Marianne, **52–54**
  and border crossings, 22, 54
  capture and murder of, 54, 172
  and Deffaugt, Jean, 54, 65, 66
  early years and family, 52
  and *Éclaireurs Israélites de France,* 52
  "*Je trahirai demain*" ("I Shall Betray Tomorrow"), 53
  and Loinger, Georges, 53, 172
  and Racine, Mila, 53, 65, 204
  rescue activities of, 52–54
  Righteous among the Nations recognition, 54
Comité de Défense des Juifs, **54–57**
  and André, Joseph, 6
  Emerson, Herbert, on, 294
  and Geulen-Herscovici, Andrée, 56, 95
  and Heiber, Maurice and Estera, 56–57
  and hidden children, 55
  history and founding of, 54–55
  and Jospa, Yvonne, 55–57, 134
  recording keeping and coding, 57
Concentration and extermination camps
  and Association of Children of the Holocaust, 9
  Bełżec (Poland), 19, 111, 152, 169, 307
  Chełmno (Poland), 100, 306
  child survivors, 9, 38, 60, 61, 100, 152
  and children's literature, 45, 46, 48
  in Croatia, 27, 42–44
  Dachau (Germany), 78, 158, 169, 197, 303, 309
  and death marches, 4, 97, 111, 168, 169, 233, 251
  diaries and journals, 67
  Edelweiss Pirates deported to, 74
  Flossenbürg (Germany), 169
  in France, 82, 92, 306
  Frank family at, 7, 82, 83, 84, 99
  Gross-Rosen (Germany/Lower Silesia), 97, 111, 184, 300, 302
  hidden children deported to, 115
  and infanticide, 127
  Janowska (Poland), 308
  Jastrebarsko (Croatia), 28, 42–44
  and *Kristallnacht,* 86
  liberation of, 169–170, 309
  and *Lore,* 174
  Majdanek (Poland), 161, 163, 169, 243, 308
  Mauthausen-Gusen (Austria), 58, 113, 167, 172, 197, 204, 304, 309

Natzweiler-Struthof (France), 82, 306
Neuengamme (Germany), 29–31, 138, 179, 305
Pawiak prison, 14, 154, 226
peipels in, 199–200
sex slavery in, 200, 222
Sisak (Croatia), 28, 29, 42–44
Sobibór (Poland), 19–21, 158, 169, 232, 307, 308
Stara Gradiška (Croatia), 28, 43
Stutthof (Germany), 100–101
Vught (Netherlands), 138, 249–250
See also Auschwitz-Birkenau extermination camp (Poland); Bergen-Belsen concentration camp (Germany); Buchenwald concentration camp (Germany); Medical experimentations; Ravensbrück concentration camp (Germany); Theresienstadt
Crematoria, 20, 56, 111, 169, 290
Czerniaków, Adam, 307

Dachau concentration camp (Germany), 158
establishment of, 303
liberation of, 169, 309
Mühldorf (subsidiary camp), 78
"priest block," 197
Daman, Jeanne, **58–60**
and *Comité de Défense des Juifs,* 55
death of, 60
early years and family, 58
and MRB (*Mouvement Royal Belge*), 59–60
and Perelman, Fela, 59
postwar activities, 60
rescue activities, 58–60
Righteous among the Nations recognition, 60
David, Janina, **60–61**
early years and family, 60
education, 61
Light over the Water, 61
passing of, 61
postwar activities, 61
A Square of Sky, 60, 61
A Touch of Earth, 61

volunteer ghetto policeman, 61
and Warsaw Ghetto, 60–61
Death camps. *See* Concentration and extermination camps
Deceptions, **62–64**
of Bouty, Pierre and Marguerite, 62
and circumcision, 63
euphemisms, 62
of Gout, Marie-Antoinette, 62–63
and passing, 63
Deffaugt, Jean, **64–66**
and Cohn, Marianne, 54, 65, 66
death of, 66
early years, 64
and Loinger, Georges, 64, 172
postwar activities, 66
and Racine, Mila, 64–65, 204
rescue activities, 64–66
Righteous among the Nations recognition, 66
Der Stürmer (Nazi newspaper), 263, 265–266
Diaries and journals, **66–68**
definitions of, 66
ghetto diaries, 67–68
and passing, 67
and resistance, 68
See also Berg, Mary; Flinker, Moshe; Frank, Anne; *Helga's Diary;* Heyman, Éva; Rubinowicz, Dawid; Rudashevski, Yitskhok; Sierakowiak, Dawid; Weiner, Pavel
Drexler, Anton, 303
Dunera boys, **68–70**
arrival in Melbourne, 69
education of, 69
and *Kindertransport,* 68, 70
postwar lives, 69–70
voyage of *Dunera,* 68–69
and World War II, 69

Éclaireurs Israélites de France, **71–73,** 129
activities of, 71, 73
and Cohn, Léo, 72
and Cohn, Marianne, 52
Gamzon, Robert, founder, 71–73, 215
history of, 71
La Sixiéme ("the Sixth"), 71, 129, 190, 215

Éclaireurs Israélites de France (Continued)
   and Lévy (Gamzon), Denise, 72
   Loinger, Georges, chief instructor of physical education, 171
   membership, 71
   and *Œuvre de Secours aux Enfants,* 190
   organizational structure, 72
   purpose of, 71, 215
   Salomon, Andrée, Deputy Commissioner to, 71, 215
   and *Union Générale des Israélites de France* (General Union of French Jews), 72
Edelweiss Pirates, **73–75**
   ages and membership, 73
   anti-Nazi opposition of, 74–75
   arrests, 74
   deported to concentration and extermination camps, 74
   and Himmler, Heinrich, 74, 219
   history of, 73–74
   and Hitler Youth, 73
   punishments for, 74
   and Schink, Barthel, 218–219
   as social outcasts, 74
   and Swing Kids, 235
Education in the Third Reich, **75–77**
   gender and misogyny, 76–77
   Hitler, Adolf, on, 75–77
   and Hitler Youth, 76
   physical fitness training, 75–76
   school curricula, 75
   teachers, 76
   textbooks, 76
Eichmann, Adolf, 16, 17, 143, 184, 191, 306, 308
Einsatzgruppen (killing squads), 289–290, 305, 306
Elli: Coming of Age in the Holocaust, **77–79**
   adaptation for young readers, 78
   on hardship and violence, 77–78
   Jackson, Livia E. Bitton, author, 77–78
   on liberation, 78
   on medical experimentation, 78
Emerson, Herbert, memorandum on refugee children in France, Belgium, and Switzerland (primary document), 293–297
   on the "children now in question," 293–294
   on children of Belgium, 294
   on children of France, 294
   on children of Switzerland, 294
   on classes of children, 294
   commentary on, 295–297
   on rescue of children, 294–295
   on safety and health of children, 295
   text, 293–295
Enabling Act, 303
Errázuriz, María, **79–80**
   arrest and torture, 79
   death of, 80
   and French Resistance, 79
   rescue activities, 79–80
   Righteous among the Nations recognition, 80
Evrard, Edmond, 2
Extermination camps. *See* Concentration and extermination camps

Final Solution, 17, 169, 290, 301, 306
Fink, Fritz. *See The Jewish Question in Education*
Flinker, Moshe, **81–82**
   death of, 82
   deportation of family to camps, 81–82
   diary of, 67, 81–82
   early years and family, 81
   on God and suffering, 81
   and liberation, 82
   publication of diary, 82
Flossenbürg concentration camp (Germany), 169
Food shortages and starvation
   at Auschwitz-Birkenau, 3, 150
   in ghetto diaries, 67
   and infanticide, 127
   in Łódź ghetto, 100, 168, 227, 284–285, 287
   and smuggling, 167, 229–231, 287
   at Theresienstad, 107
   in Warsaw Ghetto, 13, 60, 148, 229–230
Frank, Anne, **82–85**
   controversy and rights disputes, 84
   death of, 84

deportation of Frank family to Auschwitz, 84
diary of, 67, 82–85
The Diary of a Young Girl, 45, 84–85, 227, 252
in hiding, 83–84
legacy of, 84–85
in Montessori School, Amsterdam, 83
transferred to Bergen-Belsen, 84
See also Anne Frank House
Frank, Edith, 7, 82, 83, 84
Frank, Margot, 7, 82, 83, 84
Frank, Otto, 7–8, 82–84, 98–99
Freier, Recha, **85–87**
death of, 87
early years and education, 85
honors and awards, 87
and *Kristallnacht,* 86
rescue activities, 86
and Youth Aliyah, 85–87, 91, 117, 170
and Zionism, 85–87
Freund, John, testimony of (primary document), 274–280
on antisemitism, 275
commentary on, 278–280
on education, 275, 278
on friends and friendship, 275–276, 278
on German occupation of Czechoslovakia, 274–275
on illness, 277
on recreation, 276
on religion, 278
text, 274–278
on work and chores, 276–277

Gagnier, Pierre, 2
Gamzon, Robert, 71–73, 215
Garel Network, **88–90**
and Garel, Georges, 88–89, 215
and Lederman, Charles, 88, 215
and Loinger, Georges, 89
and Maison d'Izieu, 175
organizational structure, 89
origins and history of, 88–89
and Salomon, Andrée, 89, 215–216
Garnethill Hostel, **90–91**
and *Kindertransport,* 90
location, 90

origins and purpose of, 90
physical exercise and training, 91
registry, 91
and Scottish Jewish Heritage Centre project, 91
temporary lodging, 91
working-class nature of, 90
years of operation, 90
Gerlier, Pierre-Marie, **91–93**
and *Amitié Chrétienne,* 92–93
death of, 93
and Glasberg, Alexandre, 93, 101
postwar activities, 93
rescue activities, 91–93
Righteous among the Nations recognition, 93
German Workers' Party (DAP)
founding, 303
and Hitler, Adolf, 303
renamed National Socialist German Workers' Party (NSDAP), 303
Gerstein, Kurt, 307
Gertner, Ala, 309
Gestapo
and André, Joseph, 5
Cohn, Marianne, capture and execution of, 65, 66
Edelweiss Pirates, arrests of, 74
Ehrenfelder Navajo Group, public hanging of members, 218
Eichmann, Adolf, Department IV B4 head, 5
Errazuríz, María, arrest and torture of, 79
established by Hermann Göring, 303
Felix, Karol, murder of, 111
Felix, Lola, arrest of, 110
Glasberg, Vila, arrest and murder of, 102
Haining, Jane, arrest of, 106
Hart, Kitty, arrest of, 110
Heiber, Maurice and Estera, arrests of, 56
Hübener, Helmuth, arrest and execution of, 123–124
and Jewish informers, 195
Jovy, Michael, arrests and hanging of, 218–219
Küchler, Lena, torture and murder of, 152

Gestapo (*Continued*)
  Kulski, Julian Eugeniusz, arrest and imprisonment of, 154
  Leszczyńska family, arrest of, 167
  Maison d'Izieu (Jewish children's home), raid on, 175
  Mangel, Charles (father of Marcel Marceau), capture and murder of, 178
  Mont-César Abbey, raid on, 207
  Pax Hotel, 204
  Père Jacques, arrest of, 196
  Prison de Pax, 54
  Racine, Mila, torture of, 64
  raids on Jewish schools, 58–59, 95, 161, 196
  Rosenstock (Abadi), Odette, arrest and torture of, 2
  Rudashevski, Yitskhok, capture and murder of, 213
  Sendler, Irena, arrest and torture of, 225–226
  sterilization program of, 209
  and Tiefenbrunner Orphanage, 240–241
  Trocmé, Daniel, arrest and murder of, 161
  Westerweel, Johan, arrest of, 250
Getter, Matylda, **93–95**
  death of, 95
  early years and education, 93
  and passing, 93–95
  postwar activities, 94–95
  rescue activities, 93–95
  Righteous among the Nations recognition, 95
  and Sendler, Irena, 93, 94
  and Warsaw Ghetto, 93–94
  and Żegota, 93, 94
Geulen-Herscovici, Andrée, **95–96**
  and *Comité de Défense des Juifs*, 56, 95
  early years and teaching career, 95
  marriage, 96
  postwar activities, 96
  rescue activities, 95–96
  Righteous among the Nations recognition, 96
Geve, Thomas, **96–98**
  at Auschwitz, 97
  early years and family, 96–97

Guns and Barbed Wire: A Child Survives the Holocaust, 98
  and liberation, 97
  postwar activities, 97–98
  Youth in Chains, 98
Gies, Miep, **98–99**
  death of, 99
  and diary of Anne Frank, 8, 84, 99
  early years, 98
  and Frank family, 83, 98–99
  honors and awards, 99
  postwar activities, 99
  Righteous among the Nations recognition, 99
  Wallenberg Medal awarded to, 202
Glas-Wiener, Sheva, **99–101**
  Children of the Ghetto, 48, 100
  death of, 99–100
  and Łódź ghetto, 99–100
  postwar activities, 99–100
Glasberg, Alexandre, **101–102**
  and *Aliyah Bet*, 102
  and *Amitié Chrétienne*, 93, 101
  death of, 102
  early years and family, 101
  and Garel, Georges, 215
  and Gerlier, Pierre-Marie, 93
  postwar activities, 102
  rescue activities, 101–102
  Righteous among the Nations recognition, 102
Glasberg, Vila, 101–102
Goebbels, Joseph, 209, 309
Gol, Szloma, affidavit on killings at Ponary (primary document), 291–293
  on being required to wash gold fillings of the dead, 291
  commentary on, 291–293
  death counts, 292–293
  and executions, 292
  and Ponary Forest, 291–292
  text, 291
  and Vilna ghetto, 292
Göring, Hermann, 279, 303, 310
Gross-Rosen concentration camp (Germany/Lower Silesia), 97, 111, 184, 300, 302
Grynszpan, Herschel, 304

Gunden, Lois, **103–104**
   arrest of, 104
   diary of, 103–104
   early years and education, 103
   postwar activities, 104
   rescue activities, 102–103
   Righteous among the Nations recognition, 104

Haining, Jane, **105–107**
   arrest and deportation to Auschwitz, 106
   awards and memorials, 106
   death of, 106
   early years and education, 106
   missionary work, 105
   personal effects, 106
   Righteous among the Nations recognition, 106
Halverstad, Felix, 124, 232–233
Hana's Suitcase, **107–109**
   and Brady, Hana, 107–109
   Inside Hana's Suitcase (documentary), 109
   and Ishioka, Fumiko, 107–109
   Levine, Karen M. (author of nonfiction book), 109
   and Theresienstadt, 107–108
Harrer, Karl, 303
Hart, Kitty, **109–112**
   at Auschwitz, 110–111
   at Bergen-Belsen, 111
   early years and family, 109
   education, 110
   at Gross-Rosen, 111
   and liberation, 111
   marriage, 111
   postwar activities, 111
Hasvold, Nina, 191–193, 228
Hechalutz, 117, 249
Heiber, Maurice and Estera, 56–57
Heissmeyer, Kurt, 29–31, 179
Helga's Diary, **112–113**
   and Auschwitz, 112–113
   and Freiberg labor camp, 113
   and liberation, 113
   and Mengele, Josef, 112–113
   publication of, 113
   Weiss, Helga, early years and family, 112

Heydrich, Reinhard, 74, 239, 305
Heyman, Éva, **113–115**
   at Auschwitz, 113, 114
   death of, 114
   diary of, 67, 113–115
   The Diary of Éva Heyman, 45, 114
   early years and family, 113–114
   Eva Heyman: Anne Frank of Transylvania (theatrical performance), 114
   Eva.Stories project, 114–115
Hidden Child Foundation, 116
Hidden children, **115–117**
   and *Comité de Défense des Juifs*, 55, 56
   and Daman, Jeanne, 60
   diaries and journals of, 116
   First International Hidden Child Gathering, 116
   and Nazi racial ideology, 115
   and passing, 115
   and Perelman, Fela, 55
   Perl, Gabriella, 199
   reminiscences of, 45–46
   reuniting with parents, 60, 208
   and Schonfeld, Solomon, 220
   and Second Generation, 116
   and trauma, 116
   and van den Berg, Albert, 138
   and Żegota, 225
Himmler, Heinrich
   Auschwitz concentration camp established by, 305
   and Białystok children, 17
   destruction of Auschwitz gas chambers ordered by, 309
   dismantling of Sobibór ordered by, 20
   and Edelweiss Pirates, 74, 219
   and *The Jewish Quarter of Warsaw Is No More!*, 24
   and kidnapping, 141
   Kommando 1005 established by, 292
   and *Lebensborn*, 165 166
   liquidation of ghettos ordered by, 288, 308
   and medical experimentation, 29
   suicide of, 309
   Warsaw Ghetto visited by, 307

Himmler, Heinrich, on responsibility to beget children (primary document), 270–274
  on legitimate and illegitimate, 271–272, 274
  on racial hygiene (*Rassenhygiene*), 270–273
  on responsibilities of SS men, 270–271
  and selective breeding (*Lebensborn*), 270, 272, 273
  on SS men and wives of soldiers in the field, 271–273
Himmler, Heinrich, "The Difficult Decision" (primary document), 289–291
  commentary on, 289–291
  and *Einsatzgruppen* (killing squads), 289–290
  excerpts, 289
  on extermination of the Jews, 289
  on need for secrecy, 289, 290
Hirsch, Alfred (Fredy), **117–119**
  at Auschwitz, 117, 118–119, 149, 150
  death of, 119, 150
  and Jewish youth movement, 117
  and Kraus, Dita, 149, 150
  and *Maccabee Hatziar*, 117
  at Theresienstadt, 117, 118, 119, 239
  and Zionism, 117–118, 149
Hitler, Adolf
  appointed chancellor of Germany, 85, 303
  attempts to overthrow Bavaria, 303
  and *Brundibár*, 25, 26
  and child euthanasia, 36–37
  and Czechoslovakia, 278–279, 280
  declares himself Führer, 303, 304
  education views of, 75–77
  Freund, John, on, 274, 276
  and Himmler, Heinrich, 141, 289, 290
  with Hitler Youth, *120*
  Hitler Youth established by, 120
  joins German Workers' Party, 303
  and kidnapping, 141
  Leopold, King, meeting with, 207
  Mein Kampf, 209
  Nazi Party Platform of, 303
  and "Rhineland Bastards," 209
  suicide of, 240, 309
  tried and sentenced for treason, 303
Hitler Youth, **120–122**
  active service of, 121
  ages and grades, 120–121
  compulsory membership for Aryan boys, 120, 304
  designated unconstitutional, 122, 210
  Deutsches Jungvolk (German Young People), 121
  and Edelweiss Pirates, 73
  education and schools, 122
  founding of, 120
  Hitler, Adolf, with, *120*
  and Hübener, Helmuth, 122–123
  ideological nature of, 122
  and League of German Girls, 120, 163–165
  paramilitary organization, 121
  Pimpfs (youngsters), 120–121, 268
  and race, 126–127
  and "Rhineland Bastards," 210
  and *Swing Kids*, 234, 235
  and teachers, 76
  Ustaše variant of, 44
  and von Schirach, Baldur, 121
Holocaust Martyrs' and Heroes' Remembrance Authority, 258–259
Hübener, Helmuth, **122–124**
  arrest of, 123
  and Church of Jesus Christ of Latter-day Saints (LDS), 122–124
  honors and awards, 124
  trial and execution, 123–124
Hulst, Johan van, **124–125**
  death of, 125
  early years and teaching career, 124
  and *Hervormde Kweekschool* (Reformed Teacher Training College), 124–125, 232
  postwar activities, 125
  rescue activities, 124–125
  Righteous among the Nations recognition, 125
  and Süskind, Walter, 124, 232

Im Hof-Piguet, Anne-Marie, 33–34
Infanticide, **126–127**
  at Auschwitz, 167–168
  death toll, 126

and Mengele, Josef, 127, 167–168
Nazi justifications for, 126
and race, 126–127
See also Child euthanasia
International Military Tribunal (Nuremberg Trials), 184, 291–293, 300, 310

Janowska concentration camp (Poland), 308
Jasenovac Memorial Museum, 44
Jastrebarsko children's concentration camp (Croatia), 28, 42–44
Jewish Combat Organization, 180, 307, 308
The Jewish Question in Education (primary document), 263–266
   commentary on, 265–266
   on criminality of Jewry, 264–265
   Fink, Fritz (author), 263–264, 265–266
   and National Socialist state, 264–265
   on racial question, 263–264, 265–266
   on school instruction, 264
   Streicher, Julius (introduction), 263, 265–266
Jewish youth movements, **128–130**
   and *Aliyah*, 129
   and calls for resistance, 13
   Habonim, 144
   Hashomer Hatzair, 128, 129
   Hatikvah, 171
   Hechalutz, 117, 249
   influence on, 128–129
   Kashariyot, 130
   and Lapid-Andriesse, Mirjam, 158
   and Meed, Vladka, 180
   Mouvement de la Jeunesse Sioniste (Zionist Youth Movement), 52, 130, 190
   outlawed by Nazis, 130
   and Poland, 129
   and Scouting movement, 129
   and Sierakowiak, Dawid, 226
   and smuggling, 129
   and Zionism, 128–130
   Zukunft, 180
   See also Éclaireurs Israélites de France
Joffo, Joseph, **130–132**
   death of, 132
   early years and family, 130–131
   at *Moisson Nouvelle*, 131
   postwar activities, 132
   Un sac de billes (*A Bag of Marbles*), 130, 132
Jonas, Regina, **132–134**
   at Auschwitz, 134
   early years and education, 132
   at Theresienstadt, 133–134, 239
Jospa, Yvonne, **134–136**
   and *Comité de Défense des Juifs*, 55–57, 134
   death of, 136
   early years and education, 134–135
   postwar activities, 136
   rescue activities, 134–136

Kerkhofs, Louis-Joseph, **137–139**
   early years and education, 138
   and hidden children, 138
   honors and awards, 138–139
   postwar activities, 138
   rescue activities, 138–139
   Righteous among the Nations recognition, 138–139
Kertész, Imre, **139–140**
   at Auschwitz, 139–140
   death of, 140
   early years and education, 139
   Fateless (Sorstalanság), 140
   Fatelessness, 139–140
   Fiasco, 139
   Kaddish for an Unborn Child, 139
   Nobel Prize for Literature awarded to, 139, 140
   postwar activities, 139–140
Kidnapping, 88, **140–142**
   and Budisavljević, Diana, 28
   and child murder, 140
   child survivors of, 141–142
   and Himmler, Heinrich, 141
   and *Lebensborn* program, 140–141, 166, 167–168
   in *The Poisonous Mushroom*, 269
   from Poland, 140–141
   from Soviet Union, 141
   statistics, 142
   and trauma, 141–142

Kindertransport, **142–144**
   and Château de la Hille, 32
   and *Dunera* boys, 68, 70
   end of, 144
   first train, 143
   and Garnethill Hostel, 90, 144
   identity document, *143*
   and Jewish youth movement, 144
   and Kindertransport Association, 144
   meaning of the term, 142
   origins and history of, 142–143
   routes, 143–144
   and Schonfeld, Solomon, 219, 220
   and Winton, Nicholas, 144, 254
   and World Federation of Jewish Child Survivors of the Holocaust and Descendants, 256
Kor, Eva Mozes, **144–146**
   at Auschwitz, 144–146
   awards and honors, 146
   CANDLES founded by, 146
   death of, 146
   early years and family, 144–145
   and *The Girl Who Forgave the Nazis* (documentary), 146
   and Mengele, Josef, 144–146, 245–246
   testimony in trial of Oskar Gröning, 146
   and twin experiments, 144–146, 245–246
Korczak (film), 41
Korczak, Janusz, **146–149**
   Berg, Mary, on, 15
   children's books by, 148
   death of, 148, 307
   early years and family, 146
   education, 146
   "Janusz Korczak and the Children" (statue), *147*
   legacy of, 148–149
   and World War I, 147
   and Żegota, 148
Kraków ghetto, 9, 152, 307
Kraus, Dita, **149–150**
   death of, 150
   early years and family, 149
   at Hamburg labor camp, 150
   and Hirsch, Fredy, 118, 149, 150
   liberated from Bergen-Belsen, 150
   marriage, 150
   and Mengele, Josef, 149, 150
   postwar activities, 150
   at Theresienstadt, 149
Kraus, Gilbert and Eleanor, **150–152**
   death of Eleanor, 151–152
   early years and marriage, 150
   50 Children: The Rescue Mission of Mr. and Mrs. Kraus, 152
   and *Kindertransport,* 151
   legacy of, 152
   rescue activities, 150–152
   voyage to United States, 151
Kristallnacht, 32, 86, 122–123, 135, 142, 143, 215, 219, 241, 253–254, 304
Küchler-Silberman, Lena, **152–154**
   death of, 153
   death of sister, 152
   One Hundred Children, 46, 153
   passing of, 152
   postwar activities, 153
   rescue activities, 152–153
Kulski, Julian Eugeniusz, **154–155**
   arrest and imprisonment of, 154
   diary of, 154–155
   early years, 154
   and Polish Boy Scouts, 154
   postwar activities, 154–155

La Colline aux Mille Enfants, **156–158**
   and Le Chambon-sur-Lignon, 156
   Lorenzi, Jean-Louis, director, 156
   and personification of evil, 157
   reception and awards, 41, 157
   and sanctuary, 156
   and Trocmé, André, 156
Łachwa ghetto, 307
Lapid-Andriesse, Mirjam, **158–159**
   at Bergen-Belsen, 158
   early years, 158
   and Jewish youth movement, 158
   on "Lost Train," 158–159
   marriage, 159
   postwar activities, 159
Law for the Prevention of Offspring with Hereditary Defects, 209, 303. *See also* Sterilization
Łazowertówna, Henryka, 230–232

Le Chambon-sur-Lignon, **159–161**
   civil disobedience campaign, 160
   Gestapo school raid, 161
   history of, 159–160
   Huguenot Protestants of, 159–161
   liberation of, 161
   location, 159
   rescue activities, 160
   Righteous among the Nations recognition, 161, 244
   See also La Colline aux Mille Enfants; Sauvage, Pierre; Trocmé, André
Le Voyage de Fanny, **162–163**
   and Ben-Ami, Fanny, 162–163
   Doillon, Lola, director, 162
   inspiration for, 162
   reception and awards, 41, 163
League of German Girls, **163–165**
   designated unconstitutional, 165
   and Edelweiss Pirates, 73
   education and activities, 163–164
   establishment of, 163
   and Hitler Youth, 120, 163–165
   ideology and purpose, 163
   and "People's Community" (*Volksgemeinschaft*), 164
   and *Swing Kids,* 235
   war service, 164
Lebensborn, **165–167**
   establishment of, 165
   Himmler, Heinrich, on responsibility to beget children (primary document), 270, 272, 273
   and kidnapping, 141–142, 166, 168
   and liberation, 166
   meaning of the term, 165
   purpose of, 165–66
Lederman, Charles, 88, 215
Lesser, Fanny, testimony of (primary document), 297–302
   on arrival at Auschwitz, 297–298
   on beatings from camp leader, 300
   commentary on, 300–302
   on deaths at Auschwitz-Birkenau, 298
   on food, 299
   on gas chambers, 298–299
   on pregnancy, 299–300
   on roll call, 300
   on selection process, 298
   text, 297–300
   on waiting for transport, 300
Leszczyńska, Stanisława, **167–168**
   at Auschwitz, 167–168
   death of, 168
   early years and education, 167
   honors and awards, 168
   and *Lebensborn* program, 168
   in Łódź ghetto, 167
   and Mengele, Josef, 167–168
   and Perl, Gisella, 167
   postwar activities, 168
Liberation, **169–170**
   of Auschwitz, 18, 84, 169, 245, 309
   of Bergen-Belsen, 158, 169, 198, 309
   and *Brichah,* 170
   of Buchenwald, 97, 139, 169, 309
   and child survivors, 169–170
   of Dachau, 169, 309
   of Le Chambon-sur-Lignon, 161
   of Łódź ghetto, 227, 309
   of Majdanek, 169
   and Operation OVERLORD, 169
   of Ravensbrück, 309
   and reconnection of children with families, 169–170
   of Theresienstadt, 158–159, 240
   and toll of medical experimentation, 169
   of Treblinka, 169
   and Youth Aliyah, 170
   See also Reynders, Henri
Łódź ghetto
   deportations from, 306
   deportations to, 118
   in diaries and literature, 100, 226–227
   establishment of, 167, 305
   food shortages and starvation, 100, 168, 227, 284–285, 287
   liberation of, 227, 309
   liquidation of, 309
   Marysin orphanage, 99–100
   Rumkowski, Mordecai Chaim Judenrat chair, on, 286–288
   sealing of, 226, 305
   Szedlecki, Ann, testimony of, 280–285

Loinger, Georges, **171–173**
  and *Aliyah Bet,* 172
  and Cohn, Marianne, 53, 172
  death of, 173
  and Deffaugt, Jean, 64, 172
  early years, 171
  and *Éclaireurs Israélites de France,* 171
  and Garel Network, 89
  honors and awards, 172–173
  and Marceau, Marcel, 23, 172, 177–178
  marriage, 171
  and *Œuvre de Secours aux Enfants,* 64, 171–172, 177, 190, 215
  as *passeur,* 172
  postwar activities, 172
  and Racine, Mila, 172
  and smuggling, 172
  and Weill, Joseph, 171, 172
  and Zionism, 171
Lore, **173–174**
  German children as victims, 174
  reception and awards, 174
  Seiffert, Rachel, author, 173, 174
Lund, Sigrid Helliesen, 191–193
Lvov (Lv'iv) ghetto, 261, 306, 308

Maison d'Izieu, **175–176**
  and Barbie, Klaus, 175–176
  children at, 175
  and Garel Network, 175
  raid on, 175–176
  survivors, 176
Majdanek extermination camp (Poland), 161, 163, 169, 243, 308
Marceau, Marcel, **176–178**
  and border crossing, 23, 177–178
  death of, 178
  as hidden child, 177
  and Loinger, Georges, 23, 172, 177–178
  mime career, 176, 177, 178
  postwar activities, 178
  rescue activities, 177–178
Mauthausen-Gusen concentration camp (Austria), 58, 113, 167, 172, 197, 204, 304, 309
Medical experimentation, **178–180**
  and anesthesia, 180
  medico-military experiments, 179
  and Nazi ideology, 178
  racially-motivated experiments, 179
  tuberculosis experiments, 179
  See also Bullenhuser Damm; Child euthanasia; Mengele, Josef; Twins
Meed, Benjamin, 181–182
Meed, Vladka, **180–182**
  death of, 182
  early years and education, 180
  honors and awards, 182
  and Jewish youth movement, 180
  passing of, 181
  postwar activities, 181–182
  rescue activities, 180–181
  voyage to United States, 181
  and Warsaw Ghetto Resistance Organization, 181
Mengele, Josef, **182–185**
  at Auschwitz, 112, 144–146, 149, 167, 182–184, 197–198, 244, 299, 300, 301
  and Birebaum, Halina, 18
  death of, 184
  early years and education, 182
  escape to Buenos Aires, 184
  Forgiving Dr. Mengele (documentary), 146
  at Gross-Rosen, 184
  and *Helga's Diary,* 112–113
  and infanticide, 127, 167–168
  and Kor, Eva Mozes, 144–146, 245–246
  and Kraus, Dita, 149, 150
  Lesser, Fanny, testimony of, 299, 300, 301
  and Leszczyńska, Stanisława, 167–168
  and Perl, Gisella, 197–198
  and pregnancy, 4
  and selection process, 18, 112–113, 183
  and twin experiments, 144–146, 179–180, 182–183, 244–246
Minsk ghetto, 306, 308
Mischling, **185–186,** 218
  and antisemitism, 185–186
  categories, 185–186
  in literature, 45
  meaning of the term, 185
  and Nuremberg Laws of 1935, 185
  and "Rhineland Bastards," 210

and school, 186
See also "Rhineland Bastards"
Mit Brennender Sorge (Pius XI), 304
Mitterrand, François, 132, 176
Munich Conference, 304

Näf, Rösli, 32–34
National Socialist German Workers' Party (NSDAP), 303
Natzweiler-Struthof concentration camp (France), 82, 306
Neuengamme concentration camp (Germany), 29–31, 138, 179, 305
Night of the Long Knives, 303
Ninas Resa, **187–188**
  Einhorn, Lena, director, 187–188
  events of, 187–188
  Nina's Journey: A Survival Story (book), 187
  nontraditional techniques in, 188
  and Rajmic (Einhorn), Nina, 187–188
Non-Aggression Pact, 305
Nuremberg Laws, 107, 117, 178, 185, 209, 222, 273, 287, 304
Nuremberg Trials, 184, 291–293, 300, 310

Œuvre de Secours aux Enfants, **189–191**
  and Chevrier, Félix, 34–35
  in children's literature, 162
  and Éclaireurs Israélites de France, 190
  Emerson, Sir Herbert, on, 294
  fostering arrangements negotiated by, 115
  and Garel, Georges, 89, 215–216
  and Glasberg, Alexandre, 101
  and Gunden, Lois, 103
  history and founding of, 189–190
  and Le Chambon-sur-Lignon, 160
  and Lederman, Charles, 88, 215
  and liberation of France, 191
  and Loinger, Georges, 64, 171–172, 177, 190, 215
  and Maison d'Izieu, 175
  OSE homes, 34–35, 162, 172, 188, 215–216
  purpose of, 189
  and Salomon, Andrée, 190, 215–216
  Weill, Joseph, medical director, 88, 171–172
Olympic Games, Summer (1936), 304
Operation BARBAROSSA, 212, 228, 292, 306

Oslo Jewish Children's Home, **191–193**
  and antisemitism, 192
  establishment of, 191
  history of, 191–192
  and Ingebjørg Sletten-Fosstvedt, 193
  and *Nansenhjelpen,* 191
  rescue of, 192–193, 228–229
  and Sletten-Fosstvedt, Ingebjørg, 193, 228–229

Passeurs (people movers), 21–22, 53, 64, 89, 157, 161, 162, 172, 216
Passing, 67, 94, **194–196**
  challenges and dangers of, 194–195
  children's passing, 195
  and circumcision, 51, 195
  of David, Janina, 61
  and deception, 63
  definition of, 194
  documents for, 195
  and hidden children, 115
  history of, 194
  of Joffo, Joseph, 130
  of Küchler-Silberman, Lena, 152
  in literature, 45–46, 49
Pawiak prison, 14, 154, 226
Pearl Harbor, attack on, 306
Père Jacques, **196–197**
  arrest and imprisonment, 196–197
  and *Au Revoir les Enfants* (film), 196–197
  death of, 197
  early years and education, 196
  and liberation, 197
  rescue activities, 196–197
  Righteous among the Nations recognition, 197
Perelman, Chaim, 55–56
Perelman, Fela, 55–56, 58, 59
Perl, Gisella, **197–199**
  at Auschwitz, 197–198
  death of, 199
  early years and education, 197
  I Was a Doctor in Auschwitz, 199
  and liberation, 198–199
  and Mengele, Josef, 197–198
  postwar activities, 199
  and pregnant women, 167, 198

Pétain, Marshal Philippe, 92, 132, 160, 305
Piepel, **199–200**
   De-Nur, Yehiel, 199
   history and meaning of the term, 199
   and kapos, 199–200
   and *Screaming Silence,* 200, 222
Pius XI, Pope, 304
The Poisonous Mushroom (primary document), 266–270
   commentary on, 268–270
   depictions of Jewish men, 269
   depictions of Jews, 269
   excerpts, 267–268
   Hiemer, Ernst (author), 266, 268
   purpose of, 270
   Rupprecht, Philipp (illustrator), 266, 268
   Streicher, Julius (publisher), 266, 268
   use of by teachers, 269–270
Pritchard, Marion, **200–202**
   awards and honors, 202
   death of, 202
   and Dutch resistance, 200–202
   early years and education, 200
   marriage of, 202
   with Polak, Erica, *201*
   postwar activities, 202
   rescue activities, 200–202
   Righteous among the Nations recognition, 202
   Wallenberg Medal awarded to, 202
Probst, Christoph, 307

Racine, Emmanuel, 65
Racine, Mila, **203–204**
   alias (Marie Anne Richemond), 203
   arrest and torture of, 53–54, 64–65, 203–204
   border-crossing with children, 22–23, 172, 203–204
   and Cohn, Marianne, 53–54, 65, 172, 204
   death of, 172, 204
   and Deffaugt, Jean, 64–65, 204
   early years and family, 203
   honors and awards, 204
   replacements for, 204
   rescue activities, 22–23, 53–54, 64–65, 203–204
   Women's International Zionist Organization (WIZO) member, 203
Ranjitsinhji, Digvijaysinhji, **204–206**
   death of, 206
   early years, 205
   honors and awards, 206
   knighting of, 206
   A Little Poland in India (documentary), 206
   postwar activities, 205–206
   rescue activities, 205
Ravensbrück concentration camp (Germany), 4, 18, 58, 63, 107, 172, 204, 235, 249
   arrival of first prisoners to, 304
   liberation of, 309
   medical experimentation on prisoners from, 29
Reichstag fire, 303
Reigner Telegram, 307
Rémond, Paul, 1–2, 131–132
Reynders, Henri, **206–208**
   and André, Joseph, 6
   death of, 208
   early years and education, 206
   En Feuilletant mon cahier de Notes (personal notebooks), 208
   honors and awards, 208
   and liberation of Belgium, 208
   as military chaplain, 206–207
   rescue activities, 206–208
   Righteous among the Nations recognition, 208
   and van den Berg, Albert, 207–208
"Rhineland Bastards," **208–210**
   fates, 209–210
   history of, 208–209
   and Hitler Youth, 210
   and medical experimentation, 209–210
   and *Mein Kampf,* 209
   and *Mischlinge,* 210
   and *Sonderkommission 3* ("Special Commission 3"), 209
   use of the term, 208–209

Righteous among the Nations recognition
  André, Joseph, 6
  and Association of Children of the Holocaust, 9–10
  Bouty, Pierre and Marguerite, 62
  Breisjøberget, Ola, 193
  Chevrier, Félix, 35
  Cohn, Marianne, 54
  Daman, Jeanne, 60
  Deffaugt, Jean, 66
  Errazuríz, María, 80
  Gerlier, Pierre-Marie, 93
  Getter, Matylda, 95
  Geulen-Herscovici, Andrée, 96
  Gies, Miep, 99
  Glasberg, Alexandre and Vila, 102
  Gout, Marie-Antoinette, 63
  Gunden, Lois, 104
  Haining, Jane, 106
  Hasvold, Nina, 193
  and Hidden Child Foundation, 116
  Hulst, Johan van, 125
  Im Hof-Piguet, Anne-Marie, 33–34
  Jovy, Michael, 219
  Jülich, Jean, 219
  Kanabus, Feliks, 52
  Kerkhofs, Louis-Joseph, 138–139
  Le Chambon, 161
  Lund, Sigrid Helliesen, 193
  Näf, Rösli, 33–34
  Père Jacques, 197
  Pritchard, Marion, 202
  Queen Elisabeth the Queen Mother, 57
  Rauken, Ola, 193
  Rémond, Paul, 132
  Reynders, Henri, 208
  Schink, Barthel, 219
  Sendler, Irena, 226, 261
  Sletten-Fosstvedt, Ingebjørg, 193, 229
  Solvang, Martin, 193
  Sztehló, Gabor, 237
  Tanberg, Gerda, 193
  Trocmé, André, 244
  Waal, Caroline (Nic), 193
  Westerweel, Joop and Wil, 251
  and World Federation of Jewish Child Survivors of the Holocaust and Descendants, 257
Robota, Roza, 309
Roosevelt, Eleanor, 78, 199
Roosevelt, Franklin D., 308
Rosenstock (Abadi), Odette, 1–2
  arrest and torture of, 2
  marriage to Moussa Abadi, 2
  rescue activities, 1–2
  suicide of, 2
Rubinowicz, Dawid, **210–212**
  and Bodzentyn ghetto, 210–211
  diary of, 67, 210–212
  The Diary of Dawid Rubinowicz, 45, 212
  early years and family, 210
  killing of, 212
Rudashevski, Yitskhok, **212–214**
  death of, 213
  Di Goldene Keyt (The Golden Chain), 213
  diary of, 67, 212–214
  early years and family, 212
  and Operation BARBAROSSA, 212
  publications of, 213–214
  teachers of, 213
Rumkowski, Mordecai Chaim, Łódź Ghetto (primary document), 286–288
  commentary on, 287–288
  on deportation of children and elderly, 286–287
  and Germany occupation, 287–288
  on the ill, 287
  and *Judenrat* (Jewish Council), 287–288
  text, 286–287

Safirsztajn, Regina, 309
Salomon, Andrée, **215–216**
  birth of son, 216
  death of, 216
  and *Éclaireurs Israélites de France*, 215
  and Gamzon, Robert, 215
  and Garel Network, 89, 215–216
  marriage, 215
  and *Œuvre de Secours aux Enfants*, 190, 215–216
  rescue activities, 215–216
Salomon, Tobie, 215, 216
Sarnat, Ronnie, 200, 221–222. *See also Screaming Silence*

Sauvage, Pierre, **216–218**
   American Directors (with Jean-Pierre Coursodon), 217
   child Holocaust survivor, 216
   early years and family, 216–217
   Friends of Le Chambon (later Chambon Foundation) founded by, 217
   and Langlois, Henri, 217
   and Le Chambon-sur-Lignon, 216–218
   and *Lieu de Mémoire au Chambon-sur-Lignon* (museum and learning center), 217–218
   Weapons of the Spirit, 217–218
Schink, Barthel, **218–219**
   arrest and conviction for "preparation of high treason," 218
   arrest for Pirates membership, 219
   early years, 218
   Edelweiss Pirates member, 218–219
   and Ehrenfelder Navajo Group, 218
   execution of, 218, 219
   rescue activities, 218
   Righteous among the Nations recognition, 219
Scholl, Hans and Sophie, 307
Schonfeld, Solomon, **219–221**
   British Hero of the Holocaust recognition, 221
   death of, 221
   early years and family, 219
   Hasmonean High School founded by, 220
   and hidden children, 220
   and *Kindertransport,* 219–220
   National Council for Religious Education organized by, 220
   negotiation skills and successes, 220
   rabbi of Adath Yisroel synagogue (North London), 219
   rescue activities, 219–221
Screaming Silence, **221–223**
   background and inspiration, 221
   interviews with survivors, 221–222
   and piepels, 222
   Sarnat, Ronnie, filmmaker, 200, 221–222
Second Generation, **223–224**
   children of, 223–224
   definition of, 223
   differences from parent's generation, 223
   and Generations of the Shoah International, 224
   and Hidden Child Foundation, 116
   respect for child survivors, 39
   role of, 223
   and transmitted trauma, 223
   and World Federation of Jewish Child Survivors of the Holocaust and Descendants, 256
Sendler, Irena, **224–226**
   arrest and torture of, 225–226
   awards and honors, 226
   death of, 226
   early years, family, and education, 225
   and Getter, Matylda, 93, 94
   and hidden children, 225–226
   rescue activities, 224–226
   Righteous among the Nations recognition, 226, 261
   and Żegota, 49, 224–226, 261
   and Zysman, Józef, 49
Sierakowiak, Dawid, 67, **226–228**
   and Adelson, Alan, editor, 227
   diary of, 67, 226–228
   and Dobroszycki, Lucjan, editor, 227
   early years and family, 226–227
   and Jewish youth movements, 226–227
   publications of diary, 227
   and Szkudlarek, Wacław, discoverer of diary, 227
   and Turowski, Konrad, editor, 227
Sisak children's concentration camp (Croatia), 28, 29, 42–44
Sletten-Fosstvedt, Ingebjørg, **228–229**
   as antifascist, 227
   death of, 229
   escape from Norway to Sweden, 229
   journalism career, 227
   marriage, 229
   and Oslo's Jewish Children's Home rescues, 193, 228–229
   rescue activities, 228–229
   Righteous among the Nations recognition, 193, 229
   and Spanish Civil War, 227
Smuggling, **229–232**
   and *Brichah,* 170
   by children, 49–50, 229–230

and Cohn, Marianne, 52
dangers of, 230
death penalty for, 230
and deception, 62
and Deffaugt, Jean, 64–65
definition of, 229
of documents, 15, 25, 112, 167
and *Éclaireurs Israélites de France*, 71, 73
of fighters, 130
of food, 167, 229–230, 287
and Garel Network, 89, 216
and Gout, Marie-Antoinette, 62
and Gunden, Lois, 103
and Hulst, Johan van, 125
and Jewish youth movements, 129
and Jospa, Yvonne, 135
and Küchler, Lena, 152
and Leszczyńska, Stanisława, 167
in literature, 49–50
"Mały szmugler" (Łazowertówna), 230–232
and Marceau, Marcel, 177
means of, 229
and Meed, Benjamin, 181
and *Œuvre de Secours aux Enfants*, 189–190, 215, 216
and Oslo Jewish Children's Home rescues, 228–229
and *passeurs,* 172
and Racine, Mila, 202–203
and Sendler, Irena, 94, 225
and Tiefenbrunner Orphanage, 241
of weapons, 50
See also Salomon, Andrée
Sobibór extermination camp (Poland), 19–21, 158, 169, 232, 307, 308
Stalin, Joseph, 205, 285
Stara Gradiška concentration camp (Croatia), 28, 43
Starvation. *See* Food shortages and starvation
Sterilization, 78, 179, 209, 273, 303
Streicher, Julius, 263, 265–266, 268
Strippel, Arnold, 30–31, 179
Stroop, Jürgen, 24, 308
Stutthof concentration camp (Germany), 100–101

Süskind, Walter, **232–234**
    arrest and deportation to Theresienstadt, 233
    death of, 233
    and Halverstad, Felix, 124, 232–233
    and *Hollandsche Schouwburg* (Dutch Theater), 124, 232–234
    and Hulst, Johan van, 124, 232
    rescue activities, 232–234
    Süskind (film), 233–234
Süskind, Yvonne, 233
Swing Kids, **234–236**
    and antisemitism, 235
    Carter, Thomas, director, 234
    and Hitler Youth, 234–235
    and League of German Girls, 235
    storylines and insights, 234–235
    and Swing Youth (*Swingjugend*), 235
    See also Edelweiss Pirates
Szedlecki, Ann, testimony of (primary document), 280–285
    on bombing, 281–282
    commentary on, 284–285
    and curfews and personal safety, 282–283
    excerpt, 280–284
    on German occupation, 282–284
    on Łódź ghetto, 280–284
    on public hanging, 283
Szold, Henrietta, 86–87, 182
Sztehló, Gabor, **236–237**
    death of, 237
    early years and education, 236
    and Éliás, József, 236
    and liberation, 237
    postwar activities, 237
    rescue activities, 236–237
    Righteous among the Nations recognition, 237

Theresienstadt, **238–240**
    Białystok deportations to, 16, 17, 117, 118, 119
    Brundibár staged at, 25–26
    in children's literature and diaries, 107–108, 112, 247–248
    construction of, 238
    death rates, 239

Theresienstadt (*Continued*)
  establishment of, 238, 305
  first transport of Jews to Auschwitz from, 307
  food shortages and starvation, 107
  Freund, John, testimony of, 278
  and *Hana's Suitcase,* 107–108
  and *Helga's Diary,* 112
  Hirsch, Alfred, deportation to, 117, 118, 239
  Jonas, Regina, deportation to, 133–134, 239
  Kraus, Dita, deportation to, 149
  liberation of, 158–159, 240
  in literature and diaries, 240, 247–248
  location, 238
  and Nazi deceptions, 239–240
  "privileged" and "humane" reputation of, 239–240
  surrendered to International Committee of the Red Cross, 309
  Süskind family's deportation to, 233
  as transit camp, 239
  Weiner, Pavel, deportation to, 247
Tiefenbrunner, Ruth, 240, 241
Tiefenbrunner, Yona, 81, 240–242
Tiefenbrunner Orphanage, **240–242**
  establishment of, 240–241
  Flinker, Moshe, at, 81
  legacy of, 241–242
  and rescue activities, 241
Treblinka extermination camp (Poland), 18, 23, 180, 181, 212, 232
  begins operation, 307
  Białystok deportations to, 16
  first Warsaw Ghetto deportation to, 50, 307
  liberation of, 169
  Treblinka uprising, 308
  Warsaw orphans and Janusz Korczak deported to, 15, 146, *147*, 148, 307
Trocmé, André, **242–244**
  arrest and imprisonment, 243
  death of, 244
  early years and education, 242
  and *La Colline aux Mille Enfants (The Hill of a Thousand Children),* 156–157
  and Le Chambon-sur-Lignon, 159–161, 242–244

postwar activities, 244
  rescue activities, 159–161, 242–244
  Righteous among the Nations recognition, 161, 244
Trocmé, Daniel, 161, 243
Trocmé, Magda, 161, 242–244
Twins, **244–246**
  and CANDLES ("Children of Auschwitz Nazi Deadly Lab Experiments Survivors"), 146, 246
  definition of, 244
  euthanization and autopsies, 245
  Kor, Eva Mozes (and Miriam), 144–146, 245–246
  and liberation, 245
  lumbar puncture experiments, 245
  medical experimentation on, 144–146 179–180, 182–183, 244–246
  and Mengele, Josef, 144–146, 179–180, 182–183, 244–246
  Noma disease experiments, 245
  selection process, 244
  survivors, 144–146, 245–246

Van den Berg, Albert, 137–139, 207–208
Van den Berg, Rudolf, 233
Vilna Ghetto, 130, 212–213, 291–292, 306, 308
Vom Rath, Ernst, 304
Von Hindenburg, Paul, 303, 304
Vught concentration camp (Netherlands), 138, 249–250

Waal, Nice, 191–193, 228
Wajcblum, Estusia, 309
Wallenberg, Raoul, 202, 308
Wannsee Conference, 306
Warsaw Ghetto
  and Bauman, Janina, 12–14
  and Berg, Mary, 14–15
  and Birenbaum, Halina, 18–19
  deportations from, 307, 308
  establishment of, 305
  food shortages and starvation, 13, 60, 148, 229–230
  and Getter, Matylda, 93–94
  and Gutenbaum, Jakub, 9
  and infanticide, 126

and Janina, David, 60–61
Jewish Combat Organization, 180, 307, 308
and Korczak, Janusz, 146
and Kulski, Julian Eugeniusz, 148
in literature, film, and memoirs, 14–15, 23–24, 49–50, 187–188
and Meed, Vladka, 180–182
sealing of, 305
Warsaw Ghetto Resistance Organization, 181–182
Warsaw Ghetto Uprising, 9, 14, 18, 23, 24, 50, 154, 181, 187, 308
Weiner, Pavel, **247–248**
  A Boy in Terezín: The Private Diary of Pavel Weiner, April 1944–April 1945, 247
  death of, 248
  diary of, 67, 247–248
  early years and family, 247
  and liberation, 247
  postwar activities, 248
Weiss, Helga. *See Helga's Diary*
Westerweel, Johan, **248–251**
  arrest and torture, 250
  "*Avond in de Cel*" ("Evening in the Cell"), 250
  early years and teaching career, 248–249
  execution of, 250
  and Jewish youth movements, 249
  Joop Westerweel Park, 251
  resistance and rescue activities, 249–251
  Righteous among the Nations recognition, 25
  Westerweel, Wilhelmina, 249–251
White Rose (group), 307
Wiesel, Elie, **251–253**
  death of, 253
  early years and family, 251
  education, 251
  honors and awards, 252
  and liberation, 251
  Night, 46, 251–252
  postwar activities, 251–253
Winton, Nicholas, **253–255**
  death of, 255
  early years and family, 253
  honors and awards, 255
  knighting of, *254*, 255
  and *Kristallnacht*, 253–254

rescue activities, 253–255
Wallenberg Medal awarded to, 202
See also Pritchard, Marion
Women's International Zionist Organization (WIZO), 203, 216
World Federation of Jewish Child Survivors of the Holocaust and Descendants, **256–257**
  activities and events, 257
  conferences, 256–257
  establishment of, 39, 256
  and Kestenberg, Judith, 256
  mission, 255
  and Righteous among the Nations recognition, 257
  and Second Generation, 255

Yad Vashem, 219, 226, 229, 237, 244, 251, 255
  Hall of Names, *258*, 259
  Holocaust Martyrs' and Heroes' Remembrance Authority, 258–259
  See also Righteous among the Nations recognition; Yad Vashem Children's Memorial
Yad Vashem Children's Memorial, **258–259**
  founding, 258
  funding, 259
  purpose, 258, 259
  Safdie, Moshe, architect, 259
  symbolism of, 259
  view of entrance, 258
Yellow stars, 55, 95, 106, 107, 114, 130, 131, 275, 305, 306, 307
Youth Aliyah, 85–87, 91, 117, 170

Żegota, **260–261**
  activities, 260–261
  and Berman, Adolf, 226
  budget, 260
  founders, 260
  and Getter, Matylda, 93, 94
  and hidden children, 225
  history of, 260
  and Korczak, Janusz, 148
  and Sendler, Irena, 49, 224–226, 261
  and "uncircumcization" procedures, 51
  years of operation, 260

Zionism
   Betar, 128
   Dror, 128
   and *Éclaireurs Israélites de France*, 71, 215
   and Freier, Recha, 85–86, 170
   Habonim, 144
   Hashomer Hatzair, 128, 129
   Hatikvah, 171
   Hechalutz, 117, 249
   and Hirsch, Alfred, 117–118, 149
   and Jewish youth movements, 128–130
   Jüdischer Pfadfinderbund Deutschland (German Jewish Scouting Association), 117
   and Lapid-Andriesse, Mirjam, 158
   and liberation, 136, 170
   and Loinger, Georges, 171
   Maccabee Hatziar (sporting association), 117
   Mouvement de la Jeunesse Sioniste (Zionist Youth Movement), 52, 130, 190
   in Poland, 129
   and refugee children, 91
   and Salomon, Andrée, 215
   Women's International Zionist Organization (WIZO), 203, 216
   Women's Zionist Organization of America, 86
   World Zionist Congress, 85
   Youth Aliyah, 85–87, 91, 117, 170

About the Authors

Paul R. Bartrop is a multiaward-winning scholar of the Holocaust and genocide. He is professor of history and director of the Center for Holocaust and Genocide Research at Florida Gulf Coast University, Fort Myers, Florida. Across an extensive academic career, he has taught at the Richard Stockton College of New Jersey, Virginia Commonwealth University, Deakin University, the University of South Australia, and Monash University. The author, editor, or coeditor of over 25 books, his published works with ABC-CLIO include *Perpetrating the Holocaust: Leaders, Enablers, and Collaborators* (with Eve E. Grimm, 2019); *Modern Genocide: Analyzing the Controversies and Issues* (2018); *The Holocaust: An Encyclopedia and Document Collection* (2017); *Resisting the Holocaust: Upstanders, Partisans, and Survivors* (2016); *Modern Genocide: The Definitive Resource and Document Collection* (2015); *Encountering Genocide: Personal Accounts from Victims, Perpetrators, and Witnesses* (2014); *An Encyclopedia of Contemporary Genocide Biography: Portraits of Evil and Good* (2012); and *Heroines of Vichy France: Rescuing the French Jews during the Holocaust* (2019). He is currently Vice-President of the Midwest Jewish Studies Association and is a Past President of the Australian Association of Jewish Studies.

Eve E. Grimm is senior advisor to the Center for Holocaust and Genocide Research at Florida Gulf Coast University, Fort Myers, Florida. An Australian lawyer with advanced qualifications in law and a career government service as a senior attorney, she has written about the German legal profession during the Nazi period and the Holocaust. Having formerly taught in the School of Law at Monash University, Melbourne, she was a member of the legal team that provided comment on the State of Victoria's racial vilification legislation, and she was a longtime member of the B'nai B'rith Anti-Defamation Commission in Australia, during which she prepared numerous briefs relating to antisemitism. Her published work has appeared in the journal *Without Prejudice*, and she was a key contributor to *The Holocaust: An Encyclopedia and Document Collection* (2017). In 2019 she coauthored (with Paul R. Bartrop) the ABC-CLIO volume *Perpetrating the Holocaust: Leaders, Enablers, and Collaborators*.

www.ingramcontent.com/pod-product-compliance
Lightning Source LLC
Chambersburg PA
CBHW060506300426
44112CB00017B/2567